RENEWABLE ENERGY LAW

This is the first textbook to provide a clear understanding of law's role in promoting the global growth of renewable energy production and consumption.

The book introduces readers to the main legal frameworks shaping the rise of renewables at international, regional and national levels, including those which set targets for reducing greenhouse gas emissions and increasing renewable energy consumption.

Clear explanations of challenges commonly confronting renewable developments and the legal responses to them aid readers' understanding whatever their background. The author, a leading researcher in energy and environmental law, has drawn on 10 years' experience of developing and teaching research-led courses on renewable energy law to produce an authoritative but accessible work.

Readers will come away with a better understanding of how international law on climate change and sustainable development affects renewable energy, the roles of renewable energy targets and subsidies, the laws on integrating renewables into electricity networks, the legal response to public opposition to renewable energy development, the law surrounding offshore renewables, and issues raised by the decarbonisation of road transport.

Renewable Energy Law

Olivia Woolley

·HART·
OXFORD · LONDON · NEW YORK · NEW DELHI · SYDNEY

HART PUBLISHING

Bloomsbury Publishing Plc

Kemp House, Chawley Park, Cumnor Hill, Oxford, OX2 9PH, UK

1385 Broadway, New York, NY 10018, USA

29 Earlsfort Terrace, Dublin 2, Ireland

HART PUBLISHING, the Hart/Stag logo, BLOOMSBURY and the Diana logo are trademarks of Bloomsbury Publishing Plc

First published in Great Britain 2023

Copyright © Olivia Woolley, 2023

Olivia Woolley has asserted her right under the Copyright, Designs and Patents Act 1988 to be identified as Author of this work.

All rights reserved. No part of this publication may be reproduced or transmitted in any form or by any means, electronic or mechanical, including photocopying, recording, or any information storage or retrieval system, without prior permission in writing from the publishers.

While every care has been taken to ensure the accuracy of this work, no responsibility for loss or damage occasioned to any person acting or refraining from action as a result of any statement in it can be accepted by the authors, editors or publishers.

All UK Government legislation and other public sector information used in the work is Crown Copyright ©. All House of Lords and House of Commons information used in the work is Parliamentary Copyright ©. This information is reused under the terms of the Open Government Licence v3.0 (http://www.nationalarchives.gov.uk/doc/open-government-licence/version/3) except where otherwise stated.

All Eur-lex material used in the work is © European Union, http://eur-lex.europa.eu/, 1998–2023.

A catalogue record for this book is available from the British Library.

Library of Congress Cataloging-in-Publication data

Names: Woolley, Olivia, author.
Title: Renewable energy law / Olivia Woolley.
Description: Oxford ; New York : Hart, [2023] | Includes bibliographical references and index. | Summary: "This is the first textbook to provide a clear understanding of law's role in promoting the global growth of renewable energy production and consumption. The book introduces readers to the main legal frameworks shaping the rise of renewables, including setting targets for reducing greenhouse gas emissions and increasing renewable energy consumption, at international, regional and national levels. Clear explanations of challenges commonly confronting renewable developments and the legal responses to them aid readers' understanding whatever their background. The author, a leading researcher in energy and environmental law, has drawn on 10 years' experience of developing and teaching research-led courses on renewable energy law to produce an authoritative but accessible work. Readers will come away with a better understanding of how international law on climate change and sustainable development affects renewable energy, the roles of renewable energy targets and subsidies, the laws on integrating renewables into electricity networks, the legal response to public opposition to renewable energy development, the law surrounding offshore renewables, and issues raised by the decarbonisation of transport"— Provided by publisher.
Identifiers: LCCN 2022060265 (print) | LCCN 2022060266 (ebook) | ISBN 9781509936472 (paperback) | ISBN 9781509967810 (hardback) | ISBN 9781509936465 (pdf) | ISBN 9781509936489 (Epub)
Subjects: LCSH: Renewable energy sources—Law and legislation. | Renewable energy sources—Law and legislation—European Union countries. | Renewable energy sources—Law and legislation—Great Britain. | LCGFT: Textbooks.
Classification: LCC K3981.5 .W66 2023 (print) | LCC K3981.5 (ebook) | DDC 346.04/6794—dc23/eng/20230113
LC record available at https://lccn.loc.gov/2022060265
LC ebook record available at https://lccn.loc.gov/2022060266

ISBN: PB: 978-1-50993-647-2
        HB: 978-1-50996-781-0
        ePDF: 978-1-50993-646-5
        ePub: 978-1-50993-648-9

Typeset by Compuscript Ltd, Shannon
Printed and bound in Great Britain by CPI Group (UK) Ltd, Croydon CR0 4YY

To find out more about our authors and books visit www.hartpublishing.co.uk. Here you will find extracts, author information, details of forthcoming events and the option to sign up for our newsletters.

Preface

The production of energy from renewable sources is growing rapidly worldwide, driven by policy and law on reducing greenhouse gas emissions, on increasing energy security by reducing dependence on imported fossil fuels, and by the falling costs of producing energy from better established renewable technologies such as solar and onshore and offshore wind. Renewable energy's growth challenges and is likely to displace the longstanding dominance of fossil fuels in coming decades. Continued and accelerating increases in its production and consumption are vital for keeping the lights on whilst addressing environmental problems such as climate change which pose existential threats for human wellbeing. Law is central to this transition. Legal obligations and incentives to combat climate change, to make development sustainable, and to increase the proportion of alternatives to fossil fuels in energy supplies drive the turn to renewables. Legal interventions such as subsidy schemes and rules ensuring access to the networks through which electricity and gases are transported assist with securing investment in renewable energy in circumstances where investors would otherwise be deterred from financing projects. Law can act as a barrier to the expansion of renewables, but can also be used to remove barriers through legal reform. Laws on public participation in decision-making and environmental protection amongst others seek to keep the renewables rollout within publicly acceptable and environmentally sustainable parameters.

It is essential given its importance and increasing relevance that law on renewable energy should be covered in legal education, but this is easier said than done. Laws of relevance for the renewables rollout are found in several different legal subdisciplines. Understanding of non-legal matters including factors affecting decisions on investment in energy sectors, on the operation of energy networks and on sources of public opposition to renewable energy development amongst others is needed to understand why and what types of legal intervention are required and to be able to analyse their likely effectiveness. I seek in this book to make renewable energy law more accessible as a topic for legal education and research despite these challenges. I have extensive experience of addressing the complexities of teaching in this area from twelve years of developing and teaching courses on renewable energy law at the Universities of Groningen, Aberdeen and Durham and as a legal researcher working both in energy law and environmental law. I drew from that experience when writing this volume with the aim of opening up renewable energy law as a field of legal scholarship for scholars and students alike who are less well acquainted with the subject matter. I am primarily a UK and EU law scholar, but have sought to broaden the book's appeal to readers beyond these jurisdictions. I do this both by covering topics such as climate law, sustainable development and offshore renewable energy development of international relevance and by examining law's role in addressing difficulties experienced in many jurisdictions with promoting renewable energy. EU and UK law examples are used to illustrate ways in which law has been used to address the problems concerned.

The book is wide ranging, covering many of the key legal issues relating to renewables, but is not comprehensive. I felt it preferable to proceed with publication of an already substantial volume concerning a topic on which a book for supporting legal education is much needed rather than delay publication until additional chapters were available. As a result, planned content on off grid renewable electricity, renewables and heating, and renewable gases as well as sections on decarbonising marine and air transport, emissions trading and carbon taxation are not included in this first edition. I hope that it will be possible to cover these areas more fully in future editions of this work.

This book is dedicated to the memory of my mother who passed away during its preparation for publication and to my sisters, nieces, great-nieces and nephew, and friends. Thanks for always being there for me.

Olivia Woolley,
March 2023

Contents

Preface .... *v*
Abbreviations .... *xiii*
Table of Legislation .... *xv*

1. Renewable Energy Law: An Introduction 1
    I.   Introducing Renewable Energy Law 1
        A. The Book's Purpose 3
        B. The Book's Approach 5
        C. Chapter Contents 6
    II. What is Renewable Energy? 6
    III. Drivers for Renewable Energy Development 8
        A. Climate Change 9
        B. Harm to Environments and Human Health 10
        C. Energy Security 11
        D. Economic Benefits 13
        E. Sustainable Development 14
    IV. Obstacles to Renewable Energy Development 15
        A. Financial Barriers 16
        B. Carbon Lock-in 17
        C. Characteristics of Renewable Energy Sources 18
        D. Public Acceptance 19
        E. Developing World Challenges 20
    V. Defining Renewable Energy Law 21
    VI. Levels of Law 22
        Classroom Questions 23
        Scenario 23
        Suggested Reading 24

2. International Climate Change Law and Renewable Energy 26
    I.   Introduction 26
    II. The Climate Change Treaties and Renewable Energy 27
        A. Obliging State Support for Renewable Energy 28
        B. Deterring Investment in Fossil Fuel Energy 29
            (i) Nationally Determined Contributions under the Paris
                Agreement 31
        C. Market Mechanisms for Emissions Reduction 35
            (i) Market Mechanisms under the Kyoto Protocol 36
            (ii) Market Mechanisms under the Paris Agreement 38

viii CONTENTS

        D. Climate Finance 41
            (i) Unclear Commitments 42
            (ii) Low Transparency 43
            (iii) Climate Finance from Developing States 44
            (iv) Conclusion 44
        E. Technology Transfer 45
        F. Capacity Building 48
        G. Conclusion 50
           Classroom Questions 51
           Scenarios 51
           Suggested Reading 52

3. **Sustainable Development and Renewable Energy** 53
    I. Introduction 53
    II. Introducing Sustainable Development 54
    III. Sustainable Development and Renewable Energy 58
        A. The Brundtland Report 58
        B. The 1992 Rio Declaration on Environment and Development
           and Agenda 21 59
        C. The 2002 Johannesburg Declaration and Plan of
           Implementation 60
        D. Rio+20 and The Future We Want 61
        E. Sustainable Energy for All and Sustainable Development Goal 7 62
        F. International Declarations on Renewable Energy 63
    IV. Soft Law and Renewable Energy 65
    V. International Institutions for Renewable Energy 67
    VI. Renewable Energy under the Energy Charter Treaty (ECT) 71
    VII. Strengthening Support for Renewable Energy under
         International Law 73
         Classroom Questions 74
         Scenarios 74
         Suggested Reading 75

4. **Enabling Renewable Energy Growth: The Role of Targets** 76
    I. Introduction 76
    II. Greenhouse Gas Emissions Reduction Targets and
       Renewable Energy 77
    III. The Role of Targets in Promoting Renewable Energy 78
    IV. Assessing the Value of Targets for Supporting Renewable Energy:
       Key Questions 80
        A. The Target 80
        B. Holding Responsible Actors to Account 81
        C. Investor Confidence 82

V. Case Study: National Targets under the EU's Renewable
   Energy Directives 82
   A. 2001 Renewable Electricity Directive 83
   B. 2009 Renewable Energy Directive 84
      (i) Analysis 87
   C. 2018 Renewable Energy Directive 89
      (i) Proposed Amendments to the 2018 RES Directive 93
      (ii) Analysis 94
   D. Case Study Summary 96
      Classroom Questions 96
      Scenarios 97
      Suggested Reading 97

5. **Securing Investment in Renewable Energy: The Role of Subsidies** 99
   I. Support Schemes 99
   II. Investment Support 101
   III. Operating Support 102
      A. Feed-in Tariffs 104
      B. Feed-in Premiums 106
      C. Obligation/Certificate Schemes 107
      D. Allocating Support through Tenders/Auctions 108
      E. Regulatory Risk 109
   IV. Case Studies: Providing Operating Support for Renewable Energy 111
      A. Feed-in Tariff, Premium Schemes and Competitive Allocation
         (Germany) 112
         (i) Case Study Summary 113
      B. Renewables Obligation Order (ROO) (Certificate/Obligation
         Scheme, UK) 114
         (i) Case Study Summary 116
      C. Contracts for Difference (CFD) Scheme (Premium Scheme
         by Auction, UK) 117
         (i) Competitive Allocation 117
         (ii) Premium Payment 118
         (iii) Sources of Investment Risk 118
         (iv) CFD Auctions 120
         (v) Case Study Summary 121
         Classroom Questions 122
         Scenario 123
         Suggested Reading 124

6. **Transmitting Electricity** 125
   I. Introduction 125
   II. Electricity Networks and Regulation 126
      A. Transmission Systems, Distribution Systems and
         Interconnectors 126
      B. System Operation 127

CONTENTS

        C. Network Regulation 127
        D. Electricity System Regulators 128
        E. Network Operation and Markets 129
  III. Network Access Challenges 130
        A. Capacity Constraints 130
        B. From Passive to Active Management 131
        C. Consumer Participation in Electricity Systems 131
        D. Intermittency 132
        E. Network and Market Operation 133
        F. Connection Costs 134
        G. Investment Challenge 134
        H. The Regulatory Challenge 135
  IV. Legal Responses 136
        A. Network Operation 136
           (i) Market Access 139
           (ii) From Passive to Active Management 139
        B. Opening the Electricity System to New Actors 141
           (i) Smart Grids and Privacy Issues 143
           (ii) Connection Charges 144
        C. Planning 144
        D. Pro-renewables Grid Development 146
        E. Supporting Transboundary Development 147
           (i) Trans-European Energy Infrastructure Regulation
                (2022 TEEI Regulation) 148
           Classroom Questions 152
           Scenarios 152
           Suggested Reading 155

7. Planning, Licensing and Public Opposition 156
  I. Introduction 156
  II. Planning and Permitting for Onshore Wind Energy 158
  III. Concerns with Authorisation Processes for Renewable Energy
      Development 160
        A. Complexity 161
        B. Lack of Time Limits 161
        C. Public Participation Processes 162
        D. Rejection by Decision Makers 163
  IV. Reasons for Public Opposition to Renewable Energy Development 163
        A. Place-based, Visual and Amenity Concerns 164
        B. Socio-economic Factors 166
        C. Environmental Effects 167
        D. The Quality of Developmental and Decision-making Processes 168
  V. Legal Responses to Concerns with Authorisation Regimes 168
        A. Streamlining Development Consent Regimes 169
        B. 'One-stop-shops' 170
        C. Limiting Timescales for Decisions 171

	D.	Planning Policy Statements	173
	E.	Limiting Scope for the Rejection of Renewable Energy Development	174
VI.		Legal Responses to Reasons for Public Opposition	175
	A.	Early Public Engagement	176
	B.	Financial Incentives	177
		(i) Share Ownership	178
		(ii) Compensating Individuals	179
		(iii) Community Benefits	180
		Classroom Questions	181
		Scenarios	182
		Suggested Reading	183

8. Offshore Renewables 185
I.		Introduction: Offshore Power Potential	185
	A.	Fixed Offshore Wind Technology	185
	B.	Floating Turbine Technology	186
	C.	Ocean Energy Technologies Lag Behind	187
	D.	Offshore Network Development is Key for the Expansion of Offshore Wind and Ocean Energy	187
	E.	Structure of the Chapter	188
II.		Legal Foundations in Public International Law for Offshore Power Production	189
	A.	The Zoning Approach to Rights Allocation	189
	B.	Rights to Generate and Transmit Electricity	191
III.		Offshore Wind Energy and Conflict with Other Sea Uses	192
IV.		Offshore Renewable Energy and Negative Environmental Impacts	196
	A.	Duties for Environmental Protection under UNCLOS	197
	B.	Regional Seas Conventions and Plans	198
	C.	Legal Measures to Meet International Duties and Offshore Wind	200
V.		Planning for Offshore Renewables in Congested Seas	202
	A.	Marine Spatial Planning	203
	B.	Strategic Environmental Assessment	207
	C.	Environmental Impact Assessment	209
	D.	Protected Areas Assessment	211
	E.	Adaptive Management	212
		Classroom Questions	212
		Scenario	213
		Suggested Reading	215

9. Decarbonising Road Transport 216
I.		Introduction	216
II.		Promoting Renewable Fuel Consumption in Road Transport through Law	220
	A.	Setting Legal Targets for Renewable Energy in Transport	220
	B.	Promoting the Availability of Alternative Fuel Vehicles	223

	C.	Promoting Alternative Fuels 227
	D.	Infrastructure for Alternative Fuel Vehicles..................................... 229
	E.	Encouraging the Purchase of Alternative Fuel Source Vehicles 231
III.	Biofuels 232
	A.	Sustainability Concerns... 233
	B.	The EU's Legal Response to Concerns with Biofuels: The Sustainability Criteria Regime... 234
		(i) Consequences of Unsustainability in EU Law...................... 235
		(ii) The Sustainability Criteria 236
	C.	Reporting Obligations.. 238
	D.	Amendments to the Sustainability Criteria Regime........................ 239
	E.	WTO Law and the Sustainability Criteria 240
		Classroom Questions... 242
		Scenario.. 242
		Suggested Reading 243

Index.. 245

Abbreviations

ACER	The European Union Agency for the Cooperation of Energy Regulators
CDM	Clean Development Mechanism
CEF	Connecting Europe Facility
CFD	Contracts for Difference
DSO	Distribution System Operator
ECJ	European Court of Justice
ECT	Energy Charter Treaty
EEZ	Exclusive Economic Zone
ENTSO-E	The European Network of Electricity Transmission System Operators
EU	European Union
EU ETS	European Union Emissions Trading System
FIT	Feed-in tariff
GATT	General Agreement on Trade and Tariffs
GDP	Gross Domestic Product
GW	gigawatt (1000 megawatts)
HVDC	High Voltage Direct Current
ICAO	International Civil Aviation Organization
IEA	International Energy Agency
IMO	International Maritime Organization
IPCC	Intergovernmental Panel on Climate Change
IREC	International Renewable Energy Conference
IRENA	International Renewable Energy Association
ITMO	Internationally Transferred Mitigation Outcome
JI	Joint implementation
MSP	Marine spatial planning
MW	megawatt (1000 kilowatts)
MWh	megawatt hour
NDC	Nationally determined contribution
NIMBY	Not in my backyard
NPS	National Policy Statement

NREAP	National Renewable Energy Action Plan
PAC	Pre-Application Consultation
PCI	Project of Common Interest
PPA	Power Purchase Agreement
PV	Photovoltaic
RES	Renewable Energy Sources
RO	Renewables Obligation
ROC	Renewables Obligation Certificate
ROO	Renewables Obligation Order
SDG	Sustainable Development Goal
TEEIR	Trans-European Energy Infrastructure Regulation
TEC	Technology Executive Committee
TSO	Transmission System Operator
UK	United Kingdom
UN	United Nations
UNCED	United Nations Conference on Environment and Development
UNCLOS	United Nations Convention on the Law of the Sea
UNECE	United Nations Economic Commission for Europe
UNFCCC	United Nations Framework Convention on Climate Change
UNGA	United Nations General Assembly
US	United States
USSR	Union of Soviet Socialist Republics
WSSD	World Summit on Sustainable Development
WTO	World Trade Organization

Table of Legislation

Denmark

Consolidated Act No 1074 of 8 November 2011 on Renewable Energy 179

European Union

Directive 92/43/EEC on the conservation of natural habitats and wild flora
    and fauna 200, 213
    art 6(3) 202, 211–12
Directive 98/70/EC relating to the quality of petrol and diesel fuels 93, 222–23,
    229, 239
Directive 99/94/EC relating to the availability of consumer information
    on fuel economy and CO2 emissions in respect of the marketing
    of new passenger cars 231
Directive 2001/42/EC on the assessment of the effects of certain plans
    and programmes on the environment 208, 211
    art 5(1) 208
    art 9(1)(b) 208
Directive 2001/77/EC on the promotion of electricity produced from
    renewable energy sources in the internal electricity market 83, 96, 221
Directive 2003/30/EC on the promotion of the use of biofuels or other
    renewable fuels for transport 89, 221
    art 3(1) 221
Directive 2009/28/EC on the promotion of the use of energy from
    renewable sources 81, 84–89, 91–94, 96,
    137–38, 140, 222–23,
    235–36, 238–40
    Recital 60 137
    art 3(1) 85, 90
    art 3(2) 85
    art 3(4) 222, 235
    art 3(4)(c) 223
    art 3(4)(d) 239
    art 3(4)(e) 240
    art 4 86
    art 4(4) 86
    art 4(5) 86
    art 16(2)(b) 137
    art 16(2)(c) 137–38

xvi TABLE OF LEGISLATION

    art 16(3)–(8) 144
    art 16(4) 144
    art 17(1) 235
    art 17(2) 236, 239
    art 17(3) 236
    art 17(4) 237
    art 17(5) 237
    art 17(7) 238
    art 18 237
    art 18(4) 237
    art 19 236
    art 19(6) 238
    art 21(2) 239
    art 22 86
    art 22(3)(a) 170
    art 22(g)–(j) 238
    art 23 86
    art 23(4) 239
    art 23(6) 170
    art 23(7) 101
    art 25 140
    Ann I 85
    Ann IX 223
    Ann V 236
Directive 2011/92/EU on the assessment of the effects of certain public
    and private projects on the environment 159–60, 211
    art 4(1) 210
    art 6(4) 160
    art 8 160
    art 8(a) 160
    art 9 160
    Ann III 160
Directive 2014/89/EU establishing a framework for marine spatial planning 204
Directive 2014/94/EU on the deployment of alternative fuels infrastructure 230
    art 4(4) 230
    art 5(2) 230
    art 6(9) 230
Directive 2015/1513/EC relating to the quality of petrol and diesel fuels 223, 239
Directive 2018/2001/EU on the promotion of the use of energy from
    renewable sources 21, 81, 89–96,
                                                                                                                                           169, 229, 235
    art 2(24) 232
    art 2(33) 232
    art 3(1) 90, 94–95
    art 3(2) 90

art 4(3)	106
art 4(4)	109
art 6(1)	110
art 6(2)	111
art 6(3)	110
art 6(4)	110
art 14	94
art 15(1)	169–70
art 16(1)	170
art 16(4)–(6)	171
art 23(1)	93
art 24	93
art 25	90, 93, 222
art 25(1)	227–28
art 26(1)	240
art 26(2)	240
art 27(2)	223
art 29(1)	236
art 29(10)	236
art 29(3)	237
art 29(4)	237
art 29(5)	237
art 29(6) and (7)	237
art 30	237
art 30(4)	237
art 33	238
art 36	90
art 37	137
Ann IX	243
Ann VIII	239
Directive 2019/944/EU on common rules for the Internal Market for electricity	127, 140
Recital 39	142
art 3(1)	141
art 3(4)	139
art 15	141–42
art 15(2)(f)	142
art 17	141–42
art 17(2)	142
arts 19–23	144
art 32(1)	140
art 32(3)	140, 145
art 32(4)	146
art 40(1)(d)	142
art 51	146

xviii TABLE OF LEGISLATION

```
art 58(d) .................................................................................................... 146
art 58(d) and (e) ......................................................................................... 142
```
Regulation (EU) 2013/347 on guidelines for trans-European energy
infrastructure 148
Regulation (EU) 2018/1999 on the governance of the Energy Union
and climate action 93, 239
```
art 3 ............................................................................................................. 91
art 4(2) ........................................................................................................ 92
art 4(a)(2) ................................................................................................... 91
art 5 ............................................................................................................. 91
art 9 ............................................................................................................. 91
art 9(3) ........................................................................................................ 91
arts 17–28 ................................................................................................... 92
art 20 ......................................................................................................... 238
art 29(2) ...................................................................................................... 92
art 31 ........................................................................................................... 91
art 32 ........................................................................................................... 92
art 32(2) ...................................................................................................... 92
art 32(3) ................................................................................................ 92, 95
art 32(4) ...................................................................................................... 93
art 32(5) ...................................................................................................... 93
art 34 ........................................................................................................... 92
art 35(2)(d) ............................................................................................... 238
Ann I ........................................................................................................... 91
Ann IX ...................................................................................................... 238
Ann X ....................................................................................................... 238
```
Regulation (EU) 2019/1242 setting CO_2 emission performance standards
for new heavy-duty vehicles
```
art 5 ........................................................................................................... 226
art 5(3) and (4) ......................................................................................... 226
```
Regulation (EU) 2019/631 setting CO_2 emission performance standards
for new passenger cars and for new light commercial vehicles 225
```
art 1(6) and (7) ......................................................................................... 226
art 5 ........................................................................................................... 226
```
Regulation (EU) 2019/943 on the internal market for electricity 137–40
```
art 6(4) ...................................................................................................... 139
art 8(1) ...................................................................................................... 139
art 8(3) ...................................................................................................... 142
art 12 ................................................................................................... 138–39
art 16(2) .................................................................................................... 138
art 52 ......................................................................................................... 140
```
Regulation (EU) 2021/1119 establishing the framework for achieving
climate neutrality 93
Regulation (EU) 2021/1153 establishing the Connecting Europe Facility 150–51
```
art 5 ........................................................................................................... 151
art 7 ........................................................................................................... 150
```

TABLE OF LEGISLATION   xix

Regulation (EU) 2022/869 on guidelines for trans-European energy
    infrastructure 136, 147–51,
                                                                                                        158, 170, 172
    art 3 148
    art 3(4) 149
    art 3(6) 149
    art 4 149
    art 4(2) 151
    art 5(7) 149
    art 7(1) and (2) 151
    art 8 171
    art 8(5) 151
    art 9 .... 172, 177
    art 9(5) 151
    art 10 151
    art 10(1) 172
    art 16 149
    art 16(1) 149
    art 16(4) 149
    art 16(5) 150
    art 16(7) 150
    art 17 150
    art 18 150
    Ann I 148
    Ann VI 172
Treaty on the Functioning of the European Union, art 194(2) 83

International

Agreement on Technical Barriers to Trade 241
Chicago Convention 195
Convention for the Protection of the Marine Environment of the
    North-East Atlantic (OSPAR) 199, 201, 213
    art 2 199
    art 2(1)(a) 199
    art 2(1)(b) 199
    Ann V 199–200
Convention on Biological Diversity 11, 197–98, 200
Convention on Long-Range Transboundary Air Pollution 11
Convention on Migratory Species 198
Convention on the Law of the Sea 11, 22, 195,
                                                                                                        207, 212–14
    art 1(4) 197
    art 2 191
    art 3 190

xx TABLE OF LEGISLATION

art 17	193
art 21	193
arts 55–75	190
art 56	191
art 56(1)(a)	191
art 56(3)	190
art 58	193
art 58(1)	193
art 60(1)(b)	191
art 60(4) and (5)	192
art 60(7)	193–94, 196
art 76	190
art 78(2)	192
art 79	191
art 79(1)	192
art 79(4)	191
art 79(5)	193
art 86	190
art 87(1)	192
art 87(1)(c)	192
art 87(2)	193
art 136	190
art 137	190
art 192	197
art 194	197
arts 207–212	197
Ch XII	198
Pt V	190, 193–94
Pt VI	190–92
Pt XI	190
Doha Amendment to the Kyoto Protocol	27, 30
art 1	31
Energy Charter Treaty	27, 54, 71–72, 74, 111
art 1(4)	71
art 19(1)(d)	71
art 42	72
Protocol on Energy Efficiency	73
Energy Community Treaty	23
European Economic Area Agreement	23
Framework Convention on Climate Change	9, 27, 30–32, 35, 39, 43–45, 50, 73
preamble	31
art 4(1)(b)	30–32
art 4(1)(c)	28, 45
art 4(2)(b)	30
art 4(2)(d)	30

art 4(3)	42
art 4(5)	45–48
art 4(7)	31
Ann I	30
General Agreement on Tariffs and Trade	241
art I:1	241
art III:4	241
art XX	241
Johannesburg Declaration on Sustainable Development	60–62
Kyoto Protocol	27–28, 30–31, 35–38, 43–44, 47, 50–52, 73
art 2(1)(a)	28
art 2(1)(a)(iv)	28
art 3(1)	30
art 6	36
art 12	36
art 12(2)	36
art 16 ff	36
Paris Agreement	2, 9, 21, 24, 27, 29, 31–33, 35–42, 45–46, 49–51, 58, 63, 65–66, 70, 72, 77, 237
art (1)(a)	2
art 2	34
art 2(1)	32
art 2(1)(a)	2
art 2(1)(c)	41
art 2(2)	33–34
art 3	32
art 4(1)	2, 33
art 4(19)	34
art 4(2)	32, 34
art 4(3)	32–34
art 4(4)	32
art 4(9)	35
art 6	52
art 6(2)	38–40
art 6(3)	38
art 6(4)	38, 40
art 6(4)(b)	40
art 6(4)(d)	40
art 6(8)	38, 47
art 6(9)	38
art 9(2)	44
art 9(5)	43–44
art 9(7)	43
art 10	47

art 10(1) 45
art 10(2) 46–47
art 10(4) 46
art 11 49
art 13 33
art 13(11) 34, 43
art 15 34
Paris Decision 40, 42, 47
    preamble 29
    para 37(d) 40
    para 37(f) 40
    para 53 44
    para 71 49
    para 73 49
    para 73(f) 49
Rio Declaration on Environment and Development 56, 59–60, 156,
159, 201, 207
Statute of the International Renewable Energy Agency 54, 74
    art II 68
    art IV 68
Treaty on Protection and Preservation of the Marine Environment, Pt XII 197

United Kingdom

Building Regulations 2010 230
Climate Change Act 2008 78
Conservation (Natural Habitats etc.) Regulations 1994 211
Electricity Works (Environmental Impact Assessment) (England and Wales)
    Regulations 2017 210
Electricity Works (Environmental Impact Assessment) (Scotland)
    Regulations 2000 210
Environmental Assessment (Scotland) Act 2005 208
Environmental Assessment of Plans and Programmes Regulations 2004 208
Infrastructure Act 2015 179
Infrastructure Planning (National Policy Statement Consultation)
    Regulations 2009 173
Marine (Scotland) Act 2010 204
Marine and Coastal Access Act 2009 .... 203, 205, 215
    s 51(6) 205
    s 58(1) 205
    s 58(3) 205–6
Offshore Marine Conservation (Natural Habitats etc.) Regulations 2017 211
Planning Act 2008 .... 172–77, 206
    s 7 173
    s 37 176

s 47	176
ss 47 to 50	172
s 48	176
s 49	176
s 87(3)(b)	172
s 98	172
s 104(3)	174, 206
s 104(7)	175
Renewable Transport Fuel Obligations Order 2007	227
Renewables Obligation Order 2002	114
Town and Country Planning (Development Management Procedure and Section 62A Applications (England) (Amendment)) Order 2013	177
Town and Country Planning (Development Management Procedure) (England) Order 2015, reg 34	171
Town and Country Planning (Revocations) Regulations 2014	173

1

Renewable Energy Law: An Introduction

I. Introducing Renewable Energy Law

Humans have always met energy needs from renewable sources. Biomass, wind, water and solar radiation have been harnessed by civilisations to produce energy for millennia.[1] Biomass remains a principal energy source for many people in the developing world to this day.[2] Consumption of energy from renewable sources was largely displaced in states that underwent industrialisation during the eighteenth, nineteenth and twentieth centuries by energy from fossilised sources such as petroleum, coal and natural gas. The rapid global expansion of economies, populations, and urbanisation in the 8 decades following the end of the Second World War has seen further massive growth in fossil fuel consumption. As a result, fossil fuels are the dominant energy source in the world today, amounting to 81 per cent of production and consumption in 2019.[3] However, interest in renewables as a means of meeting energy demand has returned in recent decades. The best-known reason for this is the major contribution that the extraction of fossil fuels and production of energy from them are making to climate change by releasing carbon dioxide, methane, and other less prevalent but more potent greenhouse gases into the atmosphere.

The revival is at a small scale at present. Around 13 per cent of global energy production and 16 per cent of energy consumption were from renewable sources in 2018.[4] Over half of that production and consumption derives from long-established renewable sources of traditional biomass and hydropower with more recently introduced renewables technologies including for wind and solar energy and biofuels making up the

---

[1] Vaclav Smil, *Energy Transitions: History, Requirements, Prospects* (Praeger 2010) 26.
[2] United Nations, *Leveraging Energy Action for Advancing the Sustainable Development Goals* (SDG 7 Policy Brief 2021) 2021-POLICY BRIEFS.pdf (sdgs.un.org) (accessed 1 October 2022), 20–1 and 84.
[3] European Commission, *EU Energy in Figures: Statistical Pocketbook 2021* (Publications Office of the European Union, 2021) 11 and 15–17.
[4] ibid.

balance.[5] However, renewables became a leading destination for energy sector investment during the 2010s with investment in new electricity production capacity from modern renewables now consistently exceeding investment in new fossil fuel capacity.[6] Renewable electricity accounted for 75 per cent of global power sector investment in 2019 compared to 21.2 per cent in fossil fuel electricity.[7] Renewable energy use is very likely to grow significantly during the next three decades and beyond if the world's states are serious about achieving agreed goals of international climate action to which the great majority of them have committed by ratifying the Paris Climate Change Agreement including that greenhouse gas emissions should be reduced to a 'net zero' level during the second half of the twenty-first century and that the increase in global average temperature since pre-industrial times should be kept to well below 2°C and below 1.5°C if possible.[8]

Some of the growth in renewable energy to date will have been due solely to the uptake of relevant technologies by energy producers and of their output by consumers because of the attractive attributes which energy from renewable sources tends to possess. However, much of it will have happened because of legal interventions made to promote the growth in availability and use of energy derived from renewable sources and of the technologies needed for its production, transmission and consumption. Law has a major part to play in the revival of renewable energy. Laws are needed at all levels, international, regional, national and sub-national, to implement pro-renewables policies. Law can be used to encourage renewable energy production and consumption, for example by creating rights to financial support. It can also be used to lessen and remove the many barriers that would otherwise constrain its growth, for example by addressing causes of public opposition to renewable energy development. The great majority of the world's states have already introduced laws which seek to promote the renewable energy revival including by removing barriers.[9]

The appeal of renewable energy without legal intervention is only likely to increase as the cost of energy production from relevant technologies and of the technologies themselves decline through experience with their use, related efficiency gains, economies of scale in production both of energy and technologies, and the modification of energy systems and their institutions so that the positive features of renewables can be better enjoyed. However, legal intervention is likely to remain necessary in many respects during the decades ahead for reasons including:

- the continuing dominance of fossil fuel energy sources;
- related needs for very significant growth of renewable energy and for urgency in securing this growth if greenhouse gas emitting fuels are to be displaced at a rate

---

[5] REN21, *Renewables 2020 Global Status Report* (REN 21 Secretariat, 2020) 32.
[6] ibid, 165–73.
[7] ibid, 173.
[8] Paris Agreement (adopted 12 December 2015, entered into force 4 November 2016) 3156 UNTS, arts 2(1)(a) and 4(1); International Renewable Energy Agency (IRENA), *Global Energy Transformation: A Roadmap to 2050* (IRENA, 2019) 10–14.
[9] See the IEA/IRENA Renewables Policies Database at www.iea.org/policies/about (accessed 1 October 2022). See also Penelope Crossley, *Renewable Energy Law: An International Assessment* (Cambridge University Press 2019).

commensurate with the seriousness of threats posed by climate change for human well-being;
- particular needs for intervention in energy for heating and transport in which the proportion of supplies from low carbon energy remains very low;
- socio-economic lock-in to ways of living predicated on the ready availability during several decades of cheap high-density energy from fossil fuel sources; and
- inadequacies of existing systemic arrangements and laws for accommodating renewable energy.

A. The Book's Purpose

The book's purpose is to inform and educate readers about the growing bodies of laws which are being adopted to promote renewable energy's growth, to overcome constraints on this and to address problems which renewable energy's expansion creates. The book has three main aims. Its first is to aid readers' understanding of reasons why legal interventions are often needed to enable the growth of renewable energy. Its second is to advance readers' knowledge and understanding of ways in which law is being or could be used to promote renewable energy including by overcoming barriers to its use and addressing consequences of the sector's expansion. Its third is to assist readers with developing capacities to look critically at laws adopted to address commonly occurring problems encountered by the renewable energy sector as it expands. Understanding problems that relevant laws are intended to address creates a learning context in which the likely efficacy of legal responses for achieving intended aims can be assessed.

In addition, the book aims to support teaching on renewable energy law and research in this field by contributing to its development as a legal sub-discipline. The author was motivated to write a book that advances these aims by her 10 years of experience with developing and teaching courses on renewable energy law and as a researcher in the field. Law concerning renewable energy is quickly growing in importance in view of well-recognised urgent needs for replacing fossil fuel energy with renewable alternatives. Knowledge and understanding of how law can be used to enable expansion of the renewables sector are therefore of increasing value for students, policymakers and practitioners alike. However, this is not a straightforward topic for educators to develop courses on and teach or for recipients of teaching to benefit from for the following reasons. First, renewable energy law is not an established field of legal scholarship with well-defined parameters and rules for determining what lies within and without its ambit. It was therefore necessary for the author when first developing renewable energy law teaching to decide upon the scope of this emerging sub-field, and to identify its contents.

The temptation when developing a renewable energy course may be to concentrate on examining well-established legal areas such as trade law, competition law and environmental law in which issues have arisen concerning renewables. Whilst the appeal of this approach is understandable, courses which take these topics as their principal focuses may prove poor for cultivating knowledge and understanding of why law has a role in promoting renewables, of what that role is, and of how the likely contribution of laws to expanding renewable energy production and consumption can be discerned and evaluated. Instead, the author chose to concentrate on laws that drive growth of the renewables sector and that seek to enable this by overcoming the many factors constraining growth in the use of energy from renewable sources when deciding on what should fall under the sub-discipline's purview. The purpose of this exercise was not to lay exclusive claim to laws as belonging to the sub discipline. Many of the laws that it covers and which this book examines fall primarily under other fields such as climate law and environmental law. Rather, renewable energy law as a field of legal scholarship and education is concerned with determining law's role in enabling the growth of the renewables sector, and with developing bases for: identifying laws whose purpose is to promote the renewable sector's growth; analysing whether they are well designed for realising this objective; and exploring how limitations identified in current laws for promoting renewables could be remedied.

Second, acquiring command of this subject matter is a labour intensive and lengthy process. It is only through extensive reading that the author has been able to gain sufficient understanding of the contexts in which laws relating to renewables are deployed to recognise whether or not reading materials are suitable for supporting teaching and research on renewable energy law. Relevant reading materials for introducing readers not only to law used in connection with renewable energy but also the needs and challenges for integrating renewables that those laws are designed to address are spread across several legal sub-disciplines and also across several non-legal disciplines. Legal sub-disciplines in which relevant literature is found include energy law, environmental law, climate law, public international law, the law of the sea, and trade law amongst others. Non-legal disciplines in which important papers for understanding the contexts in which renewable energy development are published include economics, politics, sociology, engineering, and natural sciences including terrestrial and marine ecology. Literature in these legal sub-disciplines and non-legal disciplines must first be read and understood by the course designer to enable informed appraisal of whether or not secondary sources are likely to be useful for educational purposes.

Third, understanding of the contexts in which the rollout of renewables takes place (eg, the investment environment, the functioning of energy systems, considerations informing public responses to energy developments) is needed to teach renewable energy law in a way which enables students to think critically about its likely efficacy for supporting the rollout of renewables. Literature which examines these contexts typically derives from research in disciplines other than law and will usually, if it is presenting research results, not be aimed at supporting education for those without a background in the discipline concerned. It may therefore be too challenging for students to attain full understanding of subject matter examined in course seminars without significant support. The author has been able to acquire understanding of these contexts through broad interdisciplinary research and uses this in the book to provide foundational explanations of renewable energy law's role in different settings so that others can benefit from it when teaching, studying, and researching in the field.

To summarise, the book has been developed to address the three challenges outlined above with a view to making renewable energy law more easily accessible as a topic for course developers, students, and legal researchers alike. It defines a coherent body of legal topics linked by their relevance for enabling the growth of renewables despite the several major challenges that confront this sector's expansion. In doing so, it fills a gap in legal literature by providing what, to the author's knowledge, is the first book publication intended to perform a textbook role in support of new course development and delivery on renewable energy law. The author hopes that this product of her teaching experience will help with democratising renewable energy law as a component of legal education. The book also adds to legal scholarship in two ways. It proffers a basis for determining the parameters of renewable energy law and identifies core contents of the field. It also proposes methods in relation to each of the topics which the book examines for recognising laws that contribute to renewable energy's growth and for assessing their likely value for securing this outcome. Methods are developed by reference to the roles of renewable energy law in different contexts. For example, the purpose of laws examined in Chapter 4 is to strengthen confidence amongst investors and other actors in policy commitments made by governments to meet renewable energy targets by providing them with legal backing. The chapter identifies features that laws which provide strong support for targets in this way should possess and suggests a basis for assessing the strengths and weaknesses of relevant laws by reference to their presence or absence. The purpose of laws examined in Chapter 6 is to address challenges retarding the integration of renewable electricity into electricity networks (network access challenges). The chapter's initial review of network access challenges and of the types of intervention needed to address them aids the following explorations of how law can assist with meeting the challenges and of whether laws employed in practice to modify network operation and development are capable of doing so.

B. The Book's Approach

The book does not offer comprehensive descriptions of or proposals for laws relating to renewable energy in different jurisdictions. Books based on focused studies of challenges with introducing renewable energy in specific states and administrations and of legal responses to them are required to service these needs. Instead, it employs an approach to examining renewable energy laws which the author has developed during a decade of designing and teaching courses on this topic. The courses were taken by cohorts of students from multiple different developed and developing world jurisdictions. The author's own background is in UK and EU law, but courses that are limited to accounts of the law in these jurisdictions and of their legal peculiarities would be of limited value for such diverse groups. In view of this, the author's approach in teaching, also used in this book, is to start by identifying and exploring types of problems which efforts to introduce renewable energy tend to encounter or create wherever they are made. Commonly occurring problems are due to intrinsic characteristics of energy from renewable sources and of relevant technologies including the intermittency of energy from wind and solar sources, the fact that sources are often remote from existing networks, and the costs of renewable energy and of related technologies because of their newness. They are also due to intrinsic characteristics of fossil fuel energies and therefore of the energy systems, institutions, societies, and economies which are still dominated by them. The common nature of these problems creates much scope for those wishing to learn about how law can be used to address them to draw from experiences in jurisdictions other than their own, whilst being alert to perennial difficulties with transplanting experience from one legal culture and its socio-economic context to others.

The author employs examples from the UK and EU in examining how law can assist with addressing challenges for introducing renewable energy. Experience in these jurisdictions is useful for learning about renewable energy law as both have been proactive in promoting energy production and consumption from renewable sources. As leading proponents of renewable energy, they have also been ahead of other jurisdictions in encountering problems that pro-renewables policies can meet or create and in developing legal responses to them. The author also draws on experience from other jurisdictions with introducing renewable energy to illustrate challenges which arise and ways in which law can be used to address them. The examples used show that the type of legal responses developed in the UK and EU are not unique to them but are being employed elsewhere. As noted above, similarities in response reflect the common nature of problems raised by efforts to promote renewable energy and its integration into energy systems that were designed around qualitatively different fossil fuel energy sources.

C. Chapter Contents

The following sections introduce readers to renewable energy law by setting out essential background information for studying this topic. Section II defines renewable energy. Section III examines the main drivers for the adoption of pro-renewables policies and laws for implementing them. Section IV identifies and explains the nature of common barriers facing the growth of a new renewables sector. Knowledge and understanding of barriers are particularly important from a legal perspective as much of the law examined in this book has been introduced wholly or in part to overcome them. Section V further defines the parameters of renewable energy law as it is understood for the purposes of this book. Section VI concludes the chapter by setting out foundational legal information for following chapters on the different administrative levels at which renewable energy law is adopted.

II. What is Renewable Energy?

The term 'renewable' is used to describe energy derived from sources that are replenished at the same rate as they are used. This is in contrast to fossil fuels, the consumption of which reduces the stocks available for future generations The principal sources of renewable energy are the sun, the wind, waves, tides, tidal currents, geothermal energy and organic matter (biomass). The majority of these sources are the product, either directly or indirectly, of energy from the sun. The exceptions to this are tidal and geothermal energy which are derived respectively from the gravitational effect of the moon and from the heat of the Earth's interior. Most of these sources are fully renewable, but biomass and geothermal energy are only renewable to the extent that consumption does not exceed the capacity of the Earth and its interior to replace them. Technologies have been developed to produce energy from all these sources. Some of the technologies are well-established and widely used for commercial energy production (eg, wind and solar energy) whilst others are at an earlier stage of development (eg, wave and tidal current energy).[10]

Renewable sources can be used to meet demands for energy for electricity production, heating and transportation. Electricity can be generated from solar energy (including through photovoltaic (PV) units), through the release of water stored behind dams (hydropower and tidal barriers), through turbines driven by wind, wave and tidal currents and by the burning of biomass. In addition to meeting current demand for services such as lighting, renewable electricity is expected to have a growing role in providing energy for heating and transportation if fossil fuels consumed for these purposes are to be replaced by lower carbon alternatives. Energy for heating can be attained directly from the sun, including through its heating of the air and water, from the burning of biomass and gases derived from them in boilers, from the capture of heat produced as a by-product of electricity generated from renewable sources in combined heat and power units, and through tapping into geothermal energy. Fuels derived from a wide variety of biomass feedstocks and from organic waste can be used to power road, marine and air transportation.

A common characteristic of most renewable sources is that carbon dioxide is not emitted during the production of energy from them. The exception to this is biomass which is often described as a 'carbon neutral' energy source because carbon dioxide that organic matter absorbs during its growth is released into the atmosphere when it is burnt. 'Carbon neutral' is a controversial term with many arguing that its use conceals a complex reality with biomass burning sometimes adding to atmospheric greenhouse gas levels over the near-term timeframes in which rapid decarbonization is required because of the time taken to replace lost biomass, particularly old-growth wood, with biomass possessing an equivalent capacity for carbon storage.[11] Critics of the term also reference greenhouse gas emissions from conversion of the source material into usable energy products and from its transportation to consumers. Awareness is shown of this complexity in laws which seek to distinguish 'sustainable' bioenergy sources from sources labelled as being 'unsustainable' for reasons including their carbon footprint.[12]

Hydrogen does not occur naturally and is not a renewable fuel itself. However, it can be used as a carrier for renewable energy,[13] For example, electricity from renewables

---

[10] For a fuller explanation of renewable energy sources see Stephen Peake and Bob Everett, 'Introducing Renewable Energy' in Stephen Peake (ed) *Renewable Energy: Power for a Sustainable Future* 4th edn (Oxford University Press, 2017).

[11] Mihnea Catuti, Milan Elkerbout, Christian Egenhofer and Monica Alessi, *Biomass and Climate Neutrality* (CEPS Policy Insights, No. 2020/19, August 2020) www.ceps.eu/ceps-publications/biomass-and-climate-neutrality/ (accessed 1 October 2022).

[12] See Chapter 9, Section III.

[13] Crossley (n 9) 53–4.

8 RENEWABLE ENERGY LAW: AN INTRODUCTION

which exceeds demand at the time of generation can be used to power electrolysis of water to separate hydrogen from oxygen. Stored hydrogen can then be burnt to produce electricity when renewable sources are not sufficient to meet demand. It can also be used directly as a fuel in vehicles fitted with hydrogen fuel cells. Hydrogen has sometimes been included in legal definitions of renewable energy because of its close association with renewable power generation.[14]

It has been argued that nuclear energy should also be viewed as a renewable energy source.[15] The argument is based on revived interest in nuclear power because of its low carbon credentials, and on the substantial remaining reserves of resources required for the manufacture of nuclear fuels (primarily uranium). The argument has found little success.[16] Feedstocks for nuclear fuels, although substantial, are exhaustible. There is also much reluctance to support nuclear energy in the same way as renewable energy sources because of the potentially very significant negative effects of the former in the event of radioactive releases, still-unresolved questions about how to deal with nuclear waste and the manifest security concerns that certain states and actors may gain access to nuclear materials and technologies. Nuclear power is not included within renewable energy as defined in this book.

III. Drivers for Renewable Energy Development

The ready availability of reliable affordable energy supplies is essential for maintaining peoples' security and for the operation of economic and social systems which enhance their wellbeing. The content of energy supplies is therefore (or should be) a matter of interest for all governments. This remains the case even in national energy systems which have been deregulated in order to pass control from the state to markets. Governments use energy policies and laws to prefer certain energy sources over others where use of the preferred sources contributes to overarching policy objectives. Recent decades have seen many of the world's states adopt policies and laws in favour of increasing energy production and consumption from renewable sources. They have done this because compelling reasons demand that the content of energy supplies must be altered to address a raft of threats to the secure functioning of progressive societies including change in the Earth's atmospheric composition, accelerating worldwide environmental deterioration, localised environmental threats to public health, geopolitical turmoil and economic shocks. Renewable energy's expansion is also seen as a means of creating security and improved living conditions in states whose populations are prone to insecurity and poverty. The following paragraphs explore these reasons which are driving the widespread adoption of policies and laws in favour of renewable energy sources.

---

[14] ibid.
[15] ibid, 56–60.
[16] ibid.

A. Climate Change

The great majority of the world's states have entered into legally binding treaties under international law in which they commit to tackle climate change, describing it as a 'common concern of humankind'. The most recent of these treaties, the Paris Climate Change Treaty agreed in December 2015, had been ratified by 193 of the 197 states in the world by the end of 2021.[17] Climate change is occurring because human activities have led to change in the gaseous composition of the Earth's atmosphere and therefore of its climate system due to the release of large volumes of gases which are referred to collectively using the adjective 'greenhouse'. Greenhouse gas growth alters the Earth's climate by increasing the level of solar radiation that is trapped rather than escaping back into space. Consequences include growth in the global average temperature, alteration in historic patterns of rainfall, extreme weather events and worsening ecosystem degradation for reasons including extinction and relocation of species which are unable to cope with changed conditions. Carbon dioxide accounts for around three-quarters of current greenhouse gas emissions with the remaining quarter being made up of methane (16%), nitrous oxide (6%) and fluorinated gases (2%).[18]

The combustion of fuel to produce energy is responsible for around three-quarters of greenhouse gas emissions overall and for an even higher proportion of carbon dioxide emissions.[19] Fuel combustion as a category includes energy production by power and heating sectors, for transportation, for industrial processes, for agricultural processes, and for residential use. Greenhouse gas releases from fuel combustion are largely due to gases emitted by burning petroleum, oil and natural gas. The power and heat production sectors make the largest contribution to greenhouse gas growth (34% worldwide in 2019, 32.5% in the EU in 2019).[20] Transport's contribution is not far behind and growing, being responsible for 15 per cent of greenhouse gas emissions globally in 2019 and 30.2 per cent of emissions in the EU in 2019.[21] Manufacturing, industry and construction are together the second major contributor worldwide and the third major contributor in the EU (24% worldwide in 2019, 15.7% of emissions in the EU in 2019).[22] In addition to fuel combustion, methane is released by coal mining and by oil and gas operations.

In view of these stark statistics, decarbonisation of the energy sector provides the main focus for efforts at all levels to combat climate change with attention turning to renewable energy because either no or, in the case of carbon neutral biomass, no additional greenhouse gases are released into the atmosphere at the point of energy

---

[17] United Nations Framework Convention on Climate Change, 'Paris Agreement – Status of Ratification', https://unfccc.int/process/the-paris-agreement/status-of-ratification (accessed 1 October 2022).
[18] United States Environment Protection Agency, 'Global Greenhouse Gas Emissions Data', www.epa.gov/ghgemissions/global-greenhouse-gas-emissions-data (accessed 1 October 2022).
[19] ibid.
[20] IPCC, 'Summary for Policymakers' in Priyadarshi Shukla and others (eds) *Climate Change 2022: Mitigation of Climate Change. Contribution of Working Group III to the Sixth Assessment Report of the Intergovernmental Panel on Climate Change* (Cambridge University Press, 2022), 12; European Commission (n 3) 163.
[21] ibid.
[22] ibid.

production. Renewable sources are not the only options available for emission-free energy production. Nuclear power production has seen a revival in national policy support largely because it offers a means of producing large volumes of carbon free electricity at stable and predictable levels. Carbon capture and storage technologies offer the potential to exploit fossil fuels without greenhouse gas growth by capturing emissions at the point of production and piping them for storage underground including in depleted oil and gas fields. However, the latter is a still developing technology and both are perceived to be high-cost options for energy production whose use creates risks of significant negative impacts on human well-being. In addition, all means of producing greenhouse gas free energy will be needed in the future if gas-emitting fossil fuel production is to be eradicated.

The relationship between legal agreements made by states on combating climate change and the worldwide diffusion of renewable energy technologies is examined in detail in Chapter 2. Regional and national policies on combating climate change are also major drivers for the adoption of the renewable energy targets and laws considered in Chapter 4 and of the laws required to support renewable energy's growth examined in Chapters 5 to 9.

B. Harm to Environments and Human Health

Climate change is not the only cause of environmental concern associated with fossil fuel energy. Other problematic impacts can occur at all stages of production and consumption for different fossil fuel types. Effects include deliberate destruction of environments to access coal in strip and opencast mining, pollution of aquatic environments and drinking water due to acid runoff from mining, fracking for shale gas, leaks of crude oil from rigs and pipelines and spills from oil tankers. Air pollution from noxious gases, heavy metals and microscopic particles released from burning fossil fuels for electricity, heating and transportation is a serious enough threat to human health and environmental functioning on its own to justify their replacement with less polluting energy sources.[23] Levels of air pollution exceeding safe levels for human health are endemic in many of the world's cities.[24] IRENA projects that tackling air pollution by moving to cleaner energy sources would lead to strong human welfare gains worldwide.[25] Some of these polluting releases contribute to global warming (carbon dioxide, ozone, nitrous oxide, black carbon) whilst releases of sulphur dioxide from coal burning for electricity production lead to the acidification of rain and serious impacts from this such as forest decline and loss.

This catalogue of environmental consequences spurs calls for replacing fossil fuels with energy from renewable sources. Positive steps to tackle these problems, including

---

[23] IRENA, *Global Renewables Outlook: Energy Transformation 2050* (IRENA, 2020) 58; Frederica Perera, 'Pollution from Fossil Fuel Combustion is the Leading Environmental Threat to Global Pediatric Health and Equity: Solutions Exist' (2018) 15 *International Journal of Environmental Research and Public Health* 1.
[24] ibid.
[25] IRENA (n 23) 52.

by moving to cleaner fuels, are also required by legal duties of states and of subnational authorities at several legal levels. States party to the UNECE Convention on Long-Range Transboundary Air Pollution and its several protocols and Member States of the European Union have obligations to keep certain pollutants below specified levels and to take action when they are exceeded.[26] National and subnational laws set limits for levels of pollutants in the atmosphere, in terrestrial and marine waters, and in drinking water. Conventions ratified by many of the world's states such as the Convention on Biological Diversity and the United Nations Convention on the Law of the Sea alongside many species-specific instruments place duties on states to address sources of harm for biodiversity at large and for particular species and their habitats.

The environmental consequences of fossil fuels create interest in technologies that reduce or avoid these effects. Renewable energy technologies are often far preferable from this perspective.[27] Gases are not released directly by electricity production from renewable sources apart from biomass burning. Electric vehicles do not emit the gases or particulate matter which are major contributors to urban air pollution. Using off-grid renewable electricity production to replace reliance on diesel generators and biomass burning assists with alleviating air pollution, particularly in peoples' homes, that impacts negatively on the lives of many without access to secure centralised electricity supplies. It is unsurprising therefore that states are turning to renewable technologies in national energy and transportation policies and laws. Crossley finds that nearly half of the 113 national renewable energy laws examined in her research had addressing environmental problems as an objective including air pollution, unsustainable water use, water pollution, thermal pollution, waste and biodiversity loss.[28] We should keep in mind however the adage that 'there is no such thing as a free lunch' with energy use. Renewable energy production and consumption can also have negative environmental effects. As already mentioned, biomass burning can contribute significantly to air pollution, particularly in homes. Producing feedstock for bioenergy can lead to worse environmental effects than it avoids if this is not done sustainably.[29] Damming rivers and tidal waters to produce electricity has substantial and typically damaging impacts on river and marine ecosystems which are altered for this purpose. Care is needed with siting other means of electricity production to avoid locations where they would cause harm (eg, siting a wind farm next to a coastal breeding place for seabirds). Laws that can be used or are specifically designed to address these environmental consequences are an important part of renewable energy law as we will see in Chapters 8 and 9.

C. Energy Security

Fossil fuel resources are not evenly shared amongst states. Some such as Russia, Saudi Arabia and Venezuela have plentiful reserves whilst others must import oil and gas

---

[26] Philippe Sands and Jacqueline Peel with Adriana Fabra and Ruth Mackenzie, *Principles of International Environmental Law* 4th edn (Cambridge University Press, 2018) 259–77.
[27] IRENA (n 23) 58; Perera (n 23).
[28] Crossley (n 9) 139.
[29] See the discussion of biomass and carbon neutrality in Section II of this chapter and at Section III of Chapter 9.

from them to meet demand for these energy sources. For example, many European states and the European Union overall depend heavily on oil and gas supplies from Russia and from Central Asian states. The EU imported 96.8 per cent of its oil and petroleum products supplies and 89.7 per cent of natural gas supplies in 2019.[30] South-East Asia balances supply and demand as a region, but other Asian regions are net importers of fossil fuels.[31] Uneven distribution of fossil fuels confers geopolitical power and economic advantage on states possessing fossil fuel resources whilst leaving others economically and socially vulnerable to their actions and to disturbances in fossil fuel exporting areas. Disputes between Russia and the Ukraine through which gas pipelines pass gave European importers of gas cause for concern that supplies may be disrupted in the first decade of the twenty-first century, whilst instability in the Middle East and related risks of supply disruption are a constant source of anxiety for states which rely on oil and gas imports from the region.[32] Russia's invasion of Ukraine in 2022 led to the rapid doubling of already high oil and gas prices in the EU, and related calls for accelerated investment in green energy.[33] Means of reducing reliance on energy imports are unsurprisingly attractive to affected states. States which have fossil fuel surpluses may also choose to shore up domestic energy security by increasing non-fossil fuel energy resources domestically so that they are able to export more of their output.

Being energy secure means more than that people have the possibility of accessing energy supplies. They should also be affordable. Fluctuation in oil and gas prices can also threaten energy security, even for states with reserves of these commodities, when this leads to high prices. Means of reducing exposure to fossil fuel price volatility and related risks of harm to peoples' standards of living and national economies will appeal to many states, and not just those with net dependencies on imports.[34] Conversely, a projected long period of low prices with little prospect of volatility leading to much higher prices could depress investment in non-fossil fuel alternatives.

Renewable energy resources are also not distributed evenly. Some states possess much greater potential for commercially viable renewable energy exploitation than others. However, the renewable resource is distributed more widely than exploitable fossil fuels with every state possessing some potential for producing energy from ubiquitous sources such as solar radiation and wind. Its exploitation is also positively encouraged by global climate action as a means both of decarbonizing existing supplies and advancing adaptation by enabling the transition of socio-economic systems to a post-carbon future. In this regard, questions arise over whether it is appropriate to view energy resources whose use heightens risks of harmful climate change as secure. Energy security is therefore a major driver for renewable energy exploitation and one which operates independently from as well as alongside reducing greenhouse

---

[30] European Commission (n 3) 75 and 77.
[31] IRENA (n 23) 122.
[32] Crossley (n 9) 113–15; Matt Bonass, 'Why Renewable Energy' in Matt Bonass and Michael Rudd (eds) *Renewables: A Practical Handbook* (Globe Law and Business, 2010) 9, 11–12.
[33] OECD, *OECD Economic Outlook, Interim Report March 2022: Economic and Social Impacts and Policy Implications of the War in the Ukraine* (OECD Publishing, 2022).
[34] Crossley (n 9) 116–17; Bonass (n 32) 11–12.

gas emissions. Crossley identifies bolstering energy security in the face of diminishing national capacity to meet demand, particularly through fossil fuels, as a common reason given by states for adopting national renewable energy legislation.[35] REN 21's global status report on renewables for 2019 identifies improving energy security fears due to supplier hostility as a major reason for the adoption of pro-renewables legislation by the Ukraine and of a 100 per cent renewable electricity target for 2050 adopted by the Ukrainian city of Zhytomyr.[36] The United Arab Emirates furnishes an example of an oil-rich state which has also been proactive in exploiting renewable resources including by hosting the International Renewable Energy Agency.[37] Diversifying within renewable energy supplies can also enhance security by reducing risks from dependence on one type of renewable resource, particularly solar and wind, which derive from intermittent conditions or on particular technologies and by enabling experience to be gained with newer technologies through which learning-related reductions in costs of producing energy can be realised.[38]

D. Economic Benefits

Global transition to a low carbon economy is seen not only as an essential response to climate change, but as a driver of economic growth and creator of new jobs during the first half of the twenty-first century. Expansion of the renewables sector is expected to be a major component of this growth by creating economic demand for and employment in technology manufacturing industries and installation, operation and maintenance services. IRENA projects that losses in economic contributions and jobs due to the decline of fossil fuel industries will be outweighed by energy transition economic drivers leading to substantial net positive growth in the global economy and employment in the energy sector.[39] Economic and job opportunities through low carbon energy growth were also widely advocated for as a means of recovering from the global financial crisis in the 2010s with $190 billion support for renewable energy being made available globally under fiscal stimulus packages.[40] A similar response to economic disruption caused by COVID-19 is likely. Statements by IRENA, the IEA and the Council of the European Union on the pandemic argue for the low carbon energy transition as a spearhead of the economic response.[41]

Developing specialisations in the renewables sector has been viewed since interest in relevant technologies began to grow as a contributor to job and wealth creation.

---

[35] Crossley (n 9) 112–18.
[36] REN 21 (n 5) 182.
[37] See numerous references to renewable energy investment in the UAE in REN 21 (n 5).
[38] Crossley (n 9) 115–16.
[39] IRENA (n 23) 142–46.
[40] Crossley (n 9) 122.
[41] Council of the European Union, 'Conclusions on the response to the COVID-19 pandemic in the EU energy sector – road to recovery' (Ref 9133/20 25 June 2020); IRENA, *The Post-COVID Recovery: An Agenda for Resilience, Development and Equality* (IRENA, June 2020); International Energy Agency, *Sustainable Recovery: World Energy Outlook Special Report* (IEA, June 2020), www.iea.org/reports/sustainable-recovery (accessed 1 October 2022).

For example, the European Commission advised in 2012 that strong renewables growth to 2030 could generate over 3 million jobs, and emphasised the value for the EU's global competitiveness of maintaining its leadership in renewable technologies 'as 'clean tech' industries become increasingly important around the world'.[42] IRENA's employment report for 2019 advises that jobs in renewable energy were continuing to grow during 2018 with 11 million persons employed in the sector worldwide by the end of 2018.[43] Its modelling for the low carbon energy transition to 2050 projects fourfold growth in renewables employment to 42 million.[44] It is important to note that much of this growth is already concentrated in certain states and regions and that this concentration is likely to persist: 60 per cent of renewable energy jobs were in Asia in 2018 with 39 per cent in China alone.[45] Job concentrations are found in China, Brazil, the US, India, and the EU whilst other states and regions lag behind. However, opportunities for growth which others may take advantage of will continue to arise as the renewables sector diversifies geographically and technologically, with many technologies that will be needed for a full decarbonisation of economies still being in pre- and early commercial stages of development.

Finally, the rapidly declining costs of producing energy using well-established technologies drives increasing interest in exploiting renewable sources such as wind and solar because they are often lower-cost options for energy production than fossil fuels. See Section 1 of Chapter 5 for discussion of how renewable energy costs from better established technologies have fallen dramatically during the last decade.

E. Sustainable Development

Sustainable development has been a high-profile theme in international dialogue on tackling global problems since the 1980s.[46] It was proposed as a goal that would enable compromise between advocates of limiting economic growth and living standards due to related environmental problems that were becoming apparent in the 1970s and of economic growth and social improvements to reduce deep disparities in wealth and in qualities of life between inhabitants of developed and of developing states. Sustainable development as conceptualised by interstate agreement at Johannesburg in 2001 involves progress which advances the three pillars of the concept, economic, social and environmental, together.[47] Renewable energy's vital contribution to tackling climate change and other environmental and public health crises such as air pollution are considered above. Renewable technologies also have a central role to play in enabling future economic growth whilst respecting limits to the Earth's environmental capacity

---

[42] European Commission, 'Renewable Energy: A Major Player in the European Energy Market' COM (2012) 271 final, 2.
[43] IRENA, *Renewable Energy and Jobs: Annual Review 2019* (IRENA, June 2019).
[44] IRENA (n 23) 145.
[45] IRENA (n 43) 24–25.
[46] Sands (n 26) 217–21.
[47] United Nations, *Plan of Implementation of the World Summit on Sustainable Development* (Johannesburg, 2001) WSSD_PlanImpl.doc (un.org) (accessed 1 October 2022), para 2.

to support human exploitation. With regard to the social pillar, renewable electricity generation technologies are key to raising standards of life in developing world countries, particularly in sub-Saharan Africa. Over half of the population of sub-Saharan Africa did not have access to electricity in 2020.[48] Nearly 3 billion people were without access to clean cooking solutions, often relying instead on polluting fuel and stove combinations.[49] Off-grid electricity produced primarily from solar and wind energy provided 60 per cent of new electricity access in the 2010s.[50] That contribution is only likely to grow under the influence of the United Nations Sustainable Development Goal 7 which seeks 'to ensure access to affordable reliable sustainable and modern energy for all' by 2030.[51] The relationship between sustainable development policies and law in driving renewable energy development is examined further in Chapter 3.

IV. Obstacles to Renewable Energy Development

Renewable energy production and consumption is made possible by choices of several types of actors. Energy producers decide to invest in producing energy from renewable sources. Energy suppliers decide to purchase renewable energy from producers for provision to customers. Consumers may make a positive choice to buy energy from renewable sources, to buy an electric vehicle or to install a biomass boiler. Manufacturers decide to invest in facilities for producing technologies required for producing and consuming renewable energy and to expand them as demand for their products grows. Infrastructure owners and operators make investment decisions to adapt electricity and pipeline networks or to introduce new energy distribution facilities to anticipate or stimulate demand for a shift to renewables in energy supplies. All these changes may happen, to some extent, in the normal course of market operation without intervention being required from governments by adopting pro-renewables policies and laws. However, market operations alone will not bring about change in energy supplies from fossil fuels to low carbon energy sources including renewables at the scale and rate required by the drivers examined in Section III. IRENA advises in its 2050 roadmap that this will involve 'much stronger public sector interventions and global collaborative efforts'.[52] The main reason for this is that the growth of the renewables sector, notwithstanding its clear appeal from climate, environmental, security and economic perspectives, faces many barriers. Legal interventions in favour of renewable energy are required precisely because of the obstacles and constraints which confront efforts to implement policies that promote renewable energy directly or which drive recourse

---

[48] United Nations Economic and Social Council, 'Progress Towards the Sustainable Development Goals: Report of the Secretary-General' (Ref. E/2020/57, 28 April 2020), paras 67–72.
[49] ibid.
[50] IRENA, *10 Years: Progress to Action* (IRENA, January 2020) 14–15.
[51] United Nations, 'SDG7: Affordable and Clean Energy' (Sustainable Development Goals, Internet Site), www.un.org/sustainabledevelopment/energy/ (accessed 1 October 2022).
[52] IRENA (n 23) 55.

to it indirectly by requiring that drivers examined in Section III such as greenhouse gas growth should be tackled over a short timescale. Knowledge and understanding of the barriers are therefore essential both for understanding why renewable energy law is required and for well-founded critical analysis of the effectiveness of relevant laws for advancing renewable energy goals. The following sections outline the core challenges for expanding availability and use of renewable energy.

A. Financial Barriers

Renewable energy generating plant became the most attractive option for investment in the electricity sector during the last decade, consistently attracting more than half of the monies invested globally in electricity production from 2015 onwards – 69 per cent of global investment in power production ($283.3B) went to renewable energy developments in 2018.[53] This is partly due to financial support by states, but is increasingly the result of rapidly decreasing costs of producing electricity from renewable sources, particularly onshore wind and solar energy, with projects using these technologies being cost competitive with all forms of fossil fuel generation in 2019.[54] However, investment in generation from coal and gas still continues due to ongoing state support and to disparities within regions and even within states in the cost competitiveness of energy sources. The appeal of renewable energy is also dampened by two respects in which it compares unfavourably with coal and gas power plants. The first is that it can be difficult to integrate distributed renewable electricity into networks developed for centralised generation because systems were designed only to convey electricity directly from centralised power plants to consumers and the best renewable resources are often in remote areas far distant from grids serving communities.[55] The expense of connecting generating plant to networks can add substantially to a project's cost profile, particularly if developers are expected to bear 'deep' connection charges covering the cost of associated network modifications.[56] Secondly, initial development costs for renewable energy projects are largely fixed and incurred at the outset.[57] A high degree of confidence that revenues will be sufficient to repay monies borrowed is therefore required at the outset of projects to secure the funds needed to pursue them at affordable interest rates.

In addition, it is important to remember that renewable energy is a heterogeneous category made up of multiple technologies for extracting energy from different sources, and of different technologies for each source (eg, the constant drive to develop new turbines capable of extracting more power from the wind than current models). Only the better-established technologies have become consistently cost competitive with

---

[53] REN 21 (n 5) 154.
[54] IRENA, *Renewable Power Generation Costs in 2019* (IRENA, June 2020) 12.
[55] Marcelino Madrigal and Steven Stoft, *Transmission Expansion for Renewable Energy Scale-Up: Emerging Lessons and Recommendations* (World Bank Group Publications 2012) 3–13.
[56] ibid.
[57] Intergovernmental Panel on Climate Change, *Renewable Energy Sources and Climate Change Mitigation* (Cambridge University Press, 2012) 194.

fossil fuels. Costs for producing electricity from newer technologies such as offshore wind and concentrated solar power increasingly fall within the fossil fuel cost range, but still tend to exceed the costs of electricity from cheaper fossil fuel options as well as those of better established renewables.[58] All such technologies are likely to be needed to replace the four-fifths share of global energy consumption for fossil fuels, to prevent a future return to high carbon energy under the duress of growing energy demands from an increasing global population and to enable an increase in electricity supplies from their current level in connection with decarbonising transport, industry and heating. The failure of some supported technologies is a preferable risk to that of runaway climate change which every unit of additional fossil fuel consumption heightens.

Electricity is the low-hanging fruit of decarbonising energy supplies. Reducing emissions from transport, industry and heating is more challenging due to there being fewer and less well-established low-carbon alternatives, and limited progress has been made with moving away from high carbon energy in these sectors.[59] For road transport, responsible for over two-thirds of greenhouse gas emissions from transport,[60] this is due to a combination of: the much lower price of fuels that have benefitted from 100+ years of experience with their production and distribution compared to newer alternatives such as advanced biofuels that are still being readied for commercial application or that have not yet achieved economies of scale in production; the lower price of vehicles consuming petrol and diesel than those using alternatives, again due to the long experience with their use and resulting learning efficiencies and economies of scale; the lack of infrastructure for refuelling alternative fuel vehicles; and, for all of these reasons, the lack of popular demand for alternatives that would be required to prompt change in manufacturing sectors.[61] The much lower cost and easy availability of fossil fuels and related technologies are also the key obstacles to decarbonising marine and air transport.[62] The lack of progress with decarbonising heating and industry is partly due to cost, but also to a lack of awareness of the alternative options.[63] The weakness of state support for these sectors compared to the strength of backing for renewable electricity contributes to their slow rate of decarbonisation.[64]

B. Carbon Lock-in

In addition to factors retarding investment in renewable energy, its diffusion is hampered by the entrenchment of fossil fuels. Their 80 per cent share in global energy consumption reflects enormous sunk investment in infrastructure for energy generation, in

---

[58] IRENA (n 54) 10–17.
[59] REN 21 (n 5), 37–40.
[60] International Energy Agency, 'Transport' (Tracking Report, September 2022), Transport – Analysis – IEA (accessed 1 October 2022).
[61] IRENA, *Renewable Energy Policies in a Time of Transition* (IRENA, 2018) 13 and 38–55.
[62] ibid.
[63] ibid at 13 and 24–37.
[64] ibid at 13 and 24–55.

the extraction, refining and distribution of resources, in the design and manufacture of vehicles consuming fossil fuels, in building stock designed for fossil fuel heating, and in general into the more than a century's worth of learning and knowledge and skills acquisition that has fed into creating and maintaining the fossil fuel economy. Businesses, their shareholders and governments have corresponding vested interests in the continued utilisation of fossil fuel assets and related revenue streams and tax receipts. Economies that have become dependent on the availability of easily distributable, dense and inexpensive energy baulk at the thought of disruption to its supply. Societal practices such as commuting are based on the easy availability and affordability of fossil fuels and of vehicles that consume them whilst attitudes derived from accustomisation to the receipt of remotely produced energy without knowledge of its origins informs hostility toward renewable energy development in areas that have only been recipients of energy produced elsewhere in recent decades.

All these factors contribute to the lock-in of socio-economic systems to fossil fuel energy that must be undone to create space for renewable energy development.[65] Combinations of measures are therefore required that weaken the hold of fossil fuels alongside promoting alternative energy sources. The most immediate means available to states of destabilising the high carbon energy sector would be to follow through on commitments already made to withdraw fossil fuel subsidies whose value far exceeds that of support for renewable energy.[66] Measures for integrating the environmental costs of greenhouse gas emissions into energy prices would also assist with dispelling the perception of renewable energy as an expensive alternative and with persuading manufacturers to invest in low carbon alternatives.[67] Much broader policy and legal intervention is also required at all levels of government to enable economic and social transition and adaptation to a post-fossil fuel era.

C. Characteristics of Renewable Energy Sources

Networks of cables and pipelines transport electricity and gas to consumers. Rights to access and use them affordably are therefore essential for participation by energy producers in the markets through which electricity and gas are sold to suppliers and directly to large consumers. Integrating renewable electricity and gas into these networks and energy markets can be problematic. A reason for this is that some of the main renewable energy sources including wind and solar differ qualitatively from the fossil fuels and nuclear energy sources for which networks and arrangements developed for governing their development, maintenance and operation were designed. The main differences include:

- *Intermittency*: Fossil and nuclear energy production is controllable and predictable. Renewable electricity produced from sources such as wind and solar which depend on weather conditions are less controllable and hard to predict with accuracy.

---

[65] Gregory Unruh, 'Understanding Carbon Lock-in' (2000) 28 *Energy Policy* 817.
[66] IRENA (n 23) 62–63.
[67] REN 21 (n 5) 63–64.

- *Location*: Humans decide on the situation of nuclear and fossil fuel power and gas production units and can transport resources for producing energy to them. Sources for renewable electricity other than biomass and its derivatives are not transportable. Locations at which renewable electricity sources are found may either not be located near to a network or to one that was designed to do more than distribute energy produced elsewhere to consumers. The latter problem also arises with gas networks.
- *Scale*: Electricity and gas networks and markets in the pre-renewables era were typically connected to and used by a limited number of corporate or publicly-owned power and gas producers possessing the financial capacity to invest in and obtain funds for large capacity power and natural gas production plants. The increasing affordability of renewable power and gas technology (eg, solar panels on roofs, anaerobic digestors) makes it possible for multiple individuals, communities and small commercial operations to produce energy and sell it commercially as long as they are able to access and use networks and markets.

The qualitative differences obstruct the integration of renewables into energy systems and their markets. It will not be possible for renewable energy developers who plan to do more than meet their own energy needs to obtain funds for relevant development if they are unable to reach consumers through marketplaces and networks. Lock-in can make it difficult to address problems related to renewable energy sources' characteristics for reasons including the need to maintain security in networks which were physically developed to carry and remain dominated by energy from fossil fuels (eg, gas quality standards, voltage standards) and reluctance to alter governance arrangements that are not suited to accommodating qualitatively different energy sources.

D. Public Acceptance

Some members of the public will welcome the switch from fossil fuels to renewable energy and be willing to accept associated changes and costs including:

- The production of renewable electricity and gas in remote and rural places which are not used to producing energy locally or to development on an industrial scale.
- The inclusion of charges relating to renewable electricity and gas in prices to cover subsidies and network adaptation costs, potentially leading to higher prices for electricity and gas than would otherwise be the case.
- Higher prices for fossil fuel use due to the inclusion of charges and taxes related to carbon emissions in costs passed on to consumers.

Others may be less willing or able to accept these charges and changes even if they are supportive of the switch from fossil fuels to renewable energy and to related development in principle. Concern over changes can lead to public opposition which can lead, in turn, to the withdrawal of pro-renewables policies by governments and to the rejection of renewable energy development and of essential infrastructure for its transmission by their representatives. Public opposition has impacted significantly on renewable energy development and has led to the curtailment of renewable energy policies in many jurisdictions.[68] Laws have already been developed to address the causes of opposition and will need to increase in sophistication and reach as changes required by a low-carbon energy transition become more pronounced.

E. Developing World Challenges

The avoidance of dangerous anthropogenic interference with the climate will involve more than action by developed states to decarbonise. It also requires developing countries that are growing economically and the least developed countries that are yet to undergo significant economic growth to follow a different developmental pathway based on non-carbon-emitting and carbon neutral energy sources. The need for developing countries to embark on a low carbon energy transition or simply to avoid a fossil fuel-based stage in their development has grown during the last three decades because of carbon-intensive growth in some developing states since the early 1990s. A range of challenges need to be overcome to enable or persuade those countries classed as developing to follow a different route to that taken by developed countries during the nineteenth and twentieth centuries. The more economically advanced developing states may have acquired the ability to develop and deploy renewable energy technologies themselves but may be unwilling to do so because it would hand competitive advantage to those states who have developed on the back of cheaper and well-established fossil fuel technologies. They may also regard making commitments to replace fossil fuels with renewables as being incompatible with the fairness argument that the states primarily responsible for causing the climate crisis in the first place should take responsibility for addressing it by cutting their emissions to the extent necessary to allow others to have the same opportunities for economic and social development.[69] For those countries, the provision of financial and technological support by developed state parties as compensation (although developed states would not agree to such a description) for their consumption of much of the safe climate space may be viewed as a precondition to taking on obligations to mitigate climate change.[70]

Whilst certain developing countries may have some choice over how development is conducted, the reality for many of them, particularly the least developed countries, is that they do not have the capacity to initiate low carbon energy development. States may lack any of the factors required to exploit renewable resources including access to relevant technologies, knowledge of how they operate and are maintained, awareness of the resources available to them, a capacity to conduct or support research

---

[68] IRENA (n 61) 21 and 88; Ana Maria Gonzalez and others, 'On the Acceptance and Sustainability of Renewable Energy Projects – A Systems Thinking Perspective' (2016) 8 *Sustainability* 1171; doi:10.3390/su8111171.

[69] Philippe Cullet, 'Common but Differentiated Responsibilities' in Malgosia Fitzmaurice, David Ong, and Panos Merkouris (eds), *Research Handbook on International Environmental Law* (Edward Elgar, 2010) 161, 169–70.

[70] ibid. Sanford Gaines, 'International Law and Institutions for Climate Change' in Joshua Sarnoff (ed), *Research Handbook on Intellectual Property and Climate Change* (Edward Elgar 2016) 33, 38–39.

on development, the infrastructure required for enabling access to energy for their peoples, or the institutions needed to support the growth of a renewables sector including appropriate policy and legal frameworks.[71] States lacking a supportive policy and legal environment for renewable energy development will also struggle to attract investment even where funding is available.

V. Defining Renewable Energy Law

The drivers considered in Section III of this chapter incentivise governments to adopt policies which promote the production and consumption of energy from renewable energy sources. Giving effect to pro-renewable energy policies often requires the adoption of laws which create new rules and rights or which reform existing rules and rights for reasons including overcoming barriers discussed in Section IV of this chapter. Relevant laws collectively make up the category of renewable energy law which this book examines. The wide range of challenges and barriers confronting its growth necessitates legal action in several different areas to enable growth of the renewables sector. This book focuses on the areas in which legal intervention is most needed to effect pro-renewables policies at all levels of policy and law-making. They are covered in its chapters as follows:

- Laws adopted to pursue agreed goals of the world's states which drive renewable energy developments including those for mitigating and adapting to climate change and for making development sustainable. International treaties such as the Paris Climate Change Agreement and non-binding initiatives such as the UN's Sustainable Development Goals for 2030 create a framework within which renewable energy development takes place, and whose effectiveness for supporting renewable energy development is a key focus for renewable energy law. Relevant laws are examined in Chapters 2 and 3.
- Laws such as the European Union's Renewable Energy Directive 2018 which were adopted to create frameworks within which pro-renewables policies are given effect at regional and national levels. Their key roles include establishing and legally entrenching renewable energy targets as well as mechanisms for securing compliance with them. Relevant laws are examined in Chapter 4.
- Laws adopted to overcome barriers to renewable energy development including by weakening lock-in to fossil fuel energy. The types of barrier and legal responses to them which the book examines are: those which make it difficult to access investment in renewable energy (Chapter 5); those which make it difficult to integrate renewables into networks for transmitting energy (Chapter 6); unnecessarily

---

[71] Intergovernmental Panel on Climate Change (n 57) 195; David Ockwell and Alexandra Mallett, 'Introduction: Low-Carbon Technology Transfer – From Rhetoric to Reality' in David Ockwell and Alexandra Mallett (eds) *Low-Carbon Technology Transfer – From Rhetoric to Reality* (Routledge 2012) 3, 3–18.

complex administrative procedures (Chapter 7); and public disquiet over renewable energy development (Chapter 7).
- Laws which establish legal frameworks enabling the exploitation of renewable energy resources which are found offshore such as wind, wave, and tidal energy (Chapter 8).
- Laws adopted or used to enable renewable energy development by mitigating the negative environmental effects which exploitation of some renewable energy sources can give rise to and by avoiding and managing conflict with legal protections for the environment. Chapter 8 examines laws adopted to regulate the environmental effects of marine renewable energy. Chapter 9 examines laws adopted to regulate the environmental effects of energy production for transport from biomass.
- Law's role in enabling renewable energy growth in the road transport sector which remains heavily dependent on fossil fuel energy. The sector is examined in Chapter 9.

These areas of legal action do not cover the full extent of renewable energy law as a legal category, but acquaintance with them will provide readers with wide-ranging knowledge of law's role in supporting the growth of energy production and consumption from renewable sources.

VI. Levels of Law

Readers will encounter four levels of law in this book. First, international law governs relationships between states. It is made through two main routes. Treaties negotiated by representatives of states confer rights and place duties on states which ratify them. Rules of customary international law are legally binding on all states or sometimes on all states falling into a category (eg, enclosed sea coastal states) unless they have consistently opposed its application to them. They are not negotiated by states but come into existence when two elements are present. First, evidence is available that the substantial majority of states have adopted a common position. Second, they have done so because they consider the position to be binding on them under international law. Provisions of treaties may become rules of customary international law due to extensive support through ratification and endorsement by non-ratifying states, and therefore become binding on non-parties. For example, the entitlement for coastal states to establish exclusive economic zones in which they have certain exclusive rights under the United Nations Convention on the Law of the Sea has become recognised as a right for all states under customary international law due to widespread endorsement. It therefore governs relations between all states regardless of whether they are party to UNCLOS.

Chapter 2 concentrates on treaties of relevance to renewable energy with a particular focus on treaties concerning states' response to climate change. Chapter 3 concentrates on statements on making development sustainable which, although they have been negotiated and endorsed by most of the world's states, are not legally binding on them. They are referred to as soft law instruments to distinguish them from legally binding treaties. This does not mean that provisions of soft law instruments are legally irrelevant. They may signpost progress towards a rule of customary international law's emergence by recording interstate consensus on desirable practices such as the eradication of greenhouse gas emitting energy consumption. As discussed in Chapter 3, careful analysis of their structure and wording is also necessary. Provisions in soft law instruments may have characteristics placing them toward the harder end of the soft law/hard law spectrum whilst those in hard law instruments may be softer in character depending on the strength of commitment and the precision of the language used.[72]

Second, European Union law as a category includes treaties ratified by the Member States of the European Union which lay down its executive and legislative powers and laws adopted in exercise of those powers. They affect directly only the European Union's 27 Member States, but other European states may be required to observe or apply them to defined extents by virtue of their ratification of the Energy Community Treaty and the European Economic Area Agreement. Switzerland also applies aspects of EU energy law in line with bilateral agreements with the EU. Other regional treaty-based organisations exist such as the Association of Southeast Asian Nations (ASEAN) and the Caribbean Community (Caricom), but they do not possess independent law-making powers to the same extent as the EU.

Third and fourth, frequent references are made to national laws adopted by the law-making institutions of individual states and to laws governing areas at sub-national levels such as those adopted by the legislatures of states operating with a degree of independence from the sovereign states which they comprise (eg, the legislatures of the 50 states of the US) and by authorities with law-making powers delegated by the central government of their states (eg, the Scottish parliament).

Classroom Questions

1. What is renewable energy? Identify and describe commonly occurring characteristics of energy sources described as being 'renewable'.
2. What are the different sources of renewable energy?
3. How can renewable energy be used to meet demands for energy for the production of electricity, transport and heating?
4. Why should we exploit renewable energy when fossil fuels are still available?
5. What are the main barriers for the growth of renewable energy production? Think of some examples.
6. How can states use policy and law to overcome the barriers you identify in your answer to Question 5 with a view to promoting renewable production and consumption? Think of some examples.

Scenario

Arcadia is a small state with a varied geography. It has sunlit flatlands including desert areas that often reach high temperatures due to solar radiation in Arcadia's summer, mountainous areas with high wind speeds, a major river flowing down from

---

[72] See Section IV of Chapter 3 for further discussion of the soft law/hard law spectrum.

its mountains to its coastline, hot springs indicating subterranean volcanic activity and a coastline from which relatively shallow but frequently wild and windy coastal waters with a significant tidal range stretch out towards its maritime boundaries with its nearest neighbour, Ruritania. Arcadia's energy system is largely reliant on fossil fuels for the production of electricity and for heating and transport. Electricity and gas are transported from centralised production sites around the state through long-established grid and pipeline networks. Arcadia does not have indigenous fossil fuels and imports most of its energy supplies from Ruritania, a state with which it has not always had good relations. It's capital city, Murkyville, has an unfortunate reputation for atmospheric pollution due to its traffic-clogged streets.

Fossil fuels have served Arcadia well enough in the past, but the state's government is now looking at possibilities for replacing the fossil fuel energy mix with alternative supplies. One reason for this is that it has committed to reduce greenhouse gas emissions rapidly from the 2030s onwards in its recently submitted nationally determined contribution to global climate efforts under the Paris Climate Change Agreement. It wishes to explore possibilities for exploiting indigenous renewable energy supplies as an alternative to fossil fuels. It lacks expertise on renewables and has been reluctant to explore this route in the past due to a lack of national expertise in using renewable technologies for energy production. Its reluctance also stems from concerns over the reliability and affordability of renewables for Arcadia's peoples, some of whom live in poverty. The government's energy minister seeks guidance from the renewable engineering/legal consultancy for which you work on the following matters:

- What types of renewable resource is Arcadia likely to possess?
- How could these resources be employed to meet Arcadia's energy needs?
- Why should Arcadia consider exploiting its renewables resources when its neighbour, Ruritania, has ample supplies of oil, gas and coal?
- What barriers might Arcadia encounter in exploiting its renewable energy resources?
- Could law have a role to play in overcoming whatever challenges Arcadia may meet in switching to renewable energy?

Suggested Reading

Books

Penelope Crossley, *Renewable Energy Law: An International Assessment* (Cambridge University Press, 2019), Chapters 2, 3 and 4.

Nick Jelley, *Renewable Energy: A Very Short Introduction* (Oxford University Press, 2020), Chapters 1 and 2.

Articles and chapters

Harald Kohl and Wolfhart Dürrschmidt, 'Renewable Energy Sources – a Survey' in Roland Wengenmayr and Thomas Bührke, *Renewable Energy: Sustainable Concepts for the Energy Change* (Wiley, 2013), 4–13.

Simone Negro, Floortje Alkemade, and Marko Hekkert, 'Why Does Renewable Energy Diffuse So Slowly? A Review of Innovation System Problems' (2012) 16 *Renewable and Sustainable Energy Reviews* 3836–46.

Richard Ottinger, Lily Matthews and Nadia Czachor, 'Renewable Energy in National Legislation: Challenges and Opportunities' in Donald Zillmann and others (eds) *Beyond the Carbon Economy: Energy Law in Transition* (Oxford: Oxford University Press, 2008), 183–206.

Policy Documents

The website of the International Renewable Energy Agency (IRENA) is an excellent source of information and guidance on renewable energy development. The many useful reports for those seeking information about the renewables sector produced by IRENA include *Global Renewables Outlook: Energy Transformation 2050* (2020 Edition) and *Renewable Energy Policies in a Time of Transition* (April 2018). See: www.irena.org/.

REN 21, a body which describes itself as 'the only global renewable energy community of actors from science, governments, NGOs and industry', produces a comprehensive annual statement on the worldwide spread of renewable energy entitled *Renewables Global Status Report*. For example, see the 2021 report at: Renewables Global Status Report – REN21.

2

International Climate Change Law and Renewable Energy*

I. Introduction

Collaboration between states is often necessary to address effectively the problems and also to pursue the economic opportunities examined in Section III of Chapter 1 that are driving interest in renewable energy production. Interstate collaboration often involves the drafting and agreement of legal arrangements which variously record what participating states are obliged, expected or encouraged to contribute to international problem solving and transformative efforts. This and the following chapter examine international law agreements that states have concluded to tackle global environmental problems whilst taking advantage of opportunities that tackling them may create. Agreements on responding to the problems and opportunities concerned could either have a direct effect on renewable energy's growth because they expressly promote this or a strong indirect effect on growth in the production of energy from renewables because this is obviously central to tackling the difficulties with which the agreement is concerned.

This chapter concentrates on support provided for renewable energy development by the three treaties which frame international action on climate change. Readers may expect the climate change treaties to make detailed provision on replacing fossil fuels with renewable energy as consumption of the former for energy production is the major reason for related problems, but this is not the case. Section IIA reveals the paucity of direct support for renewable energy in the treaties. Instead, their impact on the growth of energy from renewable sources as a component of energy supplies comes as a by-product of obligations and expectations the treaties place on their parties to take measures which advance their goals. Sections IIB to IIG explore aspects of the treaties that have an indirect influence on evolution of the energy sector. This review reveals strengths but also weaknesses in their ability to promote worldwide growth of the renewables sector. It also identifies related needs for augmentation and reform of the climate change regime if it is to drive the low carbon energy transition with renewable energy at the helm that is so important for achievement of the climate treaties' goals.

The reluctance of states to make legally binding 'hard' commitments on renewable energy derives in part from the centrality of energy security to national security.

---

*This chapter updates content which was first published in Olivia Woolley, 'The Paris Climate Change Agreement: a new stimulus for international efforts to promote renewable energy development?' (2016) 28 *Environmental Law and Management* 185–200.

They have been more willing to record common positions concerning renewables in non-legally binding 'soft' law documents, many of which form part of wide-ranging statements on how to make development sustainable. Chapter 3 examines the contribution of the 'soft' law statements and of the sustainable development discourse in general to the development of law on renewable energy. It also examines support for renewable energy under the Energy Charter Treaty, the sole major hard law treaty concerning the energy sector, and through the establishment of international institutions including the International Renewable Energy Agency. Chapter 3 concludes with an overview of the state of support for renewable energy in international law and by outlining options suggested by academic commentators on how manifest deficiencies at this level of law could be remedied.

II. The Climate Change Treaties and Renewable Energy

The various sectors involved with energy creation and consumption (eg the power industry, industrial, domestic) are collectively responsible for between two thirds and three quarters of the world's greenhouse gas emissions.[1] The decarbonisation of energy supplies over a short timescale including through the replacement of fossil fuel energy by energy production and consumption from renewable sources is therefore essential for addressing climate change. Nearly all the world's States were involved with negotiating and have ratified treaties in which they commit to combat climate change. These are the UN Framework Convention on Climate Change, adopted in 1992 and ratified by 198 parties, which establishes a legal framework for the international response to climate change;[2] the Kyoto Protocol, adopted under the Framework Convention in 1997 and ratified by 192 parties, which further develops the Framework Convention's provisions on reducing greenhouse gases by placing targets on certain developed state parties;[3] the Doha Amendment to the Protocol, adopted under the Framework Convention in 2012 and ratified by 148 parties, which places more ambitious emission reduction targets on some of the developed states with targets under the Kyoto Protocol;[4] and the Paris Climate Change Agreement, adopted under the Convention in 2015 and ratified by 193 parties, which sought to revive increasingly moribund international collaboration on global warming by introducing a new legal model for climate action.[5] The key focus of agreed climate action under the treaties is on reducing greenhouse gas emissions. In addition, increasing emphasis is placed on adaptation to a climatically altered world and on support from developed and wealthier

---

[1] Hannah Ritchie and Max Roser, 'Emissions by sector' (*Our World in Data* 2020) Emissions by sector – Our World in Data (accessed 2 October 2022).
[2] United Nations Framework Convention on Climate Change (adopted 29 May 1992, entered into force 21 March 1994) 1711 UNTS 107 (FCCC).
[3] Kyoto Protocol to the United Nations Framework Convention on Climate Change (adopted 10 December 1997, entered into force 16 February 2005) 2303 UNTS 162 (Kyoto Protocol).
[4] Doha Amendment to the Kyoto Protocol (adopted 8 December 2012, entered into force 31 December 2020), UNTC A-30822.
[5] Paris Agreement (adopted 12 December 2015, entered into force 4 November 2016) 3156 UNTS.

developing states for developing states with low carbon socio-economic development through climate finance, technology transfer and capacity building measures.

This chapter looks at the contribution which the treaties and the arrangements and institutions they establish for progressing global climate action make to renewable energy's diffusion. It does so by examining four areas in which the international law on climate change can contribute most effectively to the global expansion of renewable energy production and consumption. These are as follows: obliging the promotion of renewable energy by contracting parties; diverting investment and state support away from high carbon energy development including by sending a message that the fossil fuel era is drawing to a close; using market mechanisms to create pathways to decarbonisation that are more efficient and less disruptive from an economic perspective than requiring that targets and commitments for reducing greenhouse gases be met exclusively through cuts achieved nationally by the target/duty-holder; and enhancing or creating capacity for low carbon development in the developing world through the provision of financial, technological and capacity building support.

A. Obliging State Support for Renewable Energy

The Convention and the Protocol are largely silent on the potential contribution of renewable sources to combating climate change. The former contains only a general commitment by parties to promote and cooperate on the development, application and diffusion of technologies, practices and processes that 'control, reduce or prevent' greenhouse gas emissions from the energy sector among others.[6] The Kyoto Protocol makes only a marginal advance beyond this position. Each of the developed country parties with targets under the Protocol is obliged, in achieving its target, to '[i]mplement and/or further elaborate policies and measures in accordance with its national circumstances'.[7] The list which follows of types of areas in which policies and measures could be taken includes the '[p]romotion, research, development and increased use of new and renewable forms of energy'.[8] However, there is no obligation to take steps in this particular area. Commentators have criticised this failure to promote perhaps the most effective means available to parties of reducing their greenhouse gas emissions in either instrument and have argued that promotion of renewable energy should be the main focus for any future development of the climate change regime.[9]

Some consideration was given in the climate change negotiations following the 17th Conference of Parties to the Convention at Durban in 2011 to including provisions

---

[6] FCCC (n 2) art 4.1(c).
[7] Kyoto Protocol (n 3) art 2(1)(a).
[8] ibid, art 2(1)(a)(iv).
[9] Stuart Bruce, 'International Law and Renewable Energy: Facilitating Sustainable Energy for All?' (2013) 14 *Melbourne Journal of International Law* 1, 30–35; Adrian Bradbrook, 'The Development of Renewable Energy Technologies and Energy Efficiency Measures Through Public International Law' in Donald Zillman and others (eds) *Beyond the Carbon Economy: Energy Law in Transition* (Oxford University Press 2008) 109, 128–31; Adrian Bradbrook, 'Sustainable Energy Law: the Past and Future' (2012) 30 *Journal of Energy and Natural Resources Law* 511, 517–20.

on options for decarbonising energy in a future agreement. Renewable energy was contemplated in early discussions 'as an option to increase the ambition of existing pledges and "supplementary" measures to reduce emissions before 2020'.[10] Provisions making reference to renewable energy and energy efficiency were included in the draft negotiating text annexed to the decision of the 20th Conference of the Parties to the Convention known as the Lima Call for Climate Action.[11] Paragraph 53 of the section of the text under the heading 'sources of finance' includes a proposal for the establishment of 'an international renewable energy and energy efficiency bond facility'.[12] It also proposes that parties should employ other measures for levelling the playing field between fossil fuel energy and alternative energy sources including a tax on oil exports from developing to developed countries and a 'phasing down' of high carbon investments and fossil fuel subsidies.[13]

It is unsurprising in view of the usual reluctance of states to make commitments that would surrender their control over decision making on the contents of energy supplies that these proposals do not survive in the final text of the Agreement. The only reference to energy is made in the preamble to the decision of the Conference of Parties adopting the Agreement ('the Paris Decision') which acknowledges 'the need to promote universal access to sustainable energy in developing countries, in particular in Africa, through the enhanced deployment of renewable energy'.[14] The Paris Decision also contains a statement recognising the important role of providing incentives for emission reduction activities including tools such as domestic policies and carbon pricing, but lacks any substantive commitment concerning alternative energy forms.[15] As a result, the Agreement fails to provide any direct stimulus for the growth of renewable energy consumption. Its effectiveness for promoting investment in renewables is reliant on its ability to steer energy sector investment and state support for this away from fossil fuels and to hold contracting parties to commitments made to support renewable energy in their nationally determined contributions to climate action.

B. Deterring Investment in Fossil Fuel Energy

The combustion of fossil fuels to produce energy for electricity, heating and transportation is the dominant source of the greenhouse gas emissions that are responsible for climate change. Replacing fossil fuel combustion with alternative non-greenhouse gas-emitting energy sources is therefore vital for arresting global warming. Technologies

---

[10] Bruce (n 9) 32.
[11] Mario Citelli, 'Generating Renewable Energy for the Material Realization of Sustainable Development: What Do We Need from Multilateral Cooperation, the Climate Change and the International Trade Regimes?' in Volker Mauerhofer (ed) *Legal Aspects of Sustainable Development* (Springer 2016) 373, 380.
[12] UNFCCC, 'Lima Call for Climate Action' in *Report of the conference of the parties on its twentieth session, held in Lima from 1 to 14 December 2014* (UNFCCC, Decision 1/COP 20, FCCC/CP/2014/10/Add.1, 5 Feb 2015) para 53.
[13] ibid.
[14] UNFCCC, 'Decision 1/CP.21 Adoption of the Paris Agreement' (FCCC/CP/2015/10/Add.1, 29 January 2016) preamble (Paris Decision).
[15] ibid, para 136.

for producing energy from renewable sources, particularly wind and solar energy, are frequently the most accessible and economically viable options currently available for replacing fossil fuel use. Legal duties and expectations under the climate change treaties for reducing greenhouse gas emissions (mitigation) therefore have significant potential to influence the growth of renewables. They can deter investment in greenhouse-gas-emitting energy technologies, necessitating a turn to renewables and other low carbon alternatives by states to maintain energy security and by businesses and individuals to meet their energy needs despite constraints placed on fossil fuel energy by the legally required reduction in greenhouse gas emissions. Law could therefore have a major indirect role here in driving the shift to renewables globally including by sending a message to investors in means of fossil fuel energy production or in industrial plant whose operation depends on fossil fuel consumption that their use may become unlawful or financially unviable before investment has been fully recovered. However, weaknesses in legal duties placed on states by the climate change treaties for reducing greenhouse gas production have hampered them in performing that role to date.

Signals sent by the Convention and Protocol have been too weak to alter the behaviours of the fossil fuel sector and its supporters. All states have an obligation to '[f]ormulate, implement, publish and regularly update … programmes containing measures to mitigate climate change' under the Convention, but its effectiveness is undermined by the lack of a basis for judging whether proposed state actions are sufficient to achieve the Convention's objectives or to discipline contracting parties if they are not.[16] The principal reason for this is the Convention's failure to guide parties on what they should do to meet its goal of preventing dangerous anthropogenic interference with the climate system. The only detailed direction on emissions cuts in the Convention is that the developed states listed in Annex I should aim to reduce their emissions to 1990 levels by 2000, but no trajectory is proposed for reductions beyond this less than exacting staging post.[17]

Moves to further clarify responsibilities for mitigating climate change were initiated by a provision of the Convention itself, reflecting the perception of its guidance on mitigation as being inadequate even by those who drafted the document.[18] Subsequent negotiations led to the adoption in 1997 of the Kyoto Protocol.[19] The Protocol set legally binding targets for reducing emission levels which the developed state parties listed in its Annex B were obliged to achieve in the commitment period 2008–2012.[20] Most states were required to cut between 5% and 8% of greenhouse gas emission levels from emissions levels in 1990 during the commitment period, but some states were obliged only to return to the 1990 level or to limit growth in emissions above it. A second commitment period was agreed under the Protocol for the period 2012–2020.[21] This placed legally binding targets of 20% cuts against 1990 levels on the EU states making up the majority of target-bearing parties, while non-EU target bearers

---

[16] FCCC (n 2) art 4(1)(b).
[17] ibid, art 4(2)(b).
[18] ibid, art 4(2)(d).
[19] Kyoto Protocol (n 3).
[20] ibid, art. 3(1).
[21] Doha Amendment (n 4).

had targets of between 0.5% and 24%.[22] The need to comply with their obligations under the Protocol will certainly have driven some renewable energy investment in target-holding states as part of their emission-reducing efforts. Protocol targets also drove renewable energy investment in some developing states without targets through the Protocol's market mechanisms.[23] However, the negotiating model adopted for the Protocol of agreeing emission targets for specified periods with no mechanism for raising them thereafter apart from through further agreement had major weaknesses for securing movement away from fossil fuel dependence. Few developed states outside EU members were willing to take on targets under either commitment period. The US did not ratify the Protocol whilst Canada, Japan, New Zealand and Russia, who had targets under the first commitment period, were not willing to take on targets under the second. The targets that were agreed were not always exacting. There was also little prospect of agreeing significantly higher targets for further commitment periods for developed states or of bringing in additional target holders including developing states such as China and India which had become major emitters of greenhouse gases since the Protocol was first agreed. Views of parties on how the burden for addressing climate change should be allocated had become too polarised by the time of negotiations in the 2010s for further commitments on tackling climate change for the agreement of further targets.[24]

The Convention and the Protocol are also weak on driving shifts from fossil fuels to low carbon energy sources such as renewables by developing states. The Convention gives developing states licence to increase greenhouse gas emissions if necessary in connection with meeting their 'social and development needs', whilst Article 4(7) advises that the extent to which they will effectively implement their commitments 'will take fully into account that economic and social development and poverty eradication' are their 'first and overriding priorities'.[25] Developing countries are not given carte blanche to pursue fossil-fuel-driven growth without constraint. It would not have made sense for them to take on the Article 4(1)(b) obligation to mitigate mentioned above if this were the case. However, no direction is given on the emissions trajectory that they should follow. The predictable consequence is that emissions from developing world countries have increased dramatically since 1992 with China having become the largest single state emitter by total volume of greenhouse gases in that period.[26]

(i) Nationally Determined Contributions under the Paris Agreement

If considered in isolation, the formal requirements that the Agreement places on parties for reducing emissions do not represent a significant advance from the position

---

[22] ibid, art 1.
[23] See Section IIC(i) below.
[24] Lavanya Rajamani, 'Differentiation in the Emerging Climate Regime' (2013) 14 *Theoretical Inquiries in Law* 152.
[25] FCCC (n 2) preamble, and art 4(7).
[26] Centre for Climate and Energy Solutions, 'Greenhouse Gas Emissions by Top Emitters 2018', (Global Emissions, C2ES Website), Global Emissions – Center for Climate and Energy Solutions (c2es.org) (accessed 2 October 2022).

under the Convention and Protocol. The express obligation on developed states to achieve emissions cuts is replaced with a non-binding statement of expectation that they will do so. Instead, all states take on a lowest common denominator obligation of self-determining their contribution to mitigation efforts.[27] Article 4(2) echoes the obligation to communicate and implement programmes of measures to mitigate climate change under Article 4(1)(b) of the Convention by requiring each party to 'prepare, communicate and maintain successive nationally determined contributions that it intends to achieve'. This provision could even be said to place a lower level of expectation than the Convention on contracting parties in that it requires them only to 'pursue domestic mitigation measures with the aim of achieving the objectives of' their NDCs rather than the unqualified requirement under the Convention to implement the programmes of measures communicated by them periodically.[28]

Where the Agreement does differ from its predecessors is in its clear expectation that parties' contributions will become progressively stronger from the starting point of their initial NDC. Article 3 advises that '[t]he efforts of all Parties will represent a progression over time'. Article 4(3) similarly advises that each party's NDC 'will represent a progression beyond the Party's then current nationally determined contribution and reflect its highest possible ambition'. In addition, Article 4(4) advises developing country parties that they should 'continue enhancing their mitigation efforts' and that they are 'encouraged to move over time towards economy-wide emission reduction or limitation targets in the light of different national circumstances'. These provisions make normative statements rather than imposing legally binding obligations. The legal position is therefore no different to that under the Convention with parties having no formal obligation to improve their climate change responses. Even so, it is clear that states are expected to strengthen their contributions regularly unless justification can be provided for not doing so.

The sense of commitment by the international community to addressing climate change is further reinforced by the Agreement's direction on the expected contribution of developing country parties to achieving its goal of holding the increase in global average temperatures to less than 1.5°C if possible and certainly below 2°C[29] and by the inclusion for the first time in the international climate change regime of an endpoint for mitigation efforts by reference to which the efforts of parties can be assessed. In common with the Convention, the Agreement recognises that the emissions of developing country parties are likely to increase initially. Article 4(1) notes that it will take longer for developing countries to reach a point where their growth in emissions peaks. Similarly, they are only encouraged 'to move over time towards economy-wide emission reduction or limitation targets' in contrast to developed states who, the Agreement advises, should reduce overall emissions as their default approach.[30] The Agreement does differ from the Convention, however, in envisaging that developing states will

---

[27] Paris Agreement (n 5) art 4(2).
[28] ibid.
[29] ibid, art 2(1).
[30] ibid, art 4(4).

work towards a point where their total emissions will start to decline. It is implicit in the observation that it will take longer for the emissions of developing countries to peak that this is something for which they should aim.[31] No indication is given as to how quickly this should occur, but the unabated growth of developing country emissions is unlikely to be compatible with the Agreement's goal of achieving a balance between global emissions by source and removals by sinks during the twenty-first century even if developed countries are able to transition to low carbon economies during the coming decades.[32] This goal does not envisage a complete withdrawal of greenhouse-gas-emitting actions which may leave some scope for the continued use of fossil fuel energy to the extent that the carbon released can be offset by sinks. The flexible timescale for achieving the goal also detracts somewhat from any sense of urgency that the inclusion of a destination may provide. Even so, the international community has given a clear indication that the licence given for developing states to pursue a fossil-fuel-driven expansion is not open ended. Its agreed position is that all contracting parties should reduce emissions from their energy sectors to levels below what sinks can absorb in the second half of this century.

The intent shown by the Agreement is striking when compared to its predecessors' lack of vision. The initial response by parties to the Agreement also gives hope that compliance with it will lead to massive growth in renewable energy investment. The International Renewable Energy Agency reported in December 2020 that of the nationally determined contributions submitted by state parties to the Agreement at that date, 170 of them (90%) mentioned renewables with 147 (71%) including quantified renewable energy targets.[33] However, its ability to alter investment patterns and to prompt withdrawal of support for fossil fuels is impaired by four factors which weaken its message. First, the Agreement allows states to reflect their common but differentiated responsibilities and respective capabilities in the light of different national circumstances when preparing their NDCs and determining the extent to which updated submissions should improve upon their prior position.[34] The possibility remains open, therefore, for developing states to justify lower levels of contribution than what they are capable of on grounds that the lion's share of responsibility for exposing the world to risks of dangerous climate change still lies with developed states because of their historic actions or that developed states have not provided sufficient financial and technological support for their mitigation efforts. It is also conceivable that developed states may lower their own ambition if developing states are not thought to be pulling their weight. Parties may come under peer pressure to improve their positions due to the greater transparency under the Agreement.[35] The wording 'in the light of different national circumstances' also reinforces the message that parties should reappraise and, by implication, strengthen their climate-change-mitigation activities in line with

---

[31] ibid, art 4(1).
[32] ibid.
[33] IRENA, *Renewable Energy and Climate Pledges: Five Years After the Paris Agreement* (IRENA 2019) 2–3.
[34] Paris Agreement (n 5) arts 2(2) and 4(3).
[35] ibid, art 13.

economic growth and increasing responsibility in the present for consuming what is left of the 'safe' climate space.[36] Even so, the fact that states are permitted to make proposals falling short of what they are capable of by reference to their perception of what others should be contributing weakens the impetus provided by requirements for mitigatory efforts to be escalated periodically.

Second, states are not legally bound to enhance their contributions at each five-yearly resubmission. The extent to which they respond to the Agreement's several normative expectations depends, in the absence of political will to do so voluntarily, on the presence of the following three elements: compliance by states with their obligations to provide information under the Agreement's transparency mechanism; the preparedness of other states to impose peer pressure on parties whose contributions fall short of what might be expected; and how states subject to this pressure respond. A failure to provide the information needed to support this process can also only be rectified by peer pressure itself as the Agreement does not establish a mechanism for enforcing compliance by parties with their obligations.[37] The many variables undermine the confidence that can be drawn from the Agreement itself that decarbonisation will proceed inexorably and following a reasonably predictable trajectory to the goal of balanced net emissions and temperature increases held below 2°C.

A third consideration is that parties are not obliged to implement their NDCs to the letter. Their obligation, as mentioned above, is only to pursue domestic mitigation measures with the aim of achieving the objectives of their NDCs.[38] The Agreement implies that NDCs are meant to be taken seriously with parties being required to provide information necessary to track progress made by them on their implementation, and with this information being made subject to a technical expert review, the role of which is to comment and identify areas of improvement in a facilitative non-intrusive non-punitive manner.[39] Again, however, the ability of this process to affect the behaviour of states depends on their susceptibility to peer pressure with no fallback position if parties prove immune to external opinion. The likely combined effect of the non-enforceability of NDCs and the absence of an enforcement mechanism even for the general obligation that parties do possess to effect commitments that they have made independently will be to render the NDC process ineffective for altering investor behaviour.

A fourth weakness lies in the lack of obligation for parties to communicate how the long-term goals of the Agreement will be achieved.[40] Parties are strongly encouraged to 'formulate and communicate long-term low greenhouse gas emission development strategies' but are not obliged to do so.[41] Fifty-one strategies had been submitted by July 2022, many of them following political pressure to develop long-term visions in

---

[36] ibid, arts 2(2) and 4(3).
[37] The Implementation and Compliance Mechanism established at art 15 is described as being 'facilitative in nature and function in a manner that is transparent, non-adversarial and non-punitive'.
[38] Paris Agreement (n 5), art 4(2).
[39] ibid, art 13(11).
[40] ibid, art 2.
[41] ibid, art 4(19).

time for the 26th Conference of the Parties taking place in Glasgow in November 2021.[42] Instead, the requirement to reconsider national contributions to the global climate change effort every five years is likely to introduce short-termism to parties' thinking informed by the status of climate negotiations at that time, by domestic political circumstances and by individual perception of the adequacy of contributions made by others with no guarantee of forward movement at each stage of review.[43] Clear statements of pathways towards decarbonisation and of what a decarbonised future would look like would assist with redirecting finance away from fossil fuels and towards renewable energy if proposed timescales for action are sufficiently exacting to place future cost recovery for investment in the present at risk or if the possibility of a renewables dominated future is sufficiently compelling to attract actors looking to benefit from first mover advantage. In contrast, five-yearly snapshots may give rise to a 'wait and see' attitude amongst investors with a consistent practice of emissions cuts amongst the largest state consumers of carbon emitting energy sources being required to prompt a change of course.

In summary, the international community has sent a strong signal in the Agreement that it recognises the need to decarbonise. Most NDCs include measures for increasing renewable energy generation, and the fact that parties are obliged to 'pursue domestic mitigation methods, with the aim of achieving' the objectives of their NDCs, should lead to significant growth in renewables output. However, its ability to secure movement away from investment and support for fossil fuel energy and toward renewables is impaired by the significant leeway for states to react to or ignore standards which the Agreement invites them to observe, and by the lack of legal underpinning for parties' NDCs. Its ambitious goals may appear to signal that the fossil fuel era will definitely conclude within an identifiable timescale and therefore that all future support and investment should go to renewables and other low carbon sources, but they are not backed up adequately by legally binding commitments to cut greenhouse gases.

C. Market Mechanisms for Emissions Reduction

The Kyoto Protocol established market mechanisms for use by states in meeting their commitments to contribute to reducing global greenhouse gas emissions. The Paris Agreement replaces them with alternative mechanisms. The mechanisms enable parties to keep emissions within legally binding targets or to achieve committed levels of cuts stated in NDCs by means other than reducing levels of greenhouse gases that are legally attributable to them under the climate change treaties. As considered in the following subsections, the mechanisms established under the Protocol were the climate change regime's most visible driver of renewable energy development. However, problems caused by their use led to their replacement with alternative mechanisms under the Paris Agreement. Questions remain over the Paris Agreement mechanisms as they

---

[42] UNFCCC, 'Long-term strategies portal' (UNFCCC Website) Communication of long-term strategies | UNFCCC (accessed 2 October 2022).
[43] Paris Agreement (n 5) art 4(9).

are not yet in operation, but it is hoped that opportunities they will afford for states to contribute to the Agreement's goals by obtaining credits for avoided emissions earned by low carbon energy projects will also drive investment in renewable energy.

(i) Market Mechanisms under the Kyoto Protocol

The Protocol allowed parties to meet their targets by using allowances purchased through international emissions trading to offset emissions exceeding their targets.[44] Emissions trading involves the issue of allowances to emitters to emit a stated amount of greenhouse gases under a legally established scheme. Emitters who have unused allowances because they have cut their greenhouse gas emissions may sell them to emitters who need additional allowances to cover their emissions. Scheme members are penalised when it is found at periodic assessments that their emissions are not covered by allowances. The linking of national and subnational schemes creates opportunities for international trading in emissions by enabling emitters in one jurisdiction to purchase allowances from an emitter in a different jurisdiction. The European Union's emissions trading scheme, covering stated emissions from emitters in the 27 Member States, is by its nature international. Unfortunately, emissions trading did not prove to be a significant driver for renewable energy under the Protocol as parties' targets were not exacting enough to create demand for unit transfers from other parties.[45] Parties did not need to purchase unused emission allowances to be able to meet their targets.

Parties with targets under the Protocol were also able to use credits earned through project development in other states when calculating whether they had complied with their targets. Joint implementation (JI) permitted a party with a target to derive the benefit from emissions-reducing projects in another party with a target under the Protocol.[46] This mechanism made little contribution to the spread of renewable energy with 'end-of-pipe' emission-reduction projects being preferred because credits could be earned at lower expense than through developing renewable energy infrastructure.[47] The Clean Development Mechanism (CDM) enabled parties with targets to earn credits by undertaking projects in non-target (developing) states that would result in long-term additional emissions reduction over the baseline level that would have pertained without the project.[48] In contrast to JI, around three-quarters of projects involved renewable energy production.[49] This striking difference was due in part to the requirement that projects under the CDM should contribute to sustainable development in the host country.[50] The mechanisms saw higher levels of use, despite the lack

---

[44] Kyoto Protocol (n 3) art 16ff.
[45] Geraldine Pflieger, 'Kyoto Protocol and Beyond' in Bill Freedman (ed) *Global Environmental Change* (Springer, 2014) 517, 520.
[46] Kyoto Protocol (n 3) art 6.
[47] UNEP DTU Partnership, 'JI Projects' http://cdmpipeline.org/ji-projects.htm (accessed 2 October 2022). As at 1 July 2022, 18% of the 761 projects under the mechanism were for renewable energy.
[48] Kyoto Protocol (n 3) art 12.
[49] UNEP DTU Partnership, 'CDM Projects by type' http://cdmpipeline.org/cdm-projects-type.htm (accessed 2 October 2022).
[50] Kyoto Protocol (n 3) art 12(2).

of demand by states for meeting international targets, due to the allowance for credits to be used as offsets under the EU's Emissions Trading System.[51]

The CDM has, to date, been the most obviously successful element of the international climate change regime for promoting renewable energy, but there are grounds for arguing that it was not as effective as such a mechanism could have been for driving low carbon energy development in the developing world and that the results achieved are unlikely to be long lasting. First, some aspects of the mechanism detracted from the appeal of renewable energy developments compared to alternative means of earning credits. The requirement that emissions savings should be demonstrably additional to those that would have occurred on a business-as-usual basis was harder to demonstrate than for 'end of pipe' projects that reduced greenhouse gas emissions from existing facilities (eg, capturing methane from landfill sites).[52] Such projects were also often more attractive for investors as they could realise very large volumes of credits at much lower cost.[53]

Second, the mechanism proved poor for overcoming barriers to renewable energy in the least developed countries of the developing world due to limited capacity for supporting low carbon development. Around three-quarters of projects were located in China, India, Mexico and Brazil, all of which had well-established capacities for technological innovation.[54] In contrast, only around 3% of CDM projects were located in Africa and less than 1% in the least developed countries due, in large part, to an inability to attract and support private investment.[55] CDM also proved to be a weak vehicle for technology transfer with the ability of a project to support technological development in the host state not being a condition for the issue of credits.[56] As the raison d'être for the mechanism was to promote economic efficiency by developed states in meeting their targets, it is unsurprising that its participants should have focused on opportunities for obtaining the maximum credits for the least outlay rather than on enhancing capacities for energy innovation in developing states.

---

[51] Charlotte Streck, Paul Keenlyside and Moritz von Unger, 'The Paris Agreement: A New Beginning' (2016) 13 *Journal for European Environmental and Planning Law* 3, 17.

[52] Sanford Gaines, 'International Law and Institutions for Climate Change' in Joshua Sarnoff (ed) *Research Handbook on Intellectual Property and Climate Change* (Edward Elgar 2016) 33, 45; Martijn Wilder Am and Lauren Drake, 'International Law and the Renewable Energy Sector' in Cinnamon Carlarne, Kevin Gray, and Richard Tarasofsky (eds) *The Oxford Handbook of International Climate Change Law* (Oxford University Press, 2016) 358, 366.

[53] Mario Citelli, Marco Barassi and Ksenia Belykh, 'Renewable Energy in the International Arena' (2014) 2 *Groningen Journal of International Law* 1, 25; Wilder Am and Drake (n 52), 366.

[54] Steven Ferrey, 'The Failure of International Global Warming Regulation to Promote Needed Renewable Energy' (2010) 37 *Boston College Environmental Affairs Law Review* 67, 86; Gaines (n 52) 45; Alexander Thompson, 'The Global Regime for Climate Finance: Political and Legal Challenges' in Cinnamon Carlarne, Kevin Gray, and Richard Tarasofsky (eds) *Oxford Handbook of International Climate Change Law* (Oxford University Press, 2016) 138, 145.

[55] Gaines (n 52) 45; Merylyn Hedger, 'Stagnation or Regeneration: Technology Transfer in the United Nations Convention on Climate Change' in David Ockwell and Alexandra Mallett (eds) *Low Carbon Technology Transfer: From Rhetoric to Reality* (Routledge, 2012) 211, 219; Peter Newell and Harriet Bulkeley, 'Landscape for Change? International Climate Policy and Energy Transitions: Evidence from sub-Saharan Africa' (2016) 17 *Climate Policy* 650, 657.

[56] Ferrey (n 54) 76; Gaines (n 52) 45; Dalindyebo Shabalala, 'Technology Transfer for Climate Change and Developing Country Viewpoints on Historical Responsibility and Common but Differentiated Responsibilities' in Joshua Sarnoff (ed) *Research Handbook on Intellectual Property and Climate Change* (Edward Elgar, 2016) 172, 181–182.

Third, a stable price at a high enough level for credits was required to attract investment in renewables by creating confidence that the high initial development costs would be recouped. The value of the CDM collapsed due to the long delay in entry into force of the Protocol's second commitment period, and with it lost its ability to attract investment in renewables.[57] Demand for credits from the EU ETS also declined substantially due initially to restrictions of the use of credits from certain gas destroying end of pipe projects because of doubts over their credibility and latterly due to a requirement that offsets must derive from projects in least developed countries.[58]

(ii) Market Mechanisms under the Paris Agreement

Article 6 of the Agreement identifies two ways in which parties may implement their NDCs through voluntary cooperation in addition to their own efforts. These are: the use of 'internationally determined mitigation outcomes' derived from cooperation in meeting their NDCs (referred to as ITMOs);[59] and a mechanism, bearing some resemblance to the CDM, allowing all parties to earn emission credits by supporting actions to mitigate greenhouse gases and support sustainable development in other states.[60] In addition, it defines a framework for non-market approaches to assisting with the implementation of NDCs in 'the context of sustainable development and poverty eradication'.[61]

The first point to make when considering whether these vehicles for collaboration are likely to be more effective for supporting renewable energy development than mechanisms under the Protocol is that agreement by the Paris Agreement's parties on how the mechanisms will function was only reached at the 26th Conference of the Parties to the UNFCCC in 2021.[62] Further work is needed by the parties on developing the framework for non-market approaches.[63] The institutions and detailed procedures required for registering and validating ITMOs and projects under the CDM replacement must also be established.[64] Despite this, some observations can be made about support that the mechanisms may provide for overcoming barriers to the diffusion of renewable energy.

---

[57] Hedger (n 55) 220; Newell and Bulkeley (n 55) 655–6; Wilder Am and Drake (n 52) 366.
[58] Emissions-EUETS.com, 'CERs and ERUs market as from 2013' www.emissions-euets.com/cers-erus-market-as-from-2013 (accessed on 2 October 2022).
[59] Paris Agreement (n 5) arts 6(2) and 6(3).
[60] ibid, art 6(4).
[61] ibid, arts 6(8) and 6(9).
[62] CMA, 'Report of the Conference of Parties serving as the meeting of the Parties to the Paris Agreement on its third session, held in Glasgow from 31 October to 13 November 2021. Addendum. Part Two: Action taken by the Conference of Parties serving as the meeting of the Parties to the Paris Agreement at its third session' (CMA Report, March 2022), FCCC/PA/CMA/2021/10/Add.1, Annex (Decisions 2, 3 and 4/CMA.3).
[63] ibid, Decision 4/CMA.3.
[64] Charles Di Leva and Scott Vaughan, 'The Paris Agreement's New Article 6 Rules: The promise and challenge of carbon market and non-market approaches' (International Institute for Sustainable Development, Deep Dive, 13 December 2021) The Paris Agreement's New Article 6 Rules | International Institute for Sustainable Development (iisd.org) (accessed 2 October 2022).

The first is that there is no international emissions trading mechanism of the type established under the Protocol as parties do not have legally binding targets under the Agreement.[65] However, the allowance for all states to include 'internationally transferred mitigation outcomes' (ITMOs) amongst national actions for mitigating climate change in their NDCs preserves the possibility for those supporting decarbonisation through renewable energy development to agree on an ad hoc basis with states that are less well-placed to decarbonise energy supplies to transfer resulting emission reductions to them for a financial consideration. It could also expand significantly the possibilities states have to meet their contributions to climate change mitigation by undertaking emission reduction projects in other states.[66] In particular, it incentivises the establishment and linking of domestic emission trading schemes if allowances to emit issued under them and transferred between them are accepted as ITMOs for the purposes of preparing and implementing NDCs.[67] In this regard, the 2021 decision on how transfers envisaged under Article 6.2 will be conducted accommodates government to private sector trading in markets for emission allowances.[68] It states principles that those markets and trades conducted under them will need to meet for acceptance under the Paris Agreement that units acquired in private markets credibly represent avoided emissions.

The expansion of mechanisms that place a price on carbon could assist with levelling the playing field for renewable energy globally, but only, as noted above, if it results in the prospect of high enough carbon costs to incentivise investment in renewables by making them a financially preferable alternative to continuing with existing or investing in new greenhouse gas energy production. The spread of emissions trading may not be beneficial for the renewable energy sector if a rush to link with schemes offering lower cost opportunities for covering emissions were to depress the carbon price. It may also be to the detriment of the renewables sector if subsidies are removed to prevent support external to trading systems from impairing their economic efficiency. Subsidies may be removed because reduced demand for units due to subsidy-induced switching from fossil fuels to renewables could affect the long-term incentive for investment in renewables that trading systems provide by depressing their carbon prices. However, subsidies are frequently essential for early-stage commercialisation and to support more expensive renewable technologies.

Second, the fact that the Sustainable Development mechanism was proposed by Brazil as an improved version of the CDM (describing it as CDM+) suggested that it would be expected to provide a vehicle for trading units representing avoided emissions, and, in doing so, for leveraging private investment in relevant projects.[69]

---

[65] Streck et al (n 51) 5–6.
[66] ibid, 5–7; Wolfgang Obergassel and others, 'Phoenix from the Ashes: An Analysis of the Paris Agreement to the United Nations Framework Convention on Climate Change – Part I' (2015) 27 *Environmental Law and Management* 243, 253.
[67] Torbjørg Jevnaker, and Jørgen Wettestad, 'Linked Carbon Markets: Silver Bullet, or Castle in the Air?' (2016) 6 *Climate Law* 142.
[68] CMA, 'Report of the Conference of Parties' (n 62), Decision 2/CMA.3.
[69] Andrei Marcu, 'Carbon Market Provisions in the Paris Agreement (Article 6)' (CEPS Special Report No 128, January 2016) www.ceps.eu/publications/carbon-market-provisions-paris-agreement-article-6 (accessed 2 October 2022), 13.

Direction in the Agreement that the mechanism should 'incentivize and facilitate participation in the mitigation of greenhouse gas emissions by public and private entities ...' and in the Paris Decision that the mechanism should build on '[e]xperience gained with and lessons learned from existing mechanisms and approaches adopted under the Convention and its related legal instruments' reinforced this impression.[70] The rulebook agreed in 2021 clearly envisages private involvement in the development and financing of Article 6.4 projects as well as under Article 6.2 through participation in emissions trading schemes.[71]

Third, the basis for operation of the Sustainable Development mechanism set out in the Paris Decision requires that proposals for activities should be able to demonstrate the 'additionality' of emissions savings that they are expected to realise over a business-as-usual scenario.[72] Further conditions are included in the Agreement that the mechanism should both 'contribute to the reduction of emission levels in the host Party' and 'deliver an overall mitigation in global emissions'.[73] Additionality and contribution to reducing emissions levels in the host Party are to be demonstrated for project registration under the Rules agreed in 2021 for the Article 6.4 mechanism's operation.[74] Demonstrating additionality is essential for confidence that projects supported under this mechanism will contribute to realising the Paris Agreement's goals. However, it was less easy for new build renewable energy projects to satisfy a similar requirement under the CDM than for projects involving emissions reductions from existing plant.[75] Both conditions could also limit the extent to which the mechanism is capable of driving renewable energy development and related technology transfer in the least developed countries as they have fewer emissions to reduce than other states.

Fourth, the scope of activities that would be regarded as ITMOs and that would fall under the sustainable development mechanism encompasses not only the individual projects supported by the JI and CDM mechanisms, but also the implementation of policies, plans and programmes, potentially allowing very large numbers of credits to be earned from sector-wide interventions.[76] The allowance for all parties to transfer ITMOs and to undertake activities under the Sustainable Development mechanism also expands possibilities for states to support renewable energy development in other states including for technologically literate developing country parties such as China and India to benefit from supporting poorer developing countries.[77]

It can be surmised from the rough outlines of cooperation mechanisms in Article 6 of the Agreement that they may maintain and build on incentives provided under the Protocol that enjoyed some success with supporting renewable energy development.

---

[70] Paris Agreement (n 5) art 6(4)(b); Paris Decision (n 14) para 37(f).
[71] CMA, 'Report of the Conference of Parties' (n 62); Di Leva and Vaughan (n 64).
[72] Paris Decision (n 14) para 37(d).
[73] Paris Agreement (n 5) art 6(4)(d).
[74] CMA, Report of the Conference of the Parties' (n 62), Decision 3/CMA.3.
[75] Wilder Am and Drake (n 52) 366.
[76] Obergassel and others (n 66) 253; Daniel Bodansky, 'The Paris Climate Change Agreement: A New Hope?' (2016) 110 *The American Journal of International Law* 288.
[77] Obergassel and others (n 66) 253.

They also potentially expand the range of renewable-energy-related projects from which benefits may be derived through cooperation. However, operation of the mechanisms appears in July 2022 to be some way off with institutions and detailed arrangements for their functioning still to be developed.[78] The actual effectiveness of the new mechanisms for renewable energy will only become apparent when they are finally operational.

D. Climate Finance

One of the goals of the parties to the Paris Agreement is to make 'finance flows consistent with a pathway towards low greenhouse gas emissions and climate-resilient development'.[79] Adequate finance flows are needed to fund investment in the massive programmes of low and zero carbon development required to meet the Agreement's goals of limiting temperature growth to 1.5°C if possible and certainly below 2°C, fostering climate resilience and low greenhouse gas development, and reaching net zero greenhouse gas emissions by 2050. This is particularly the case for energy-related investments in view of the significant proportion of global greenhouse gas emissions for which fuel combustion is responsible. The mobilisation and transfer of climate finance by wealthier more technologically advanced states to less wealthy developing states is vital for enabling low carbon energy investment in them, particularly in the least developed countries.[80] Financial transfers are also seen as important for responding to the perceived unfairness that developing countries are now unable to follow the same pathway to growth that rich well-resourced developed states have followed because the former have used up the atmosphere's 'safe' capacity for absorbing carbon dioxide.

The three climate change treaties record agreements that climate finance must be provided to support low carbon development in developing states and related commitments. However, for various reasons, including flaws in the relevant legal provision, several difficulties have been experienced with realising the potential of arrangements for climate finance to enable low carbon energy development – and the growth of renewable energy as part of this – in the developing world. At the Glasgow Conference of Parties in 2021, climate finance flows were recognised to be falling far short of the promised minimum level of provision both in the level and types of finance being provided.[81] The opportunity afforded by the adoption of the Paris Agreement and development of its Rulebook to address some of these difficulties was taken up to an extent, but some of the most serious flaws with legal provision remain unaddressed. The following sections outline some of the principal problems with existing legal provision and its implementation for securing adequate flows of climate finance.

---

[78] Di Leva and Vaughan (n 64); Joanna Depledge, Miguel Saldivia, and Cristina Peñasco, 'Glass Half Full or Glass Half Empty?: The 2021 Glasgow Climate Conference' (2022) 22 *Climate Policy* 147, 153–54.
[79] Paris Agreement (n 5) art 2(1)(c).
[80] Depledge (n 78) 151–52.
[81] ibid, 151.

(i) Unclear Commitments

What developed states are required to do to comply with their obligations on climate finance is unclear from the vague wording of the relevant provisions of the Convention and Protocol.[82] The expenditure covered by the obligation to meet the 'agreed full incremental costs' of measures by developing states to implement their obligations under the Convention is not defined.[83] The amount of support to be provided and how the burden for financing this should be shared amongst developed states are not specified. The parties made a belated attempt to clarify the position at the Copenhagen Conference of Parties in 2009 by agreeing that developed states should mobilise $100 billion of funding annually by 2020, but this agreement is also difficult to effect due to a lack of guidance on how responsibility for raising this amount should be allocated amongst developed states.[84]

The obligation for developed states to provide financial support under the Paris Agreement is no better defined than corresponding provisions under the Convention and Protocol with the developing country call for the expected annual contribution to be stated in the Agreement having met strong opposition.[85] The goal of $100 billion mobilisation by 2020 is repeated in the non-binding Paris Decision, but does not add detail to the promise made under the Copenhagen Accord or offer guidance on how the responsibility for providing this level of finance or the higher amount which the decision advises should be mobilised from 2025 should be shared amongst contributing states.[86] Indeed, the relevant paragraph of the decision leaves it unclear whether the post-2025 burden will fall on developed states alone or will be spread more widely amongst states possessing the capacity to support others.

What counts as climate finance is also unclear. This is not defined in any of the treaties or in the Paris Agreement Rulebook. Article 4.3 of the Convention obliges developed country parties to provide 'new and additional financial resources', but grounds for distinguishing new and additional financial resources from existing funding streams have not been developed. The lack of definition has led to debate about whether sources used by parties when providing information on their contributions can properly be regarded as climate finance.[87] Should this be limited, as developing countries argue, to non-repayable transfers? The inclusion of loans is particularly controversial as interest levels, even where below commercial rates, and repayment obligations, could see more monies coming back to developed states than were provided in climate finance in the first place.[88]

---

[82] Thompson (n 54) 141.
[83] FCCC (n 2) art 4(3).
[84] UN Doc. FCCC/CP/2009/L.7, 18 December 2009. Thompson (n 54) 156–57.
[85] Alexander Zahar, 'The Paris Agreement and the Gradual Development of a Law on Climate Finance' (2016) 6 *Climate Law* 75, 82–83; Obergassel and others (n 66), 257–58.
[86] Paris Decision (n 14) para 53.
[87] Hao Zhang, 'Implementing Provisions on Climate Finance under the Paris Agreement' (2019) 9 *Climate Law* 21, 31–35.
[88] ibid, 35.

(ii) Low Transparency

Insufficient obligations for reporting on climate finance and a resulting lack of transparency have made it difficult to establish how much support has been provided, whether claimed support satisfies obligations of developed states, and whether the funding that has been transferred to developing countries has had any positive effect.[89] A lack of clarity creates fertile ground for parties to argue about whether or not sufficient support has been provided rather than concentrating on enabling renewable energy development. In the same vein, the fact that developing states were not obliged under the Convention and Protocol to identify assistance required by them or to account for what they received allowed scope for them to complain that support was inadequate without being clear about what backing they require for the creation of a renewable energy capacity.[90]

The Paris Agreement and its Rulebook strengthen developed country obligations for reporting on climate finance and technology transfer.[91] Developed states are required to report qualitatively and quantitatively every two years on finance provided and mobilised by them.[92] This information will be made subject to a Technical Expert Review.[93] Efforts made to comply with financing responsibilities will also be examined by all parties 'in a facilitative, multilateral consideration of progress'.[94] Compliance with enhanced obligations should improve significantly the transparency and predictability of planned and delivered climate finance flows from developed states individually. However, problems due to lack of clarity on individual responsibility for contributing to the agreed annual total finance and over what counts as climate finance remain.

The Paris Rulebook advises that developing states should report on climate finance received, but they are not obliged to do so.[95] That leaves open scope for debate over the adequacy of climate finance received by them. They are also not required to report on how climate finance is used.[96] Concerns arise that, without information on this, transferred monies may be used for purposes other than enabling low carbon development or lost due to corruption. Transparency and engagement on monies received would therefore assist both with building confidence in finance providers, and with incentivising developing states to create attractive environments for attracting low carbon investment.[97]

---

[89] Thompson (n 54) 151–53; Zahar (n 85) 83–86.
[90] Zahar (n 85) 86.
[91] Paris Agreement (n 5) arts 9(5) and 9(7); CMA, 'Identification of the information to be provided by Parties in accordance with Article 9, paragraph 5, of the Paris Agreement', 15 December 2018, Dec 12/CMA.1, FCCC/PA/CMA/2018/3/Add.1.
[92] ibid.
[93] Paris Agreement (n 5) art 13(11).
[94] ibid.
[95] CMA, 'Modalities, procedures and guidelines for the transparency framework for action and support referred to in Article 13 of the Paris Agreement', Decision 18/CMA1, FCCC/PA/CMA/2018/3/Add.2., para 134.
[96] ibid, para 132.
[97] Zhang (n 87) 35–36.

(iii) Climate Finance from Developing States

Expectations under the Convention and Protocol of transfers purely from a developed North to an undeveloped South do not correspond with changed economic realities.[98] Brazil, India and China have become economic powers in their own right; they have burgeoning capacities for technological innovation but are under no obligation to afford financial and technological support to others. Any assistance that they do offer could pass under the radar as developing country parties are not obliged to report on this.[99]

With regard to the flow of support, the Agreement is notable for encouraging developing state parties to provide climate finance.[100] In addition, the description of the new minimum level of climate finance to be agreed before 2025 as 'collective' implies that the better-off developing country parties as well as developed states may come under pressure to contribute to this.[101] Inclusion of developing state parties within the frame of possible contributors to climate finance represents a significant departure from the bifurcated world of the Kyoto Protocol, but falls short of the express broadening of the donor pool that developed state parties called for in negotiations leading to the Agreement as recognition of changed economic circumstances since the early 1990s.[102]

(iv) Conclusion

The many uncertainties mentioned above have allowed the serious business of establishing low carbon economies in the developing world to become mired in debate and recrimination. Developing states argue that funding provided has been inadequate whilst developed states attribute problems not to failings on their part but to a lack of the enabling environments required for recipients of support to benefit from it including by attracting private investment.[103] The perception of inadequate support has been used by developing countries to oppose calls made on them in climate negotiations to take a more active role in mitigating climate change.[104] The resulting effect on the diffusion of renewable energy technologies has been two-fold: more limited progress with the spread of renewable energy in the developing world than might otherwise have been achieved through developed world support; and a broader weakening of the impetus provided by the international climate change regime for decarbonising energy supplies due to the disengagement of states responsible for an increasing proportion of the world's greenhouse gas emissions and with growing capacities for technological innovation from the global effort to mitigate climate change.

---

[98] David Ockwell and Alexandra Mallett, 'Introduction: Low Carbon Technology Transfer – From Rhetoric to Reality' in David Ockwell and Alexandra Mallett (eds) *Low Carbon Technology Transfer: From Rhetoric to Reality* (Routledge, 2012) 3; Philippe Cullet, 'Common but Differentiated Responsibilities' in Malgosia Fitzmaurice, David Ong and Panos Merkouris (eds) *Research Handbook on International Environmental Law* (Edward Elgar, 2010) 161, 176; Shabalala (n 56) 191.
[99] Paris Agreement (n 5) art 9(5).
[100] ibid, art 9(2).
[101] Paris Decision (n 14) para 53.
[102] Bodansky (n 76) 310.
[103] Thompson (n 54) 150; Shabalala (n 56) 172–74.
[104] Shabalala (n 56) 173 and 187–93.

E. Technology Transfer

Technology development and transfer worldwide are of fundamental importance for the replacement of fossil fuel technologies with renewable technologies as the dominant sources of energy supplies. Technology development and transfer involves more than the provision of hardware for producing renewable energy from technologically advanced states to those at lower levels of development. It also involves helping less advanced states with creating enabling environments for renewable energy technology that can attract investment in relevant development, and with acquiring the capacities necessary to adopt technologies received and to become innovators themselves in adapting them to meet indigenous energy needs.[105]

The need for action on widespread access to technologies enabling decarbonisation and adaptation to the consequences of climate change are recognised in the climate change treaties. All parties to the UNFCCC are obliged to '[p]romote and cooperate in the development, application and diffusion, including transfer, of technologies, practices and processes' for controlling, reducing or preventing greenhouse gases in all relevant sectors including energy and transport.[106] The key role of technologically advanced states and their nationals in making a worldwide diffusion of low carbon technologies possible is recognised by the obligation placed on developed states to 'take all practicable steps to promote, facilitate and finance, as appropriate, the transfer of, or access to, environmentally sound technologies and know-how to other parties … to enable them to implement the provisions of the Convention'.[107] The obligation for developed countries extends to the provision of support for 'the development and enhancement of endogenous capacities and technologies' of developing countries.[108] Despite the legally binding nature of these commitments, discussion over how to give effect to them proceeded slowly. It took until 2010 for the parties to the Convention to agree on the establishment of a Technology Mechanism for implementing them.[109] This consists of the Technology Executive Committee whose role is to identify and develop policy on issues facing technology development and transfer and the Climate Technology Centre and Network which is responsible for promoting implementation of the Convention's obligations in line with the TEC's policies.

The Paris Agreement also makes provision on technology development and transfer. The parties seek to accelerate work on this strand of climate action by stating a shared long-term vision 'on the importance of fully realizing technology development and transfer in order to improve resilience to climate change and to reduce greenhouse gases'.[110] They also take on a common obligation to 'strengthen cooperative action

---

[105] Nicola Sharman, 'Inter-State Climate Technology Transfer under the UNFCCC: A benefit-sharing approach' (2022, Early View) *Review of European, Comparative and International Environmental Law* 1, 5–6.
[106] UNFCCC (n 2) art 4(1)(c).
[107] ibid, art 4(5).
[108] ibid.
[109] UNFCCC, 'Information on Climate Technology Negotiations' (UNFCCC Climate Technology website) Climate Technology Negotiations (unfccc.int) (accessed 2 October 2022).
[110] Paris Agreement (n 5) art 10(1).

on technology development and transfer'.[111] A Technology Framework is established 'to provide overarching guidance to the work of the Technology Mechanism'.[112] The framework was adopted at the first conference of parties to the Paris Agreement at Katowice in 2018.[113] It provides strategic guidance to the Technology Mechanism on advancing the Paris Agreement's long-term vision in line with its key themes of innovation, implementation, enhancing enabling environments and capacity building.

Provision on technology transfer under the climate change treaties has supported projects involving renewable energy production and/or the creation of enabling environments for attracting investment in and capacity building for pursuing renewable energy development in developing states.[114] A UNFCCC report on technology needs in parties' nationally determined contributions under the Paris Agreement refers to projects involving Nauru, Thailand, Brunei, South Korea, the United Arab Emirates and Uruguay amongst others.[115] However, technology transfer from technologically advanced to less advanced states is viewed as inadequate to date for enabling the uptake of low carbon development in the latter. It has often proved to be ineffective when it has been provided for enabling developing states to become low carbon economies in their own right.[116]

Successful technology development and transfer is complex. It involves simultaneous action on promoting technological innovation, creating conditions to enable the diffusion of technologies from the minority of technologically advanced states to states with very different and often undeveloped and unattractive investment environments, creating capacities needed for adopting transfers and translating then into long-term indigenous technological capabilities and making finance available for all of those steps.[117] Careful and country-specific analysis is needed as to why technology transfer remains at a low level in many developing country jurisdictions and of how it could be enhanced. Whilst recognising this, commentators have identified weaknesses in legal provision for this aspect of climate action under the climate change treaties that may have contributed to low levels of international technology transfer to date. First, high-level and vague provisions in the Convention and the Paris Agreement leave many questions about what developed state parties and more technologically advanced developing states are obliged or expected to do. It is not clear what steps are envisaged by the obligation to 'promote, facilitate and finance, as appropriate, the transfer of, or access to, environmentally sound technologies and know-how to other Parties' under the Convention.[118] The failure to define clearly what technology transfer involves, or to

---

[111] ibid, art 10(2).
[112] ibid, art 10(4).
[113] CMA, 'Technology framework under Article 10, paragraph 4, of the Paris Agreement', Decision 15/CMA.1, FCCC/PA/CMA/2018/3/Add.2, 15 December 2018.
[114] UN Climate Technology Centre and Network, *Technology and Nationally Determined Contributions*, UNFCCC (Report, 2021), TT:CLEAR (unfccc.int) (accessed 2 October 2022).
[115] ibid.
[116] Sharman (n 105) 6–7.
[117] ibid, 6.
[118] FCCC (n 2) art 4(5).

specify the financial support that should be provided for this, further hampered initial efforts to effect this work stream. This has contributed to the 18 years it has taken for the Technology Mechanism to be established.[119,120] Provision on technology transfer is enhanced marginally by the Paris Agreement's vision of what this process is intended to achieve, but this high-level statement still lacks the detail required to pin developed states down to specific commitments or to judge the adequacy of the support provided by them.[121] It appears from the description of the Technology Framework in the Paris Decision that its role will be to address some of the weaknesses with the existing arrangements under the Convention.[122] It is expected to facilitate not only the identification of developing states' technology needs to enable a more focused approach to technology transfer, but also the 'enhanced implementation of their results ... through the preparation of bankable projects'.[123] Importantly, its role also includes 'the enhancement of enabling environments for and the addressing of barriers to the development and transfer of socially and environmentally sound technologies'.[124] Work on implementing the Technology Framework is still ongoing under the UNFCCC; whether it will improve outcomes remains to be seen.

Second, financial support including from climate finance will be needed for the conduct of most technology transfer initiatives. A lack of coordination between the two strands of climate action adds to difficulties with securing investment for technology transfer due to already noted legal difficulties affecting flows of climate finance.[125] developed state parties of the Convention and all parties to the Paris Agreement have an obligation to provide financial support to developing country parties for implementing the technology transfer article.[126] However, agreement has never been concluded on the level of finance and on how responsibility for meeting it should be shared. Instead, rather heavy reliance fell on the Kyoto Protocol's market mechanisms as a vehicle for transferring renewable and other low carbon technologies to the developing world.[127] The mechanisms were useful for transferring hardware for individual projects, but not for the capacity building work that would enable recipient states to adopt the transferred technologies and develop technological innovation abilities themselves. The non-market mechanisms in Article 6(8) of the Paris Agreement were agreed on in part to address this problem, but discussion continues as to how they will operate.[128]

---

[119] Gaines (n 52) 38–40; Shabalala (n 56) 177–83.
[120] ibid, 46–48; ibid, 187–94.
[121] Paris Agreement (n 5) art 10.
[122] Paris Decision (n 14) para 67.
[123] ibid, para 67(a).
[124] ibid, para 67(d).
[125] Sharman (n 105), 5; Chaewoon Oh, 'Contestations over the Financial Linkages Between the UNFCCC's Technology and Financial Mechanism: Using the Lens of Institutional Interaction' (2020) 20 *International Environmental Agreements* 559.
[126] UNFCCC (n 2) art 4(5); Paris Agreement (n 5) art 10(2).
[127] Sharman (n 105) 6.
[128] See section IIC(ii).

Third, the Agreement makes no reference to the effect of intellectual property rights on technology transfer. Developing country views that the existence of such rights obstruct the transfer of technological knowhow and developed country arguments that other factors, particularly the lack of supportive policy and legal frameworks for technology investment and innovation, are to blame have become proxies for wider discontents over the functioning of the climate finance and technology transfer provisions.[129] Silence on this issue, as with developing country reporting, leaves continued space for it to be raised as a barrier to low carbon development in future negotiations on whether and to what extent developing country parties should take on fuller responsibility for mitigating climate change.[130]

F. Capacity Building

The preceding sections identify problems with mechanisms for climate finance and technology transfer that have limited their support for renewable energy development. To the extent that support has been provided, its effectiveness is further impaired where confidence is lacking in the ability of states to provide a stable investment destination due to the absence of appropriate policy and legal frameworks and of coherent regulatory frameworks for renewable energy. Private investors may be unwilling to finance projects in such circumstances even when official development aid is available from the climate change regime's funding bodies.[131] States may also be unable to take advantage of projects involving the transfer of renewable energy hardware to them where they lack the innovation capacity required to adopt and adapt the technology provided to them.[132] Without this, any investments that are made may not enable the host state to achieve long-term sustainability in its energy supplies. The key response to this situation is for states with established capacities for technological innovation to provide developing countries with the long-term support required to cultivate their own capabilities for supporting renewable energy in policy and law and for adopting, adapting, manufacturing and deploying technologies made available to them. In this regard, there is a need for close coordination between capacity building and climate action on technology development and transfer.

Capacity building has been a feature of the climate change regime from its inception.[133] Article 4(5) of the Convention obliges developed country parties to

---

[129] Gaines (n 52) 34; Shabalala (n 56) 173–74.
[130] Gaines, ibid 34.
[131] ibid, 43–47; Ana Pueyo and others, 'How to Increase Technology Transfers to Developing Countries: A Synthesis of the Evidence' (2012) 12 *Climate Policy* 320, 332–36.
[132] Rob Byrne and others, 'Energy Pathways in Low Carbon Development: the Need to Go Beyond Technology Transfer' in David Ockwell and Alexandra Mallett (eds) *Low Carbon Technology Transfer: From Rhetoric to Reality* (Routledge, 2012) 123, 124–27; Anne-Marie Verbeken, 'Low Carbon Technology Transfer under the Climate Change Convention: Evolution of Multilateral Technology Support' in David Ockwell and Alexandra Mallett (eds) *Low Carbon Technology Transfer: From Rhetoric to Reality* (Routledge, 2012) 143, 150–51 and 160.
[133] UNFCCC, 'Capacity Building in the Negotiations' Capacity-building in the negotiations | UNFCCC (accessed 2 October 2022).

'support the development and enhancement of endogenous capacities and technologies of developing country Parties' in connection with the provision of technological support. However, as with technology transfer itself, the parties have been slow to transfer general commitments into detailed programmes for action. A framework for capacity building was established in 2001 by a decision of the Marrakesh conference of parties to the Convention,[134] but the workstream has continued to hold a lower profile than other areas of interstate action under the international regime despite periodic reappraisal of how its status could be enhanced.[135]

With this unpromising backdrop in mind, the inclusion of a standalone provision for capacity building in the Paris Agreement may be one of its most valuable contributions to improving support for renewable energy development in the developing world.[136] The article itself mostly consists of statements recording a consensus on the desirability of support for capacity building to enable climate change mitigation and adaptation action by developing states including by acquiring abilities to facilitate technology development, dissemination and deployment and to access climate finance. Of more significance is the establishment of the Paris Committee on Capacity Building, a new meta-institution with a broad remit to address gaps in and enhance existing efforts in this area in all aspects of the climate change regime for which such support is required.[137] The Paris Committee was given responsibility for overseeing and managing a workplan for 2016–2020 on capacity building.[138] This includes 'exploring how developing country Parties can take ownership of building and maintaining capacity over time and space', a preferable approach for having a lasting effect to developed-state led capacity building initiatives conducted on an ad hoc basis only when funding is available.[139] The follow-up workplan for 2021–2024 identifies three priority areas for capacity building action: achieving coherence and coordination in capacity building efforts under the UNFCCC; identifying capacity gaps and needs; promoting awareness; raising knowledge and stakeholder engagement.[140]

Capacity building has evolved quickly as an area of climate action following the stronger focus under the Paris Agreement. Much remains ambiguous about what states are expected to do to support capacity building under the Paris Agreement.[141] Significant questions arise, answers to which will differ for each different state recipient, over the capacity building efforts needed to support national climate action and how capacities can be built effectively. Even so, it is clear from interaction between states that action in this area under the climate change regime will

---

[134] UNFCCC, 'Decision 2/CP.7 'Capacity building in developing states' (21 January 2002) FCCC/CP/2001/13/Add.1.
[135] UNFCCC, 'Capacity Building in the Negotiations' (n 133).
[136] Paris Agreement (n 5) art 11.
[137] Paris Decision (n 14) para 71.
[138] ibid, para 73.
[139] ibid, para 73(f).
[140] UNFCCC COP, 'Review of the Paris Committee on Capacity-Building', Dec. 9/CP.25, FCCC/CP/2019/13/Add.2, para 9.
[141] Sonja Klinsky and Ambuj Sagar, 'The Why, What and How of Capacity Building: Some Explorations' (2022) 22 Climate Policy 549.

continue to grow in importance for supporting decarbonisation and adaptation in developing states and renewable energy development under them. Klinsky and Sagar identify capacity building as a major destination of overseas development assistance ($10B annually).[142] Numerous requests for capacity building support in connection with renewable energy projects have been included in nationally determined contributions submitted by parties to the Paris Agreement.[143] The states' performance of the energy projects concerned is typically made conditional in the relevant NDCs on the receipt of capacity building support from more technologically advanced states.[144]

G. Conclusion

Looked at in isolation, the Paris Agreement does not inspire confidence that it will provide much more of an engine house for an international diffusion of renewable energy than the UNFCCC and the Kyoto Protocol. It does not directly promote renewables. It encourages but does not ensure that states will progressively increase their climate change mitigation efforts including by pursuing low carbon energy development. It leaves plenty of scope for argument both over how the burden of responding to climate change should be shared amongst contracting parties and on whether the developed world has atoned for its sins sufficiently by providing financial, technological and capacity building support to derail whatever motive force the Agreement may provide for displacing fossil fuel energy by renewable alternatives. Longstanding problems with arrangements for climate finance and technology transfer, the international climate change regime's main channels for supporting low carbon energy development and innovation in the developing world, have only partially been addressed. Finally, even where states do make strong commitments to support renewable energy in their NDCs, they cannot be forced to stand by them to the letter. However, it does at least create a framework for ongoing negotiations that may lead to a progressive strengthening of international support for renewables including by allowing public and private actors that have promoted the replacement of fossil fuels with renewable energy to place pressure on contracting parties that prove more reticent to alter their energy-consuming behaviours. Commitments to increase renewable energy production feature in almost all states NDCs. The mechanisms established under Article 6 have promise as vehicles for supporting renewable energy investment whilst action on capacity building will help engender the capabilities required for developing states to become producers of renewable energy and perhaps even independent technological innovators in the renewables sector.

---

[142] ibid.
[143] Mizan Khan, David Mfitumukiza and Saleemul Huq, 'Capacity Building for Implementation of Nationally Determined Contributions under the Paris Agreement' (2020) 20 *Climate Policy* 499, 505.
[144] ibid.

Classroom Questions

1. Why and in what respects is international collaboration on tackling climate change and its consequences a driver for renewable energy development?
2. Consider critically legal provision made under the three climate change treaties for:

    (a) promoting the growth of renewable energy directly (e.g. by obliging states to exchange fossil fuel energy for renewable energy);
    (b) promoting the growth of renewable energy indirectly (e.g. by obliging states to reduce emissions of greenhouse gases).

    How and to what extent is this legal provision likely to secure growth in the renewables sector?

3. Identify the mechanisms introduced by the Paris Agreement which allow states to include greenhouse gas emissions avoided through steps taken in other jurisdictions than their own in their periodic statements on greenhouse gas emissions reduction attributable to them. How may each of the mechanisms support renewable energy growth, and particularly in developing states? In answering this question, draw from comparable experience with market mechanisms under the Kyoto Protocol.
4. Why is legal provision in the following areas important for supporting renewable energy development in developing states?

    (a) climate finance
    (b) technology transfer
    (c) capacity building

Consider critically the support current legal provision in these areas makes for supporting renewable energy development. How, if at all, could this support be improved through further development and reform of the relevant laws?

Scenarios

1. Techinvest, a bank which invests in new technological opportunities, would like to know about investment possibilities that the ratification by states of the UNFCCC and the Paris Agreement may give rise to. It asks you for guidance on the legal strength of commitments made by parties under these Agreements, including by submitting nationally determined contributions, for undertaking renewable energy development and for reducing greenhouse gas emissions from the energy sector. To what extent can it draw confidence from them that significant investment in renewable energy will follow over the coming decades within individual state parties to the treaties and cumulatively?
2. Ragusa, a small but wealthy developed state, is a party to the UNFCCC and the Paris Agreement. It has a high carbon footprint due to the consumption of fossil fuel energy by its citizens. Sadly, it has few indigenous renewable energy resources with which to replace them, being rather flat and with a typically dull and cloudy climate. Ragusa has heard about possibilities for state parties to the Paris Agreement to contribute to the global climate effort by acquiring credits

for emission-reducing activities in jurisdictions other than their own. Advise Ragusa on the relevant opportunities under the Paris Agreement offered by its Article 6 mechanisms. Draw, if necessary, when doing so, from experience with the market mechanisms under the Kyoto Protocol.

Suggested Reading

Book chapters

Sanford Gaines, 'International Law and Institutions for Climate Change' in Joshua Sarnoff (ed) *Research Handbook on Intellectual Property and Climate Change* (Edward Elgar 2016) 45.

David Ockwell and Alexandra Mallett, 'Introduction: Low Carbon Technology Transfer – From Rhetoric to Reality' in David Ockwell and Alexandra Mallett (eds) *Low Carbon Technology Transfer: From Rhetoric to Reality* (Routledge 2012) 3.

Dalindyebo Shabalala, 'Technology Transfer for Climate Change and Developing Country Viewpoints on Historical Responsibility and Common but Differentiated Responsibilities' in Joshua Sarnoff (ed) *Research Handbook on Intellectual Property and Climate Change* (Edward Elgar 2016) 172.

Martijn Wilder Am and Lauren Drake, 'International Law and the Renewable Energy Sector' in Cinnamon Carlarne, Kevin Gray, and Richard Tarasofsky (eds) *The Oxford Handbook of International Climate Change Law* (Oxford University Press 2016) 358.

Articles

Joanna Depledge, Miguel Saldivia, and Cristina Penasco, 'Glass Half Full or Glass Half Empty?': The 2021 Glasgow Climate Conference' (2022) 22 *Climate Policy* 147, 153–54.

Mizan Khan, David Mfitumukiza and Saleemul Huq, 'Capacity Building for Implementation of Nationally Determined Contributions under the Paris Agreement' (2020) 20 *Climate Policy* 499.

Nicola Sharman, 'Inter-State Climate Technology Transfer under the UNFCCC: A benefit-sharing approach' (2022) *Review of European, Comparative and International Environmental Law* 5–6.

Charlotte Streck, Paul Keenlyside and Moritz von Unger, 'The Paris Agreement: A New Beginning' (2016) 13 *Journal for European Environmental and Planning Law* 3.

Charlotte Streck, Moritz von Unger and Nicole Krämer, 'From Paris to Katowice: COP24 Tackles the Paris Rulebook' (2019) 16 *Journal for European Environmental and Planning Law* 165–90.

Hao Zhang, 'Implementing Provisions on Climate Finance under the Paris Agreement' (2019) 9 *Climate Law* 21.

Policy

IRENA, *Renewable Energy and Climate Pledges: Five Years After the Paris Agreement*, 2019, International Renewable Energy Agency: Abu Dhabi.

3

Sustainable Development and Renewable Energy

I. Introduction

Public international law's contribution to the growth of renewable energy is not limited to the climate change treaties. This chapter examines other respects in which it urges and sometimes requires states and their nationals to use renewable technologies and support growth in the production and consumption of energy from them. Its main focus is on the discourse in international environmental policy and law on Sustainable Development.[1] This discourse has dominated interstate dialogue since the 1980s on how to enjoy continued economic growth and address social problems of poverty and inability to meet basic needs for an adequate standard of life whilst preserving environmental capacities to support life. Section II of this chapter examines the emergence and evolution of the sustainable development discourse during the last 30 years. Promoting renewable energy is seen as a main means of moving forwards on all of sustainable development's fronts by enabling sustainable economic and social development, by bringing clean energy within reach of people currently without access to electricity and modern energy facilities for cooking, and by displacing unsustainable energy sources such as fossil fuels and biomass harvesting when this exceeds capacities for regrowth.[2]

Despite unanimous support for sustainable development as a concept, states have been less willing to conclude legally binding agreements on actions required of them to make sustainability a reality. This is particularly the case for the sources and security of state energy supplies. The importance of access to affordable energy for maintaining the functioning of economies and societies makes states very reluctant to compromise their sovereignty on how energy needs are met. Much of the international endorsement for renewable energy related to sustainable development has therefore been made through non-binding multi-state declarations and through resolutions of the

---

[1] For introductions to the topic, see Alan Boyle and Catherine Redgwell, *Birnie, Boyle and Redgwell's International Law and the Environment* 4th edn (Oxford University Press, 2021) 116–29; and Philippe Sands and Jacqueline Peel with Ruth Mackenzie and Adriana Fabra, *Principles of International Environmental Law* 4th edn (Cambridge University Press, 2018) 217–29.

[2] See Chapter 1, section III E.

United Nations. The statements and resolutions are examples of 'soft law', a category used by legal scholars to distinguish certain provisions of international agreements, for example because of their presence in a non-legally binding instrument, their vagueness and their unenforceability from 'hard law' provisions.[3] Section III examines states' support in relevant documents for the development and diffusion of renewable energy technology. We will look at the disappointingly slow progress made between initial statements in the 1980s and the interstate Rio Declaration of 2012 followed by a more proactive and ongoing period of support under the Sustainable Energy for All initiative and in connection with the UN's Sustainable Development Goal 7 of ensuring access to affordable, reliable, sustainable and modern energy for all. In view of its prevalence, we will also consider the strengths and weaknesses of soft law for enabling the growth of the renewables sector. Soft law has obvious limitations due to the lack of legal obligation, but it does have merit as a way of moving international dialogue on renewable energy forwards when states are not willing to make harder commitments.

Institutions with renewable energy remits were established under the United Nations in parallel with dialogue in the 1990s and 2000s, but lacked the support and powers required to drive worldwide growth in the renewables sector. Disappointment in general with the slow progress of dialogue on renewable energy despite its obvious advantages for making development sustainable and the notable lack of a high-profile international institution with a renewable energy focus prompted a Germany-led interstate initiative to fill this gap. The result was the establishment by treaty in 2009 of the International Renewable Energy Agency (IRENA), an organisation intended to provide an international repository of expertise and guidance for states and their nationals on exploiting notionally vast opportunities for producing renewable energy.[4] Section V of this chapter considers the valuable contribution made by IRENA to renewable energy's growth as a proportion of world energy supplies whilst recognising that its ability to drive the sector's growth is limited by its lack of authority to require parties to use renewable energy.

The chapter then goes on to examine support for renewable energy under legally binding international agreements concerning the energy sector. Section VI considers pro-renewable commitments made in the Energy Charter Treaty, the leading international agreement concerning the energy sector.[5] Section VII concludes the chapter by reviewing criticisms made by commentators of the weak support provided by international law for renewable energy and by looking at ways suggested by them of enhancing backing for worldwide expansion of the renewables sector.

II. Introducing Sustainable Development

Sustainable development emerged as a concept during the 1980s in response to a number of global problems and to political difficulties with finding consensus on addressing

---

[3] See section IV below for further discussion of the Soft/Hard Law terminology.
[4] Statute of the International Renewable Energy Agency (adopted on 26 January 2009, entered into force on 8 July 2010) 2700 UNTS 45.
[5] Energy Charter Treaty (adopted on 17 December 1994, entered into force on 16 April 1998) 2080 UNTS 95.

them.[6] The 1970s and 1980s saw growing concerns over environmental deterioration in general and with global environmental problems that became apparent during these decades such as ozone depletion, climate change and the exhaustion of fish stocks. There was no settled position on how to address these concerns, however, with irreconcilable conflict emerging between persons arguing for 'limits to growth' to prevent socio-economic development from further transgressing environmental limits to entertain human demands, and others who expressed confidence in humanity's ability to overcome constraints through its ingenuity and technological advances.

In addition, these decades saw growing awareness both of gross disparities in wealth and access to food and other essential resources between the world's developed and developing states, and that gaps between standards of life were often increasing due to worsening poverty, environmental degradation, inappropriate exploitation of resources and armed conflict. The interests of developing states in improving living standards through development came into conflict with calls from developed states for stronger global environmental protection. Developing states understandably viewed it as inequitable that they should be required to accept constraints on their future development in respect of environmental problems caused by states that had become wealthy and technologically advanced by exploiting the resources to which other less developed states were now to be denied access. As with the debate on responding to environmental problems, the differing views on which states should bear responsibility for responding to them and how seemed irreconcilable.

Something was needed to move international dialogue on addressing problems facing the world beyond the impasse it had reached of fundamental disagreement between both advocates of limits to growth and of 'promethean' optimism and States calling for higher environmental standards with those bridling against limits on their future development. Sustainable development does this by aspiring to a milieu in which economic and social development for all can proceed whilst environmental limits are respected. Sustainable development's roots lie in the 1972 Declaration of the UN Conference on the Human Environment (Stockholm Declaration) which calls for the integration of environmental considerations into development planning to 'ensure that development is compatible with the need to protect and improve environment' as well as for technological and financial assistance to developing countries to remedy environmental harm caused by underdevelopment and natural disasters.[7] It was not until the following decade that it became a focus for international dialogue following the publication in 1987 of *Our Common Future* (the Brundtland Report) by the UN-initiated World Commission on Environment and Development.[8] The report urges the adoption of sustainable development which it defines as 'development that meets the needs of the present without compromising the ability of future generations

---

[6] Marie-Claire Cordonier Segger and Ashfaq Khalfan, *Sustainable Development Law: Principles, Practices, and Prospects* (Oxford University Press, 2004) 15–24.
[7] United Nations, *Report of the UN Conference on the Human Environment*, Ref. A/CONF.48/14/Rev.1, 5–16 June 1972, 3–5 (the Stockholm Declaration).
[8] World Commission on Environment and Development, *Our Common Future* (Oxford University Press, 1987).

to meet their own needs'.[9] It expresses confidence that constraints from environmental limits can be overcome through technological progress and social reorganisation, stating that '[t]he concept of sustainable development does imply limits – not absolute limits but limitations imposed by the present state of technology and social organization on environmental resources and by the ability of the biosphere to absorb the effects of human activities. But technology and social organization can be both managed and improved to make way for a new era of economic growth'.[10]

The 1992 Rio Declaration on Environment and Development took forwards the Brundtland Report's recommendations by setting out principles that states should observe in order to make development sustainable.[11] It is not legally binding, but has been and remains a strong influence on the formulation of international law rules on environmental protection as a record of the agreed position between all of the world's developed and developing states on how sustainable development can be realised.[12] The Rio conference also published Agenda 21, a plan of action for implementing sustainable development.[13] Both documents place an emphasis on reconciling economic growth and environmental sustainability whilst tackling poverty. Principles 3 to 5 of the Rio Declaration encapsulate these aims by advising respectively that '[t]he right to development must be fulfilled so as to equitably meet developmental and environmental needs of present and future generations', that 'environmental protection shall constitute an integral part of the development process and cannot be considered in isolation from it' and that '[a]ll States and all people shall cooperate in the essential task of eradicating poverty as an indispensable requirement for sustainable development, in order to decrease the disparities in standards of living and better meet the needs of the majority of the people of the world'.

International gatherings to review progress with sustainable development and to refresh aims and plans have taken place at 10-yearly intervals since the 1992 Rio Conference. In 2002, the World Summit on Sustainable Development was held in Johannesburg, South Africa. The resulting declaration reaffirms states' commitment to pursuing sustainable development, but gives greater weight to combatting social inequity between the developed and developing worlds with environmental concerns having a lower profile.[14] The accompanying Johannesburg Plan of Implementation also describes poverty eradication as the 'greatest global challenge facing the world today', placing it alongside changing unsustainable patterns of production and consumption and protecting and managing the natural resource base of economic and social development as 'overarching objectives of, and essential requirements for, sustainable

---

[9] ibid, Chapter 2: Towards Sustainable Development, para 1.
[10] ibid, An Overview by the World Commission on Environment and Development, para 27.
[11] United Nations, *Rio Declaration on Environment and Development*, UN Doc A/CONF 151/6/Rev 1, (1992) 31 ILM 874 (Rio Declaration).
[12] Jane Holder and Maria Lee, *Environmental Protection, Law and Policy* 2nd edn (Cambridge University Press, 2007) 220–27.
[13] United Nations Sustainable Development, *United Nations Conference on Environment and Development*, Rio de Janeiro, Brazil, 3 to 14 June 1992: Agenda 21, Agenda21.doc (un.org) (accessed 2 October 2022). (Agenda 21).
[14] Cordonier-Segger and Khalfan (n 6), 25–44.

development'.[15] The Rio +20 conference of 2012 in Rio de Janeiro maintained the strong emphasis on poverty eradication as an objective in its outcome document, *The Future We Want*, whilst repeating commitments to advancing the three pillars of sustainable development together.[16]

The negotiation and agreement of goals has also been used to back the fine words and aspirations expressed in conference declarations with statements of objectives to be pursued within set timescales of making development more sustainable to the extent stated within the prescribed period. Eight Millennium Development Goals to be reached by 2015 were agreed to by nearly all the United Nations' Member States in 2000.[17] Objectives concerned the eradication of poverty and hunger, access to primary education, gender equality, reduced child mortality, improved maternal health, more effective responses to endemic diseases such as malaria and AIDS, ensuring environmental sustainability and establishing a global partnership for development. The Millennium Development Goals were succeeded in 2015 by 17 Sustainable Development Goals.[18] This is a package adopted by UN Member States which builds on and augments the impetus provided by the Millennium Development Goals by introducing more specific aims and supporting them with sub-goals and indicators of progress on achieving objectives. For example, the key role of access to energy in advancing economic, social and environmental goals is recognised by the adoption of a goal concerning access to affordable, sustainable, secure and modern energy supplies for all.[19] The Sustainable Development Goals are to be met by 2030. UN states were not legally obliged to achieve the Millennium Development Goals. Nor are they bound to achieve the Sustainable Development Goals. However, support for the latter from indicators may make it easier for other states and civil societies to apply peer pressure on states whose performance, when measured against indicators, is notably poor.[20]

It is doubtful despite having been a goal of international action on social and environmental problems since the 1980s that states are legally bound to act in accordance with sustainable development as a principle of customary international environmental law.[21] The room for debate over what pursuing sustainable development obliges or forbids states to do allowed by its flexibility, a product of its role in bringing together groups with diametrically opposed views, impedes its progress from highly influential

---

[15] *Johannesburg Plan of Implementation*, Report of the *World Summit on Sustainable Development*, Johannesburg, South Africa, 4 Sept 2002, UN Doc. A/CONF. 199/20, paras 2 and 7.

[16] *The Future We Want*, Outcome of the *Rio +20 United Nations Conference on Sustainable Development*, Rio de Janeiro, Brazil, 20–22 June 2012, A/CONF.216/L.1.

[17] United Nations General Assembly, Resolution 55/2, 'United Nations Millennium Declaration', 8 September 2000, UN Doc A/RES/55/2.

[18] United Nations General Assembly, Resolution 70/1, 'Transforming Our World: The 2030 Agenda for Sustainable Development', 21 October 2015, UN Doc A/RES/70/1.

[19] ibid, 19.

[20] Details of the goals, supporting targets, and indicators is at United Nations, 'Do you know all 17 SDGs?', (United Nations, Department of Economic and Social Affairs) THE 17 GOALS | Sustainable Development (un.org) (accessed 22 October 2022).

[21] Boyle and Redgwell (n 1) 125–29.

concept to legal obligation.[22] That said, some elements of sustainable development including the integration of environmental considerations into decision making and related procedural requirements for environmental impact assessment and interstate consultation may well have become rules of customary international law. See Boyle and Redgwell's view that 'although international law may not require development to be sustainable, the precedents suggest that it does require development decisions to be the outcome of a process which promotes sustainable development'.[23] Sustainable development's influence on international discussion on addressing environmental problems whilst tackling poverty, hunger and the unfair distribution of benefits and burdens from past and present resource use between states remains undimmed. For example, climate action under the Paris Agreement is stated as taking place 'in the context of sustainable development and efforts to eradicate poverty'.[24]

III. Sustainable Development and Renewable Energy

Renewable energy was mentioned in the Brundtland Report and is referred to in documents produced at the subsequent international summits on sustainable development because its greater use provides an obvious means of reducing environmental harm associated with fuel combustion by avoiding and displacing fossil fuel consumption whilst enabling more sustainable economic activity. Renewable energy also has a key role in alleviating poverty and improving quality of life, including by bringing supplies to communities not currently benefiting from energy services, reducing the significant time spent on collecting firewood by those currently reliant on energy sources found in localities, and improving air quality in homes by replacing wood burning for heating and cooking.[25] As considered in the following paragraphs, the Brundtland Report and the documents produced by subsequent summits all encourage the growth of renewable energy production in general terms. However, their broad-brush endorsements, the lack of progress from warm words to detailed statements on how the worldwide rollout of renewables should proceed, and their continued support for fossil fuels as a means of progressing economic and social goals has led legal scholars to question their value for promoting a shift to renewable energy.

A. The Brundtland Report

The Brundtland Report of 1987 is strongly supportive of renewable energy, describing it as the 'foundation of the global energy structure during the 21st Century' and referring to steps to 'shift the energy mix more towards renewables' alongside increasing energy efficiency as the most urgent policy measures for the world's states to take on

---

[22] ibid.
[23] ibid, 128.
[24] Paris Agreement (adopted 12 December 2015, entered into force 4 November 2016) 3156 UNTS I-54113.
[25] See Chapter 1, section III E.

combating climate change.[26] The report's section on renewables advises that they 'offer the world potentially huge primary energy sources, sustainable in perpetuity and available in one form or another to every nation on Earth', but advises that 'it will require a substantial and sustained commitment to further research and development if their potential is to be realized'.[27] It identifies key steps for promoting renewable energy 'in the short run' including the removal of hidden subsidies for conventional fuels, giving renewable energy a higher profile in national energy policies including through publicly funded research and development programmes, the creation of 'social and institutional frameworks that will ease these sources into energy supply systems' and large-scale financial and technical assistance to enable developing states to take advantage of potentially massive solar and biomass energy resources.[28] The relatively strong and detailed language we see in the report compared to that of declarations agreed following interstate negotiation and compromise at the Rio, Johannesburg and Rio+20 conferences reflect its origin as the work of an UN-established independent advisory commission.[29]

B. The 1992 Rio Declaration on Environment and Development and Agenda 21

The declaration agreed at the 1992 UN Conference on Environment and Development in Rio does not mention renewable energy, but guidance that states should reduce and eliminate unsustainable patterns of production and consumption and cooperate to strengthen endogenous capacity for sustainable development including through the development, diffusion, and transfer of 'new and innovative technologies' provides encouragement for pro-renewables policies.[30] Renewable energy is referred to in Agenda 21, the non-binding comprehensive plan of action for implementing sustainable development that was developed and endorsed by states participating in the conference to guide future decision-making on development at all governmental levels, and by the public and private sectors.[31] Its section on 'Energy development, efficiency and consumption' begins by stating that the need to control atmospheric greenhouse gases means 'growing reliance on environmentally sound energy systems, particularly new and renewable sources of energy' and therefore that existing constraints to 'increasing the environmentally sound energy supplies required for pursuing the path towards sustainable development, particularly in developing countries, need to be removed'.[32]

---

[26] World Commission on Environment and Development (n 8), Chapter 7 'Energy: Choices for Environment and Development', paras 25 and 88.
[27] ibid, para 74.
[28] ibid, paras 87–88.
[29] Adrian Bradbrook, 'The Development of Renewable Energy Technologies and Energy Efficiency Measures through Public International Law' in Donald Zillman and others (eds) *Beyond the Carbon Economy: Energy Law in Transition* (Oxford University Press, 2008) 109, 111; Mario Citelli, Marco Barassi and Ksenia Belykh, 'Renewable Energy in the International Arena: Legal Aspects and Cooperation' (2014) 2 *Groningen Journal of International Law* 1, 2.
[30] Rio Declaration (n 11), Principles 8 and 9.
[31] Agenda 21 (n 13).
[32] ibid, 'Chapter 9 – Protection of the Atmosphere', paras 9.9–9.12.

Article 9.12 sets out actions that governments should undertake to 'increase the contribution of environmentally sound and cost-effective energy systems, particularly new and renewables ones' including cooperation on identifying environmentally sound, economically viable energy sources, promoting 'the research, development, transfer and use of technologies and practices for environmentally sound energy systems including new and renewable energy systems with particular attention to developing countries' and reviewing current energy supplies to 'determine how the contribution of environmentally sound energy systems as a whole, particularly new and renewable energy systems' could be increased in an economically efficient manner including by overcoming barriers.[33] These statements give clear guidance that states should review possibilities for introducing renewable energy production and consumption where possible and to aid this including by identifying and removing barriers and creating conducive systems for renewable development. However, it is important to note that Agenda 21 is not legally binding and the wording it uses does not create a sense of obligation that would require states to ensure the national growth of renewable energy. The quite high-level statements provide some basis for reviewing state action (eg, has a review of current energy supplies to spot low carbon opportunities been conducted?), but largely lack the detail required to hold states to account about their performances.

C. The 2002 Johannesburg Declaration and Plan of Implementation

The 10-year review of progress with sustainable development at Johannesburg in 2002 brought together representatives of all the world's states. The documents setting out agreements reached by them at the conference, the Johannesburg Declaration on Sustainable Development and the Plan of Implementation of the World Summit on Sustainable Development, are therefore authoritative on states' collective willingness to collaborate on pursuing sustainable development at that time including by promoting renewable energy.[34] They do display some positive developments in international willingness to promote renewable energy as a key future energy source. The Plan of Implementation calls on governments, relevant regional and international organisations and other relevant stakeholders to take a wide range of steps on supporting renewables and other energy sources for sustainable development including more developed to developing world support through finance, technology transfer and capacity building and consideration of sustainable energy options in all relevant areas of policy making.[35] Alternative energy technologies should be developed and disseminated with the aim, inter alia, 'of giving a greater share of the energy mix to renewable energies'.[36] Actors are also called on '[w]ith a sense of urgency [to] substantially

---

[33] ibid, para 9.12.
[34] *Johannesburg Declaration on Sustainable Development*, in Report of the *World Summit on Sustainable Development*, Johannesburg, South Africa, 26 Aug–4 Sept 2002, A/CONF 199/20; Johannesburg Plan of Implementation (n 15).
[35] Johannesburg Plan of Implementation ibid, para 20.
[36] ibid, para 20(c).

increase the global share of renewable energy sources with the objective of increasing its contribution to total energy supply'.[37] A separate section on poverty eradication calls on actors to facilitate achievement of the Millennium Development Goals including that of halving the number of persons in poverty by 2015 by improving access to reliable, affordable, economically viable socially acceptable and environmentally sound energy services and resources.[38] Suggested ways of doing this include rural electrification, decentralised energy systems and the increased use of renewable energy.[39]

Commentators on energy under the sustainable development dialogue conclude that the Johannesburg Plan gives stronger support for renewables than preceding statements. For example, Bradbrook argues that it is apparent even from 'a cursory comparison of paragraph 20 with the terms of Agenda 21 ... that the cause of renewable energy ... has improved dramatically over the decade between UNCED and the WSSD'.[40] The Johannesburg Plan does represent progress from Agenda 21 in the strength of its pro-renewables statements and the greater detail it offers on steps that governments and others should take to enable growth on their use. The linkage of its expectations with Millennium Development Goals and with the Committee on Sustainable Development's resolution on energy for sustainable development did create some basis for critical review of states' actions.[41] Even so, it falls far short of providing legally strong support for the renewables sector. The Declaration and Plan are not legally binding documents. States do not commit to take steps in support of renewable energy under them. On the contrary, provisions which offer indicative lists of actions that governments and others 'would' take if they were committed to achieving stated objectives and which call on them to take action are less strong than corresponding statements in Agenda 21 of what Governments 'should' do to promote renewable energy. A proposal to include a target for the proportion of renewable energy supplies in overall energy consumption would have made a material difference to the Plan's influence, but met with opposition.[42] In addition, renewable energy is often referred to in the Plan's provisions as one option amongst others including 'advanced fossil fuel technologies' for achieving aims, thereby weakening the normative thrust provided by its stronger statements of support for increasing renewables in energy supplies.

D. Rio+20 and The Future We Want

Bradbrook, in a 2008 review of public international law on renewable energy, expresses hope based on progress from Agenda 21 to the Johannesburg Plan that the way forward for international support for renewables through the sustainable development

---

[37] ibid, para 20(e).
[38] ibid, para 9.
[39] ibid, para 9(a).
[40] Bradbrook (n 29) 122–24. See also Citelli (n 29) 3; Stuart Bruce, 'International Law and Renewable Energy: Facilitating Sustainable Energy for All' (2013) 15 *Melbourne Journal of International Law* 18, 32–33.
[41] Johannesburg Plan of Implementation (n 15) paras 1 and 20.
[42] Bradbrook (n 29) 123; Bruce (n 40) 33.

dialogue lies through 'small increments, with successive conferences and summits taking progressively stronger measures in support of renewable energy and energy efficiency, with a view ultimately to achieving a binding convention'.[43] It is disappointing, therefore, that paragraph 20 of the Johannesburg Plan, described by Bradbrook as 'a significant step forward' was followed by the weak section on Energy under *The Future we Want*, the outcome document of the Rio+20 sustainable development summit which took place in 2012.[44] The conference and outcome documents were widely viewed as disappointing, particularly on sustainable development as a vehicle for addressing environmental problems facing the world.[45] One consequence of this is the lack of support for renewable energy, references to which are lukewarm compared to stronger statements in the Johannesburg plan. The strongest statement recognises that 'improving energy efficiency, increasing the share of renewable energy and cleaner and energy-efficient technologies are important for sustainable development, including in addressing climate change'.[46] Renewable energy is viewed throughout as one option alongside other 'cleaner' energy technologies including 'cleaner fossil fuel technologies' for supporting development. Even a proposal to head the relevant section 'Sustainable Energy' was opposed by developing countries.[47] The main disappointment, as noted above, is that the conference was not able to build on the growing international consensus between 1992 and 2002 apparent from the stronger statement of the Johannesburg conference on renewables by adding 'harder' detail on how broad support for renewables in Agenda 21 and the Johannesburg Plan should be implemented such as targets and agreed levels of developed state support for developing states' uptake of renewables through climate finance, technology transfer and capacity building.

E. Sustainable Energy for All and Sustainable Development Goal 7

The UN General Assembly sought to mobilise international cooperation on clean energy outside of multilateral fora on sustainable development by declaring 2012 to be the International Year of Sustainable Energy for All.[48] A further resolution of the General Assembly in March 2013 declared 2014–2024 to be the UN Decade of Sustainable Energy for all (UN General Assembly Resolution 67/215).[49] The organisation Sustainable Energy for All was established to coordinate and mobilise States and public and private actors to increase the share of new and renewable energy sources

---

[43] ibid, 124.
[44] *The Future We Want* (n 16) paras 125–9; Citelli (n 29) 4; Bruce (n 40) 21.
[45] Although note that scholars also identify some positive developments for environmental protection alongside disappointments. For example, see Ann Powers, 'The Rio +20 Process: Forward Movement for the Environment?' (2012) 1 *Transnational Environmental Law* 403.
[46] *The Future We Want* (n 16) para 128.
[47] Raymond Clémençon, 'Welcome to the Anthropocene: Rio +20 and the Meaning of Sustainable Development' (2012) 21(3) *Journal of Environment and Development* 311, 322.
[48] United Nations General Assembly, Resolution 65/151, 'International Year of Sustainable Energy for All', 16 February 2011, UN Doc A/RES/65/151.
[49] United Nations General Assembly, Resolution 67/215, 'Promotion of New and Renewable Sources of Energy', 20 March 2013, UN Doc A/RES/67/215.

in energy supplies.[50] It is an independent organisation with a formal working relationship with the United Nations. The UN's Sustainable Development Goals for 2030, adopted in September 2015, include a goal dedicated to energy (SDG7)[51] to '[e]nsure access to affordable, reliable, sustainable and modern energy for all'. One of its targets is to 'increase substantially the share of renewable energy in the global energy mix' by 2030. The Member States of the United Nations committed to adopting the resolution by setting out the sustainable development agenda for 2030 and its goals and targets to work tirelessly for their full implementation.[52] Sustainable Energy for All's principal focus is now on working 'in partnership with the United Nations and leaders in government, the private sector, financial institutions, civil society and philanthropies to drive faster action towards the achievement of Sustainable Development Goal 7 ... in line with the Paris Agreement on climate'.[53]

The Sustainable Energy for All initiatives and the adoption of SDG7 show awareness amongst states that broadening access to and altering the composition of energy supplies are central to progress on sustainable development. However, their promotion of renewable energy has been disappointing to date. The resolution launching the decade of sustainable energy for all recognises that the share of 'new and renewable sources of energy in the global energy supply' is low and stresses the need for it to be increased, but does not offer detail such as timelines, targets and specific measures for promoting renewables.[54] SDG7 also lacks detail on the level of increase for renewables to be achieved by 2030 and does not support this general requirement with detail on steps to be taken to enable achievement of the ambitious 2030 aim.[55] Calzadilla and Mauger criticise the goal's ambiguity.[56] Definitions of 'access to', 'modern' and 'sustainable' are not provided. They also note the lack of ambition of the renewable energy goal, criticising its failure to recognise that substantial growth of renewable energy is already occurring and to consider how further substantial increases could be secured.[57]

F. International Declarations on Renewable Energy

Some interstate meetings have produced declarations recognising the value of renewable energy and the desirability of promoting the growth in its consumption. The developed states making up the G8 adopted a Plan of Action following the 2005 meeting in which

---

[50] Sustainable Energy for All, 'Who We Are', (Sustainable Energy for All website), Who we are | Sustainable Energy for All (seforall.org) (accessed 2 October 2022).
[51] See n 20.
[52] United Nations General Assembly, Resolution 70/1 (n 18), 3 at para 2.
[53] See n 50.
[54] United Nations General Assembly (n 49) para 6.
[55] Paola Calzadilla and Romain Mauger, 'The UN's New Sustainable Development Agenda and Renewable Energy: The Challenge to Reach SDG7 While Achieving Energy Justice' (2018) 36 *Journal of Energy and Natural Resources Law* 233; Stuart Bruce and Sean Stephenson, 'SDG7 on Sustainable Energy for All: Contributions of International Law, Policy and Governance' (UNEP/CISDL Issue Brief 2016), 7–8.
[56] Calzadilla and Mauger (n 55) 236–37.
[57] ibid.

they undertook to promote change in energy uses including by enabling the further development and commercialisation of renewable energy.[58]

Regular international conferences have also been held since 2004 at which representatives of governments, businesses, non-governmental organisations and civil society groupings gather to explore how renewable energy can be promoted. These biennial events, called International Renewable Energy Conferences, are set up by REN21 in collaboration with a host city and country. REN21 describes itself as a 'global renewable energy community of actors' made up of representatives from business, governments, civil societies, science and academia which aims to 'enable decision-makers to make the shift to renewable energy happen' by pooling experience, promoting collaboration, and giving guidance on key issues.[59] It describes IRECs as international high-level policy events at which REN21 'invites leaders from government, the private sector and civil society to meet and discuss policies and experiences' in order to build 'collective know-how to advance renewables at the international, national and sub-national levels'.[60] The conferences which have been held to date are: Bonn (2004), Beijing (2005), Washington DC (2008), Delhi (2010), Abu Dhabi (2013), Cape Town (2015), Mexico City (2017) and Seoul (2019).[61] The next IREC will be held in Madrid in 2023.

These conferences and also declarations from sustainable development conferences have undoubtedly raised the profile of renewable energy. IRECs, in particular, aid the growth of renewable energy. Each event produces a full report of the conference and a declaration of delegates. For example, the declaration of the 2019 Seoul IREC recognises in clear terms the role of renewable energy in addressing climate change; tackling transboundary air pollution (with a related call for interstate collaboration on producing enhanced policies and regulations at national, regional, and global levels); making urban living sustainable with a related need for the integration of thinking on renewable energy development into policies and laws for urban planning; enabling achievement not just of SDG7, but of the other SDGs; and leaving no-one behind when accessing sustainable energy supplies including by promoting mini-grid development.[62] This is certainly useful for reminding delegates and non-attendees of the role of renewable energy in advancing several shared international goals, and will hopefully have a pro-renewables influence on decision-making in corporations and governments to which attendees belong and on efforts in science, academia and civil societies to support and promote the low carbon energy transition. Bruce describes the 'normative influence' of statements made by delegates to IRECs including representatives of state governments as 'considerable and demonstrative of the direction of international renewable energy discourse and policy'.[63] However, the statements are not legally binding and do not

---

[58] Bradbrook (n 30) 124–26.
[59] REN21, 'Who we are' (REN21 Website), Who we are – REN21 Renewable energy for the 21st Century (accessed 2 October 2022).
[60] REN21, 'About REN21 Events', (REN21 Website) About REN21 Events – REN21 (accessed 2 October 2022).
[61] REN21, 'IRECS', (REN21 Website), www.ren21.net/irecs/ (accessed 2 October 2022).
[62] KIREC Seoul 2019, 'Declaration', 25 October 2019, 191030_KIREC-Seoul-2019-Declaration_FINAL.pdf (ren21.net) (accessed 2 October 2022).
[63] Bruce (n 40) 43–44.

evince any intention on the part of those making them to be bound in law to increase renewable energy production and consumption in the ways they describe.[64]

IV. Soft Law and Renewable Energy

The instruments reviewed in section III have a 'soft law' nature. 'Soft law' is used as a term to distinguish certain agreements made by states from 'hard law' agreements. How soft law and hard law in public international law can be distinguished from each other and the consequences of making that distinction have long been a focus for legal scholarly debate.[65] Some scholars question whether the label 'law' is appropriate for any statement made in an instrument to which the parties have not agreed to be legally bound.[66] They view them as more akin to policy statements than to law. Other scholars are more flexible when distinguishing between 'soft' and 'hard' law and attributing consequences to the distinction, preferring to assess laws against a spectrum extending from extremely soft at one end to extremely hard at the other and using criteria to assess where a provision should be placed on that spectrum.[67] Abbot and Snidal's ground-breaking analysis of 2000 identifies three qualities to enable assessment of what they call the legalisation of international relations.[68] These are the precision of rules, the degree of obligation for parties endorsing them and the delegation to a third party of authority to review the performance of parties against the endorsed standard.[69] Soft law is viewed as beginning 'once legal arrangements are weakened along one or more of the aforementioned dimensions resulting in a large variation in institutional design ...'.[70] Provisions in the statements examined in section III may be viewed as soft with regard to the degree of obligation because they feature in agreements by which parties are not legally bound, but may be seen as possessing qualities, such as agreement on a target for altered behaviour, that situate them further towards the hard end of the spectrum. Conversely, provisions in hard law instruments which are viewed as hard with regard to the degree of obligation because parties agreed to be bound by the instrument in which they feature may be towards the soft end of the spectrum overall because of low precision on what is to be done and the lack of provision for third party review of performance by parties leading to some form of penalty where this falls short. As we saw in Chapter 2, the Paris Agreement on

---

[64] Ibid.
[65] Gregory Shaffer and Mark Pollack, 'Hard vs. Soft Law: Alternatives, Complements, and Antagonists in International Governance' (2010) 94 *Minnesota Law Review* 706.
[66] ibid, 712–13.
[67] ibid, 715–17.
[68] Kenneth Abbott and Duncan Snidal, 'Hard and Soft Law in International Governance' (2000) 54 *International Organization* 401; Shaffer and Pollock (n 65) 714; Maximilian Wanner, 'The Effectiveness of Soft Law in International Environmental Regimes: Participation and Compliance in the Hyogo Framework for Action' (2021) 21 *International Environmental Agreements: Politics, Law and Economics* 113, 116–17.
[69] ibid.
[70] Wanner (n 68) 116.

Climate Change combines provisions with hard characteristics with those that are softer in terms of precision, obligation and enforceability although they feature in a binding legal instrument.[71]

The fact that all the statements concerning sustainable development and renewable energy tend towards the soft end of the spectrum because they are not legally binding on the states and other actors who agreed them raises questions about their likely effectiveness for driving worldwide growth in the renewables sector. The usefulness of soft law for advancing objectives has, as with its parameters, long being a matter of academic debate. Some argue that it is no more valuable than supportive policy statements for promoting outcomes.[72] However, other commentators identify general merits of soft law as a category.[73] States are highly sensitive about the security of energy supplies and are keen to preserve their sovereignty over energy policy. Negotiations for soft law agreements can be useful in such circumstances as a means of enabling dialogue and agreement on common positions. The lack of hard legal commitment at the end of the process can enable a freer and less legalistic dialogue. Soft law negotiations could therefore be conducive for the emergence of normative positions and for commitments that tend towards hardness in some cases. Some scholars see value in soft law as a potential stepping stone to hard law commitments.[74] Others argue that it is wrong to view it as subservient to hard law, and that it could, depending on the objectives pursued, be better than hard law for securing effective outcomes in some circumstances.[75] Further discussion of the merits of those positions lies outside the scope of this book, but we can say from the review in Section III of this chapter that statements made to date on renewable energy are distinctly soft on all three of Abbott and Snidal's criteria.[76] They are imprecise, imparting little sense of a commitment beyond a substantial increase in the role of renewables to meet energy needs. There is no basis in law for a third-party review of performance against supportive statements on renewables. Even if there were, a benchmark against which to assess this that a target or a more clearly worded promise would provide is lacking. That is not to say that the dialogue to date has been without benefit for the growth of renewable energy. Its profile has remained high as an alternative to fossil fuel energy and commentators argue that the soft law discussions could yet provide a launching point for more detailed commitments.[77] It must also be borne in mind that these statements are not made in isolation. They are made alongside and may have more positive influences on renewable energy's growth when combining with other commitments (eg, to combat climate change) than those anticipated when statements are viewed in isolation.[78]

---

[71] Lavanya Rajamani, 'The 2015 Paris Agreement: Interplay Between Hard, Soft and Non-Obligations' (2016) 28 *Journal of Environmental Law* 337.
[72] Shaffer and Pollock (n 65) 712–13.
[73] ibid, 719–21.
[74] For example, see Francesco Sindico, 'Soft Law and the Elusive Quest for Sustainable Global Governance' (2006) 19 *Leiden Journal of International Law* 829, quoted in Shaffer and Pollock (n 65) 724–25.
[75] Shaffer and Pollock (n 65) 725–27.
[76] Bradbrook (n 29) 128–9; Bruce (n 40) 27–34.
[77] Bruce (n 40) 51–52.
[78] Leslie-Anne Duvic-Paoli, 'From Aspirational Politics to Soft Law? Exploring the International Legal Effects of Sustainable Development Goal 7 on Affordable and Clean Energy' (2021) 22 *Melbourne Journal of International Law* 1.

That said, it is hard to conclude that the soft law statements made on renewables to date have been anything other than lacklustre.

V. International Institutions for Renewable Energy

The growth of renewable energy as a proportion of energy supplies and its integration into energy systems is made difficult by the continued dominance of fossil fuels in global energy supplies and by worldwide socio-economic carbon lock-in. Energy law scholars writing in the 2000s argued that the establishment by states of an international institution dedicated to promoting renewable energy production and consumption and with authority to pursue this goal was needed as a counterweight to the entrenchment of carbon-emitting energy sources and to international energy institutions founded in and before the 1970s such as the International Energy Agency, OLADE (the Latin American Energy Organisation), and the Organisation of the Petroleum Exporting Countries (OPEC) whose main focus remained on fossil fuel energy.[79] In 2000, the G8 forum for the world's leading economies called for a task force to examine how challenges to enable renewable energy development in developing states could be overcome.[80] The task force's report led to the establishment of the Renewable Energy and Energy Efficiency Partnership, a public-private partnership for supporting low carbon market development in developing countries.[81] REEEP had some success in supporting early renewable energy growth in the developing world. The Plan of Action adopted by the G8 at the Gleneagles summit in 2005 expressed support for increasing renewable energy as part of efforts to tackle climate change and make development sustainable by turning to clean energy technologies.[82] The Plan advises that '[w]e will promote the continued development and commercialisation of renewable energy' including by supporting the first IREC (in Bonn, 2004) and the work of REEEP, and through working with the International Energy Agency on producing 'implementing agreements on renewable energy' and on research into the 'challenges of integrating renewable energy sources into networks'.[83] However, these initial steps fell short in the view of Adrian Bradbrook, one of the leading early energy law scholars, of the backing needed for serious global progress on replacing fossil fuels with renewables. Bradbrook argued in 2008 that 'the lack of an entity with the express purpose and function of promoting' renewable technologies has been '[a] significant weakness in the current international institutional arrangements for the promotion of renewable energy ...'.[84]

---

[79] Indra Overland and Gunilla Reischl, 'A Place in the Sun? IRENA's Position in the Global Energy Governance Landscape' (2018) 18 *International Environmental Agreements* 335, 337.
[80] Thijs van de Graaf and Kirsten Westphal, 'The G8 and G20 as Global Steering Committees for Energy: Opportunities and Constraints' (2011) 2 (Special Issue) *Global Policy* 19, 22 and 30.
[81] Binu Parthan and others, 'Lessons for Low-Carbon Energy Transition: Experience from the Renewable Energy and Energy Efficiency Partnership (REEEP)' (2010) 14 *Energy for Sustainable Development* 83.
[82] G8 Gleneagles 2005, 'Gleneagles Plan of Action: Climate Change, Clean, Energy and Sustainable Development' Registry Document (utoronto.ca) (accessed 2 October 2022).
[83] ibid, paras 16 and 17.
[84] Bradbrook (n 29) 127.

The UN was an early mover on renewable energy through its organisation of the UN Conference of New and Renewable Sources of Energy in Nairobi in 1981.[85] However, this early interest was not followed by effective measures for promoting renewable energy.[86] Dialogue on renewable energy within the UN continued following the conference under the newly founded UN Committee on the Development and Utilisation of New and Renewable Energy Sources. This met every two years until it was replaced in 1994 by a similar committee but with a development focus under the UN's Economic and Social Council. The new committee's remit was subsequently subsumed by the Committee on Sustainable Development, a backwards step for focused action on renewables as renewable energy was only one amongst many interest areas for an institution with general responsibility for considering how to make progress on sustainable development following the 1992 Rio Conference.[87] In parallel, agencies of the UN, particularly the UN Environment Programme, the UN Development Programme, and the regional economic commissions, had responsibilities for promoting renewable energy in connection with their performance of established functions throughout this time.[88] However, none of them had an exclusive focus on or a mandate to support renewable energy and there was no move towards interagency cooperation on renewable energy.[89]

It was not until the 2000s that states which had been proactive in promoting renewable energy (particularly Germany), frustrated with the UN's inaction, took the initiative themselves to establish an agency outside the UN.[90] The Statute of the International Renewable Energy Agency was agreed in 2009 and received rapid approval by states. IRENA had 168 state parties as at July 2022 with a further 16 states having initiated the process leading to ratification.[91]

IRENA's objective is to promote 'the widespread and increased adoption and the sustainable use of all forms of renewable energy'.[92] The activities that it will undertake to advance this goal, listed in Article IV of the Statute, generally aim to facilitate the expansion of renewable energy by gathering and disseminating knowledge, providing advice to states on renewable energy technology and on institutions and legal and financing structures to support the development of renewable energy sectors, and by promoting research and development in renewable energy.[93] IRENA is not itself a research centre and does not provide funding for RE projects. IRENA's medium-term strategy of 2018 explains the mission of the agency in the five-year period from

---

[85] Sylvia Karlsson-Vinkhuyzen, 'The United Nations and Global Energy Governance: Past Challenges, Future Choices' (2010) 22 *Global Change, Peace and Security* 175, 182.

[86] Glen Wright, 'The International Renewable Energy Agency: A Global Voice for the Renewable Energy Era' (2011) 2 *Renewable Energy Law and Policy* 251, 252–53.

[87] Karlsson-Vinkhuyzen (n 85) 182.

[88] ibid.

[89] ibid.

[90] Wright (n 86) 253–54; Overland and Reischl (n 79) 336; Johannes Urpelainen and Thijs van der Graaf, 'The International Renewable Energy Agency: A Success Story in Institutional Innovation?' (2015) 15 *International Environmental Agreements* 159.

[91] Statute of the International Renewable Energy Agency (n 4).

[92] ibid, art II.

[93] ibid, art IV.

2018 to 2022 as being to 'play a leading role in the ongoing transformation of the global energy systems as a centre of excellence for knowledge and innovation, a global voice of renewable energy, a network hub for all stakeholders and a source of advice and support for countries'.[94] This is to be advanced by providing: (i) 'authoritative knowledge and analysis on renewables-based energy transformation at global, national and sectoral levels'; (ii) 'relevant timely, high-quality information and access to data on renewable energy'; (iii) 'an inclusive platform for all stakeholders to foster action, convergence of efforts and knowledge sharing for impact on the ground'; and (iv) support for 'country-level decision-making to accelerate the renewables-based transformation of national energy systems, advance strategies to diversify energy sources, reduce global emissions and achieve sustainable development'.[95]

IRENA performs the first two of these strategic objectives by operating as a repository of knowledge and expertise on renewable energy technologies and the challenges of integrating them within energy systems.[96] Its wide membership, now including more than 90% of the world's states, also enables it to perform the third objective of providing a platform to foster action on the ground to promote renewables by collaboration between member countries. Initiatives referred to on IRENA's website illustrate its role in bringing together and working with different states and their energy stakeholders on the formulation and implementation of plans for deploying renewable energy technologies.[97] IRENA has worked under its Clean Energy Corridors initiative with participating states to support the integration of renewable power into national systems and promote its cross-border trade including by supporting the creation of regional markets. It works under this initiative with members in Africa belonging to the East and South African power pools, with members in west Africa in collaboration with the Economic Community of West African states (EcoWAS) and with members in Central America in collaboration with the Central American Integration System (SICA). EcoWAS and SICA are treaty-based regional organisations which seek through collaboration to realise benefits for individual member states. IRENA's Global Geothermal Alliance brings together governments, businesses and other stakeholders to support the deployment of realisable geothermal potential. Support for country-level decision making, the fourth objective, is delivered through IRENA's renewables readiness assessment tool.[98] IRENA has garnered much experience with helping states to assess domestic prospects for renewable energy deployment, identifying issues to be addressed and concrete responses to them and assisting states with implementing the guidance provided. Renewables readiness assessments are initiated by states that wish to work with IRENA on exploring how their renewable energy potential could be exploited. Reports of assessments conducted for Paraguay, Botswana, Belarus, Tunisia, Albania and Jordan were published by IRENA in 2021.[99]

---

[94] International Renewable Energy Agency, 'Medium-term Strategy 2018–2022: Report of the Director General', IRENA Doc A/8/11, 13 January 2018, para 9.
[95] ibid, para 10.
[96] See IRENA's website at IRENA – International Renewable Energy Agency (accessed 2 October 2022).
[97] ibid under 'Our Work'.
[98] IRENA, 'Renewable Readiness Assessment' (IRENA webpage) Renewable Readiness Assessment (RRA) (irena.org) (accessed 2 October 2022).
[99] IRENA, 'Publications' (IRENA webpage) Publications (irena.org) (accessed 2 October 2022).

Commentators are generally positive about the potential for IRENA to promote the growth of renewable energy internationally where states have political will to achieve changes in their energy supplies.[100] Improved knowledge may also promote political willingness to act by showing how apparently insurmountable barriers to renewable energy's expansion could be overcome and by increasing transparency internationally on sources of funding for renewable energy projects. However, it must be noted that IRENA does not have any substantive powers to require the use of renewable energy or to develop new instruments that oblige states to act (such as the agreement of targets with states).[101] Its role is purely facilitative; it cannot drive the growth of renewable energy where there is a failure by states to act.

International institutions other than IRENA continue to have important influences on renewable energy's worldwide diffusion. The G20 forum, a group of major economies combining G7 members with economies, inter alia, those of China, India, Indonesia, Brazil, Mexico and Saudi Arabia, which have seen massive growth in the last 50 years, brings together the world's major economies, its major producers and consumers of energy, its major emitters of greenhouse gases and its major likely investors (and hosts of private investors) in green energy.[102] It is potentially very well placed, therefore, to provide a framework for more intrusive efforts on replacing fossil fuels with renewables than have been pursued to date. Clean energy remains on the group's agenda with dialogue informed by an Energy Transitions Working Group. The 'Sustainable Energy Transition' is one of three main pillars to be examined under Indonesia's Presidency of the G20 in 2022.[103] In addition, energy transition is still a key focus for the United Nations. Responsibilities for energy activities continue to be fragmented amongst UN Agencies, but UN Energy, set up in 2004, serves to engender collaboration between different parts of the UN and its Member States on energy-related issues.[104] UN Energy's main current focus is on the implementation of Sustainable Development Goal 7 including the performance of its sub-goal on renewable energy production. Similarly to IRENA, UN Energy has an 'epistemic' role as a provider of information and expertise, an instigator of partnerships and a facilitator of initiatives.[105] Current work within the G20 and the UN will undoubtedly be of some value for promoting renewable energy's growth, but there is a persistent theme in both cases. The need to switch to clean energies such as renewables as a matter of urgency is clearly recognised. Soft support to engender renewable and other carbon-free energies is readily proffered. However, the hard support from institutions with appropriate legal powers that is also needed to drive change at a scale and rate commensurate with the threat posed by climate change is not forthcoming. That must change if the fossil fuels still making up 80 per cent of global energy supplies are to be displaced within the short time frame still available for remaining within the Paris Agreement's temperature goals.

---

[100] Overland and Reischl (n 79) 335–37; Urpelainen and van der Graaf (n 90) 162–71.
[101] Urpelainen and van der Graaf (n 90) 168; Bruce (n 40) 45.
[102] Philip Andrews-Speed and Xunpeng Shi, 'What Role Can the G20 Play in Global Energy Governance? Implications for China's Presidency' (2016) 7 *Global Policy* 198, 201–2.
[103] G20, 'Presidency of Indonesia' (Website), G20 Presidency of Indonesia (accessed 2 October 2022).
[104] UN Energy, 'About UN Energy', (UN Energy Website), Newabout – UN – Energy (accessed 2 October 2022).
[105] ibid under 'What We Do'.

VI. Renewable Energy under the Energy Charter Treaty (ECT)

The Energy Charter Treaty is the sole major legally binding treaty concerned with the energy sector.[106] It was adopted in 1994, entered into force in 1998 and has 54 parties, mostly European states and states from the former USSR.[107] The Energy Charter Treaty focuses on investment protection and facilitating trade in energy and energy services. It was created to enable the development of energy industries in former USSR states with a view to gaining access to their rich hydrocarbon resources. Given this focus, it is unsurprising that the original ECT has little to say on renewable energy. It contains only one provision that mentions renewable energy. Article 19 on Environmental Aspects requires Contracting Parties to 'strive to minimize in an economically efficient manner harmful environmental impacts … from all operations within the Energy Cycle in its Area …'. One amongst a range of steps that states are meant to take in light of this commitment is to: '(d) have particular regard to improving energy efficiency, to developing and using renewable energy sources, to promoting the use of cleaner fuels and to employing technologies and technological means that reduce pollution'.[108] Bruce describes this provision as, at most, placing a weak and therefore hard-to-enforce form of conduct obligation on parties, one which is further undermined by the word 'strive' and by the strong emphasis on the need to act in a cost-effective manner.

Whilst the original ECT makes only weak provision on obligatory support by its parties for the growth of renewable energy, its provisions on investment protection apply to and therefore provide support for everything falling under its definition of Energy Materials and Products including energy produced from renewable sources.[109] A significant proportion of cases heard under the Energy Charter Treaty's dispute resolution provisions have been brought by investors in renewable technologies in response to claimed infringements of their investments.[110] Often claims concern policies, laws and administrative decisions, for instance the removal of a subsidy, that impair the utility or reduce the value of an already-made investment. Investment protections under the Treaty also apply to fossil fuel energy technologies. This gives rise to concerns that the prospect of compensation claims by fossil fuel investors over laws that impact negatively on existing fossil fuel investments may deter parties to the Energy Charter Treaty and their nationals from acting against climate change.[111]

---

[106] Energy Charter Treaty (n 5).
[107] International Energy Charter, 'The Energy Charter Treaty' (webpage), Energy Charter Treaty – Energy Charter (accessed 2 October 2022).
[108] Energy Charter Treaty (n 5), art 19(1)(d).
[109] ibid, art 1(4).
[110] Andrei Belyi, 'The Energy Charter Process in the Face of Uncertainties' (2021) 14 *Journal of World Energy Law and Business* 363, 371.
[111] ibid, 370–71; Paul Thiessen, 'Reforming the Energy Charter Treaty for Sustainability?' (2022) 40 *Journal of Energy and Natural Resources Law* 465.

In 2017 the Energy Charter Conference, the governing and decision-making body for the Energy Charter process, confirmed the launch of discussions on modernisation of the Energy Charter Treaty. Those discussions bore fruit on 24 June 2022 when an agreement in principle was reached by negotiators to the Treaty. The proposed revisions were communicated to contracting parties in June 2022 for adoption by the Energy Charter Conference. They will not enter into force thereafter until they have been ratified by three-quarters of the Energy Charter Treaty's parties.[112] The revisions seek to make the Treaty more supportive of investment in renewables and other non-fossil fuel energy sources.[113] Definitions are updated to include previously excluded energy materials and products such as biomass and biogas amongst those benefitting from investment protection. More regular reviews of schedules of energy materials and products will better enable the Conference to react to technological change. Parties are given the option to exclude, with support from a decision of the Conference, investment protection for fossil fuels in their territories where this does not fit with their energy and climate policy goals. The EU and the UK announced that they would take advantage of this to exclude new fossil fuel investments from 15 August 2023 and existing investments from 10 years after entry into force of the revisions. Great emphasis is also placed on parties' rights to advance legitimate public policy goals through regulation such as protecting the environment and mitigating climate change. The direct support for renewable energy has not been enhanced with investment support remaining the Treaty's main purpose. However, new provisions are included which call for or place duties on parties to observe commitments under multilateral environmental treaties including the UNFCCC and the Paris Agreement. Parties reiterate commitments to contribute to sustainable development and principles of responsible business conduct in their energy investment and trade activities, agreeing as part of this not to encourage trade by unilaterally reducing environmental standards.

The revisions were viewed as not having gone far enough in their support for low carbon energy by Contracting Parties who are also Member States of the European Union to align the Treaty with the Paris Agreement objectives and the European Union's Green Deal policy and law package. Several of them had given notice of their intention to withdraw from the Treaty by November 2022. Withdrawal takes effect one year after notice is given. This reaction led to postponement of a vote on the proposed revisions to April 2023. It appears from this trend that the Energy Charter Treaty's influence may be significantly impaired unless additional reforms are tabled which further weaken support for fossil fuel investment and strengthen support for renewables and other law carbon energy sources.[114]

---

[112] Energy Charter Treaty (n 5) art 42.

[113] See the summary of revisions at International Energy Charter, 'Public Communication explaining the main changes contained in the agreement in principle (Ad Hoc Meeting of the Energy Charter Conference, 24 June 2022), Modernisation of the Treaty – Energy Charter Treaty (accessed 2 October 2022).

[114] International Institute for Sustainable Development, 'Energy Charter Treaty Withdrawal Announcements Reflect Reform Outcome is Insufficient for Climate Action' (International Institute for Sustainable Development website, 7 November 2022) www.iisd.org/articles/statement/energy-charter-treaty-withdrawal-announcements (accessed 16 November 2022).

VII. Strengthening Support for Renewable Energy under International Law

Commentators on the status of international law on renewable energy tend to agree with Bradbrook's conclusion that the mixture of soft law declarations and of weak references in Conventions are of limited effect and that stronger legal intervention is needed if international law is to make a meaningful contribution to the growth of renewable energy production.[115] They also examine options for strengthening international law in this field. Options for hard law approaches considered in their work include:

(a) the adoption of a separate convention on renewable energy, and particularly the agreement by parties of targets for increasing renewable energy consumption and reducing the carbon intensity of their energy sectors;
(b) the adoption of a Protocol of the Energy Charter Treaty on Renewable Energy (the Energy Charter Treaty already has a Protocol on Energy Efficiency); and
(c) the adoption of a Protocol to the United Nations Framework Convention on Climate Change on Renewable Energy or strengthening references to renewable energy and other means of decarbonising energy supplies in legal instruments establishing the international climate change regime. The possibility of strengthening references to renewable energy was discussed in negotiations for a successor to the Kyoto Protocol[116] and could provide an alternative focus to agreeing further emissions reductions. However, as noted in Chapter 2, the agreement made in Paris in December 2015 does not promote low carbon energy directly.[117]

These approaches would be desirable because they would place binding obligations on states with regard to renewable energy production. However, it seems unlikely that such international instruments will be developed without the stimulus of a significant worsening of climate change or for energy security reasons. States are reluctant to surrender sovereign powers in general, and this is particularly the case with regard to energy because the availability of secure and affordable energy supplies is central to the functioning of their socio-economic systems.

Bradbrook and Bruce also suggest a soft law statement of renewable energy principles, going beyond the vague encouragements and exhortations of past soft law statements, as a means by which the slow journey towards rules of international law on renewable energy could be progressed.[118] This seems the most likely development in view of the UNGA's resolutions concerning the decade of sustainable energy for all. Whilst a further soft law instrument would not commit states to act, a clear statement of principles concerning renewable energy could promote the harmonisation of national laws and the eventual emergence of customary international rules or general principles of law recognised by civilised nations on renewable energy.

---

[115] Bradbrook (n 29); Bruce (n 40); Adrian Bradbrook, 'Sustainable Energy Law: The Past and the Future' (2012) 30 *Journal of Energy and Natural Resources Law* 511, 517–20.
[116] Chapter 2, section IIA.
[117] ibid.
[118] Bradbrook (n 29); Bruce (n 40).

Classroom Questions

1. What does sustainable development involve? Why is the international discourse on making development sustainable of relevance for renewable energy development?
2. How have international soft law declarations on sustainable development been used to promote renewable energy development?
3. Consider the potential advantages and limitations of soft law for securing the growth of the renewable energy sector. Have the actual uses of soft law you identify in your answer to question 2 realised the potential advantages of soft law in practice?
4. Consider critically the support provided by the Energy Charter Treaty for renewable energy. How, if at all, will this be enhanced by reforms agreed to the Energy Charter Treaty?
5. What are IRENA's roles and responsibilities? Examine its strengths and weaknesses for promoting renewable energy.
6. How, if at all, could international law be made more effective for securing increases in renewable energy?

Scenarios

1. The United Nations General Assembly has resolved to convene a 10+ years follow-up international summit on making development sustainable to Rio +20. You are part of the legal team for Coralia, a small island developing state. Coralia has a strong interest in seeing a global shift to renewable energy and other non-carbon energy sources, possessing excellent renewable electricity resources itself and being under significant threat from rising sea levels if greenhouse gas emissions are not reduced to zero with urgency. The head of the Coralia delegation seeks information from you on prospects for making progress on support for renewable energy under the UN's sustainable development discourse. You are asked to advise on the following:

    (a) How and to what extent has the international dialogue on sustainable development under the United Nations committed to support the production and consumption of renewable energy?
    (b) What are the options for progressing beyond the current legal position on support for renewable energy under the sustainable development discourse? What are the relative merits and disadvantages of the options for securing real progress on support for renewable energy?

2. The Coralian government is also looking at whether becoming a ratifying party to one or more of the international energy treaties could aid Coralia in its goal of becoming 100 per cent renewable. It seeks your advice on whether Coralia would be aided in pursuing its renewable energy goal by:

    (a) ratifying the IRENA Statute and become a member of IRENA, or
    (b) ratifying the Energy Charter Treaty.

Suggested Reading

Book chapters

Adrian Bradbrook, 'The Development of Renewable Energy Technologies and Energy Efficiency Measures through Public International Law' in Donald Zillman, Catherine Redgwell, Yinke Omorogbe, and Lila Barrera-Hernandez (eds) *Beyond the Carbon Economy: Energy Law in Transition* (Oxford University Press, 2008) 111.

Martijn Wilder Am and Lauren Drake, 'International Law and the Renewable Energy Sector' in Cinnamon Carlarne, Kevin Gray, and Richard Tarasofsky (eds) *The Oxford Handbook of International Climate Change Law* (Oxford University Press, 2016) 358.

Articles

Stuart Bruce, 'International Law and Renewable Energy: Facilitating Sustainable Energy for All' (2013) 15 *Melbourne Journal of International Law* 18.

Paola Calzadilla and Romain Mauger, 'The UN's New Sustainable Development Agenda and Renewable Energy: The Challenge to Reach SDG7 While Achieving Energy Justice' (2018) 36 *Journal of Energy and Natural Resources Law* 233.

Leslie-Anne Duvic-Paoli, 'From Aspirational Politics to Soft Law? Exploring the International Legal Effects of Sustainable Development Goal 7 on Affordable and Clean Energy' (2021) 22 *Melbourne Journal of International Law* 1.

Paul Thiessen, 'Reforming the Energy Charter Treaty for Sustainability' (2022) 40 *Journal of Energy and Natural Resources Law* 465, doi: 10.1080/02646811.2022.2040214, 5–12.

Johannes Urpelainen and Thijs van der Graaf, 'The International Renewable Energy Agency: A Success Story in Institutional Innovation?' (2015) 15 *International Environmental Agreements* 159.

Policy

Agenda 21, Report of the UNCED, I (1992) UN Doc A/CONF 151/26/Rev1, (1992) 31 ILM 874, paras 9.9 and 9.12.

Johannesburg Plan of Implementation, Report of the *World Summit on Sustainable Development*, Johannesburg, South Africa, 4 Sept 2002, UN Doc A/CONF 199/20, paras 9 and 20.

The Future We Want, Outcome of the *Rio +20 United Nations Conference on Sustainable Development*, Rio de Janeiro, Brazil, 20–22 June 2012, A/CONF 216/L1, paras 125 to 129.

United Nations, 'Do You Know All 17 SDGs?', (United Nations, Department of Economic and Social Affairs, Webpage) THE 17 GOALS | Sustainable Development (un.org) (accessed 9 October 2022).

4

Enabling Renewable Energy Growth: The Role of Targets

I. Introduction

Many of the world's states have made some form of commitment in national policy and law to achieve the growth of renewable energy as a proportion of national energy consumption by a specified percentage and by a specified date.[1] In addition, some states (mostly developed or fast-growing developing economies) have made commitments in national policy and law to achieve an absolute reduction in greenhouse gas emissions for which the state is responsible or in the carbon intensity of national economic activity. Such commitments may serve, albeit indirectly, as a driver for the growth of renewable energy production because it is a leading option for reducing emissions from the energy sector.[2] These commitments may be made in policy statements only but are sometimes reinforced by being made legally binding. The European Union, a regional organisation established by treaties adopted by its 27 Member States, has made commitments in policy and law both to increase renewable energy consumption and to reach net zero greenhouse gas emissions by 2050.[3] In federal systems such as the US, states may have adopted relevant targets with higher ambition than those adopted at the national level. For example, California, the world's sixth-largest economy, has targets of 60 per cent renewable electricity in electricity retail sales by 2030 and 100 per cent electricity from renewable or other zero carbon sources in electricity retail sales by 2045.[4]

The chapter considers the role of such commitments in supporting the growth of renewable energy production and consumption. It will begin by considering both the

---

[1] Details of renewable energy targets adopted by states are included in country profiles at the website of the International Renewable Energy Agency (IRENA). See IRENA – International Renewable Energy Agency (accessed 2 October 2022), under 'Our Work' and 'Countries'.

[2] Grantham Research Institute on Climate Change and the Environment, 'Climate legislation – countries, regions, territories', www.lse.ac.uk/GranthamInstitute/countries/ (accessed 2 October 2022).

[3] European Commission (Climate Action), 'European Green Deal', European Green Deal (europa.eu) (accessed 2 October 2022).

[4] US Energy Information Administration, 'California' (US Energy Information Administration, March 2022) U.S. Energy Information Administration – EIA – Independent Statistics and Analysis (accessed 9 October 2022).

general role that such targets can play, and the questions that should be answered to assess whether a target is able to provide a meaningful framework for expansion of the renewables sector. As the discussion reveals, the legal status of targets and the extent to which they are supported by legal mechanisms enabling actors responsible for achieving them to be held to account for their performance are key considerations when assessing whether a target is likely to act as an effective driver for achieving its stated aim. A case study is used to furnish examples both of how targets and underpinning legal frameworks can support the renewables sector and of how applying the analytical approach suggested in sections II and III to them can aid understanding of their strengths and weaknesses for securing stated aims. The case study examines commitments made by the European Union and its Member States for the growth of renewable energy consumption by 2001, 2020 and 2030, and support offered for them by related Directives and Regulations. It reveals certain strengths in the approaches employed to give the targets 'teeth', but also weaknesses which hamper their ability to give confidence that measures necessary to achieving the desired outcome will be maintained.

II. Greenhouse Gas Emissions Reduction Targets and Renewable Energy

Many of the world's states have adopted climate change laws and policies.[5] Some amongst them have made stronger commitments on tackling climate change including by taking on legal duties to achieve specified levels of greenhouse gas emissions cuts by a specified date. For example, seven of the G20 member states (Canada, the European Union, France, Germany, Japan, Republic of Korea, and the United Kingdom) have made legal commitments to cut national emissions to net zero by 2050 in line with the Paris Agreement's net zero goal.[6] The other G20 members have also committed to net zero but only in policies or executive statements. Twenty-four US States and the District of Columbia have also set specific greenhouse gas emissions targets in statute or by executive order.[7] Greenhouse gas emissions targets may not commit to increase renewable energy specifically, but the impetus they provide for moving away from greenhouse gas emitting energy is almost certain to be a major driver for the growth of energy production and consumption from renewable sources as leading low carbon alternatives.

This chapter focuses on targets for increasing renewable energy consumption, but the approach it suggests for assessing the seriousness of a government's commitment

---

[5] Grantham Research Institute on Climate Change and the Environment, 'Climate Change Laws of the World' (LSE, Database) Climate Change Laws of the World (climate-laws.org) (accessed 4 October 2022).
[6] United Nations Climate Action, 'Net Zero Coalition' (UN Website), Net Zero Coalition | United Nations (accessed 4 October 2022).
[7] Centre for Climate and Energy Solutions (C2ES), 'U.S. State Greenhouse Gas Emissions Targets' (C2ES Website) U.S. State Greenhouse Gas Emissions Targets – Center for Climate and Energy SolutionsCenter for Climate and Energy Solutions (c2es.org) (accessed 4 October 2022).

could equally be applied to targets in law for cutting greenhouse gases. Analysts of the likely efficacy of national legal frameworks for promoting renewable energy should have in mind the framework for relevant efforts provided by overarching greenhouse gas targets alongside those for increasing the proportion of renewable energy in energy supplies. Climate change mitigation targets may assume heightened importance in jurisdictions such as the UK which have made legal commitments to reduce greenhouse gases but not to increase renewable energy. The author has used the UK's Climate Change Act 2008 in teaching as a case study on the ability of a greenhouse gas emission reduction target to secure growth in renewable energy alongside the EU law examples used in this chapter.

III. The Role of Targets in Promoting Renewable Energy

Targets for renewable energy production or consumption can contribute to the growth of the renewables sector by:

- Forcing governments to act in order to meet the target.
- Creating a framework for the development of detailed programmes and packages of measures for renewable energy. Commentators describe 'a clear long-term energy strategy (strategic planning)' as being 'conducive to investments as investors favour a long-term framework with a clear vision'.[8]
- Creating a framework for the development of reporting and review regimes for on-going scrutiny of governmental progress on renewable energy.
- Engendering confidence in investors that the renewables sector will enjoy governmental support within a specified timeframe. Leal-Arcas and Minas describe the 'main purpose of a framework that includes renewable energy mandatory targets' as being to 'provide the business community with the long-term stability and legal predictability it needs to make confident and rational investments in the renewable energy sector'.[9]
- Supporting the growth of particular technologies and/or renewable energy in particular sectors where express governmental backing would create confidence in a hitherto unheralded sector (eg, national targets under EU law for renewable energy in transport).[10]

---

[8] Friedemann Polzin and others, 'Public Policy Influence on Renewable Energy Investments – A Panel Data Study Across OECD Countries' (2015) 80 *Energy Policy* 98, 106.

[9] Rafael Leal-Arcas and Stephen Minas, 'The Micro Level: Insights from Specific Policy Areas: Mapping the International and European Governance of Renewable Energy' (2016) 35 *Yearbook of European Law* 621, 661. See also Wenfeng Liu and others, 'The Effectiveness of China's Renewable Energy Policy: An Empirical Evaluation of Wind Power Based on the Framework of Renewable Energy Law and its Accompanying Policies' (2021) 57 *Emerging Markets, Finance and Trade* 757, 766–77.

[10] See Section VB below.

- Introducing long-termism to policy-making by setting targets with concluding dates going beyond the electoral cycle. As noted above, the prospect of stable, predictable long-term commitment can increase investor confidence by reducing regulatory risk and therefore borrowing costs.[11]

Targets for reducing greenhouse gases are also likely to contribute to the growth of the renewables sector in the ways identified above due to the significant proportion of emissions from fuel combustion, to the widespread availability of energy from renewable sources and to the increasing appeal of wind and solar electricity in terms of cost, but do so indirectly as other options for reducing greenhouse gas emissions are available (eg, nuclear, carbon capture and storage and shifting from high carbon fossil fuels such as coal to natural gas as a lower carbon fossil fuel).

The use of targets to promote renewable energy growth can also give rise to concerns:

- Targets can end up as a constraint on growth that could actually be achieved where they are not ambitious enough. For example, there was much political debate over the low ambition shown by the EU's initially agreed goal of 27 per cent renewable energy by 2030, hence the agreement of a higher goal of 32 per cent as being more representative of the EU's capabilities.[12]
- Targets may break down an ultimate goal into shorter timeframes (eg, 20 per cent renewable energy by 2020 under the EU as a stepping-stone towards 80–95 per cent overall decarbonisation by 2050 under the EU's 2020 Climate and Energy policy). Breaking down a long-term aim into stages may assist with governmental planning, monitoring progress and making the change required tangible for affected policy makers, businesses, and populations. However, action to achieve short-term targets may also be unhelpful for achieving the longer-term goal of complete decarbonisation (eg, support flowing into the cheapest technologies in the 2020s may result in a loss of focus on supporting technologies needed to achieve higher levels of decarbonisation in the 2030s). Ideally, shorter-term targets should be developed within the context of longer-term overarching targets within a legal framework enabling and requiring reflection on whether the short-term goal and plans for meeting it are compatible with the long-term aim.
- General targets will need to be supplemented with more detailed programmes of measures if they are to assist a broad range of renewable technologies including those which are not commercially viable at the time of the target's adoption but may become the technologies of the future with support. Risks arise with general targets that attention will be directed to the lowest cost best established renewable energy technologies at the expense of other options and to the easier to decarbonise electricity production sector instead of energy consumption for transport and heating.

---

[11] Polzin (n 8) 106.
[12] See Section VC below.

IV. Assessing the Value of Targets for Supporting Renewable Energy: Key Questions

Targets may look very good on paper, but it is necessary to consider them critically to establish whether they are likely to offer support for the growth of renewables in practice. Investors will only draw confidence from targets which impose real and effective obligations on actors to back renewable energy development. Governments may find it all too easy to ignore promises to promote renewables without legal backing if they were made by preceding administrations or if other policy goals become more pressing. It is important therefore to consider whether a target has any legal (or other) underpinning.[13] Can those subject on the face of it to a duty/obligation to meet a target be held to account for a failure to do so including by the imposition of penalties? Are the potential penalties large enough to have a deterrent effect (eg, encouraging compliance)?[14] Can action be taken to hold persons to account *before* the date when the target must be met?[15] This is particularly important for renewable energy's growth as the ability to pursue a claim for missing a final target gives little comfort for efforts to decarbonise by a specified date unless the penalty has a sufficient deterrent effect on its own to secure compliance from the date of the target's adoption.

Key questions include:

A. The Target

- Is it clear what the target requires an actor to do?
- Who is bound to achieve the target or observe the duty? Is this clear?
- By when is the target to be achieved? Is this clear?[16]
- Is the target legally binding? Alternatively, is it supported by some non-legal (e.g. moral or cultural) commitment?[17]

---

[13] Commentators distinguish between targets made in a context (eg, a strong supportive legal framework) evidencing a credible commitment and targets sending only a relatively weak signal of commitment when assessing a target's likely capability of creating investor confidence in the renewables sector. See Nana Obeng-Darko, 'Why Ghana will not Achieve its Renewable Energy Target for Electricity: Policy, Legal and Regulatory Implications' (2019) 128 *Energy Policy* 75, 79; and Nancy McCarthy and Heath Henderson, *The Role of Energy Laws in Expanding Energy from Non-Traditional Renewables* (2014, Inter-American Development Bank, IDB Working Paper Series No. IDP-WP-540).

[14] Marjan Peeters and Thomas Schomerus, 'Modifying our Society with Law: The Case of EU Renewable Energy Law' (2014) 4 *Climate Law* 131, 133; Angus Johnston and Eva van der Marel, 'How Binding are the EU's "Binding" Renewables Targets?' (2016) 18 *Cambridge Yearbook of European Legal Studies* 176, 206–7.

[15] Johnston and van der Marel (n 14) 189.

[16] Obeng-Darko (n 13) 77.

[17] McCarthy and Henderson (n 13).

- Where the target itself is not legally binding, is it supported by obligations to take action contributing to achievement of the target? Are the obligations worded clearly enough to secure achievement of the target?[18]
- Is the target/duty holder also obligated to develop and implement a strategy and programmes for achieving the target/duty?[19]
- Does the target law create arrangements for reviewing the likely fitness of the strategies/programmes for achieving the target/duty? Is the review to be conducted by a body with appropriate expertise? Is the target/duty holder obliged to revise the strategy and programmes in response to comments from the reviewing body?[20]
- What is the legal status of the target law? Does its legal status or legal provision made under the target law limit scope for legislators to reduce or revoke the target subsequently?

B. Holding Responsible Actors to Account

- Is the target supported by sub-obligations that facilitate monitoring of performance by the actor holding the duty to achieve it (eg, developing and updating programmes of measures for implementing the target, periodic reporting by the target holder on actions)?
- Have institutional arrangements been established for periodic monitoring of and comment on on-going performance against the ultimate target?
- Is the target's achievement supported by requirements to meet interim targets?
- What consequences if any flow from an actor falling short of the rate of renewable energy growth and/or greenhouse gas emissions reduction required to achieve the target? Can a target/duty holder be held to account for an interim shortfall and by whom?
- Is interim enforcement before national/regional courts possible? By what means, at what cost, and with what ease (eg, is justice likely to be accessible?).
- If interim enforcement is possible, can penalties be applied and do they represent a serious enough threat (eg, size of the penalty, likelihood of it being imposed, likely duration of proceedings) to secure compliance by the target/holder?
- Can action be taken for a failure to achieve the target itself at the date of expected achievement?

---

[18] See, eg, the discussion of the obligation to take 'effectively designed measures' under the EU's 2009 Renewable Energy Directive at Johnston and van der Marel (n 14) 189–93.

[19] As McCarthy and Henderson note (n 13), legally binding targets 'in and of themselves provide only limited reduction' in investment risk. Accompaniment of targets with detailed statements on how they will be given effect to is vital for creating confidence that a stable and predictable environment for investment in renewable technologies will emerge. See also Polzin (n 8) 106 and Leal-Arcas and Minas (n 9) 661.

[20] Legal provisions concerning the preparation, review, reporting on implementation, and monitoring implementation of plans for effecting targets are of central relevance for analysis of the EU's 2009 and 2018 Renewable Energy directives at Sections VB and VC below.

- What consequences flow from a failure to meet the target? Can penalties be applied? Are they likely to have a deterrent effect on the target holder, thereby ensuring action ahead of time to prevent the relevant legal obligations from being breached (eg size of the penalty, likelihood of it being imposed, likely duration of proceedings)?

C. Investor Confidence

- In view of the answers to the above questions, is the target capable on its own of creating confidence in investors that the renewables sector will enjoy positive public support over a defined timeframe?
- Does it create confidence in renewables in general only or in renewables for particular sectors or particular technologies?

The two questions concerning investor confidence cannot be answered with a simple yes or no response. Capability to create confidence is better understood as extending on a spectrum from unlikely to engender confidence to likely to do so. Where a target should be placed on the spectrum is a matter of judgment informed by answers to all of the questions concerning the target and related provision for holding responsible actors to account. A target which is legally binding, accompanied by a duty to formulate and implement programmes of measures for its achievement which are then reviewed and must be revised if they are found to be inadequate, supported by obligations to report on progress with meeting the target, backed-up by arrangements for reviewing progress which, if this is judged to be deficient, oblige the target holder to remedy the shortfall, and enforceable by the imposition of penalties large enough to have a deterrent effect will be very likely to instil confidence in investors. The fewer of these qualities which a target possesses, the less likely it becomes that it will be judged capable of attracting investment in the renewables sector.

V. Case Study: National Targets under the EU's Renewable Energy Directives

The European Union and its institutions use powers conferred on them by treaties negotiated and ratified by the EU's Member States to adopt policies and laws concerning energy production and consumption.[21] It has adopted policies on renewable energy during the last three decades as part of wider efforts to combat climate change and advance other policy goals including technological leadership and energy security. Its policy statements set as their focal points goals for increasing the proportion of energy in EU energy supplies that derives from renewable sources by a set date

---

[21] For an introduction to EU competences in energy policy and law making see Kim Talus, *Introduction to EU Energy Law* (Oxford University Press, 2016) 7–14.

(2010, 2020, and 2030 respectively). The case study examines the three main laws adopted through the EU legislative process to pursue its renewable energy policy goals. The EU experience with effecting targets through laws is of interest because of the variety of legal approaches used to support targets with mechanisms for scrutinising and where necessary securing improvement in the performance of actors responsible for promoting the renewables sector. Achievement of overall EU goals on renewables depends on the combined success of its individual Member States in advancing the EU objective. However, Member States are unwilling to surrender control over their decision-making authority to the EU level. Indeed, the Treaty on the functioning of the European Union's section on energy policy marks out 'a Member State's right to determine the conditions for exploiting its energy resources, its choice between different energy sources and the general structure of its energy supply' as ground on which EU policy and law may not trespass.[22] Creativity is therefore needed in legal design to support progress toward EU goals whilst respecting the sensitivity of Member States to intrusion from EU law on national energy policy and law.

The European Council, the group of heads of state of the 27 Member States, defines the European Union's policy agenda. The European Commission, the executive branch of the European Union, drafts laws and is responsible for the day to day running of the Union. The legislature is made up of the European Parliament and the Council of the European Union, a body made up of ministers for each of the 27 Member States with membership changing depending on the topic under examination (eg, national energy ministers will review proposed energy laws). The Court of Justice of the European Union, the Union's judicial branch, is responsible for interpreting EU treaties and laws. Readers who wish to know more about the European Union and its institutions as a source of law are directed to authoritative sources on this topic as referenced below.[23]

A. 2001 Renewable Electricity Directive[24]

The European Commission made its first formal policy statement on renewable energy in a green paper of 1996,[25] and followed this in 1997 with a White Paper setting out a Community Strategic Action Plan for renewables.[26] The dialogue initiated by the White Paper led to the adoption in 2001 of the EU's Renewable Electricity Directive.[27]

---

[22] Treaty on the Functioning of the European Union of 13 December 2007, consolidated version [2012] OJ C326/47, art 194(2).
[23] Robert Schütze, *An Introduction to European Law*, 3rd edn (Oxford University Press, 2020); Catherine Barnard and Steve Peers, *European Union Law*, 3rd edn (Oxford University Press, 2020).
[24] Commentaries on the Directive are also available at Johnston and van der Marel (n 14) 179–84; and Theodoros Iliopoulos, 'Dilemmas on the Way to a New Renewable Energy Directive' (2018) *European Energy and Environmental Law Review* 210, 211.
[25] Commission, 'Energy for the future: renewable sources of energy – Green Paper for a Community Strategy' COM (96) 576 final.
[26] Commission, 'Energy for the future: renewable sources of energy – White Paper for a Community Strategy and Action Plan' COM (97) 599 final.
[27] Council Directive 2001/77/EC of 27 September 2001 on the promotion of electricity produced from renewable energy sources in the internal electricity market [2001] OJ L 283/33 (the 2001 Directive).

The Directive's goal was to secure a 22.1 per cent share of electricity produced from renewable sources in total EU electricity consumption by 2010. It sought to achieve this by requiring Member States to set a national indicative target for renewable electricity consumption in 2010.[28] In doing so they were obliged to take into account reference values set out in an Annex to the Directive representing the EU's view on the contribution each Member State should be able to make to its overall objective. Member States also had an obligation to take 'appropriate steps to encourage greater consumption of electricity produced from renewable energy sources in conformity with the national indicative targets'.[29] However, Member States were not obligated either to set targets that would ensure achievement of the EU's objective or to achieve their national indicative targets under EU law. It is unsurprising in view of the lack of clear legal obligation to make contributions sufficient to realise the Directive's goal that Member States' performance was somewhat patchy.[30] A few states hit their indicative targets for electricity with their strong performance securing achievement of the EU's overall goal of 12 per cent energy from renewable sources in energy supplies,[31] but 15 out of 27 states did not.[32] This outcome led to the view that more intrusive legal measures would be required to ensure that all Member States should contribute in a spirit of solidarity to increasing renewable energy consumption in the EU under the successor law on renewable energy.[33]

B. 2009 Renewable Energy Directive[34]

In March 2007, the European Council agreed to increase renewable energy consumption to 20 per cent of overall energy consumption in the EU by 2020.[35] This agreement formed part of the 20/20/20 strategy that sought to reduce the EU's greenhouse gas emissions to 80 per cent of 1990 levels by 2020. The other key plank of this strategy was to increase the efficiency of energy consumption by 20 per cent by 2020. Improving energy efficiency is valuable in itself for reducing emissions from energy production and use. It also makes it easier to achieve commitments on renewables as growth in this sector will take place against a backdrop of shrinking demand for energy.

---

[28] ibid, art 3(2).
[29] ibid, art 3(1).
[30] Hans van Steen, 'The Determination and Enforceability of National Renewable Energy Targets' in Paul Hodson and Christopher Jones (eds) *Renewable Energy Law and Policy in the European Union* (Claeys and Casteels 2010) 43, 43–45.
[31] Eurostat, 'Statistics in Focus 44/2012, Environment and Energy' https://ec.europa.eu/eurostat/documents/3433488/5585312/KS-SF-12-044-EN.PDF/d3dbfde0-5af8-4510-856b-287a6f015665 (accessed 2 October 2022) referenced in Alessandro Monti and Beatriz Romera, 'Fifty Shades of Binding: Appraising the Enforcement Toolkit for the EU's 2030 Renewable Energy Targets' (2020) 29 *Review of European, Comparative and International Environmental Law* 221, 229.
[32] Commission, 'Renewable Energy Progress Report' COM (2013) 175 final, 4.
[33] Commission, 'Renewable Energy: Progressing towards the 2020 target' COM (2011) 31 final, 3–4.
[34] Commentaries on the Directive are also available at Johnston and van der Marel (n 14), 185–97; and Iliopoulos (n 24), 212.
[35] Council of the European Union, 'Presidency Conclusions: 8/9 March 2007' Ref 7224/1/07/Rev 1.

The Commission was invited by the European Council to prepare legal instruments to implement its political commitments. A new Directive for renewable energy was proposed in January 2008,[36] and was adopted after passing through the European legislative process in April 2009.[37] It entered into force in June 2009, and Article 27(1) required Member States to transpose it into their national legislations by 5 December 2010. The Directive's goal was to secure the achievement of a 20 per cent share of energy from renewable sources in Community energy consumption by 2020. There were two key differences between the 2009 Directive and its predecessor. The first was that it imposed national targets on Member States to achieve increases in renewable energy consumption that were legally binding at the EU level. Second, the targets under the 2009 Directive were for increasing the contribution of renewable sources to energy consumption for heating and cooling and transportation in addition to electricity. It was for Member States to decide on how their targets were met. Greater weight could be placed on electricity generation than on energy for heating and cooling and transport or vice versa. However, the Directive also set a separate national target for 10 per cent of energy consumed for transport to come from renewable sources. Accordingly, all Member States were obliged to increase renewable energy consumption for transport as part of their efforts to decarbonise national energy supplies.[38]

The principal obligation of each Member State was to achieve a national target for the proportion of renewable energy in energy consumption by 2020.[39] The national targets, as set out in Annex I to the 2009 RES Directive, added up to a 20 per cent share of renewable energy for the EU as a whole. Half of the total additional increase in renewable energy over consumption levels achieved under the 2001 Directive for achievement of the overall 2020 target was shared between Member States equally, but the Commission allocated the second half among them according to their GDP per capita. It also modified targets to take into account efforts made by Member States that had already achieved significant growth in renewable energy consumption.[40] The targets varied significantly as a result. Sweden's was highest at 49 per cent whilst Malta's was lowest at 10 per cent.

Steady progress by Member States in increasing renewable energy consumption was required throughout the period covered by the Directive if the 2020 targets were to be met. In view of this, and to provide backing for the effectiveness of the principal obligation, Article 3(2) of the Directive set an indicative trajectory of growing consumption levels that Member States were expected to follow during specified periods. The indicative trajectories were not legally binding. However, Member States were obliged by Article 3(2) to introduce measures that were 'effectively designed' to ensure

---

[36] Commission, 'Proposal for a Directive of the European Parliament and of the Council on the promotion of the use of energy from renewable sources' COM (2008) 19 final.
[37] Council Directive 2009/28/EC of 23 April 2009 on the promotion of the use of energy from renewable sources and amending and subsequently repealing Directive 2001/77/EC and 2003/30/EC [2009] OJ L140/16 (the 2009 RES Directive).
[38] 2009 RES Directive, ibid, art 3(1).
[39] ibid.
[40] The basis on which targets were calculated is explained in Commission, '2020 by 2020 Europe's climate change opportunity' COM (2008) 30 final, 7–8. See also van Steen (n 30) 55–61.

that the growth in renewable energy consumption followed their indicative trajectories. Infraction proceedings could therefore have been brought against a state which failed to make sufficiently serious efforts to achieve its target in principle, although the wording 'effectively designed' allowed much scope for debate over the adequacy of adopted measures.[41]

Member States were required under the 2009 RES Directive to prepare and submit national renewable energy action plans (NREAPs) by June 2010 documenting how they intended to achieve their targets including by collaboration with other states and imports.[42] The NREAPs were also to state the intended contribution of renewable energy generation in each sector (electricity/heating/transport) to the achievement of the overall national target. The Commission had the power to make recommendations in response to NREAPs.[43] Member States were not legally bound to implement recommendations, but not doing so could have been used as evidence of a failure to introduce 'effectively designed' measures in the event that a Member State fell below its indicative trajectory. Each Member States also had an obligation to resubmit its NREAP if it fell below its indicative trajectory.[44] In addition, Member States were required to submit detailed national reports on progress toward the national renewable energy target every two years.[45] The Commission analysed the national submissions and reported on overall progress to the European Council and Parliament.[46]

Good provision may have been made under the Directive to ensure transparency over steps taken to achieve goals, but questions arose over whether any legal consequences likely to secure improvement in a Member State's performance would flow from a report revealing that this was not sufficient to reach the State's 2020 target. As noted above, Member States were not legally obliged to reach their indicative trajectories. The obligation to take measures 'effectively designed' would also be challenging to enforce because the phrase is not defined. The national target obligation could not be enforced until after 2020 when it fell due.[47] As a result, weight was placed on the deterrent effect of legal outcomes and penalties that a failure to meet a national 2020 target would trigger for securing adequate performance by Member States before 2020. A major omission in this regard was that the Directive did not itself specify penalties for a failure by a Member State to achieve its 2020 targets.[48] When calculating the merits of meeting or not meeting their targets, States would have been aware that the European Commission had the power to initiate infringement proceedings against states that failed to achieve their 2020 target,[49] but would also have known

---

[41] van Steen (n 30) 62–5; Johnston and van der Marel (n 14) 189–93.
[42] 2009 RES Directive, art 4.
[43] ibid, art 4(5).
[44] ibid, art 4(4).
[45] ibid, art 22.
[46] ibid, art 23.
[47] See discussion of the weight this places on legal provision designed to secure the performance of commitments ahead of when they fall due in Johnston and van der Marel (n 14) 177 and 189.
[48] ibid, 202.
[49] European Commission, 'Infringement procedure', Infringement procedure | European Commission (europa.eu) (accessed 2 October 2022).

that such proceedings often do not proceed beyond the pre-judicial stage and, if they do, can take four or more years until judgment is given by the European Court of Justice (ECJ).[50] In addition, they would have known that the Commission may refer a Member State back to the ECJ if it fails to rectify the position following a judgment which finds it in breach of EU law, and that it may request at that point for a lump sum fine and/or a daily payment to be awarded as financial penalties. However, the size of penalties is not fixed.[51] They are determined individually based on assessment by the European Court of Justice of the breach under consideration including the perceived significance and severity of the infringement.[52] States might therefore have gambled on any proceedings being resolved long before that stage was reached, and, if financial penalties were imposed, on their being less expensive to pay than the cost of investing additional monies in supporting the growth of renewable energy when deciding on whether or not to meet their targets in full.[53] Considerations of interstate solidarity and of not harming relations with other Member States by 'free-riding' on their efforts would be likely to feature in deliberation by states struggling to meet their targets over whether to act in this manner.

(i) Analysis

The legal framework created by the Renewable Energy Directive 2009 for establishing the EU's 20 per cent by 2020 renewable energy policy goal in law and promoting its achievement through Member State efforts had some attributes that would have helped with creating confidence amongst investors in the renewables sector. Most notably, the replacement of the 2001 Directive's non-binding indicative targets with legally binding targets for Member States sent a strong message for the growth of renewable energy production in the EU. This was backed up by improvements on the legal support provided by the 2001 Directive for holding Member States to account including: the obligation to prepare programmes of measures for realising the target and to resubmit them if national progress fell below the required trajectory; the opportunity for the Commission to comment on the adequacy of programmes before their adoption; the obligation on Member States to undertake measures effectively designed to secure progress in line with a trajectory leading to achievement of the 2020 target; obligations to report periodically on national progress on increasing the proportion of renewables in energy supplies with progress to be reviewed by the Commission and compared against the desired trajectory identified in the Directive; and the fact that the 2020 targets, because they were legally binding, could be enforced through infringement proceedings potentially leading to a substantial fine.

---

[50] Johnston and van der Marel (n 14) 206–09.
[51] Dorien Bennink, Harry Croezen and Margaret van Valkengoed, *The Accountability of European Renewable Energy and Climate Policy* (CE Delft report, April 2011), www.cedelft.eu/publicatie/the accountability of european renewable energy and climate policy/1143 (accessed 2 October 2022); see also Johnston and van der Marel (n 14) 206–09.
[52] European Commission (n 49).
[53] This is one aspect of a broader debate about whether the prospect of infringement proceedings poses a sufficient deterrent threat to secure Member State compliance with EU law. See Peeters and Schomerus (n 14), 133–35.

We have also seen that there are some weaknesses in legal provision under the Directive which would have weakened somewhat its ability to inspire investor confidence in future Member State support for renewables. Member States were not required to make the changes to their programmes recommended by the EU. The standard to be met by the obligation to take effectively designed measures was not defined, leaving scope for debate over the adequacy in law of steps taken by Member States. It was also not mandatory to rectify the position if progress fell below the indicative trajectory other than by submitting a new plan. Finally, the likely duration and uncertain outcome of infringement proceedings impairs the ability of legally binding targets to deter non-compliance. In summary, the 2009 Directive compares well to its predecessor on the legal support it affords for performance of the EU's renewable energy policy goal. However, there are grounds for questioning whether this support was quite as compelling as the adoption of legally binding targets might have led many to believe.[54]

Whatever the strengths and weaknesses of the Directive's legal design, statistics published in 2022 revealed that renewables accounted for 22.1 per cent of EU energy consumption in 2020, exceeding the 2009 Directive's goal by 2.1 per cent.[55] Of the 27 EU Member States only France fell below its nationally binding renewable energy target set in the 2009 Directive. Some Member States (Luxembourg, Belgium, Slovenia, the Netherlands and Ireland) were only able to reach their targets by arranging statistical transfers of renewable energy from Member States who had exceeded their targets. The 2009 Directive encouraged States to cooperate in this way by permitting them to use cooperation mechanisms for working together on increasing the proportion of renewables in EU energy overall.[56] EU consumption of renewables in energy for transport in 2020 also exceeded the 2009 Directive's 10 per cent goal.[57] Out of the 27 Member States, 15 failed to reach the 10 per cent level with seven (Greece, Croatia, Cyprus, Latvia, Lithuania, Poland and Romania) falling below it by more than 1 per cent. The slow progress on renewable transport suggests that stronger legal intervention than a standalone target is needed to drive significant growth in renewables for this sector.

These statistics do not themselves enable us to draw conclusions about the contribution of legally binding targets to the performance of individual Member States. We can take note, however, that they represent an improvement on the individual and combined performances of Member States when operating under indicative goals which did not bind at the EU level set by predecessors to the 2009 Directive. Achievement of the overall target by 26 out of 27 Member States compares favourably with the failure of 15 out of 27 Member States to achieve their indicative targets under the 2001 Electricity Directive.[58] The improvement of performance against their indicative trajectories by several Member States from the first half of the 2010s could also

---

[54] Monti and Romera (n 31) 230.
[55] Eurostat, *Renewable Energy Statistics* (Eurostat January 2022) Renewable energy statistics – Statistics Explained (europa.eu) (accessed 2 October 2022).
[56] For information on the cooperation mechanisms see Olivia Woolley, 'Renewable energy consumption' in Martha Roggenkamp, Edwin Woerdman and Marijn Holwerda (eds) *Essential EU Climate Law*, 2nd edn (Cheltenham, Edward Elgar, 2021) 98, 114–18.
[57] Eurostat (n 55).
[58] See Section VA above.

suggest an influence with data recorded in the 2015 progress report indicating that nine states would miss their 2020 targets.[59] Performance against the 10 per cent transportation target, although still disappointing, represents a significant improvement over levels reached under non-binding indicative targets set by the 2003 Biofuels Directive.[60] 22 out of 27 Member States fell below their indicative targets in 2010 compared to 15 out of 27 in 2020 with half of those falling short within one percentage point of 10 per cent.[61]

C. 2018 Renewable Energy Directive

The Commission initiated discussion of the policy and legal framework for climate and energy in the period from 2021 to 2030 in January 2014.[62] This led to agreement by the European Council in October 2014 on an EU-wide target of at least 27 per cent energy from renewable sources in overall energy consumption by 2030.[63] The Commission's proposal, endorsed by the Council, called for a different approach from the previous Directive. It records the Commission's views that European and national targets may have driven 'strong action by the Member States and growth in emerging industries', but that they did not always fit well with EU policy goals for undistorted competitive energy markets.[64] In addition, the proposal expresses concerns over the affordability of energy for consumers and businesses, over the effect of energy costs on the competitiveness of the EU's economy, and that binding targets may have been responsible for impairing the cost effectiveness of national efforts to implement Union climate and energy policy including by requiring states to develop renewable energy to a specified level even when this was not the most cost effective means open to them for reducing greenhouse gas emissions.[65]

The Commission's proposal for reconciling these concerns with ensuring the further growth of renewable energy was to replace legally binding national targets for Member States with an overall Union target for renewable energy, thereby allowing Member States more flexibility in deciding on how to meet greenhouse gas reduction targets most cost effectively whilst imposing a collective responsibility for ensuring growth of renewables consumption. The overall Union target would be backed up by rigorous European-level governance arrangements to keep individual and collective progress by Member States towards its achievement under review.

---

[59] Commission, 'Renewable energy progress report', COM (2015) 293 final, 5.
[60] Council Directive 2003/30/EC of 8 May 2003 on the promotion of the use of biofuels or other renewable fuels for transport [2003] OJ L 123/42.
[61] Commission, 'Renewable energy progress report', COM (2013) 175 final, 4.
[62] Commission, 'A policy framework for climate and energy in the period from 2020 to 2030', COM (2014) 15 final.
[63] European Council, 'Conclusions on 2030 Climate and Energy Policy', SN 79/14, 23 and 24 October 2014, www.consilium.europa.eu/uedocs/cms_data/docs/pressdata/en/ec/145356.pdf (accessed 2 October 2022).
[64] Commission, COM (2014) 15 final (n 62).
[65] ibid. Alexander Bürgin, 'National binding renewable energy targets for 2020, but not for 2030 anymore: Why the European Commission developed from a supporter to a brakeman' (2015) 22 *Journal of European Public Policy* 690.

The 27 per cent target was widely criticised as lacking in ambition. The Commission, the Parliament and the Council reached political agreement in June 2018 on a higher target of at least 32 per cent energy from renewable sources in overall energy consumption by 2030.[66] A proposal for a new renewable energy directive was published by the Commission in November 2016 as part of a wider package of laws to implement climate and energy policy for 2021–2030 and beyond under the Clean Energy for All Europeans programme.[67] The 2018 RES Directive received legislative approval in December 2018.[68] Member States were required to have transposed it into national laws by 30 June 2021.[69] The Directive enshrines the 32 per cent target in law,[70] but takes note of views that changing circumstances could render it inadequate. It provides that the Commission will review the target (and others set under it) 'with a view to submitting a legislative proposal by 2023 to increase it' where change in the cost of renewable energy production, change in the Union's commitments for decarbonisation under international law, or decline in the Union's energy consumption would justify an increase.[71]

The most notable difference between the 2018 RES Directive and its predecessor is that it does not place legally binding national targets on Member States at the European level. Instead, they each have obligations to 'set national contributions to meet collectively' the Union target for 2030 and to 'collectively ensure' its achievement.[72] The expectation that Member States will achieve a Union target without setting their individual responsibilities for ensuring that it is met in European law raises questions about how they can be held to account for perceived inadequacy of their contributions to its realisation. What is there to prevent failure to achieve the overall EU target or the poor performance of individual states without having national legally binding targets at the European level?

The Commission proposed in its policy statement of 2014 to plug the gap left by the absence of national targets by establishing overarching Union governance for all policy areas contributing to its goal of a 40 per cent reduction of greenhouse gas emissions compared to 1990 levels by 2030.[73] A governance regulation was proposed as part of the Clean Energy for all Europeans legislative programme,[74] and was adopted in December 2018.[75] As a regulation, it has almost immediate direct legal effect.

---

[66] Commission, 'Europe leads the global clean energy transition: Commission welcomes ambitious agreement on further renewable energy deployment in the EU' (Press Release, 14 June 2018) http://europa.eu/rapid/press-release_STATEMENT-18-4155_en.htm (accessed 2 October 2022).

[67] Commission, 'Proposal for a Directive of the European Parliament and of the Council on the promotion of the use of energy from renewable sources' COM (2016) 767 final.

[68] Directive (EU) 2018/2001 of the European Parliament and of the Council of 11 December 2018 on the promotion of the use of energy from renewable sources [2018] OJ L 328/82 (the 2018 RES Directive).

[69] 2018 RES Directive (n 68) art 36.

[70] 2009 RES Directive (n 37) art 3(1).

[71] 2018 RES Directive (n 68) arts 3(1) and 25.

[72] ibid, arts 3(1) and 3(2).

[73] Commission, COM 2014 15 final (n 62).

[74] Commission, 'Proposal for a Regulation on the Governance of the Energy Union', COM (2016) 759 final.

[75] Regulation (EU) 2018/1999 of the European Parliament and of the Council of 11 December 2018 on the Governance of the Energy Union and Climate Action, amending Regulations (EC) No 663/2009 and (EC) No 715/2009 of the European Parliament and of the Council Directives 94/22/EC, 98/70/EC, 2009/31/

It required each Member State to prepare and submit a draft integrated national energy and climate plan for 2021 to 2030 to the Commission by the end of 2018 with the final plan to be notified to the Commission and published by the end of 2019.[76] The plans were to state the contribution that the Member State would make to achieving the Union target on renewable energy together with the interim trajectory that would be followed to achieve its planned contribution in line with milestones specified in the Regulation.[77] Detailed prescribed information on national policies and measures that would be pursued and taken to realise the proposed contribution was also to be provided.[78]

The Commission had the power to issue country specific recommendations for revising the draft plans.[79] Article 31 of the Governance Regulation also empowered the Commission, if it assessed collective ambition shown by Member States' plans to be inadequate for achievement of the 2030 target, to issue recommendations calling on those states whose contributions were deemed to be insufficient to increase their ambition. States falling below their expected contribution were to be identified by application of a formula set out in Annex II to the Regulation. Member States were obliged to take due account of the Commission's recommendations when finalising their plans but were not obliged to apply them if they chose not to.[80] This initial stage of review is crucial for achieving the EU's overall target. If Member States' planned contributions were to fall short of the EU goal at the outset, the Directive does not oblige them to increase their contributions during the period of plan implementation. The potential gap between planned national contributions and the Union goal is a consequence of the shift from EU-allocated legally binding targets adding up to the overall EU target under the 2009 RES Directive to national self-determination of efforts under the 2018 Directive with non-binding recommendations being the Commission's main tool for making up the shortfall. The initial process of review, recommendation and revision succeeded in securing an increase in commitments needed to attain the Union goal. Draft Member State plans showed collective ambition amounting to between 30.4 and 31.9 per cent of energy from renewables in Union energy consumption. Final plans submitted at the end of 2019 following the Commission's review of drafts and recommendations showed collective ambition amounting to between 33.15 and 33.7 per cent.[81] That initial experience gives confidence in the arrangements introduced by the 2019 Directive for scrutinising Member State plans, but the legal vulnerability would be tested again if a future increase in the 32 per cent goal was to necessitate the preparation of revised plans showing greater ambition in increasing renewable energy consumption.

EC, 2009/73/EC, 2010/31/EU, 2012/27/EU and 2013/30/EU of the European Parliament and of the Council, Council Directives 2009/119/EC and (EU) 2015/652 and repealing Regulation (EU) No 525/2013 of the European Parliament and of the Council [2018] OJ L 328/1.

[76] ibid, arts 3 and 9.
[77] ibid, arts 4(a)(2) and 5.
[78] ibid, art 3 and Annex I.
[79] ibid, arts 9 and 31.
[80] ibid, art 9(3).
[81] Commission, 'An EU-wide assessment of National Energy and Climate Plans', COM (2020) 564 final, 2.

Member States have extensive biennial reporting obligations during the period covered by the plan including on progress made on increasing renewable energy consumption.[82] The Directive also sets reference points, corresponding to the indicative trajectory of the 2009 RES Directive, against which progress by Member States with effecting their contributions and by the Union with increasing renewable energy consumption toward 32 per cent can be assessed. The reference points are 18 per cent by 2022, 43 per cent by 2025 and 65 per cent by 2027.[83] The Commission has authority under the Governance Regulation to take action if actual Member State contributions fall short of planned levels. Recommendations may be made to a Member State if the Commission concludes through interim review that it is making insufficient progress towards implementing its climate plan, and to all states if it concludes that the Union is at risk of not meeting its target based on an aggregate interim assessment of combined Member State performance.[84] As with the stage of plan review, Member States are obliged to take recommendations into account and in subsequent reports to explain either how they were followed or give reasons for why they were not followed.[85] However, they are not obliged to implement them. In addition, the Commission has an obligation if collective national measures on renewable energy are assessed to be insufficient to achieve the 2030 target to 'propose measures and exercise its power at the Union level' to ensure its achievement.[86] Observance of the obligation could potentially lead to proposals for measures and action aimed at closing a gap between cumulative Member State ambition and performance and the Union's overall goal, but this catch-all provision does not guarantee that Member State action to fill gaps can be compelled.

Member States are obliged to improve their performance on increasing renewable energy production and consumption in stated circumstances. Where Member States combined progress reports reveal that growth in EU renewable energy as a proportion of energy supplies is below an EU reference point for 2030, Member States whose progress on achieving renewable energy growth set out in their plans has fallen below the rate expected by the EU reference points must 'ensure that additional measures are implemented within one year following the date of reception of the Commission's assessment in order to cover the gap'.[87] Indicative measures that could be taken are listed, including national measures to increase deployment of renewable energy, making a voluntary financial payment to the Union renewable energy financing mechanism and using the Directive's cooperation mechanisms. As with the obligation to take measures effectively designed to follow the trajectory under the 2009 RES Directive, this is an obligation to take measures intended to secure an outcome rather than a duty to keep to the 2018 Directive's reference points per se. However, the expectation that measures taken will be sufficient to close the gap in a context where the shortfall is known sets a clearer backdrop for assessing their adequacy than the effectively designed duty.

---

[82] Regulation 2018/1999 (n 75), arts 17 to 28.
[83] ibid, arts 4(2) and 29(2).
[84] ibid, art 32.
[85] ibid, art 34.
[86] ibid, art 32(2).
[87] ibid, art 32(3).

Explanation must be provided in the next national progress report to be submitted after a reference point has been missed of how the gap will be covered.[88] Member States also have a clearly worded obligation to take additional measures 'sufficient to cover the gap' within one year where its proportion of renewable energy falls below its target under the 2020 Directive over a whole year.[89] This is known as the no backsliding provision.

The Union target and Member States' contributions to this focus on the overall level of renewable energy in national consumption. Accordingly, there is no repeat of the separate legally binding target for renewable energy in transport under the 2009 RES Directive. Member States are required, however, to provide separate details of estimated sectoral trajectories in their plans. With regard to transport, they must also set an obligation on fuel suppliers to ensure a minimum level of 14 per cent renewable energy in fuel supplies by 2030.[90] In addition, the 2018 RES Directive makes specific provision, albeit through an obligation of conduct rather than result, for mainstreaming renewable energy in heating and cooling.[91] Member States must endeavour to increase the share of renewable energy in that sector by an indicative 1.3 per cent as an annual average for the periods 2021 to 2025 and 2026 to 2030. They must also lay down the necessary measures to ensure that district heating and cooling systems contribute to this increase.[92]

(i) Proposed Amendments to the 2018 RES Directive

There has been a radical increase in the EU's ambitions on decarbonisation since the 2018 RES Directive was adopted. Its goals have increased from a 40 per cent reduction in greenhouse gas emissions against 1990 levels in 2030 to 55 per cent and from an 80 to 95 per cent reduction in emissions in 2050 to complete decarbonisation by that date. The 55 per cent and 100 per cent goals are enshrined in law by the EU's first overarching law on climate change adopted in 2021.[93] The law establishes procedures for reviewing the compatibility of EU law with its decarbonisation goals. In July 2021, the European Commission presented its 'Fit for 55' package of revisions to its existing climate laws aimed at bringing them into line with the higher targets.[94] The package included a proposal for amendments to the 2018 RES Directive.[95] The draft revisions proposed an increase in the 2030 renewable energy target from 32 per cent to 40 per cent of renewables in EU energy supplies. Negotiations were ongoing in

---

[88] ibid, art 32(5).
[89] ibid, art 32(4).
[90] 2018 RES Directive (n 68), art 25(1).
[91] ibid, art 23(1).
[92] ibid, art 24.
[93] Regulation (EU) 2021/1119 of 30 June 2021 establishing the framework for achieving climate neutrality and amending Regulations (EC) No. 401/2009 and (EU) 2018/1999 (European Climate Law) [9.7.2021] OJ L243/1.
[94] European Council, 'Fit for 55' (European Council Website) Fit for 55 – The EU's plan for a green transition – Consilium (europa.eu) (accessed 2 October 2022).
[95] European Commission, 'Proposal for a Directive amending Directive (EU) 2018/2001, Regulation (EU) 2018/1999 and Directive 98/70/EC and repealing Council Directive (EU) 2015/652', COM (2021) 557 final.

early 2023 for a 45 per cent renewables target for 2030 in light of Russia's invasion of Ukraine and the related need for the EU to end its reliance on Russian fossil fuel exports. The draft directive also proposes higher targets for sectors of energy consumption. The indicative target for renewables in energy for heating and cooling in the 2018 RES Directive is replaced by an obligation for each Member State to increase the share of renewables in energy consumed for these purposes by at least 1.1 per cent annually starting from a 2020 baseline. The level of the obligation on reducing the greenhouse gas intensity of transport fuels to be placed by Member States on fuel suppliers is increased to at least 13 per cent by 2030. An indicative target is to be introduced by Member States for the consumption of renewables in energy used by industry.

It was at least envisaged in the 2018 RES Directive that the EU's ambition on renewable energy may be increased, and that climate and energy plans would need to be revised by Member States and then reviewed by the Commission with a following round of recommendations from the Commission, responses to recommendations by Member States, and submission of final draft plans. Draft updates to Member States' integrated national climate and energy plans must be submitted by 30 June 2023 with finalised updated plans to be submitted by 30 June 2024.[96] Member States are required in their updated plans to modify planned contributions to Union targets including for renewable energy 'in order to reflect' the Union's increased ambition.[97]

(ii) Analysis

The 2018 RES Directive retreats from the credibility enhancing legally binding targets of the 2009 RES Directive. It moves back towards the indicative targets approach of the 2001 Directive which was criticised for failing to back the EU's policy ambition for increasing renewable electricity with the legal rigour required to create confidence in its achievement.[98] However, the 2018 RES Directive's detailed provisions on review, reporting and revision move it further forwards toward the end of the spectrum indicating good capabilities for enhancing investor confidence than the 2001 Directive. The EU target itself, viewed in isolation, is not convincing. Contributions to the target are not formally allocated for Member States as they were under the 2009 RES Directive. The meaning and therefore the enforceability of the obligation held in common by Member States to 'collectively ensure that the share of energy from renewable sources' reaches 32 per cent in 2030 are in doubt.[99] However, this weak European focus is compensated for by stronger legal provision on obligations for Member State duty holders to take action contributing to achievement of the target and on reviewing and where necessary challenging progress made with attracting investment in renewables at the national level. On the positive side, more detailed plans for national contributions to EU renewables growth than NREAPs must be prepared. They are examined and commented on under a process which compares commitments offered to an indicative

---

[96] 2018 RES Directive (n 68), art 14.
[97] ibid.
[98] See section IVA above.
[99] 2018 RES Directive (n 68), art 3(1).

assessment of what a Member State should be able to contribute. Detailed comments made by the Commission must be taken into account by Member States when finalising plans. As experience with preparatory planning in relation to the 32 per cent target would suggest, the lack of an obligation to implement recommendations may be balanced by political pressures likely to result where a Member State is reluctant to pull its weight on efforts to meet a shared political commitment. Rigorous reporting obligations for both Member States and the Commission enable progress to be monitored by EU institutions, other Member States and civil societies with related potential for ongoing political pressure at European and domestic levels including from obligations to take into account and respond to further recommendations where a Member State's performance against its plan for increasing renewable energy proves deficient.

In addition to the web of procedural obligations, substantive obligations to take measures designed to achieve a specified outcome are triggered when deficient performance threatens achievement of the EU's overall goal. As noted above, the obligation for Member States falling below the trajectory needed to effect their plans to implement additional measures within a year with the express purpose of covering the gap potentially affords a basis for infraction proceedings if there is a significant failure in recovering lost ground.[100] This obligation makes a particular contribution to reinforcing the 2018 EU target. The threat that planned national contributions will become de facto targets if the trigger of collective contributions falling below a reference point for the EU target occurs incentivises Member States to prevent this situation from arising.

The above obligation and related prospect of Member State action to achieve their planned contributions being compelled helps significantly with creating confidence that measures for promoting renewables will be taken. However, we should not ignore aspects that compromise the confidence creating potentialities of the EU target and its supporting legal framework. There is no guarantee where initial plans and/or subsequent performance are inadequate that they will be improved. Member States are not obliged to apply recommendations. The fact that the obligation is triggered only where collective progress falls below a reference point could see a two-speed expansion of renewables in the EU with the strong performance of some states making up for poor contributions by others. The ultimate weakness with legal provision for securing achievement of the EU target also remains: if Member States collectively do not improve plans sufficiently in line with recommendations to enable the EU goal's achievement, then no means exist for the EU to compel improvement in their contributions. Member States are only clearly obliged to achieve the contributions set out in their plans. The shortfall scenario was avoided for the 32 per cent goal by Member State responses to recommendations, but the risk of a shortfall emerging when Member States prepare revised plans to meet the higher target for 2030 remains. Member States are, of course, obligated collectively to ensure achievement of the EU target.[101] However, questions arise over what that commitment requires them to do individually and over its enforceability.

---

[100] Regulation 2018/1999 (n 75), art 32(3).
[101] 2018 RES Directive (n 68), art 3(1).

D. Case Study Summary

Experience with the three directives illustrates ways in which law can be used to support targets and their strengths and weaknesses for engendering confidence that governmental promises to increase growth in renewable energy production have substance. We have seen three different means of allocating state responsibility for achieving a regional goal supported variously by obligations for planning, reporting, and taking measures calculated to achieve an outcome, by provision for review against a legally established standard and related requirements to respond to comments, and by the prospect of punishment in the event that obligations are not complied with. We have also seen how weaknesses in the legal entrenchment of targets themselves and in support provided by underpinning mechanisms can impair their intrinsic ability to drive sectoral growth. The 2001 Directive was blighted by a lack of legal clarity over what states were required to contribute to an EU goal. The 2009 Directive rectified this omission through setting clear and legally binding targets, but the supporting legal arrangements are undermined by limited requirements for responding to critical comments and by uncertainty concerning the consequences of default. The 2018 Directive strengthens provision for reporting on, review of and response to critical comment concerning Member State policy and law on renewables but restores the pursuit of an EU goal without specifying Member State contributions which proved problematic under the first instrument. It remains to be seen whether the 2018 Directive's much more exacting regimes on transparency and making up for inadequate performance avoids the 2001 Directive's lacklustre results.

Classroom Questions

1. How can targets for increasing renewable energy/reducing greenhouse gases be used to support the growth of renewables?
2. Identify key considerations for assessing the effectiveness of targets and of target-setting laws for supporting the growth of renewable energy.
3. Identify ways in which law can be used to support targets including by enabling persons responsible for achieving a target to be held to account.
4. Case Study (EU Law): A client has a broad interest in investing in renewable energy in EU Member States. You are asked by the client on whether targets for promoting renewable energy under the EU's 2018 Renewable Energy Directive (2018/2001/EC) are likely to offer effective support for supporting the growth of the renewables sector? In particular, the client asks you to answer the following questions:

    (i) What targets for renewable energy growth do Member States have under the law? Are they clear (who/what/when)? What is their legal status?
    (ii) Are the targets supported by arrangements for reporting on progress? Are these arrangements for reporting useful for holding Member States to account? Who reviews the reports?
    (iii) Are the targets supported by arrangements for the interim review of progress (eg, benchmarks of expected progress by particular dates)? Can legal action be taken for a failure to meet an interim target?

(iv) What consequences flow from a failure to meet the final target? Are they useful for holding Member States to account? Can penalties be imposed? If so, are they sufficient to have a deterrent effect (e.g. incentivising compliance with the target rather than risk being penalised for a default)?

(v) In view of your answers to these questions, are the targets capable of creating investor confidence in the renewables sector in the EU?

Scenarios

Basalto, an island state in the mid-Atlantic, has adopted a renewable energy law. The law includes a duty for the government of Basalto to secure an increase in the proportion of renewable energy in national energy consumption from the level in 2020 to 40 per cent by 2030. A client investment bank is considering renewable energy investment in Basalto. It has asked you to advise on the degree of confidence that can be drawn from the target and related renewable energy law that Basalto's policy goal will be followed by commensurate action and therefore by investment opportunities.

- What features of the law should you examine when answering your client's question?
- How would the absence or presence of the following features affect your advice:
  (i) An obligation for the Basaltan government to prepare programmes of measures for implementing the target.
  (ii) An obligation for the Basaltan government to adopt measures effectively designed to secure progress at the rate needed to achieve the ultimate goal.
  (iii) Obligations to report on progress made in following an indicative trajectory leading to achievement of the goal.
  (iv) Obligations to take measures to remedy the shortfall if a review of progress finds that the rate of renewable energy growth is not adequate to secure the target's achievement.

The duty to reach 40 per cent renewable energy by 2030 is enforceable under Basaltan law. What questions should you seek to answer when considering whether confidence in the likelihood of compliance with the target can be drawn from its potential enforceability before Basalto's courts?

Suggested Reading

Book chapters

Olivia Woolley, 'Renewable Energy Consumption' in Martha Roggenkamp, Edwin Woerdman and Marijn Holwerda (eds) *Essential EU Climate Law*, 2nd edn (Cheltenham, Edward Elgar, 2021) 98.

Articles

Theodoros Iliopoulos, 'Dilemmas on the Way to a New Renewable Energy Directive' (2018) *European Energy and Environmental Law Review* 210.

Angus Johnston and Eva van der Marel, 'How Binding are the EU's 'Binding' Renewables Targets?' (2016) 18 *Cambridge Yearbook of European Legal Studies* 176.

Rafael Leal-Arcas and Stephen Minas, 'The Micro Level: Insights from Specific Policy Areas: Mapping the International and European Governance of Renewable Energy' (2016) 35 *Yearbook of European Law* 621.

Alessandro Monti and Beatriz Romera, 'Fifty Shades of Binding: Appraising the Enforcement Toolkit for the EU's 2030 Renewable Energy Targets' (2020) 29 *Review of European Comparative and International Environmental Law* 221.

Policy

European Commission, 'A Policy Framework for Climate and Energy in the Period from 2020 to 2030', COM (2014) 15 final, pp. 1–7 and 12–14.

5
Securing Investment in Renewable Energy: The Role of Subsidies

I. Support Schemes

The cost of producing electricity from some renewable technologies has declined rapidly in the last decade. IRENA reported in 2022 that the global average levelised cost of electricity production (GALCofE) fell between 2010 and 2021 by 88 per cent for utility-scale solar power, by 67 per cent for onshore wind and concentrated solar power and by 60 per cent for offshore wind and that the GALCofE was now lower by 11 per cent for new utility-scale solar power and hydropower and by 39 per cent for onshore wind than for the cheapest new fossil-fuel-fired power generating option.[1] The competitiveness of these better-established renewable technologies in electricity markets with other power-generation technologies makes them increasingly attractive to investors even without incentives from public support as confidence grows in the ability to recover development costs and turn a profit from projects using these technologies through the sale of electricity in markets.

However, care is needed with attempting to draw conclusions about the appeal for investors for renewable energy technologies as a whole from global average figures. The costs position and therefore the confidence of developers in recovering development expenses and making a profit will very for each project depending on factors such as its location (eg, the quality of the resource available for power production varies significantly depending on factors such as wind speeds, solar radiation etc.) and experience in the relevant market with renewable energy investment. The size of a project has an impact on its financial viability. Renewable energy developments often have much lower generating capacities then fossil fuel power plant and are therefore less able to benefit from economies of scale. The maturity of technologies is also a key consideration with newer renewable energy technologies not yet having benefited from the regular experience with their deployment in large scale developments that have

---

[1] IRENA, *Renewable Power Generation Costs in 2021* (IRENA 2022) 17.

enabled significant cost reductions for solar and wind energy. For renewable projects using well-established solar and wind energy technologies, levelised costs of energy may be higher, sometimes much higher, than the global average, leaving them less able to compete with new generating facilities using alternative technologies or with incumbent power producers. Newer technologies, whose commercial use on a large scale is not yet established, will typically struggle to compete and therefore to gain a foothold in markets and access to the opportunities that affords for reducing production costs by learning from doing.

Other factors that may disadvantage renewable electricity developments in the eyes of potential backers include the uncertainty of overall revenues from intermittent generating plant; and the fact that existing energy companies may be unwilling to redeploy substantial asset bases to the renewables sector because of sunk investment (financial and psychological) in their current fossil fuel business models. In addition, a large proportion of renewable electricity project expenditure derives from fixed up-front development costs, with operating costs being minimal due to 'fuels', excluding biomass-based energy, being freely available, whereas the proportion of fixed up-front costs for fossil fuel projects is smaller with a higher proportion of variable operating costs, mostly for fuel. Projects with a high proportion of fixed up-front costs may be thought of as riskier by investors because they are less able to adapt to volatile electricity market prices (eg, they need stable electricity prices at minimum levels over lengthy timeframes to be able to cover initial expenditure). In contrast, fossil fuel businesses can hedge against fluctuations in coal/gas prices.

Means of producing renewable energy in industry, heating, cooling and transportation are also disadvantaged by higher production costs and lower availability of renewable alternatives compared to fossil fuels such as petroleum and natural gas that have benefitted from several decades of experience with technologies for their production and consumption.[2] The fall in the costs of renewable electricity production is also changing the position here, making electrification based on renewable sources an increasingly attractive alternative to sticking with the status quo. However, it must be borne in mind that consumers must also purchase the equipment needed to produce energy for meeting these needs (eg, a new electric or hydrogen-fuelled car, a heat-pump or a biomass boiler) and that costs for these items may be higher for the non-fossil fuel consuming technologies than for manufacturers of equipment that have already realised efficiencies through decades of use and the establishment of worldwide capacities for their production enabling fully realised economies of scale for production costs. Concerns of this nature are naturally relevant not only for the consumer looking to replace equipment to meet energy needs for transport, heating, cooling, or in industry and for equipment producers but also for producers of energy whose marketability depends on consumer choices.

Investors may be put off from investing in projects because of concerns that they would not be able to recover monies invested and a reasonable profit margin through

---

[2] IRENA, *Remap: Roadmap for a Renewable Future (2016 edition)* (IRENA, 2016) 106–20; IRENA, *Global Energy Transformation: A Roadmap to 2050: 2019 Edition* (IRENA, 2019) 32.

energy sales alone. Alternatively, they may only be willing to loan money for such projects at interest rates that developers would find prohibitive. In view of this, governments with policies for increasing renewable energy production and consumption use financial incentives (support schemes) to attract investment in projects for producing renewable energy and technologies which consume it (eg, biomass boilers) in circumstances where it would not be provided under normal market conditions.

This chapter considers the main approaches which governments employ to support renewable energy development financially. Consideration of them is grouped under two headings: measures used to enhance access to funding for the development of technologies to the point where they are ready for commercialisation ('investment support'); and measures which enable the recovery of development costs once renewable technologies are operational ('operating support'). The section on operating support describes common characteristics of three scheme types used worldwide to support renewable energy developments: feed-in tariffs; obligation and certificate schemes (also known, particularly in the U.S., as renewable portfolio schemes);[3] and premium schemes. Commonly occurring strengths and weaknesses of these scheme types for creating investor confidence in projects are examined. Case studies of the principal support schemes for renewable electricity projects introduced by the UK Government during this century as well as Germany's experience with feed-in tariffs provide examples of how these scheme types have been used in practice and further illustrate characteristics which can affect their utility for attracting investment in the renewables sector.

II. Investment Support

Financial backing for research into and the development of early-stage renewable energy technologies and for the trialling of pre-commercial prototypes is often hard to obtain because of the high risk that monies invested will not be recovered.[4] Alternatively, investors may only be prepared to provide capital at rates of return that would make it difficult to recover development costs through energy sales without substantial operating support (see section III below). States use measures, collectively referred to as 'investment support', to make it easier for innovators to develop new renewable energy technologies and to encourage consumers to use them through the provision of public financial support.[5]

---

[3] Craig Hart and Dominic Marcellino, 'Subsidies or Free Markets to Promote Renewables?' (2012) 3 *Renewable Energy Law and Policy* 196, 198–200.

[4] Katy Hogg and Ronan O'Regan, 'Renewable Energy Support Mechanisms: An Overview' in Matt Bonass and Michael Rudd (eds) *Renewables: A Practical Handbook* (Globe Business Publishing Ltd. 2010) 31, 35–39.

[5] ibid; Commission, 'Review of European and national financing of renewable energy in accordance with Article 23(7) of Directive 2009/28/EC', SEC (2011) 131 final, 4–6; Commission, 'European Commission guidance for the design of renewable support schemes – Accompanying the document Communication from the Commission: Delivering the internal market in electricity and making the most of public intervention' SWD (2013) 439 final, 11–12; Zeineb Abdmouleh, Rashid Alammari and Adel Gastli, 'Review of Policies Encouraging Renewable Energy Integration and Best Practices' (2015) 45 *Renewable and Sustainable Energy Reviews* 249.

Grant schemes provide funding to developers for the development and testing of eligible renewable energy technologies. The provision of long-term public loans enables them to access investment at much lower rates of return then would be available to them through private finance. Alternatively, guarantees of repayment from public bodies in the event that a borrower defaults may enable developers to access private finance more cheaply. Long-term grants are also used to encourage the purchase of renewable technologies by domestic and business consumers. For example, Member States of the European Union offer investment grants to promote the take up of renewable energy heating systems such as biomass boilers.[6]

In addition to making public funds available, governments provide tax incentives and reductions to support investment by reducing the financial burden on developers. These may include reduced corporate tax rates, tax holidays and tax credits.[7] Reduced tax rates can also be used to encourage the consumption of renewable energy rather than fossil fuels. The use of biofuels in road transport is commonly promoted by applying lower rates of fuel tax to them compared to petrol or by allowing tax offsets for their consumption.[8]

Investment support is generally viewed as playing a supporting role to operating support, its main function being to enable technologies to reach the point where they are capable of commercial-scale operation. Its key contribution, in addition to creating the space for new technologies to progress from idea, initial design or laboratory-based experiment via the prototype stage to possible deployment, is to lower the costs of those initial stages (eg, by making funds available at lower rates than are available from private lenders) so that costs to be recouped through operation are less daunting. However, the European Commission, in its guidance of 2013 on support for renewable energy, encourages the wider use of investment support in place of operating support because it does not distort the operation of energy markets.[9]

III. Operating Support

States use measures, collectively described as operating support, to attract investment in projects using renewable energy technologies that have matured sufficiently for commercialisation. This is often done by providing in law that renewable energy generators will receive a set price from a legally obligated purchaser for the electricity that they produce or an additional sum on top of revenues realized through sales of electricity in the market (feed-in tariffs and feed-in premiums). The aim in both cases is to give confidence that overall revenues received will enable project cost recovery

---

[6] Commission, SEC (2011) 131 final (n 5), 6, 9–10. Current information on Member State support schemes can be found at: Renewable energy policy database and support: Start (res-legal.eu) (accessed 4 October 2022).
[7] Hogg and O'Regan (n 4) 37–39.
[8] Commission, SEC (2011) 131 final (n 5) 6.
[9] Commission, SWD (2013) 439 final (n 5) 11–12.

and profitability. Another common legal approach is to combine an obligation for sectoral actors such as electricity/gas/transport fuel suppliers to include a proportion of renewable energy in their supplies with a requirement that this should be demonstrated by them by obtaining certificates provided to the original producers of the renewable energy. This creates a potentially desirable combination of a legally required market for renewable energy and of additional revenue from the sale of certificates (obligation/certificate schemes). Subsidies may be made available as of right to qualifying technologies or through competitive measures such as tenders and auctions in which developers submit tenders or bids for support. Sections III.1 to III.4 below offer fuller comment on the strengths and weaknesses of these support scheme types and of competitive allocation for attracting investment in renewable energy projects. Case studies in Section IV examine uses of the scheme types to support electricity in Germany and the UK.

The use of operating support can be more controversial than investment support for the following reasons:

- Operating support distorts market competition directly. It is disliked by those who view undistorted markets as the most cost-efficient means of meeting energy needs. For example, the European Commission sees subsidies as necessary measures for pursuing the EU's renewable energy policy, but ones which do not sit well with its goal of an EU-wide fully competitive internal energy market.[10]
- The costs of such schemes often fall directly on electricity sector companies who then pass them on to consumers in energy bills. Rising energy bills are often attributed, rightly or wrongly, to governmentally imposed renewable energy costs. Resulting public opposition can lead to subsidies being reduced or withdrawn and to wariness of policymakers over introducing new support schemes.[11]
- Some argue that schemes such as FITs are bad in the long-term for the development of renewable energy because they remove producers from market pressures and therefore from competitive drivers for increasing technological efficiency and related reduction in production costs.[12] By the same token, they argue that schemes which combine some additional revenue for renewable generators with market exposure are preferable for promoting the long-term growth of renewable energy.[13] Others view the use of feed-in tariffs more positively, arguing that market avoiding schemes create a space for technological improvement in which possibilities for reducing production costs can be explored. They contrast this with the risk that schemes which expose subsidy recipients to market pressures may deter investment

---

[10] ibid, 3–8.
[11] Leah Stokes, 'The Politics of Renewable Energy Policies: The Case of Feed-in Tariffs in Ontario, Canada' (2013) 56 *Energy Policy* 490.
[12] Commission, SWD (2013) 439 (n 5), 5 and 7–9; Doerte Fouquet and Thomas Johansson, 'European Renewable Energy Policy at Crossroads – Focus on Electricity Support Mechanisms' (2008) 36 *Energy Policy* 4079; Sirja-Leena Penttinen, 'The First Examples of Designing the National Renewable Energy Support Schemes under the Revised EU State Aid Guidelines' (2016) 37 *European Competition Law Review* 77.
[13] ibid.

or mean that this is only available at higher rates of interest than those available for plant supported by feed-in tariffs, thereby leading to higher cost renewable energy for consumers.[14] It has also been argued (with some support from analysis of past technological change) that the drive for increasing profit which is intrinsic to corporate behaviour in capitalist economies should motivate a search for increasing efficiency by renewable generators in order to maximise financial gain whilst benefiting from a feed-in tariff.[15]

The main purpose of operating support schemes is to enable access to finance for renewable energy projects in circumstances where investors would otherwise not be willing to invest by addressing investors' perception of risk.[16] Common sources of investor risk perception include:

- *Price risk* – that revenue received from renewable energy production will not cover project costs.
- *Route to market risk* – that a buyer will not be found for energy produced by the generating plant. Generators benefitting from subsidies which expose them to market pressures such as premiums and certificate sales under certificate/obligation schemes will only receive the subsidy if they can find a buyer for the electricity in the first place.
- *Volume risk* – that the volume of energy production will not be sufficient to cover development costs OR, with regard to intermittent electricity in particular, that financial penalties will be levied where actual output falls short of volumes which the generator has already committed to place on the market (balancing risk).[17]
- *Allocation risk* – when tenders/auctions are used to distribute support, that the funding needed for a project will not be obtained. Allocation risk is particularly likely to deter investment where costs must be incurred up front before a tender or auction bid can be submitted (eg, for undertaking environmental impact assessment, obtaining planning permission, making a grid connection).

A. Feed-in Tariffs[18]

Common features: Under FIT schemes, an actor specified by law (typically a system operator or supplier) has a legal obligation to purchase all energy produced by specified types of renewable generating plant at a fixed price and for a fixed period of

---

[14] Hogg and O' Regan (n 4), 39–42; Fouquet and Johansson (n 12), 4084–85. Volkmar Lauber, 'The European Experience with Renewable Energy Support Schemes and Their Adoption: Potential Lessons for Other Countries' (2011) 2 *Renewable Energy Law and Policy* 120, 126–32.

[15] Aviel Verbruggen and Volkmar Lauber, 'Basic Concepts for Designing Renewable Electricity Support Aiming at a Full-scale Transition by 2050' (2009) 37 *Energy Policy* 5372, 5378–39; Lauber (n 14) 129–30.

[16] Hogg and O'Regan (n 4), 33–34 and 39–44.

[17] Corinna Klessmann, Christian Nabe and Karsten Burges, 'Pros and Cons of Exposing Renewables to Electricity Market Risks – A Comparison of the Market Integration Approaches in Germany, Spain, and the UK' (2008) 36 *Energy Policy* 3646.

[18] This section draws on discussion of the feed-in tariff scheme type in published work including Klessmann et al (n 17); Fouquet and Johansson (n 12); Verbruggen and Lauber (n 15); Hogg and O'Regan

time, the price and period also being specified in the law. For example, see Germany's Act on Granting Priority to Renewable Energy Sources 2000 (EEG) under which the system operators were required to pay fixed rates for electricity from renewable sources, typically over a 20-year period.[19] The electricity purchased was sold by them on the market and costs shared amongst Germany's transmission system operators and eventually passed on to consumers. This FIT scheme came to an end in August 2014 for most generating plant over 500kw despite enormous success with supporting the growth of renewable electricity production due to public and political concerns of the type mentioned below.[20]

Benefits: They provide stable long-term support for renewable energy development and therefore generate investor confidence. For these reasons, they are particularly effective for securing investment in new technologies. The tariff rate and time period for payment must be set correctly to achieve these effects. Degression, a term meaning the reduction of rates available to new claimants annually to reflect declining development costs, reduces risk of overpayment. FITs arguably stimulate innovation through developers being given a space within which to pursue efficiency gains. Some argue that the guaranteed receipt of a set amount for a set time discourages efficiency enhancement, but others counter that, for most businesses, the profit motivation will drive efficiency gains in order both to improve margins between the cost of energy production and feed-in tariff rates and to ensure that they are maintained once the period of support ends.[21]

Concerns (raised by the European Commission and others) include that: they may result in higher energy prices due to the absence of a stimulus to innovate and cut prices that exposure to the market provides; that they have a significantly distorting effect on the functioning of energy markets; the potential of windfall profits for renewable energy producers if tariff rates are set too high or production costs drop unexpectedly; and that higher costs and windfall profits may lead to public opposition not only to feed-in tariff schemes, but in general to legal interventions in favour of renewables leading to higher energy prices.[22] In addition, the fact that FIT payments are received irrespective of demand means that producers can be unresponsive to market conditions.[23] As a result, market prices have sometimes been negative on very

---

(n 4); Toby Couture and Yves Gagnon, 'An Analysis of Feed-in Tariff Remuneration Models: Implications for Renewable Energy Investment' (2010) 38 *Energy Policy* 955; Lauber (n 14); Hart and Marcellino (n 3); Stokes (n 11); Commission, SWD (2013) 439 (n 5); Olivia Woolley, 'Replacing Fossil Fuel Generation with Renewable Electricity: is Market Integration or Market Circumvention the Way Forward' in Raphael Heffron and Gavin Little (eds) *Delivering Energy Law and Policy in the EU and US: A Reader* (Edinburgh University Press 2016) 179; Marcella Nicolini and Massimo Tavoni, 'Are Renewable Energy Subsidies Effective? Evidence from Europe' (2017) 74 *Renewable and Sustainable Energy Reviews* 412, 413–14; and Yuliya Karneyeva and Rolf Wüstenhagen, 'Solar Feed-in tariffs in a Post-grid Parity World: The Role of Risk, Investor Diversity and Business Models' (2017) 106 *Energy Policy* 445, 446–47.

[19] Hart and Marcellino (n 3), 201–03.

[20] Henning Thomas, 'Transforming the German Feed-in-tariff System: Legal Aspects from a Regional Perspective' in Marjan Peeters and Thomas Schomerus (eds) *Renewable Energy in the EU* (Edward Elgar 2014) 75.

[21] See nn 12–15 above.

[22] Stokes (n 11); Penttinen (n 12).

[23] Commission, SWD (2013) 439 final (n 5) 9.

windy days during which demand is low. Note that the claim that FITs lead to higher energy prices is open to debate. Evidence suggests that they may offer a cheaper means of attracting investment than schemes giving market exposure to generators because investors are willing to provide funds at lower rates of return due to the steady guaranteed revenue.[24]

B. Feed-in Premiums[25]

Common features: The premium scheme type offers a potential alternative to FIT and certificate/obligation schemes for supporting renewable energy development using technologies which are ready for commercial deployment, but which have not yet achieved cost competitiveness with fossil fuel energy. Electricity from generating plant supported under such schemes is sold into markets, but the risks associated with exposure to price volatility are tempered by the payment of a premium (typically by the operators of transmission systems or by electricity suppliers) for each unit of sold electricity. The payment may be fixed at a specified level or may be a 'floating' amount that falls as electricity and carbon prices increase. Such scheme types may require subsidy recipients to pay monies received by them for each unit of electricity that exceeds the prescribed amount to the subsidy provider. The aim is to avoid situations where receiving electricity revenues and a premium would lead to a much higher recovery than is necessary for a generator to cover development costs because of a high market price. See Section IVB below for discussion of such a requirement under the UK's Contracts for Difference scheme. Repayment requirements may be included in a scheme design to address public concerns over 'windfall profits' for subsidy recipients but may make the premium scheme type less of a stimulus for renewable energy development by established generating companies than the certificate/obligation scheme type for reasons discussed in the following section.

Premium schemes are likely to become the dominant scheme type in the European Union due to strong support from the European Commission. Its guidelines on state aid in the field of energy and the environment for the period 2014 to 2020 advised that aid should be granted as a premium in addition to the market price from 1 January 2016 save for low-capacity/small-scale developments that may continue to receive FITs.[26] The 2018 RES Directive confirms the guidance by requiring that Member States, when using direct price support schemes to support electricity from renewable sources other than small-scale and demonstration installations, should do so in the form of a market premium (Art 4(3)).

---

[24] See sources at n 15 above.

[25] This section draws on discussion of the premium scheme type in published work including Klessmann et al (n 17), Couture and Gagnon (n 18) 960–64, Commission SWD (2013) 439 final (n 5) 8–9, Erik Gawel and Alexandra Purkus, 'Promoting the Market and System Integration of Renewable Energies through Premium Schemes – A Case Study of the German Market Premium' (2013) 61 *Energy Policy* 599 and Woolley (n 18).

[26] Commission, 'Guidelines on State Aid for Environmental Protection and Energy 2014–2020', 2014/C 200/01, 25, para 125.

Benefits: The scheme type provides a happy medium between feed-in tariff schemes and certificate/obligation schemes with regard to price risk. In contrast to FIT schemes, the premium scheme type combines the market exposure, which some argue is needed to drive renewable energy producers to improve efficiency with a lower level of price risk than under the certificate/obligation scheme type because they offer a steadier revenue stream for energy which has found a buyer.[27]

Concerns: That the scheme type leaves risks intact or only partially addressed which may deter investment, particularly by smaller generators and for newer technologies. Route to market risk and related price risk are present as premiums are only paid for electricity sold in markets.[28] Indeed this risk may be higher than under certificate/obligation schemes as renewable energy production is not dragged upwards by an obligation to include a specified amount of energy from renewable sources in their supplies. See the case study on the UK's contracts for difference scheme at section IVC below under which a legal response, a mandatory buyer of last support, was introduced to address concerns that producers with CFDs would not be able to benefit from them if a market for their electricity was not found. In addition, some price risk remains for smaller-scale generators who do not sell electricity in markets themselves, but do so through wholesalers who take on risks of market operation on behalf of generators in return for purchasing electricity at discounted prices.[29]

C. Obligation/Certificate Schemes[30]

Common features: Some states have enacted laws which oblige electricity sector actors (usually suppliers, but sometimes also producers and consumers) to include a specified proportion of electricity from renewable sources in their overall production, supply or consumption.[31] Compliance with the obligation is demonstrated by the provision of certificates. These are issued to renewable electricity producers who may sell them either together with or separately from electricity to obligated actors. The idea behind such schemes is that the receipt of two separate revenue streams should enable developers of renewable electricity installations to recover monies invested in them. This type of scheme is also widely used in connection with energy for transportation with suppliers of fuel being obliged to include a proportion of energy from renewable sources in their supplies.[32] Obligation schemes can be technology neutral or can give differing levels of support for different technologies (a practice known as banding). This is generally done by providing that well-established technologies such as onshore wind will receive

---

[27] See discussion of the debate over the merits of market exposure above.
[28] Gawel and Purkus (n 25) 607–08.
[29] ibid, 607; Klessmann et al (n 17), 3652 and 3656; Lauber (n 14) 130–31.
[30] This section draws on discussion of the certificate/obligation or renewable portfolio standards scheme types in published work including Fouquet and Johansson (n 12); Verbruggen and Lauber (n 15) 5739–41; Hogg and O'Regan (n 4) 42–44; Lauber (n 14); Commission, SWD (2013) 439 final (n 5), 10–11; Woolley (n 18); and Nicolini and Tavoni (n 18), 413–14.
[31] Commission, SWD (2013) 439 final (n 5), 10–11 and 25.
[32] Commission, SEC (2011) 131 final (n 5), 6 and 10.

fewer certificates for each unit of energy produced than newer technologies such as wave and tidal energy that require stronger initial support to become established.

Claimed benefits: The scheme type combines (potentially generous) support for renewable energy with market exposure, thereby reducing price risk whilst encouraging renewable energy producers to innovate and drop prices (in theory) with corresponding benefits for consumers. The obligation acts as a driver in general for renewable energy development although this may tend to favour better established lower cost technologies and larger-scale projects (with resulting economies of scale) unless banding or some similar intervention is made to promote newer technologies.[33] The reason for this is that chances of deriving a profit through the two revenue streams increase as the initial development costs decrease. As the case study of the UK's Renewables Obligation at section IVB below reveals, this scheme type has tended to attract investment in the renewables sector from well-resourced incumbent energy companies who are willing and able to accept risks of occasional loss in view of the potential for significant profits through selling certificates when market prices are high.[34]

Concerns: Both revenue streams (energy prices and certificate sales) are highly variable. This double exposure to markets creates significant investment risk for developers that monies expended on a project and an attractive profit margin will not be recouped.[35] As noted above, the scheme type may work better for incumbents who are more able because of existing asset bases and revenue streams to take a financial hit than new market entrants. It also tends to encourage investment in the cheapest well-established renewables. There is also some evidence to suggest that costs of investment and therefore of energy can be higher for projects supported by certificate/obligation schemes due to higher interest charges for monies loaned because of the greater exposure to price risk.[36]

D. Allocating Support through Tenders/Auctions

Governments often choose to make renewable energy support available through competitive processes. Developers are invited to submit tenders or bids in auctions stating the price that they would like to receive for energy produced by the supported plant. The government will then choose those which meet competition conditions. Typically, the preference will be for the lowest-priced bids because they place the least financial burden on the public purse and/or on consumers. Allocating subsidies through competitive processes is seen as a means of driving down the cost of renewable energy production in addition to greater market exposure.[37] They can also be used to channel revenues to large projects and preferred technologies.

Competitive allocation has its uses, but can also add to a perception of renewable energy projects as risky by investors where a project's viability depends on securing a

---

[33] Lauber (n 14), 126–31.
[34] ibid, 130–31.
[35] ibid, 126–31.
[36] Commission, SWD (2013) 439 final (n 5), 10–11.
[37] ibid, 6–7.

subsidy (see the reference to allocation risk above).[38] Tenders and auctions can also introduce risks of lost development costs where, as is often the case, a project needs to be reasonably well-advanced (having obtained its licence, undergone an environmental impact assessment) before a subsidy can be applied for.[39] These additional sources of risk add to those already present for subsidies with market exposure. See the case study on the UK's Contracts for Difference scheme below for an illustration of the additional investment risks associated with subsidies made available through competitive allocation.

The use of auctions to distribute renewable energy funds will come under close scrutiny in the EU during the remainder of this decade and the start of next. This is because the EU's State Aid guidelines for energy and the environment requires that subsidies for generating plant of 1MW or over (6MW or 3 units for onshore wind) should be made available through competitive processes under all new schemes submitted for State Aid approval from the start of 2017.[40] The 2018 RES Directive reinforces this guidance by obliging Member States to ensure that support for electricity is granted 'in an open, transparent, competitive, non-discriminatory, and cost-effective manner' save where dealing with small-scale installations and demonstration projects.[41]

E. Regulatory Risk

In addition to the risk factors examined at Section III above, potential developers and investors in the renewables sector will also consider regulatory risk when assessing whether a subsidy gives them sufficient confidence in the prospects of profiting from their initial outlay to proceed with their plans. Regulatory risk covers the possibility that governments may subsequently alter the terms on which support is provided after the investment has been made.[42] Regulatory risks often arise in connection with developing countries whose investment environments may be perceived in general as uncertain from political, legal and macro-economic perspectives.[43] However, there have also been several well-known instances of subsidy scheme alteration after an award has been made or investment in a sector committed in developed countries.[44]

---

[38] David Toke, 'Renewable Energy Auctions: How Good are They?' (2015) 8 *International Journal of Sustainable Energy Management and Planning*, 43–56.
[39] Natalie Kozlov, 'Contracts for Difference: Risks Faced by Generators under the New Renewable Support Scheme in the UK' (2014) 7 *Journal of World Energy Law and Business*, 282, 283–84.
[40] Commission, State Aid Guidelines (n 26) para 126.
[41] Directive (EU) 2018/2001 of the European Parliament and of the Council of 11 December 2018 on the promotion of the use of energy from renewable sources [2018] OJ L 328/82 (the 2018 RES Directive), art 4(4).
[42] Anatole Boute, 'Regulatory Stability and Renewable Energy Investment: The Case of Kazakhstan' (2020) 121 *Renewable and Sustainable Energy Reviews* 109673, 1–2; UNEP Finance Initiative, *Financing renewable energy in developing countries: Drivers and Barriers for Private Finance in sub-Saharan Africa* (UNEP February 2012) Financing_Renewable_Energy_in_subSaharan_Africa.pdf (unepfi.org) (accessed 5 October 2022), 44–45.
[43] UNEP Finance Initiative (n 42), 44–45.
[44] Daniel Behn and Ole Kristian Fauchald, 'Governments under Cross-fire? Renewable Energy and International Economic Tribunals' (2015) 12 *Manchester Journal of International Economic Law* 117, 119–27.

Legal design flaws in subsidies such as setting significantly more generous rates for renewable energy technologies than they require to cover development costs and success with attracting investment far exceeding expectations have left developed states facing scheme funding problems and with fears that public discontent may necessitate a subsidy's reduction or withdrawal for schemes under which costs are passed on to consumers. For example, rates paid and the duration of support under Spain's feed-in tariff scheme for solar energy had to be reduced for subsidies already awarded in 2010 due to growth in renewable investment at a scale and rate far exceeding the electricity system's ability to absorb new generating capacity.[45] One reason for this was the limited capacity of distribution system operators to pass on scheme costs to consumers leading to a huge deficit in payment for electricity provided by generators. Sudden change in the terms on which subsidies are offered can also affect renewable energy growth by reducing workload and revenues for businesses established in the expectation of long-term government support for a renewable energy sub-sector at previously stated levels. For example, a sudden reduction in the feed-in tariff rates offered for solar panels by the UK government was reported to have harmed the nascent development of a skilled supply chain for providing and installing this renewable technology in the UK.[46]

Concerns for funders over the reliability of support offered by governments can lead them to increase interest rates charged on capital loaned substantially.[47] Confidence amongst investors in the predictability of government support can therefore make a significant difference for the financial viability of renewables and for growth in their use. Law is used in a number of ways to create the investor confidence in support stability required for monies to be loaned at more affordable rates. First, laws can make it more difficult for the government concerned to change its position including by imposing penalties for doing so. EU law promotes confidence in support schemes offered by its Member States by obliging them to publish long-term schedules stating expected support over a five-year period including timing, frequency of tendering and expected capacity, budgetary or technological limits on funding availability.[48] The effectiveness of support schemes and their distributional effects on different consumer groups must be assessed every five years with the results of the assessment being taken into account in subsequent scheme revisions.[49] A Member State which was to revise 'the level of, and the conditions attached to, the support granted to renewable energy projects ... in a way that negatively affects the rights conferred thereunder and undermines the economic viability of projects that already benefit from support' would be in breach of EU law and exposed to the prospect of Commission-initiated proceedings potentially leading to a fine.[50] Legally binding national targets for increasing the proportion

---

[45] Behn and Fauchald (n 44) 120–23.

[46] Fiona Harvey, 'Solar Companies to sue UK Government for £140M over feed-in tariff cuts' (Guardian newspaper, 23 January 2013) Solar companies to sue UK government for £140m over feed-in tariff cuts | Solar power | The Guardian (accessed 4 October 2022).

[47] Corinna Klessmann and others, 'Policy Options for Reducing the Costs of Reaching the European Renewables Target' (2013) 57 *Renewable Energy* 390, 394–95.

[48] 2018 RES Directive (n 41) art 6(3).

[49] ibid, art 6(4).

[50] ibid, art 6(1).

of energy from renewable sources in energy supplies also assist with creating confidence in the likely continuity of support for renewable energy although, as examined in Chapter 4, their ability to have this effect depends on the strength of the supporting legal regimes for securing compliance with them.[51]

In addition, states enter investment treaties to give confidence to nationals from participating states that the terms on which investments are made in host states will not be changed arbitrarily.[52] A main purpose for developing and developed states to conclude investment treaties is to leverage investment which would not otherwise be made due to a lack of confidence in the host state's investment environment. The Energy Charter Treaty's provisions on investment were also intended to perform that function by giving nationals of developed west European states the confidence to conduct and finance development in energy rich states previously forming part of the Soviet Union.[53] Many of the cases heard under the Energy Charter Treaty's dispute resolution mechanism have involved claims that states have failed to provide fair and equitable treatment to investors by other parties due to ex-post alteration of support offered for renewable energy.[54]

Second, problems experienced with feed-in tariffs necessitating change have often been due to subsidies being made available in law to any actor falling under the relevant law's definition of persons entitled to support. The need for *ex post* intervention can be reduced by better defining and placing limits on the available support in law. See Boute's discussion of reducing regulatory risks associated with subsidies by limiting quantities of supported output, providing finite budgets or setting maximum electricity volumes for competitive allocations and restricting scheme access to generators in defined locations where connecting new power plants does not necessitate major network upgrade works.[55] Including provisions that allow change in the terms on which subsidies are provided when this is justified by a change in circumstances since the scheme was introduced can also be used to avoid the rigidity that makes disruptive change unavoidable. In this regard the EU's 2018 RES Directive allows Member States to 'adjust the level of support in accordance with objective criteria, provided that such criteria are established in the original design of the support scheme'.[56]

IV. Case Studies: Providing Operating Support for Renewable Energy

The following case studies of the three operating support scheme types discussed above and used by Germany (Feed-in tariff) and the United Kingdom (Certificate/

---

[51] Chapter 4, Section IV.
[52] Anatole Boute, 'Combating Climate Change through Investment Arbitration' (2012) 35 *Fordham International Law Journal* 613.
[53] Energy Charter Treaty (adopted on 17 December 1994, entered into force on 16 April 1998) 2080 UNTS 95.
[54] Boute (n 42) 2–4.
[55] ibid, 3–4.
[56] 2018 RES Directive (n 41) art 6(2).

Obligation, Premium and Competitive Allocation) illustrate how risks associated with them have arisen in practice.

A. Feed-in Tariff, Premium Schemes and Competitive Allocation (Germany)[57]

Germany's experience with supporting renewable electricity under the EEG 2000 provides a good case study of the feed-in tariff and premium scheme types and of competitive allocation of subsidies. It shows that feed-in tariffs can be very effective for attracting investment in renewables, but that their use and success can give rise to concerns, particularly over the costs that financing feed-in tariffs can give rise to pressure for subsidy reform. It also illustrates the discomfort that policymakers who subscribe to the economic theory that undistorted market competition offers the best route to cheaper and more secure energy may feel with using subsidies and other market-interfering methods to promote renewable energy growth. Their antipathy to market intrusion manifests in policy goals, whilst accepting subsidies as a necessary evil for establishing renewable energy capacities in the near term, to lessen and eventually eliminate that intrusion over time.

Germany made available a classic feed-in tariff scheme between 2000 and 2014 under the often-reformed EEG 2000.[58] The scheme guaranteed the purchase of electricity produced by renewable energy technologies specified in law at governmentally set fixed prices for a duration of 20 years. Germany's transmission system operators were obligated to pay the subsidies. They recouped monies paid through a combination of selling the electricity purchased from renewable generators in markets and including unrecouped costs in a surcharge borne by consumers.[59] The system operators were also obligated to guarantee access to networks for renewable generators and to give priority access to renewable electricity over power from other sources.[60]

The investor confidence produced by mandatory purchase and guaranteed returns for a guaranteed period drove significant growth in renewable electricity in Germany. This increased from 6.2 per cent of electricity supplies in 2000 to 25.8 per cent in 2014.[61] However, the scheme's popularity led to significant growth in the cost of financing its operation for system operators and therefore for the public and for its industries.[62] Resulting concerns over support for renewable energy and its economic effects led to

---

[57] The case study draws from academic comment on electricity subsidy schemes used in Germany since 2000 including Klessmann et al (n 17), Lauber (n 14), Hart and Marcellino (n 3), Gawel and Purkus (n 25), Thomas (n 20), Matthias Lang and Annette Lang, 'The 2014 German Renewable Energy Sources Act Revision – From Feed-in Tariffs to Direct Marketing to Competitive Bidding' (2015) 33 *Journal of Energy and Natural Resources Law* 131; Penttinen (n 12); Merethe Leiren and Inken Reimer, 'Historical Institutionalist Perspective on the shift from Feed-In Tariffs towards Auctioning in German Renewable Energy Policy', (2018) 43 *Energy Research and Social Science* 33; and Johannes Saurer and Jonas Monast, 'Renewable Energy Federalism in Germany and the US' (2021) 10 *Transnational Environmental Law* 293.

[58] Gesetz für den Vorrang Erneuerbarer Energien, Federal Law Gazette 2000, part I, 305.

[59] Klessmann et al (n 17) 3650; Saurer and Monast (n 57) 300; Leiren and Reimer (n 57) 35.

[60] ibid. See also Chapter 6, section IVA.

[61] Lang and Lang (n 57).

[62] Thomas (n 20) 76–78; Lang and Lang (n 57) 131–33; Saurer and Monast (n 57) 300; Leiren and Reimer (n 57) 35–37.

calls for the EEG's reform. Exemptions were granted from the surcharge for Germany's energy-intensive industries because of fears that their economic competitiveness with equivalent industries in states not subject to a similar surcharge would suffer.[63] This domestic political pressure coincided with increasing opposition from the European Commission to the use of subsidy schemes that removed renewable energy generators from market exposure on grounds including distortion of electricity market competition, obstruction from national policy and legal interventions of Europe-wide energy markets' emergence, concerns that technologies removed from market exposure would not undergo competition-driven production efficiencies in order to maximise profit and, in connection with this, that feed-in tariffs were causing higher electricity prices than would be the case under subsidies paid in addition to revenue from electricity sold in markets as a premium.[64] In addition, competition-related questions arose over whether the exemption for energy-intensive businesses was unlawful under EU law on state aid.[65] Its guidelines on state aid in the fields of energy and the environment for 2014–2020 advised that, save for small-scale developments, FIT schemes should be replaced as they came up for renewal of state aid approval, by schemes under which support was provided on top of electricity sold in markets (whether through premiums or certificates).[66]

These influences have driven three stages of evolution in German support for renewable electricity.[67] First, the addition of a voluntary option for subsidy recipients to choose premium payments on top of directly marketed electricity rather than a feed-in tariff. Second, the direct marketing premium scheme replaced the feed-in tariff as the sole source of support in 2014 except for small renewable projects which remain eligible for the feed-in tariff.[68] Under this scheme, project operators are paid a sum by the relevant transmission system operator on top of each unit of electricity sold in markets. This is the difference between a specified level and an average monthly market price, the idea being that overall revenues will be consistently close to those required for the project concerned to cover costs and make a profit.[69] Third, premiums are now made available through auctions under which developers submit bids stating the specific revenue level by reference to which premiums will be calculated, with lowest bidders succeeding in obtaining support which is now limited by the German government to maximum amounts for particular technologies.[70]

(i) Case Study Summary

The switch from a subsidy type with very low risks of non-recovery for investors to one in which price risk is low, but other types of risk of non-cost recovery

---

[63] Saurer and Monast (n 57) 301; Leiren and Reimer (n 57) 36.
[64] See section IIIB above. See also Saurer and Monast (n 57) 301–02, Leiren and Reimer (n 57) 37–38.
[65] Saurer and Monast (n 57) 301; and Leiren and Reimer (n 57) 37–38.
[66] Commission, State Aid Guidelines (n 26).
[67] Thomas (n 20); Lang and Lang (n 57); Penttinen (n 12) 81; Saurer and Monast (n 57) 301–03; Leiren and Reimer (n 57) 36–38.
[68] See Lang and Lang (n 57) 137 for details of projects still eligible for the feed-in tariff.
[69] Gawel and Purkus (n 25) 600–02.
[70] Lang and Lang (n 57) 137–39.

114 SUBSIDIES FOR RENEWABLE ENERGY

(eg, route-to-market risk) are present will inevitably affect investor confidence in the renewables sector. The introduction of further investment risks associated with the auction of subsidies from deliberately limited budgets such as non-availability of support and incurring advance development costs without certainty of support will have a further impact. Indeed, the auction process seems designed to dampen growth in renewable electricity partly to address difficulties posed by this for the functioning of the wider electricity system and partly to address the cost concerns mentioned above.[71] Germany's experience therefore illustrates problems that very effective support for renewable energy may engender in terms of system functionality and public acceptability. However, questions arise over whether the responses adopted will maintain the growth in renewable energy required to achieve a rapid decarbonisation of Germany's electricity sector. The increase in renewable energy production continued to grow, reaching nearly 40 per cent by 2018,[72] but more of this growth is likely to have come from investment by utilities which are better able to bear the transaction costs and risks of auction processes than from smaller businesses and community-level investment. A consequence of this is that the acceptance of renewable energy development that investment by non-traditional actors associated with localities engendered may diminish as major commercial developers without a community connection take their place.[73]

One lesson from this account must be that strategies for renewable energy support which aspire to the full decarbonisation needed for combatting climate change must consider challenges associated with systemic ability and public willingness to accept the switch to a different and potentially higher cost system in policy and legal design from the outset. The problem here may lie as much with political failures to explain both the short-term and long-term costs and benefits of shifting away from fossil fuel energy to renewable energy and the relative merits of removing and exposing renewables from market competition as with the legal design of Germany's FIT schemes.

B. Renewables Obligation Order (ROO) (Certificate/Obligation Scheme, UK)[74]

The ROO was introduced in 2002 and frequently amended subsequently.[75] It was withdrawn in 2017 on its complete replacement by the Contracts for Difference scheme examined in Section IVC. It required licensed UK electricity suppliers to source a specified proportion of electricity they provided to customers from eligible renewable sources. Suppliers discharged the obligation by obtaining certificates of

---

[71] ibid, 133; Penttinen (n 12) 81.
[72] Saurer and Monast (n 57) 302.
[73] Leiren and Reimer (n 57) 37–38.
[74] The case study draws from critical analysis of the Renewables Obligation presented in Geoffrey Wood and Stephen Dow, 'What Lessons Have Been Learned in Reforming the Renewables Obligation? An Analysis of Internal and External Failures in UK Renewable Energy Policy' (2011) 39 *Energy Policy* 2228 and in Bridget Woodman and Catherine Mitchell, 'Learning from Experience? The Development of the Renewables Obligation in England and Wales 2002–2010' (2011) 39 *Energy Policy* 3914.
[75] The Renewables Obligation Order 2002 (SI 2002/914).

renewable electricity production directly from producers or indirectly through a certificate market. Producers received monies from certificate sales in addition to the price obtained for electricity supplied. Suppliers who failed to supply enough certificates to cover their obligation were required to pay a 'buy-out' price to Ofgem at the year end. The resulting buy-out fund was then redistributed amongst electricity suppliers each year with the size of shares being determined by their relative success in meeting the obligation.[76]

Two problems were experienced with the scheme during its early years, both of which this scheme type is prone to in general. The first was that the level of the obligation was set too low with the result that it was met before the year end and that the price of certificates was lowered because of a lack of scarcity. This problem was addressed by amending the mechanism by which the level of obligation was recalculated each year to ensure that it exceeded anticipated renewable electricity production (also known as creating 'headroom'), thereby preventing certificate prices from crashing.[77]

Second, the scheme was effective for attracting investment in the lowest-cost technologies for producing electricity such as onshore wind because they offered greatest potential of making a significant profit from the scheme but was ineffective for attracting investment in less developed technologies producing electricity at higher costs due to less experience with their use. This has been addressed by 'banding', a practice under which less developed technologies are given more certificates for each unit of electricity produced in recognition of the higher level of financial support they need to attract investment.[78] Under agreed banding levels for the period 2013 to 2017, 0.9 of a certificate was awarded for each MWh of onshore wind increasing to 2 ROCs (declining to 1.8 in 2016–17) for each MWh of offshore wind and 3 ROCs for each MWh generated from tidal stream and wave power.[79]

The RO was closed to new generating plant from 2017 on its replacement by the Contracts for Difference scheme. Rights to receive ROCs accrued to the date of closure have been grandfathered (ie, developments already accredited under the RO will continue to receive support under the scheme for however many years remain of the 20-year term for which this is provided). Generators were able to choose between ROs and CFDs from 2014 to 2017. The Government seeks to maintain confidence in the scheme by confirming that the current arrangements, driven by 'headroom', will continue until 2027 and that it will buy certificates itself at a fixed price from 2027 to 2037 when the scheme ends.[80]

---

[76] Woodman and Mitchell (n 74) 3915.
[77] ibid, 3916–19.
[78] ibid, 3919.
[79] Department for Business, Energy and Industrial Strategy and Ofgem, Renewables Obligation banding levels 2013–17', Calculating Renewable Obligation Certificates (ROCs) – GOV.UK (www.gov.uk) (accessed 4 October 2022).
[80] Ofgem, *Renewables Obligation: Guidance for Generators that receive support or would like to receive support under the Renewables Obligation (RO) scheme* (Guidance document, April 2019) www.ofgem.gov.uk/system/files/docs/2018/09/renewables_obligation_guidance_for_generators_september_2018_0.pdf (accessed 4 October 2022).

116 SUBSIDIES FOR RENEWABLE ENERGY

Notwithstanding the improvements mentioned above, the Renewables Obligation was criticised by academic commentators on grounds that it had not reduced risks for investors sufficiently to secure growth rates in renewable energy enabling the Government to meet its commitments on renewable energy consumption.[81] The introduction of 'headroom' stabilised certificate prices whilst banding strengthened the position of newer technologies. However, two fundamental risks remained throughout: the lack of a guaranteed route to market for energy sales and the lack of certainty both over market prices and prices for certificates. As a result, the scheme continued to benefit energy from cheaper established renewables (particularly onshore wind) even after banding and from large-scale developments that benefit from economies of scale. It also favoured established large power companies able to take risks that expenditure would not be recovered, proving weak in contrast for attracting market entry by new developers. The articles referred to above compare the scheme unfavourably with the Feed-in Tariff scheme type for promoting increases in renewable energy production, particularly from new technology developments conducted by non-incumbent electricity producers.

(i) Case Study Summary

The UK's experience with the Renewables Obligation highlights difficulties which can arise for attracting investment in renewable energy when support schemes still leave developers significantly exposed to the risk that revenues from generation and from the subsidy may not be sufficient to cover development costs. This is particularly the case for new market entrants, for smaller generation projects and for those using less-well-established technologies, all of which are less well able than incumbent generating companies with substantial existing asset bases and revenue streams to take on risks of loss-making development on the off-chance of making large profits if market and certificate prices are both high.

The experience also illustrates both the need for careful legal design of support schemes to ensure that they are capable of attracting support for the renewables sector in circumstances when this may not otherwise be forthcoming; and how legal reform can be used to address weaknesses in a scheme. We have seen that the initial Renewables Obligation contained features, insufficient scarcity of certificates to generate investment-supporting prices throughout the year and insistence by the UK government on strict technology neutrality when the scheme was introduced, which undermined its effectiveness for attracting financial support. Legal reforms in the shape of headroom and banding improved the scheme's appeal for investment, particularly in new technologies and projects by new market entrants. It is to be regretted that valuable experience with supporting renewable energy in the UK gained from years of trial and error with the RO were completely abandoned in favour of the Contracts for Difference scheme, a new and much more complex set of arrangements for allocating support.

---

[81] Wood and Dow (n 74); Woodman and Mitchell (n 74).

C. Contracts for Difference (CFD) Scheme (Premium Scheme by Auction, UK)[82]

The CFD scheme ran in parallel with the Renewables Obligation until 2017. It has been the sole support scheme available for new renewable energy generators in the UK (above 5MW) since April 2017. The legal foundation for the scheme is contained in the Energy Act 2013, but with much of the detail having been provided in following regulations. To date, four funding rounds have taken place under the scheme: in 2015, 2017, 2019 and 2022. The fifth round is due to be held in 2023.

(i) Competitive Allocation

Under the initial scheme design, it was envisaged that renewable energy developers would apply for support from three funding pots:

- *Established technologies* such as onshore wind, solar (funding for this pot was only made available in CFD allocation round one and in round four, but with eligibility limited to projects of 5MW maximum capacity and below);
- *'Less established' technologies* such as offshore wind, wave and tidal. A minimum amount of the budget was ring-fenced for wave and tidal energy only in CFD allocation round one. The UK Government announced in June 2018 that remote island onshore wind would be differentiated from other onshore wind projects to allow *onshore* wind farms in the Scottish islands to seek funding from this pot because of the particular difficulties with producing and transmitting electricity from these locations.[83] Offshore wind was removed from this pot in round four, having become much better established since 2014 and was given its own funding pot in view of the UK's policy ambitions for massive offshore wind energy generation.
- *Conversions of fossil fuel generating plant to run on biomass.* No funding was provided for this pot in the early allocation rounds and it has since been abandoned.

The UK Government advised before funding round one that the budget for established technologies would be limited to ensure competition between applicants. Applicants

---

[82] The case study draws from information made available by the UK Government at 'Electricity Market Reform: Contracts for Difference' (UK Government website, last updated February 2017) www.gov.uk/government/collections/electricity-market-reform-contracts-for-difference (accessed 4 October 2022). It also draws from critical analyses of the Contracts for Difference scheme presented in Kozlov (n 39), Penttinen (n 12), Brodies, Electricity Market Reform: Comparing Contracts for Difference to the Renewables Obligation, (September 2013, briefing document produced by law firm) Microsoft Word – 18397399_5.DOC (rackcdn.com) (accessed 4 October 2022); Ross Fairley, 'All Change in Green Energy: Results of the first Contracts for Difference auction', *In-House Lawyer* (May 2015) All change in green energy: results of the first Contracts for Difference auction – The In-House Lawyer (inhouselawyer.co.uk) (accessed 4 October 2022); and Marijke Welisch and Rahmatallah Poudineh, 'Auctions for Allocation of Offshore Wind Contracts for Difference in the UK' (2020) 147 *Renewable Energy* 1266.

[83] Department of Business, Energy and Industrial Strategy, 'Contracts for Difference: Stakeholder Bulletin' (UK Government website, June 2018) CfD_stakeholder_bulletin – June_2018.pdf (publishing.service.gov.uk) (accessed 4 October 2022).

were to submit sealed bids stating the strike price that they would be willing to accept and the contracts were to be awarded by auction to the lowest bidders. All applicants for funding from the budget for 'less established' technologies would receive funding based on administrative strike prices published in December 2013 or would also be asked to submit sealed bids stating the strike price acceptable to them if applications exceeded available funding. Contracts awarded have been based solely on sealed bids because of applications exceeding the budget under all the auctions to date.

(ii) Premium Payment

Generators who are awarded a CFD enter a contract with a counterparty established by statute which is responsible for paying the premium. The scheme provides recipients of support with a premium for each unit of electricity sold by them in electricity markets. The premium amounts to the difference between a reference wholesale price (reflective of average market price levels during periods for which payments are claimed under a contract) and a 'strike price' (a figure specified in the contract for difference which is intended to reflect the cost of investing in a particular low carbon technology). The generator pays monies back to the counterparty if the reference wholesale price exceeds the strike price. The hope is that the guaranteed receipt of a long-term relatively stable price will encourage investment in renewable energy projects (contrast this stability with the full exposure to market volatility under the Renewables Obligation scheme). Licensed electricity suppliers have obligations to fund the scheme by making payments to the counterparty but, in contrast to the Renewables Obligation, they do not have obligations to include a specified proportion of renewable energy in their supply portfolios.

(iii) Sources of Investment Risk

As with other premium schemes, risk that revenue received from electricity sold in markets will not cover development costs is lower than under schemes such as the Renewables Obligation which give generators greater exposure to market volatility. However, several areas of risk remain which may combine to discourage potential investors from financing renewable energy projects where support from a Contract for Difference would be required to make the development attractive to them. Some of the possible sources of risk are listed below to add detail to the main categories of premium scheme characteristics identified in Section IIIB which may impair their effectiveness for attracting investment in the renewables sector.

- *Price risk* – This is much reduced compared to the Renewables Obligation, but some risk remains that developers will not be able to recover their costs because the market price they receive together with payments under the CFD do not cover them, particularly for generators who sell electricity to wholesalers at below the market reference price rather than selling energy themselves into markets (receiving lower prices because the wholesaler bears the market risk).
- *Route to market risk (1)* – In contrast to the Renewables Obligation, there is no legal obligation on suppliers to supply a proportion of renewable energy. Much will

therefore depend, for actual volumes of renewable energy generation supported by CFDs, on whether strike prices set under the CFDs enable renewable generators both to sell energy into the market at competitive prices and to cover their costs, thereby encouraging investment in renewable generation.

- *Route to market risk (2)* – The ability of generators to benefit from CFD support depends on their ability to find a sale for their electricity. However, concerns arose when the scheme was being designed that generators (particularly those with small-scale plant using new technology) with CFDs would not be able to benefit from them because they were unable to conclude power purchase agreements with suppliers. To address this concern, the UK Government proposed that 'offtakers of last resort' should be appointed who would be obliged to take uncontracted power produced by a CFD holder, albeit at a discount to the market reference price to ensure that this would be seen as a 'last resort'.[84]

- *Allocation risk (1)* – As noted at IVC(i) above, there is no guarantee that renewable generators will receive support under the scheme. Willingness to invest may be impaired by the lack of firm knowledge about strike prices (and therefore about prospects of recovering development costs) until auctions have been held. Evidence from the first CFD auction suggests that the auction process, coupled with limited budgets, can result in a major risk of exclusion from support under the scheme, particularly for smaller generators that are less able to submit low bids because they lack the revenues/asset base to absorb a loss.[85] The fourth allocation round responded to this by limiting support in the established technologies pot to projects with capacities of 5MW and below. Investor confidence has also been affected by the infrequency of allocation rounds, the lack of a set timetable for years ahead with each round to date being arranged on a one-off basis and variation in the monies provided for funding rounds as budgets are agreed separately for each round. The unpredictability in timing and funding makes it harder for developers to plan ahead and hampers the emergence of supply chain businesses for renewable energy development and operation.[86] The UK Government plans to address these concerns in part by holding annual auctions with the fifth allocation round taking place in 2023.[87]

- *Allocation risk (2)* – Developers can only apply for a CFD when development proposals are well-advanced (ie, planning permission has been obtained and grid connection agreements made with the network operator). This may put off developers and investors as substantial costs are incurred for environmental assessment and securing grid access without a guarantee that the project will obtain a CFD. As Fairley notes, the scheme favours 'bigger developers who are generally more able to carry the cost of developing a project up to the point of planning and grid

---

[84] Ofgem, 'Offtaker of last resort' (Ofgem Website) Offtaker of Last Resort (OLR) | Ofgem (accessed 4 October 2022).
[85] Fairley (n 82).
[86] Welisch and Poudinet (n 82), 1267, 1268, 1273.
[87] UK Parliament, Statement made by Kwasi Kwarteng, Secretary of State for Business, Energy and Industrial Strategy', Statement UIN HCWS600, 9 February 2022.

[connection] in order to qualify to bid in a CFD action and live with the risk of being unsuccessful'.[88]

- *Complexity risks* – The transaction costs of such a complex arrangement are high. The CFD proposals can be compared unfavourably in this respect with the simplicity both of FIT and premium schemes and of the Renewables Obligation that was available to all renewable energy units meeting statutory definitions.
- *Repayment risk* – The fact that generators must repay monies to the counterparty when the reference price is above the strike price could affect the solvency of small producers, particularly those which are selling energy under PPAs at a sizeable markdown from market prices. The fact that renewable generators will be unable to benefit from higher yields in certain market conditions may also put off more entrepreneurial investors.
- *Cost recovery risk* – The CFDs run for 15 years rather than the 20-year support for RO projects, with the potential consequence that it will be harder for developers to recover project development costs over the shorter timescale.[89]
- *Funding availability risk* – The CFD scheme competes with other subsidies within an overall cap on the budget for funding for energy development (the levy control framework).[90] The government also negotiates individual CFDs with larger developments (eg, new nuclear, large offshore wind). CFDs such as the contract agreed in 2013 for the new nuclear power station Hinkley Point C (£92.50, double the current wholesale price of electricity) will eat into funds that could have gone to multiple smaller renewable energy projects at lower cost.

(iv) CFD Auctions

The first CFD auction was held in February 2015. 2GW of renewable electricity was supported including 750MW of onshore wind, 72MW of solar PV and 1.1GW of offshore wind. The auction used a 'pay as clear' system. This means that the strike price awarded for successful generators under the auction are raised to the highest strike price for a successful participant in the auction round for a project type for the year that the project type requests support to commence (eg, all onshore wind expected to receive support from 2018–2019 receives a strike price of £82.50). The low budget of the auction (compared to the Renewables Obligation), led to fierce competition and strike prices at lower levels than administrative strike prices. Some technology types lost out as a result with solar receiving a strike price for 2015–2016 of £50, too little in practice for the projects concerned to be constructed. Experience with the auction evidences some of the concerns mentioned above, particularly allocation risk.[91]

---

[88] Fairley (n 82).
[89] Welisch and Poudinet (n 82), 1268.
[90] Department for Business, Energy, and Industrial Strategy, 'Levy Control Framework' Levy Control Framework (LCF) – GOV.UK (www.gov.uk) (accessed 4 October 2022).
[91] For information about the first allocation round see UK Government, 'Contracts for Difference (CfD): first allocation round' (UK Government website) Contracts for Difference (CfD): first allocation round – GOV.UK (www.gov.uk) (accessed 4 October 2022).

The second auction was due to be held in October 2015 but was postponed. Amber Rudd, then the Secretary of State for Energy and Climate Change, announced in November 2015 that there would be a further auction in 2016 and one more before the end of the parliament (May 2020). No auction took place in 2016. Instead, the UK Government announced in November 2016 that a second allocation round would commence in April 2017. This round did not offer funding for technologies in the 'established' band such as onshore wind and solar PV. A total of £290 million was made available for specified technologies in the 'less established' band only. The auction was held in August 2017 and the results announced on 11 September. The auction resulted in support for three very large offshore wind farms (including the 1.4GW Hornsea 2 scheme) with offshore wind accounting for 97 per cent of supported technology. A noteworthy feature of the auction was that the strike price for offshore wind projects for 2022–2023 (57.50) was less than half the strike price for projects due to commence operation in 2017/2018 under the first auction.[92]

The third allocation round was significantly less generous than its predecessor with total funding of £65 million. Funding was limited again to less-established technologies, with the great majority of support going again to offshore wind projects.[93] In contrast, £280 million was made available for the fourth round auction in 2022 with support being provided for multiple small solar farms and onshore wind farms in Scotland as well as a number of Scottish remote island wind and tidal energy projects under the less-established funding pot. The largest share of funds again went to offshore wind with five projects totalling nearly 7GW maximum capacity receiving support. A floating offshore wind project received support for the first time under this round.[94]

(v) Case Study Summary

Analysis of the UK's CFD scheme highlights strengths and weaknesses of the premium scheme type. Such schemes tend to expose developments to lower price risk than the certificate/obligation scheme type and therefore to reduce this major source of concern for investors to an acceptable level. However, the analysis shows that the premium scheme type is not a panacea. The requirement, as with the certificate/obligation scheme, for developers to find a buyer for their electricity in order to receive the premium creates a risk that the development will not find a route to market. Again, this is particularly the case for projects using newer technologies, small-scale commercial developments and new market entrants who, in contrast to incumbent producers, may not have corporate links to supply companies.

---

[92] For information about the second allocation round see UK Government, 'Contracts for Difference (CfD): second allocation round' (UK Government website) Contracts for Difference (CfD): second allocation round – GOV.UK (www.gov.uk) (accessed 4 October 2022).
[93] For information about the third allocation round see UK Government, 'Contracts for Difference (CfD): third allocation round' (UK Government website) Contracts for Difference (CfD): Allocation Round 3 – GOV.UK (www.gov.uk) (accessed 4 October 2022).
[94] For information about the fourth allocation round see UK Government, 'Contracts for Difference (CfD): fourth allocation round' (UK Government website) Contracts for Difference (CfD) Allocation Round 4: results – GOV.UK (www.gov.uk) (accessed 4 October 2022). For further information on floating offshore wind energy see Chapter 8, section IB.

The case study also shows the importance of careful legal design for support schemes and of how law can be used to address design problems. Legal provision for a buyer of last resort addressed the route to market risk mentioned above to an extent. In contrast, a substantial residual price risk remains for smaller-scale electricity generators who sell electricity to wholesalers at a below market price rather than attempt to participate directly in markets themselves. Such developers may be left out of pocket even after receiving a premium because this is calculated as the difference between the strike price and the average market price for electricity.

With regard to subsidies allocated competitively rather than as of legal right, the case study displays some of the claimed strengths and weaknesses of such an approach for supporting renewable energy. The allocation risk of not obtaining a contract and therefore of not recouping costs incurred to be able to participate in an auction is likely to act as a deterrent for initiating projects, especially those using newer technologies which may struggle to compete in auctions with better-established bidders. The dramatic drop in strike price sought by offshore wind projects in auction round two compared to round one is due to rapidly declining production costs as the technology's efficiency and scale of deployment increase but may also be attributable to the need for bidders to be competitive in auctions by submitting bids at the lower end of the remuneration likely to be needed by them to cover development costs.

In connection with the impact of the auction design, the case study also shows that schemes may be intentionally poor for supporting certain types of renewable energy development. For example, a government's policy on support may prefer large-scale developments using better-established technologies because they are perceived to offer greater potential for economies of scale and production efficiency and therefore to be lower cost. This chapter does not look critically at such policy choices, its focus being on assisting readers with identifying where, as with the Contracts for Difference scheme, a subsidy may not be well-designed for attracting investment in projects likely to be perceived by developers as risky. Even so, it is legitimate to question whether an approach of boosting renewable energy in the short term by concentrating only on certain technologies will be effective for realising the wholesale decarbonisation of energy that will be needed during the twenty-first century if the international community's commitment to net zero greenhouse gases by 2050 is to be achieved.

Classroom Questions

1. Why can it be challenging to attract investment in renewable energy development? How can subsidies assist with attracting investment?
2. What type of subsidies are used to provide: (a) investment support; (b) operating support? When are they usually provided and for what purposes?
3. Identify the main characteristics and the strengths and weaknesses for promoting the growth of renewable energy production of the following types of operating support schemes:
   (i) Feed-in tariffs
   (ii) Obligation/certificate schemes
   (iii) Premium schemes

4. Why are subsidies sometimes made available through competitive processes (e.g. tenders/auctions)? Are there any potential downsides of competitive allocation for attracting investment in renewable energy?
5. Identify and compare the strengths and weaknesses of the three schemes reviewed in the case studies for attracting investment in renewable energy.

Scenario

Tidaltech has developed a new technology for producing electricity from tidal streams. The technology has been trialled successfully and is now ready for its first deployment in small-scale commercial projects. Tidaltech predicts that it would struggle to cover its development costs, including the costs of repaying monies borrowed from investors, through electricity sales alone. Tidaltech is therefore looking at public support made available by a number of states with significant potential for electricity production from tidal streams. Inventato, an island state, offers a guaranteed feed-in tariff payment over a 20-year term for tidal stream electricity at a level that should enable Tidaltech to cover its development costs with a small profit margin as long as it can secure investment at a low enough rate of interest to make payments affordable. Fabricado, an archipelago, offers guaranteed feed-in premium payments over a 20-year term for tidal stream technology to be paid on top of monies received for electricity sold in markets under power purchase agreements. The premium is available to all projects using tidal stream power technology as of right (ie, applicants do not have to participate in a competitive bidding process to secure support). The premium to be paid is the difference between the average weekly electricity market price and an administratively set strike price. Fabricado's administrative strike price for tidal stream is set at the same level as the price to be paid for each unit of electricity under Inventato's feed-in tariff. However, recipients of premiums under this scheme are not required to pay monies to the subsidy provider if the market price exceeds the strike price, meaning that Tidaltech could make a substantial profit when electricity market prices are high.

Tidaltech is drawn towards Fabricado's scheme because of the potential for making higher profits from developments using its new technology but is cautious about making a choice between development in Inventato and in Fabricado as it only has the resources to undertake commercial developments in one of the two jurisdictions. Advise Tidaltech on the potential benefits and disadvantages of Inventato's feed-in tariff scheme and Fabricado's feed-in premium scheme for reducing risks that it will not be able to recoup its development costs from investment in the two jurisdictions.

Suggested Reading

Articles

Zeineb Abdmouleh, Rashid Alammari and Adel Gastli, 'Review of Policies Encouraging Renewable Energy Integration and Best Practices' (2015) 45 *Renewable and Sustainable Energy Reviews* 249.

Craig Hart and Dominic Marcellino, 'Subsidies or Free Markets to Promote Renewables?' (2012) 3 *Renewable Energy Law and Policy* 196.

Volkmar Lauber, 'The European Experience with Renewable Energy Support Schemes and Their Adoption: Potential Lessons for Other Countries' (2011) 2 *Renewable Energy Law and Policy* 120.

Temitope Onifade, 'Hybrid Renewable Energy Support Policy in the Power Sector: The Contracts for Difference and Capacity Market Case Study' (2016) 95 *Energy Policy* 390.

Policy

European Commission, 'European Commission guidance for the design of renewable support schemes – Accompanying the document Communication from the Commission: Delivering the internal market in electricity and making the most of public intervention' SWD (2013) 439 final.

Michael Taylor, *Energy Subsidies: Evolution in the global energy transformation to 2050* (IRENA, Technical Paper 1/2020) Energy subsidies: Evolution in the global energy transformation to 2050 (irena.org) (accessed 9 October 2022).

6

Transmitting Electricity

I. Introduction

Electricity is typically transported from where it is produced to consumers via cable networks, also referred to as grids. Exceptions to this include consumption by generators of self-produced electricity and the direct supply of power to consumers from dedicated generating plant. Cable networks are regarded as essential infrastructure because of their role in ensuring that people, public services and economies have access to secure energy supplies. Having access to them is essential for generators to be able to sell their output to consumers and is therefore vital for the growth of renewable electricity production. Certainty of network access and related costs of connecting generating plant to networks and of using them to transmit and distribute electricity are central considerations for renewable generating plant developers when deciding if a proposed project is feasible and financially viable.

In practice, difficulties are already being encountered – or are anticipated as the scale of its production grows – with integrating renewable electricity into networks.[1] These difficulties have already retarded and will continue to constrain growth in its production if they are not addressed. They are due primarily to the fact that renewable electricity, particularly from variable sources and from remote locations, may not fit well with networks that were designed to transmit and distribute predictable output from centralised high-capacity power plants consuming transportable and manageable fossil fuels such as coal and gas. Laws for network development and operation based on the assumption of a system carrying only electricity produced by a small number of centralised power stations from predictable supply sources may also act as barriers to integrating widely distributed and often variable energy from renewable sources into electricity systems.

---

[1] International Energy Agency-Energy Technology Systems Analysis Programme & International Renewable Energy Agency, *Renewable Energy Integration in Power Grids: Technology Brief* (IEA-ETSAP & IRENA Technology Brief E15, April 2015) Renewable Energy Integration in Power Grids (irena.org) (accessed 9 October 2022).

In view of the above, the main aim of legal interventions in favour of renewable electricity with regard to cable networks is to overcome problems that would otherwise prevent it from reaching consumers and being sold in markets. This chapter seeks to assist readers with understanding why such problems arise and how law can be used to address them. Section II provides introductory information on types of electricity networks, on how they are structured and operated and on typical actors and institutions involved with their operation and development to familiarise readers with terminology used when considering this topic. Section III identifies and explains commonly arising and anticipated problems with integrating renewable electricity into networks developed to carry centralised fossil fuel power. Ways in which law is being or could be used to address these problems are then examined in Section IV. They are categorised by reference to the degree of intervention required to address the problem, ranging from altering current network operation practices to the development of new transboundary infrastructure. The review of legal responses is supported by examples from laws of the European Union and its Member States in view of extensive experience which they have already accrued with tackling grid-based obstacles to renewable electricity expansion in policy and law.

II. Electricity Networks and Regulation

A. Transmission Systems, Distribution Systems and Interconnectors

High-capacity power plants are usually connected to transmission systems for long-distance transmission at high voltage to consumers. Transmission systems tend to have a monopoly over transmitting electricity in a state or region as the enormous capital investment involved in their development makes it uneconomic to construct competing networks. For example, there were only 35 such systems in the European Union's 28 Member States in September 2019 with four of them in Germany and four in the United Kingdom due to the historical development in these countries of separate regional grids.[2] Lower capacity distribution systems take electricity from transmission lines to meet demand from connected consumers and distribute it to them at lower voltage levels. Distribution systems are also monopolies, but there are many more of them because of their role in serving particular communities. There were around 2,400 such systems in the EU's 28 Member States in September 2019.[3]

Transmission and distribution systems tend to lie within national borders as they were often first developed as public facilities by states.[4] Initial public development is

---

[2] ENTSO-E, 'ENTSO-E Member Companies' (ENTSO-E website) Member Companies (entsoe.eu) (accessed 9 October 2022).

[3] Giuseppe Prettico and others, *Distribution System Operators Observatory 2018* (European Commission, JRC Science for Policy Report, 2019) https://publications.jrc.ec.europa.eu/repository/bitstream/JRC113926/jrc113926_kjna29615enn_newer.pdf (accessed 9 October 2022), 10–15.

[4] Erik van der Vleuten and Vincent Lagendijk, 'Transnational infrastructure vulnerability: The historical shaping of the 2006 European "Blackout"' (2010) 38(4) *Energy Policy* 2042.

not always the case though. Electricity networks in the US were often developed by private actors in response to local and regional demand prior to the last quarter of the twentieth century.[5] This has resulted in patchworks of network development for which legal intervention at State and Federal levels is required to secure cooperation between their operators on matters of public policy goals such as countrywide energy security and renewable energy integration.[6]

Standalone networks are increasingly being linked by interconnector cables which allow the trade of electricity between them. For example, the UK has several offshore interconnectors that link it with the electricity systems of Belgium, France, the Netherlands, Norway, and Ireland.

B. System Operation

It is essential for security of supply that an appropriately resourced and experienced actor is established in law as the party responsible for the maintenance and operation of each transmission and distribution system. Legal frameworks governing electricity networks impose duties on the licensed actor aimed at maintaining security of the electricity system including by modifying networks in line with changing patterns of generation and consumption. For example, EU law requires Member States to put in place laws for appointing transmission and distribution system operators, and prescribes the duties which national laws should impose on them.[7] Legal ownership of a system and the legal right to operate it may lie with different actors, but a permit for network operation is unlikely to be granted unless the legal relationship between owner and operator is such that the latter will be able to discharge its duties for developing, maintaining and operating the network even though it is not the network's legal owner (eg, guarantees to fund grid development by the operator from the owner).

C. Network Regulation

Electricity networks remain heavily regulated in liberalised electricity systems in which competition has been introduced to power generation and supply. Continued regulation of network operation is required for the following reasons:[8]

- There is limited scope to introduce competition due to the enormous capital investment required for network development. The lack of competition raises concerns that network operators may exploit their monopoly position by overcharging

---

[5] Paul Joskow, 'Transmission Policy in the United States' (2005) 13 *Utilities Policy* 95.
[6] ibid.
[7] Directive (EU) 2019/944 of 5 June 2019 on Common Rules for the Internal Market for electricity and amending Directive 2012/27/EU [2019] OJ L158/125, Chapters IV and V.
[8] Paul Joskow, 'Lessons Learned from Electricity Market Liberalization' (2008) 29 (special issue 2) *The Energy Journal* 9.

customers for the use of grids or by investing heavily in infrastructure without regard to efficiency in the knowledge that those who pay to access their grids have no alternative but to use them.

- The constant maintenance and development of grids is essential for the secure functioning of energy systems, and to accommodate change in the nature of energy supplies (eg, through the growth of energy from renewable sources).
- Collusion between generators and transporters, particularly where they have a common corporate owner, could otherwise prevent the emergence of competition in the electricity market (ie, the corporate group books capacity on the network to carry the energy that it produces to the exclusion of other producers).

As noted above, system operators in liberalised systems are made subject to prescribed duties to ensure that networks are properly maintained and adapted and that there is no discrimination between customers seeking network access (save where the law positively requires this to serve some policy objective).

D. Electricity System Regulators

The establishment of a regulator with responsibility for ensuring observance by system operators of their duties as part of its remit is common under liberalised electricity systems.[9] Regulatory independence is a typical requirement under liberalised systems to prevent markets from being distorted, save where permitted in law, by governmental use of regulatory authority to pursue policy goals.[10] For example, the EU Electricity Directive 2019 requires Member States to establish independent regulators and sets out the responsibilities and powers they must possess.[11] Most importantly for integrating renewable electricity, regulators control the amount that network operators can charge for the use of their systems ('regulated tariffs'). Accordingly, they control the extent to which system operators can recover what they spend on grid maintenance and development through payments from grid users. In practice, regulators periodically review system operator proposals for both network development and related growth in the level of tariffs they can charge for system use to cover the costs of proposed development.[12] The regulator decides on the amount of money the system operator can recover over a set period (five years in the UK) for use of the network, with the decision effectively placing a limit on development that the system operator is able to conduct.[13]

---

[9] ibid, 13, 23–25.
[10] ibid.
[11] Directive 2019/944/EU (n 7), Chapter VII.
[12] Dierk Bauknecht and Jan-Peter Voß, 'Network Regulation' in Barbara Praetorius and others (eds) *Innovation for Sustainable Electricity Systems: Exploring the Dynamics of Energy Transitions* (Physica-Verlag 2009) 191.
[13] ibid. See also Aileen McHarg, 'Evolution and Revolution in British Energy Network Regulation: From RPI-X to RIIO' in Martha Roggenkamp and others (eds) *Energy Networks and the Law: Innovative Solutions in Changing Markets* (Oxford University Press 2012) 313.

E. Network Operation and Markets[14]

Consumers contract with suppliers for the supply of electricity in retail markets. Suppliers contract with generators in advance of when electricity is produced to ensure that they can meet demand from their consumer portfolios. Large consumers (eg, cement, paper, glass, metallurgy industries) may contract for electricity supplies with generators directly. Electricity trades between generators and suppliers/large consumers can take place months and even years ahead of production or closer to this including on the day of generation itself. Trading is conducted directly between generator and supplier/large consumer through over the counter trades or is done through electricity exchanges with the latter typically allowing trading through futures (weeks/months ahead of generation), day ahead and on the day (intra-day) markets.

Generators and suppliers must book capacity in transmission and distribution systems to ensure that electricity which they have agreed to supply can be conveyed through cable networks to consumers.[15] Capacity booking is typically organised by the transmission system operator for the whole network including distribution systems connected to the transmission system. Capacity is made available for blocks of time by the TSO including through auctions where demand may exceed capacity to carry electricity. Auctions are described as explicit when conducted independently from electricity trading and implicit when electricity trading and capacity allocation are combined.

The input and output of electricity into systems must be kept in balance.[16] A failure to do so can result in system breakdown and the loss of supplies. TSOs are usually responsible for keeping electricity systems in balance. One way in which they do this in liberalised systems is by running balancing markets in which they and other actors are able at short notice to procure generation or demand reduction or increase as necessary to balance inputs and outputs where generation falls below or exceeds the level which generators committed to produce.[17]

As discussed in the following section, the relationship between markets and system operators presents several problems for renewable electricity growth including over the ability of generators to sell their product in markets and the greater likelihood for renewable generators that they will be subject to imbalance penalties because sources such as wind and solar are intermittent.

---

[14] Anna Creti and Fulvio Fontini, *Economics of Electricity: Markets, Competition and Rules* (Cambridge University Press 2019). See also Ignacio Perez-Arriaga and others, 'Transmission and Distribution Networks for a Sustainable Electricity Supply' in Ibon Galarraga, Mikel Gonzalez-Eguino and Anil Markandya (eds) *Handbook of Sustainable Energy* (Edward Elgar 2011) 116.

[15] ibid.

[16] Letha Tawney, 'Revolutionizing the Electricity Sector: Renewable Energy and Low Carbon Grid Infrastructure' in Frauke Urban and Johan Nordersvard (eds) *Low Carbon Development: Key Issues* (Routledge, 2013) 154.

[17] Creti and Fontini (n 14) 136–54.

III. Network Access Challenges

Transmission and distribution networks experience difficulties with accommodating rapidly growing demand for the direct connection of renewable generating plant to them and for the carriage of renewable electricity. This may be due to physical constraints or to longstanding operational practices for the network. Problems also arise because rules for network and market operation that were designed and adopted before significant demand for network access from renewables constrain growth in its production. The main network access challenges are described in the following paragraphs.

A. Capacity Constraints[18]

Networks that were designed to accommodate predictable volumes of electricity travelling in one direction from relatively controllable generating stations may not have the capacity to accept renewable energy. For example, distribution systems may have only the capacity needed to meet expected demand from end consumers. It would not have been envisaged when they were designed that generating plant would wish to connect to them. However, renewable energy production often happens in areas lying closer to distribution systems than transmission systems, and requests are being made to connect wind and solar facilities directly to distribution grids. In addition, capacity issues may arise when volumes of electricity being produced by renewable plant are larger than may have been envisaged during network development or where this causes electricity to flow in an unanticipated direction. For example, grids developed to carry electricity from centralised generating plant to remote areas of low population (eg higher altitude areas) may now be expected to convey sometimes very large volumes of wind electricity to areas of major consumption.

Much work is needed to adapt networks to provide enough capacity for the new energy sources (eg upgrading networks, bypassing them). The need for this work can raise difficulties with attracting the typically large investment required and with securing regulatory support for increased network charges (see the investment and regulatory challenges below). In advance of such works, legal measures of the type discussed at Section IV A below which require network operators to make pro-renewables changes in network operation can be used to try and prevent capacity constraints from restricting the growth of renewable energy production.

---

[18] IEA-ETSAP & IRENA (n 1) 5–7; Paul Lehmann and others, 'Carbon Lock-Out: Advancing Renewable Energy Policy in Europe' (2012) 5 *Energies* 323, 332–38; LeRoy Paddock and Karyan San Martano, 'Energy Supply Planning in a Distributed Energy Resources World' in Donald Zillman and others, *Innovation in Energy Law and Technology* (Oxford University Press, 2018) 371, 372–80.

B. From Passive to Active Management[19]

Distribution systems have been operated passively to date. The only purpose that they have served is to distribute energy to consumers. They are now faced with requests from renewable generators to connect to their networks and to feed electricity into them. Accordingly, distribution system operators must become active managers of inputs to and outputs from their systems. This creates difficulties for them with adapting to new practices. It also creates difficulties in law as duties and rules developed with passive management in mind may not be consistent with new expectations.

There was only a limited need for cooperation (mostly operational) between TSOs and DSOs under the fossil fuel dominated energy system in which electricity flowed only from centralised power plants to consumers. Much greater coordination between TSOs and DSOs in the planning and development of future networks is required because of the more active role that distribution systems are playing in accommodating renewable energy (and in connection with demand-side measures and smart grids).[20] However, requirements for TSO/DSO collaboration under existing regulatory frameworks is often limited because of the past relationship between them. Institutions capable of facilitating TSO/DSO collaboration such as bodies representing the tens to hundreds of DSOs operating in many states may also be lacking because of the former passivity of distribution system operation.

C. Consumer Participation in Electricity Systems[21]

New technologies are driving radical change in the role of electricity consumers in electricity systems. Historically, all but the largest consumers would have been passive recipients and consumers of electricity produced elsewhere in a top-down relationship with generators, system operators and suppliers. Affordable renewable electricity technologies now enable consumers not only to meet their own demand, but also to participate in markets by selling excess capacity. The term 'prosumer' is used to describe this new class of actors. This ability can have network advantages such as reducing the need for upgrades to ensure that demand is met, but also contributes to problems for distribution systems with capacity and the shift from active to passive management. It requires the adaptation of electricity markets, of arrangements for securing network capacity and of balancing markets to accommodate prosumers as market participants. This may be done directly or, as will more likely be the case for small producers, through single actors who aggregate generation from multiple low-level producers to

---

[19] Perez-Arriaga (n 14); IEA-ETSAP & IRENA (n 1) 5–7; Lehmann (n 18) 332–38; Paddock (n 18) 379–80.
[20] See Section III C.
[21] Lehmann (n 18) 332–38; Paddock (n 18) 372–79; Fereidoon Sioshansi, 'Innovation and Disruption at the Grid's Edge' in Fereidoon Sioshansi (ed) *Innovation and Disruption at the Grid's Edge: How Distributed Resources are Disrupting the Utility Business Model* (Academic Press, 2017) 1.

make substantial bids in markets (aggregators). It also makes legal change necessary to recognise possibilities created by renewable and other technologies for electricity system participation and to address barriers to this to the extent that the priority consideration of maintaining system security allows for this.

In addition, 'smart grid' technologies provide consumers with real time information about their electricity costs and enable them to switch on electricity consuming devices remotely when costs are low.[22] They equip consumers individually and collectively to assist with meeting challenges posed by renewable electricity intermittency (see Section III D) and network constraints through informed demand management, and potentially to benefit financially from this by selling prospective reduced demand directly or through aggregators in balancing markets. Again, however, such technologies are disruptive of the status quo. Significant modification of networks, particularly distribution systems, will be required to accommodate them. Their introduction challenges market and regulatory rules which make no prior provision for active consumer involvement with demand management. In addition, massive growth through digitalisation in electricity company knowledge about peoples' consumption habits raises moral and legal questions about individual privacy.[23] Significant legal reforms are required to ensure that law facilitates these technological developments where their use is desirable whilst addressing concerns associated with them.

D. Intermittency[24]

Inputs and offtakes from electricity networks *must* be kept in balance. Keeping networks in balance can become more difficult as volumes of renewable electricity grow because some renewable energy sources, including wind and solar energy, are intermittent. This means that the amount of energy produced varies because of the variable weather conditions affecting their production. TSOs are usually made responsible for keeping the network for which their system is the main component in balance as part of their overarching duty to maintain security of supply. It will fall to them therefore to lead on responding to security threats posed by growing intermittency. Responses may include the integration of electricity storage options (eg, batteries, hydrogen), developing and/or enhancing interconnections with systems that benefit from stable renewable sources, and introducing the information technologies required for consumers to participate in balancing as prosumers and through demand management. Works required for some of these options raise the investment and regulatory

---

[22] IRENA, *Smart Grids and Renewables: A Guide for Effective Deployment* (Working Paper, November 2013) www.irena.org/publications/2013/Nov/Smart-Grids-and-Renewables-A-Guide-for-Effective-Deployment (accessed 9 October 2022); International Energy Agency, *Technology Roadmap: Smart Grids* (Report, 2011) Technology Roadmap – Smart Grids – Analysis – IEA (accessed 9 October 2022).
[23] IRENA (n 22) 18–19; IEA (n 22) 39–40; Christian Hoerter, Nils Feyel and Alexandria Awad, 'The Smart Grid: Energy Network of Tomorrow – Legal Barriers and Solutions to Implementing the Smart Grid in the EU and US' (2015) 8 *International Energy Law Review* 291.
[24] Tawney (n 16) 151–54; Lehmann (n 18) 332–38.

challenges discussed below. The temptation may also be strong for network operators, in view of legal duties to maintain secure network operation, to limit network access for renewable electricity.

Electricity storage options were once limited, but technological improvements and declining costs are making battery storage more available for individual and business consumers.[25] The storage of power from electricity by using it for electrolysis of water to separate hydrogen from oxygen during periods of high renewable electricity production and low cost for storage and release when renewable output is lower and costs higher is also an option.[26] As with renewable generating plant, there is a clear role for subsidies to enable storage development when this would not be financially viable. However, questions over the market and legal status of electricity storage would need to be settled to enable emergence of a financial case for storage. Market rules may need adaptation to enable participation by stored electricity actors. The legal status of storage would also need to be settled as it may be unclear whether this is regarded in law as generation, distribution or a separate activity. The label attached to the activity may have legal ramifications including potentially constraining those with interests in generation from owning storage where it is viewed as a network activity and vice versa for network operators where it is viewed as generation.[27]

E. Network and Market Operation

Market operation and confirming network capacity requirements with system operators would typically have taken place no later than the day before planned generation and transmission when networks were carrying electricity largely from predictable sources. However, closure of markets and of network registrations a day before electricity production presents difficulties for renewable generators who will not have an accurate idea of production from intermittent sources until a couple of hours before the production time.[28] It may prevent the sale of and network access for renewable electricity where production exceeds volumes expected the day before. Renewable generators may also incur balancing costs where production falls short or exceeds predicted output. This is another factor that will feature in their upfront thinking on a project's financial viability as it places renewable developments at a disadvantage compared to predictable fossil fuel power. Moving closure times for market operation and network registration closer to the time when knowledge of intermittent renewable

---

[25] IEA-ETSAP & IRENA (n 1) 11–12; Tawney (n 16) 156–57; Matthijs van Leeuwen and Martha Roggenkamp, 'Regulating Electricity Storage in the European Union: How to Balance Technical and Legal Innovation' in Donald Zillman et al (eds), *Innovation in Energy Law and Technology* (Oxford University Press, 2018) 154.

[26] Ruven Fleming and Joshua Fershee, 'The 'Hydrogen Economy' in the United States and the European Union: Regulating Innovation to Combat Climate Change' in Donald Zillman et al, *Innovation in Energy Law and Technology* (Oxford University Press, 2018) 137.

[27] Van Leeuwen and Roggenkamp (n 25) 164–66.

[28] Lehmann (n 18) 332–38; Tawney (n 16) 155.

electricity production firms up, to the extent that network security allows, would be required to address these constraints.

F. Connection Costs[29]

Developers of renewable power projects must reach an agreement with a system operator to connect the new generating plant to the operator's network. The system operator charges the developer for works required to make the connection. Such charges can be prohibitively expensive for renewable projects, and particularly where system operators seek to recover not only costs for the connection but also those for related upgrades to existing networks from the developer. This practice is described as 'deep' connection charging. 'Shallow' charging occurs where renewable project developers bear only the costs of connection. Regulation of charging practices by system operators may be needed to prevent them from retarding renewable energy development.

Under shallow charging, system operators will need to secure investment required to conduct upgrade works rather than being recompensed by renewable developers. To obtain backing at a reasonable rate, they will need to show regulatory approval for recovery of the costs of network upgrades through use of system charges. As with all such development, connection-related construction raises significant challenges for system operators with attracting investment and securing regulatory approval for the recovery of costs.[30]

G. Investment Challenge[31]

Massive investment is required to support programmes of upgrades and new development to equip grids for decarbonised energy supplies. Costs for electricity network development in the EU to 2030, much of which is needed to integrate renewable energy, are estimated to be €152 billion.[32] System operators under liberalised systems will first seek financial support for such development through inclusion of related costs in charges for using their networks. Confirmation by the regulator that the network charge may be increased enables system operators to secure investment from financiers at low rates due to strong confidence in repayment. However, a range of challenges described in the following paragraph from the regulatory relationship may make it difficult for system operators to obtain all the backing they need through this channel. Support from state and regional institutions may also be required in such circumstances to assist operators with leveraging affordable finance.

---

[29] IEA-ETSAP & IRENA (n 1) 23, 27–28.
[30] See section III G below.
[31] Lehmann (n 18) 332–38.
[32] Edwin Haesen and others, *Investment Needs in Trans-European Energy Infrastructure up to 2030 and Beyond* (Ecofys Report for the European Commission, July 2017) DOC_1 (europa.eu) (accessed 9 October 2022).

H. The Regulatory Challenge[33]

Incentive regulation has provided the standard regulatory model internationally during the period of energy market liberalisation of the last 35 years.[34] It incentivises network operators to behave as if they were subject to competition by rewarding them for increasing efficiency in and reducing the costs of their operation. Typically, the amount that the operator can charge for use of the network is capped. This provides the operator with an incentive to 'beat the cap' (and thus realise a profit) by making greater efficiency savings than the regulator assumed in setting the price cap. Incentive regulation is effective for promoting economic efficiency, but not for incentivising network operators to incur major costs in connection with network upgrades to accommodate renewable energy. On the contrary, TSOs and DSOs have tended to cut back on network modifications and research and development under the incentive regulation model to maximise their profitability (the amount by which they 'beat the cap').

The growth of renewable electricity production presents a particular challenge to long-standing regulatory approaches for 'passive' distribution grids. Regulation has tended to focus on cost-cutting, but a much more proactive approach is demanded both of regulators and regulatees to ensure the adaptation of networks to accommodate renewable energy and to make related modifications.

In addition, national regulators have sometimes proved unwilling to support transboundary projects including those required to address the intermittency challenge mentioned above and to connect remote renewable generation to consumers (eg, offshore wind energy).[35] National regulators tend to be guided by duties in the laws establishing them, often including a duty to promote the interests of national consumers. They may therefore be reluctant to confirm financial support for development in the following instances:

- where it is being conducted for the benefit of two or more states or for a region;
- where it is hard (as it invariably is with transboundary projects) to establish the costs and benefits for national grid users and energy consumers with any precision; and
- where significant risks are perceived with delivery of a project and/or with realisation of projected benefits for national consumers (eg, projects use innovative technology or they will be constructed in the expectation of future demand, but with no guarantee that their full capacity will be used).

This reluctance can prevent transboundary projects from being conducted by system operators or their appointees because development costs cannot be recovered

---

[33] Lehmann (n 18) 332–38; Bauknecht and Voß (n 12) 191–201.
[34] ibid; McHarg (n 13) 313–22.
[35] European Commission, 'Impact Assessment Accompanying the Document Proposal for a Regulation on Guidelines for Trans-European energy Infrastructure and Repealing Decision No 1364/2006/EC', SEC (2011) 1233 final, 12–15; Olivia Woolley, 'Overcoming Legal Challenges for Offshore Electricity Grid Development: A Case Study of the Cobra and Kriegers Flak Projects' in Martha Roggenkamp and Olivia Woolley (eds) *European Energy Law Report IX* (Intersentia 2012) 169, 182–87.

without regulatory agreement that they can be included within national network tariff charges.

IV. Legal Responses

A range of practical and legal responses can be used to address network access challenges. First, network operations can be altered to increase scope for renewable energy integration by positive discrimination in its favour over electricity from other sources and by shifting from passive to active network management. Laws governing network operation can be reformed to require that pro-renewable and proactive operating approaches should be employed. Legal responses relating to network operation are considered in section IVA.

Second, policymakers, legislators, and regulators can take steps to modify existing laws, regulatory policies and regulatory roles which obstruct renewable electricity production due to a simple lack of appropriate legal provision for new types of activity and actor (eg, aggregation). Relevant legal approaches are considered in section IV B.

Third, legal requirements for network planning can be used to require that system operators identify needs for physical modification of networks to accommodate renewable energy, ideally long before constraints arise. Ways of equipping network planning law to support renewable energy integration are considered in section IV C.

Fourth, alteration in law (or by policymakers and/or regulators directly where existing law allows for this) of the duties of regulators and of the relationship with regulated networks can be used to alleviate constraints on development financing discussed under the regulatory challenge (section III H) where planning processes identify needs for network development. Means in policy and law of lessening financing constraints stemming from the regulatory relationship are considered in section IV D.

Fifth, new relationships between regulators and regulated systems can be created where necessary to tackle challenges associated with developments involving more than one state such as interconnectors and large-scale supergrid projects. The EU's Trans-European Energy Infrastructure Regulation of 2022 is considered in section IV D(i) as an example of a law which ensures support for transnational developments. This section also considers the EU's Connecting Europe Facility as an example of interstate financial support for major infrastructure development where backing from national regulators may not be sufficient, on its own, to raise funds required for a project.

A. Network Operation

Laws governing network operation can be reformed to require that operators integrate renewable electricity to the extent that system security allows. Modified operating practice offers an option for integrating renewables, typically during the early stages of growth in their production, whilst needs for network modification are explored. At a basic level, general requirements that access must be provided for renewable electricity direct operators' attention to practices which may prevent this. Clearer legal direction may also be given to ensure that renewable energy intermittency is not used as justification for limiting access.[36] For example, the EU's 2009 Renewable Energy Directive required Member States to provide renewable electricity with either guaranteed or priority access.[37] States were able to provide the former where intraday markets existed, allowing the sale of electricity on the day of production by guaranteeing network entry for traded power. Priority access involves admitting renewable electricity to networks as and when it is produced even if this is at a time when it is not possible to sell it through already closed markets. The 2009 RES Directive gives the mandatory purchase of electricity under feed-in tariff schemes as an example of when priority access has been provided.[38] The obligation under EU law to provide for guaranteed or priority access in national law ceased on 1 July 2021, the date on which the Directive was repealed.[39]

Laws requiring positive discrimination in favour of renewable electricity production by network operators can also be used to ensure that it is integrated in network flows to the full extent possible. Dispatch involves scheduling the order in which generating stations with access to a network at a point in time should produce scheduled electricity.[40] This is often set by reference to the order in which bids were accepted in a market. In some electricity systems, the system operator is responsible for 'dispatching' generating stations. Law can therefore be used to ensure the carriage of renewable electricity by requiring that it should be given priority in dispatch. For example, the EU's 2009 Renewable Energy Directive required Member States to introduce priority dispatch for renewable energy where system operators had this responsibility.[41] Self-dispatch by generators rather than the system operator is typically the practice under more sophisticated market arrangements combining electricity sales and allocation of network capacity. It is also a possibility under such arrangements to secure priority dispatch for renewable energy by requiring that the operator of the relevant market or actors responsible for their own dispatch act accordingly even if this would depart from market scheduling.[42] The EU's 2019 Electricity Regulation defines priority dispatch 'with regard to the self-dispatch model [scheduling arranged through markets by market actors], [as] the dispatch of power plants on the basis of criteria which are

---

[36] See section IV D(i).
[37] Directive 2009/28/EC of 23 April 2009 on the promotion of the use of energy from renewable sources and amending and subsequently repealing Directives 2001/77/EC and 2003/30/EC [2009] OJ L140/16, Recital 60, art 16.2(b).
[38] ibid.
[39] Directive 2018/2001 of 11/12/2018 on the promotion of the use of energy from renewable sources [2018] OJ L382/82, art 37.
[40] Victor Ahlqvist, Par Holmberg and Thomas Tangerås, 'Central versus Self-Dispatch in Electricity Markets' (Research Institute of Industrial Economics, IFN Working Paper No.1257, 2018) Microsoft Word – Central_Decentral_EPRG_AhlqvistHolmbergTangerås_190327b (cam.ac.uk) (accessed 9 October 2022).
[41] Directive 2009/28/EC (n 37) art 16(2(c).
[42] Emissions-EUETS.com, 'Self-Dispatch System' Self-Dispatch System (Electricity Balancing Market) – Emissions-EUETS.com (accessed 9 October 2022).

different from the economic order of bids and, with regard to the central dispatch model [order decided on by System Operators], the dispatch of power plants on the basis of criteria which are different from the economic order of bids and from network constraints, giving priority to the dispatch of particular generation technologies'.[43] Priority is to be given when dispatching renewable electricity by system operators 'to the extent permitted by the secure operation of the national electricity system' but only for power produced by renewable facilities with a generating capacity of 400kW or less or by demonstration projects. The effect of this measure will therefore be limited largely to domestic-scale power generation (eg, solar panels on a roof) and to pre-commercial deployments for innovative technologies.[44]

One reason for imposing priority dispatch is that system operators may otherwise be tempted to look to electricity from intermittent renewables before electricity from other sources when it is necessary to curtail grid access temporarily for some generators to prevent congestion or to maintain system balance. Another way of preventing this would be to make clear in law that system operators must not curtail renewable electricity as a first choice unless this is necessary for system security. In this regard, the EU's 2009 Directive requires Member States to 'ensure that appropriate grid and market-related operational measures are taken in order to minimise the curtailment of electricity produced from renewable energy sources'.[45] They must also ensure that system operators report to their national electricity system regulators where renewable electricity is curtailed to maintain system security on curtailments and on planned corrective measures to avoid them in the future.[46] The 2019 Electricity Regulation takes a similar tack, advising as a general principle that '[t]ransaction curtailment procedures shall be used only in emergency situations, namely where the transmission system operator must act in an expeditious manner and redispatching or countertrading is not possible' and should be 'applied in a non-discriminatory manner'.[47]

Measures such as priority access and dispatch raise concerns in liberalised electricity systems that the perceived ability of competitive markets to promote efficiency and lower cost in electricity production and thereby to promote the growth of renewable electricity (by driving reductions in the cost of its production) will be impaired by their use.[48] They may therefore be seen as a necessary evil to be departed from as soon as policy goals for promoting early stage renewable sector growth have been achieved. The influence of these concerns is apparent from the much more limited use of relevant measures made in the EU's clean energy for all package of laws of 2018 and 2019. The laws do not impose special requirements for access by renewables. Instead, all states are required to ensure that markets and arrangements for booking system capacity allow generators to participate and register as near to

---

[43] Regulation (EU) 2019/943 of 5 June 2019 on the internal market for electricity [2019] OJ L158/54 (the 2019 Regulation), art 2(20).
[44] ibid, art 12.
[45] Directive 2009/28/EC (n 37) art 16(2)(c).
[46] ibid.
[47] Regulation EU 2019/943 (n 43) art 16(2).
[48] European Commission, 'Impact Assessment accompanying a proposal for a Directive on common rules for the Internal Market in Electricity' SWD (2016) 410 final Part 3/5, 4–16.

the time of generation as possible.[49] Provisions on priority dispatch and curtailment remain but are applicable only to small-scale generation (below 400 kW).[50] All generators apart from such small-scale producers are required to participate in balancing markets and to bear related costs.[51]

Whether or not this greater market exposure is beneficial for the growth of renewable electricity and for the EU's efforts to decarbonise energy supplies remains to be seen. However, similar questions to those considered in the chapter of this book on subsidies arise over how the growth of renewable energy as the principal thrust of greenhouse gas emissions reduction will be affected.[52] Some renewable technologies are now competitive and likely to survive when used in developments with access to good conditions for their production, but less-well-developed technologies may struggle when support is reduced as may established technologies used in more marginal projects. Is this rapid return to undistorted market discipline wise in view of significant expectations on renewable electricity to displace not only still dominant fossil fuel electricity but also the near monopolies of fossil fuel heating and transport?

(i) Market Access

As discussed above,[53] early market closure can prevent the sale of renewable electricity when it exceeds projected levels. It also leaves renewable generators more exposed to imbalance penalties than fossil fuel generators. Law can be used to address this situation, to the extent that system security allows, by requiring market operators to reduce the time gap between market closure and the point of production and transmission. The EU's Electricity Regulation of 2019 requires market operators to 'allow market participants to trade energy as close to real time as possible' in markets held on the day when electricity is to be generated (intraday markets) and markets in which participants offer to produce power or reduce demand at short notice to prevent electricity systems inputs and outputs from getting out of balance (balancing markets).[54]

(ii) From Passive to Active Management

The operation of distribution networks must shift from historical passivity to active management to accommodate renewable energy integration whilst maintaining network security.[55] Behavioural change amongst distribution system operators is required with regard to the management of flows on their networks, network

---

[49] See sections IVA(i) and IVB.
[50] Regulation EU 2019/943 (n 43) art 12.
[51] Directive (EU) 2019/944 (n 7) art 3(4).
[52] Chapter 5.
[53] See section III E.
[54] Regulation 2019/943 (n 43), arts 8(1) and 6(4).
[55] See section III B.

planning processes, and interaction with actual and potential network users and with the operators of the transmission systems to which their systems are connected. Different types of legal intervention can be used to promote required change in DSO culture. First, this can be done by modifying legal duties of the actor responsible for system operation. For example, DSOs were subject to a much lighter planning obligation than TSOs under the EU's 2009 Electricity Directive.[56] The 2019 Directive ends this imbalance by giving DSOs an obligation to publish a network development plan every two years which should provide transparency on planned investment and network needs for services such as demand response and storage in the next five to ten years.[57] Particular emphasis should be given in the plan to infrastructure required to connect new generating capacity and new loads such as electric vehicles.[58]

The second way involves modifying laws governing distribution network operation and/or requiring that regulations be modified by the regulator so that they facilitate and incentivise active management by DSOs. Active management of network flows involves not only the control of access, but also an ability to alleviate network congestion where this arises by using flexibility services such as distributed generation, energy storage and demand response. The EU's 2019 Electricity Directive calls on Member States to allow and provide incentives to DSOs to procure flexibility services including congestion management.[59]

Creating institutional support for DSOs offers a third way of aiding the cultural shift from passivity to active management. For example, an organisation of transmission system operators, ENTSO-E, was created in the EU in 2009 to promote collaboration between TSOs. Their collaboration includes work on removing differences between networks by developing common EU-wide codes for network operation. An equivalent organisation for DSOs was not viewed as necessary at this time. The 2019 Electricity Regulation fills this gap by establishing an EU DSO entity whose tasks include to facilitate the integration of renewable energy resources, distributed generation and other resources embedded in the distribution network such as energy storage.[60]

Creating this body also assists with improving interaction between DSOs and TSOs. Significant emphasis is placed on coordination between transmission system and distribution system operation as a responsibility for this new entity and as an additional responsibility for the organisation of TSOs. This is to be achieved in part by involvement of the DSO organisation with ongoing development of the common network codes for EU electricity system operation. In the EU example, enhanced duties of DSOs and TSOs are also used to require cooperation between them to enable effective participation of market participants connected to the grid in retail, wholesale and balancing markets.

---

[56] Directive 2009/72/EC of 13 July 2009 concerning common rules for the internal market in electricity and repealing Directive 2003/53/EC [2009] OJ L 211/55, art 25.
[57] Directive (EU) 2019/944 (n 7), art 32(3).
[58] ibid.
[59] ibid, art 32(1).
[60] Regulation EU 2019/943 (n 43) art 52.

Measures of this kind will secure some behavioural change in distribution and transmission systems operations. Whether or not this is sufficient to realise the full potential of renewable electricity as part of energy sector decarbonisation remains to be seen. Key factors for integration in liberalised systems under which system operators have been separated from other elements of the energy chain and privatised are the extents to which: governments and regulators are willing to use whatever legal authority they may have to intervene in system operation; system operators respond to direction on how to perform their legal duties and to regulatory and financial incentives including, for example, linking higher charges for system use with the growth of distributed generation. A reappraisal of carefully constructed legal relationships between government, regulator, operator and system users introduced to promote competition and efficiency in electricity production will be needed. This should include the possibility of enhanced governmental powers and a return to public ownership if possibilities for securing change through tools available under liberalised systems prove inadequate.

B. Opening the Electricity System to New Actors

Renewable power and 'smart' digital information technologies disrupt electricity systems. The former technologies enable consumers, communities and other small-scale producers to meet their own electricity demand and to benefit financially by making excess production available for sale. This may be done through markets or net metering, a practice in which the value of electricity fed into the grid is deducted from the consumer's bill.[61] The latter technologies facilitate consumer involvement in electricity systems including by responding in consumption choices (eg, when to charge an electric vehicle) to shifting electricity prices and offering demand response as a valuable commodity in markets to maintain system balance. Provision in law must be made to allow for the integration of actors and activities that were not envisaged when legal frameworks were enacted to govern electricity systems. Without this, they may be excluded from making positive contributions to the functioning of electricity systems undergoing a low carbon transition by a failure of law to keep pace with technological change. The following paragraphs identify four ways in which law can be used to make the necessary provision.

First, basic permission is needed for particular classes of actors to participate in systems. For example, the EU's 2019 Electricity Directive requires Member States to ensure that national laws do 'not unduly hamper ... consumer participation' including through demand response, investments into flexible electricity, storage and electromobility.[62] Similar requirements are imposed to enable system participation by storage operators and demand response in the EU.[63] Laws in the US state of California

---

[61] Paddock and San Martano (n 18) 371, 373.
[62] Directive (EU) 2019/944 (n 7) art 3(1).
[63] ibid, arts 15 and 17.

and the Canadian state of Ontario make similar provision for the integration of prosumers, demand response and storage in their electricity systems.[64]

Second, market operators should be required to allow participation by consumers offering generation and demand response and of storage operators in markets. For example, EU law makes clear that consumers are entitled to be active in electricity systems including through market participation.[65] It encourages this by requiring Member States to ensure that markets accept minimum bid sizes of 500kW or less, a level allowing participation by some domestic-scale generators.[66] Access for small-scale generators is not unconditional as all trading actors become responsible for keeping the system in balance and are therefore subject to penalties where their offering is not in line with accepted bids.[67]

The administration and expense involved and expertise required for effective participation in markets is likely to deter small-scale providers of generation, demand response and storage from direct market participation in practice. Instead, an emerging class of actors known as aggregators purchases services offered by small-scale actors (usually at a discount to market price levels to reflect that the aggregator takes on market risk) and participates in markets as a wholesaler of multiple offerings.[68] EU law requires Member States to ensure that aggregators can participate in electricity systems and markets and that consumers have the option to sell power and services through them as well as directly.[69]

Third, TSOs and DSOs have a significant role in enabling access for new actors as the parties responsible for system connection for new power plants and access to networks for electricity produced by them, as procurers of services to keep systems in balance, and in view of often close connections between market and network operation. This is also the case for regulators whose relationship with system operators can, as we have seen, constrain network modification to integrate new activities.[70] EU law requires TSOs and DSOs to include new activities when procuring ancillary services such as system balancing and to work with regulators in order to establish technical requirements for their participation in markets.[71] Regulators also have a general obligation to help achieve the integration of small and large-scale electricity production from renewable sources and to facilitate network access for new renewable generation capacity and storage including by removing barriers that could prevent this.[72]

Fourth, electricity system change creates incompatibilities with existing law and raises questions about its interpretation. Reform of existing laws will be needed to

---

[64] José Márquez and Margarita González Brambila, 'Regulation of Electricity Storage, Intelligent Grids, and Clean Energies in an Open Market in Mexico' in Donald Zillman and others, *Innovation in Energy Law and Technology* (Oxford University Press 2018) 172, 179–83.
[65] Directive (EU) 2019/944 (n 7) art 15.
[66] Regulation (EU) 2019/943 (n 43) art 8(3).
[67] Directive (EU) 2019/944 (n 7) art 15(2)(f).
[68] ibid, Recital 39; Sioshansi (n 21).
[69] Directive (EU) 2019/944 (n 7) art 17.
[70] Section III H.
[71] Directive (EU) 2019/944 (n 7), arts 17(2) and 40(1)(d).
[72] ibid, arts 58(d) and (e).

address matters which legislators could not have anticipated when they were enacted. Examples from EU law show the kinds of difficulties which can arise. Questions have been asked about whether the storage of hydrogen produced using excess renewable electricity to power electrolysis should be regulated under the law relating to electricity or gas sector storage, particularly when the purpose of storage is to produce electricity at a later date.[73] With regard to electricity sector storage, storage operators may 'consume' electricity by storing it when prices are low (eg, when renewable output exceeds demand) and release the same electricity when prices are higher. Commentators have noted that treating storage operators both as producers and consumers of electricity for such transactions may lead to them being double charged for system use and/or for tax purposes and that this may dissuade actors from becoming storage operators.[74]

(i) Smart Grids and Privacy Issues

Smart grid technology could create a new type of electricity system in which consumers play an active role, particularly through responding to electricity market prices and managing their demand. It has an important role to play in making electricity systems more efficient and better able to cope with the intermittency of some renewable power sources. States worldwide have recognised its value by introducing major Smart grid policy initiatives.[75] A typical starting point for such initiatives is to require in law that existing electricity meters are replaced with smart meters which are able to provide consumers with real-time information on their electricity consumption costs.[76] For example, laws requiring smart meter installation and recognising new categories of actors in law such as smart meter installers and data managers have been enacted in the EU, at federal level in the US and Australia and in US and Australian states.[77] However, such rollouts must be handled with care to avoid causing a consumer backlash. Smart meters can raise privacy concerns because of the detailed access they give to system operators, suppliers and meter owners and readers about a consumer's energy consumption habits.[78] The digitalisation of networks also raises separate concerns over the vulnerability of essential infrastructure to cyberattacks.[79]

---

[73] Fleming and Fershee (n 26) 150–53.
[74] Van Leeuwen and Roggenkamp (n 25) 165–66.
[75] IRENA (n 22); Marilyn Brown and Shan Zhou, 'Smart Grid Policies: An International Review' (2013) 2 *WIREs Energy Environ* 121.
[76] Maria Tuballa and Michael Abundo, 'A Review of the Development of Smart Grid Technologies' (2016) 59 *Renewable and Sustainable Energy Reviews* 710.
[77] Kenneth Zame and others, 'Smart Grid and Energy Storage: Policy Recommendations' (2018) 82 *Renewable and Sustainable Energy Reviews* 1646; Hoeter, Feyel & Awad (n 23); Lee Godden and Anne Kallies, 'Smart Infrastructure: Innovative Energy Technology, Climate Mitigation, and Consumer Protection in Australia and Germany' in Donald Zillman and others, *Innovation in Energy Law and Technology* (Oxford University Press 2018) 391.
[78] IRENA (n 22) 18–19; Hoerter, Feyel and Awad (n 23).
[79] IRENA (n 22) 19.

In addition to requiring their installation and creating related roles and responsibilities, law can be used to support smart grid rollouts by addressing the privacy concerns mentioned above. Law's main contribution to addressing these concerns is to establish credible controls on the acquisition, management and transfer of data harvested from smart meters. Laws adopted as part of smart technology programmes in the EU, the US and Australia have three main strands of regulation.[80] First, limits are placed on data which can be gathered legally. Californian law requires that the design of smart meters should adhere to legal limits, with data minimisation and anonymity techniques being built into the equipment itself.[81] Second, the storage of data is subject to controls aimed at ensuring privacy and cybersecurity. EU law requires Member States to put in place rules ensuring efficient and secure data access, data protection and security which should be backed up by periodic compliance checks.[82] Third, data may only be made available to third parties by the initial recipient with the customer's express consent. Californian law requires that the customer should have information about who the data will be passed to and how it will be used before giving consent to this. It also requires that the recipient should make contractual commitments with the customer to maintain data security.[83]

(ii) Connection Charges

The European Commission frowns on 'deep' charging because the related expense may deter renewable generators from investing in affected projects.[84] It calls for system operators to use 'shallow' charging instead under which renewable energy developers bear only the costs of connection. The 2009 Renewable Energy Directive contained measures concerning costs for connection to and using networks.[85] Important among them with regard to the costs problem was Article 16(4) which required Member States to review system operators' charging policies for connections and related network upgrades every two years with a view to ensuring 'the integration of new producers ...'. This provision also permitted Member States to require System Operators to bear all or part of the costs of such work.

C. Planning

Operational measures and legal reform may enable renewable electricity integration to a limited extent without network modification. However, network upgrades and new development will be required to accommodate significant growth of the renewable

---

[80] ibid, 18–20; Hoerter, Feyel and Awad (n 23); Godden and Kallies (n 77); Tuballa and Abundo (n 76); Zame et al (n 77).
[81] Hoerter, Feyel and Awad (n 23) 298.
[82] Directive (EU) 2019/944 (n 7) arts 19–23.
[83] Hoerter, Feyel and Awad (n 23) 299.
[84] Commission, 'European Commission guidance for the design of renewables support schemes', SWD (2013) 439 final, 5 November 2013, 16–17.
[85] 2009 RES Directive (n 37) arts 16(3) to 16(8).

power sector including by introducing the smart grid technology required for decision-making by consumers. The importance of maintaining security of supply has always required transmission system operators to think several years ahead about changes required to accommodate evolving generation patterns and to meet future demand from consumers. In view of this, network planning is a key aspect of transmission system operator duties in electricity systems. However, detailed planning has not been as necessary historically for distribution systems as generating stations were not connected to them and as there was little consumer involvement in systems. Rigorous planning requirements will need to be introduced as part of distribution system operators' responsibilities if distributed renewable power is to be integrated into networks.[86] In this regard, the EU's Electricity Directive 2019 requires Member States to ensure that distribution system operators should produce a network development plan at least every two years.[87]

Planning processes for transmission and distribution system operators alike will need to possess certain qualities to facilitate renewable electricity integration as part of a low carbon energy transition. First, plan preparation should take place well ahead of when planned development is envisaged in view of long lead-in times both for infrastructure development and for that of generating plant. Planning ahead promotes development of renewable energy generating plant by giving confidence that the infrastructure will be available to carry new sources of electricity generation.

Second, planning should consider not only anticipated generation feeding into networks but also the potential for demand to be met through storage (including from electric car batteries), through growing network efficiency, and through demand management. Growth in consumption from electric vehicles and heating will need to be anticipated if networks are to be ready for significant growth of the share of electricity for meeting energy demand as a whole. An important benefit of taking all these possibilities into account is that self-generation, demand management and storage may avoid needs for developing new transmission and distribution infrastructure by counterbalancing demand growth with ways of meeting this which do not involve the construction of new network infrastructure.[88]

Third, the cost of integrating renewable energy varies depending on the location. It may be more expensive to connect generating plant to a part of a network which is already congested than where capacity is available. Indeed, distributed generation may avoid network upgrades if sited appropriately by alleviating congestion in other parts of the network.[89] Renewable generation from wind and solar is not fully flexible as energy can only be produced from them where the resource is available in sufficient strength for a project's financial viability. Even so, providing information in plans on where networks are congested and where they have capacity can assist with promoting development in locations where it is likely to be most efficient for network development

---

[86] Paddock and San Martano (n 18) 383–34.
[87] Directive (EU) 2019/944 (n 7) art 32(3).
[88] Perez-Arriaga (n 14) 125; Lehmann (n 18) 332–38.
[89] ibid.

and operation.[90] Differentiated charges for connecting distributed renewable generation to the network depending on associated costs and other devices such as fast tracking connection and licensing applications could also be used to promote development in less congested areas to the extent that the relevant legal framework allows discrimination between different classes of system user.[91]

Fourth, the fact that system operators do not know for certain how demand from generators and consumers will evolve is a perennial difficulty for network development. This problem can be exacerbated under liberalised systems due to mandatory separation of corporate interests in system operation and generation. Related risks of wasted investment and unused capacity are unavoidable, but they can be minimised by requiring better interaction between distribution system operators, transmission system operators, generators, governments, regulators and representatives of new system actors such as storage operators, aggregators and prosumers. EU law recognises the need for better communication amongst all systemic actors. Distribution system plans must be based on consultation with all relevant system users and system operators.[92] Similarly, TSO plans should be based on existing and forecast supply and demand after consulting all the relevant stakeholders.[93]

D. Pro-renewables Grid Development

Access to very substantial financial backing will be required to deliver planned network upgrades for integrating renewable electricity. The willingness of regulators to allow for the recovery of development costs through use of system charges is a key factor in the ability of system operators to secure finance at reasonable rates. As discussed at section III H, the incentive regulation model does not fit well with circumstances in which major modification to networks is needed, and particularly when it concentrates on promoting economic efficiencies. Modification by regulators of the regulatory model so that this is better equipped to support renewable energy integration offers a direct means of alleviating this problem. Regulators may choose to alter the model themselves if they have the legal authority to do so, and particularly where their legal duties require them to act in ways conducive to the growth of the renewables sector. For example, regulators' duties in EU law include helping to achieve 'the integration of large and small-scale production of electricity from renewable sources and distributed generation in both transmission and distribution networks', and facilitating access to the network for new generation capacity and energy storage facilities including by removing barriers to electricity from renewable sources.[94] States may also have preserved authority to instruct national regulators on policy matters, to the extent that regulatory independence allows, under the national law which establishes the regulator.

---

[90] Paddock and San Martano (n 18) 387–88; Lehmann (n 18) 332–38.
[91] ibid, 388–89; Perez-Arriaga (n 14) 128.
[92] Directive (EU) 2019/944 (n 7) art 32(4).
[93] ibid, art 51.
[94] ibid, art 58(d).

Movement away by the UK's electricity sector regulator from a classic economic efficiency oriented regulatory model in the 2010s to one which promotes 'green' development by system operators offers an example of regulatory reform aimed at integrating renewables. Ofgem replaced its longstanding regulatory model (RPI-X) with the RIIO model ('Revenue using Incentives to deliver Innovation and Outputs').[95] RIIO incentivises system operators to achieve publicly desired outputs such as accelerating the rate of connection for renewable energy plant to networks by offering them financial incentives.

E. Supporting Transboundary Development

National regulators may be particularly reluctant to support projects that cross national boundaries for the reasons discussed in section III H. Such projects can also be hampered where conflicts arise between the laws of the states applying to them. For example, much scope for legal conflict between national laws is raised by plans of the North Sea's coastal states to collaborate on the development of a North Sea electricity grid to transmit offshore wind electricity from marine areas under the jurisdiction of producing states across one or more marine borders to the consuming state.[96] States involved with transboundary projects can address these difficulties by creating new governance regimes which tackle the particular problems faced by this class of developments. Legal provision required under new governance regimes to support transboundary development may include obligations for national system operators and regulators to cooperate with each other and with their counterparts in the other involved states on delivering projects which the regime endorses, and reforms aimed at streamlining development consent and licensing processes for transboundary projects including by reducing or taking other steps to overcome differences between national laws. Transboundary development would also be assisted by agreement between participating states and national actors on sets of rules for the development and operation of an interconnector and network which treat it as it actually is, a single piece of infrastructure, rather than separating it for legal purposes into a patchwork of parts to which different national laws apply.

The following section focuses on the EU's Trans-European Energy Infrastructure Regulation of 2022 (replacing the 2013 Regulation). The Regulation's purpose is to facilitate transboundary development by requiring that specified procedures be applied in decision-making by regulators on allowing cost recovery by system operators and in permitting procedures for energy infrastructure which has been identified as being of strategic significance for regions of the EU. The EU can adopt laws establishing alternative structures for governing transboundary development because of

---

[95] McHarg (n 13).
[96] Woolley (n 35); Olivia Woolley, Peter Schaumberg and Graham St Michel, 'Establishing an Offshore Electricity Grid: A Legal Analysis of Grid Developments in the North Sea and in US Waters' in Martha Roggenkamp et al (eds) *Energy Networks and the Law: Innovative Solutions in Changing Markets* 180, section II B.

the policy-making and legislative powers which Member States have granted to its institutions under EU Treaties. Woolley examines the possibility of States not belonging to a supranational legal order such as the EU and also for EU Member States that prefer to base collaboration on their remining national legal authority to support transboundary collaboration on infrastructure by entering into a treaty under international law which creates a specific regime for the conduct of envisaged projects in a 2013 article.[97]

(i) Trans-European Energy Infrastructure Regulation (2022 TEEI Regulation)

The current TEEI Regulation entered into force in June 2022.[98] It largely has the same structure and makes similar provision to the preceding Regulation of 2013,[99] but has been modified to place greater emphasis on renewable energy because of the EU's much increased ambition on decarbonisation and on improving regional energy security following Russia's invasion of the Ukraine. It promotes the development of infrastructure that overcomes the intermittency, capacity and distance challenges examined in section III of this chapter by the growth of energy from renewable sources in energy supplies. Its provisions seek to address national regulatory reluctance to support transboundary development. They also seek to combat difficulties with obtaining legal consents for such developments, and to lessen the investment challenge by providing access for relevant developments to EU funding mechanisms. The following sections explain key aspects of the Regulation.

Selecting Projects of Common Interest – The 2022 Regulation applies to development in nine priority energy corridors and three priority thematic areas.[100] The priority corridors focus on improving electricity interconnections between Member States for reasons including the better integration and transmission between them of renewable electricity and on developing infrastructure for transboundary transmission of offshore renewable electricity and to enable growth in hydrogen as an energy source. The thematic areas include advancing the EU-wide rollout of smart grid technology alongside work on creating transboundary networks for carbon dioxide transmission to storage sites and on using smart gas grid technology to improve access for low carbon and renewable gas sources to pipeline networks.

The Regulation establishes a mechanism for selecting projects of common interest (PCIs).[101] Regional groups (made up of Member States representatives, TSOs,

---

[97] Olivia Woolley, 'Governing a North Sea Grid Development: The Need for a Regional Framework Treaty' (2013) *Competition and Regulation in Network Industries* 73.

[98] Regulation 2022/869 of 30 May 2022 on guidelines for trans-European energy infrastructure, amending Regulations (EC) No 715/2009, (EU) 2019/942 and (EU) 2019/943, Directives 2009/73/EC and (EU) 2019/944 and repealing Regulation (EU) 347/2013 [2022] OJ L 152/45.

[99] Regulation (EU) No 347/2013 of 17 April 2013 on guidelines for trans-European energy infrastructure and repealing Decision No 1364/2006/EC and amending Regulations (EC) No 713/2009, (EC) No 714/2009 and (EC) No 715/2009 [2013] OJ L115/39.

[100] 2022 TEEI Regulation (n 97) Annex I.

[101] ibid, art 3.

national regulatory authorities and representatives from the Commission, ACER and ENTSO-E) prepare lists of PCIs choosing from projects proposed to them by developers which fall under one or more of the priority electricity corridors or thematic areas. Projects are selected by reference to criteria set out in Article 4. The European Commission uses the regional lists to prepare and adopt a final list.[102] The process is repeated every two years. The fifth Commission list of projects of common interest was adopted in November 2021 and entered into force in April 2022.[103] The first list under the new regulation is to be adopted by 30 November 2023. Note that projects may only be added to the lists of PCIs with the approval of the Member States to whose territory the project relates.

Priority projects are included within the ten-year network development plans of TSOs.[104] Article 5(7) requires certain action to be taken (including the selection of third parties to finance and construct developments) if the construction of a priority project does not proceed in accordance with its implementation plan. National regulatory authorities and the Commission are given powers to intervene if stated circumstances occur (eg a 26-month delay beyond the date when the project was to commence operation under its implementation plan).

Enabling Investments with Cross-border Impacts – Section III H explains the reluctance that national regulators may feel with allowing revenue recovery by system operators for transboundary projects because of difficulties with allocating accurately the costs and benefits of transboundary projects to the electricity systems undertaking them or that will benefit from them even if they are not directly involved. That reluctance is related to duties commonly borne by national regulators to be mindful of the interests of consumers who will ultimately bear the costs of development which TSOs are allowed to recover though use of system charges. Article 16 of the 2022 TEEI Regulations helps with removing this obstacle by guiding national regulators on cost allocation for PCIs. It advises that the TSOs or other project promoters 'of the Member States to which the project provides a net positive impact' shall bear the 'efficiently incurred investment costs' of PCIs. This may mean that TSOs of systems in states other than the states in which a project is being conducted may bear some of the costs (eg, because a system benefits through a reduction in congestion). The costs should be paid for by network users through tariffs for network access in the relevant Member States (eg, regulators should allow the costs to be included within TSO charges for network use) to the extent that they are not covered by congestion or other charges.[105]

The project proposers submit an 'investment request' to the relevant TSOs which includes a request for them to undertake a cross-border cost allocation.[106] The TSOs

---

[102] ibid, art 3(4).
[103] European Commission, 'Key cross border infrastructure projects', (Commission, Energy Website) Key cross border infrastructure projects (europa.eu) (accessed 9 October 2022).
[104] 2022 TEEI Regulation (n 98) art 3(6).
[105] ibid, art 16(1).
[106] ibid, art 16(4).

that benefit from the development are identified by the proposers by undertaking an 'energy system wide cost-benefit analysis', the methodology for which is to be developed in accordance with Article 11 by ENTSO-E for electricity and ENTSO-G for gas. This requirement seeks to overcome the difficulty that Regulators have had with identifying exactly who benefits from major network projects which has made them reluctant to support such projects.

Article 16 also seeks to overcome difficulties for transboundary projects due to national regulators making decisions independently of each other by requiring them to coordinate their decisions and to make them within a set timescale. Decisions on the allocation of investment costs to system operators should be made within six months of the date on which the last investment request was received by a national regulator.[107] If the regulators cannot agree on cost allocation within the six-month period, the decision will be made by ACER. This ensures that national regulatory reluctance will not impede the implementation of PCIs.[108]

Section III H on 'Regulatory Challenges' also notes the reluctance that national regulators may feel over allocating support to projects which are perceived by them as being 'risky' because they will be using technology which has not been used previously in largescale developments or represent anticipatory expenditure on infrastructure in advance of current demand or firm commitments for its use (eg, seeking to encourage renewables investment by advance provision of the infrastructure required for transmitting it from producers to consumers). The 2022 TEEI Regulations' Article 17 responds to this concern by allowing Member States and national regulatory authorities to 'grant appropriate incentives' to projects whose promoters incur 'higher risks for the development, construction, operation or maintenance of a project of common interest … when compared to the risks normally incurred by a comparable infrastructure project'.[109]

Finally, Article 18 advises that certain PCIs involving electricity and hydrogen infrastructure can access financial assistance under the Connecting Europe Facility (CEF). The CEF was developed by the EU to support major infrastructure projects that may otherwise struggle to secure the funds required from private investors. The CEF for the period 2021–2027 is established in law by a 2021 EU Regulation.[110] This latest iteration of the CEF offers particular support for transboundary renewable energy projects.[111]

An interesting feature of the 2022 TEI Regulations is that PCI status may be accorded to projects involving non-EU states if criteria are met including 'a high level of convergence of the policy framework of the third country or countries involved'

---

[107] ibid, art 16(5).
[108] ibid, art 16(7).
[109] ibid, art 17(1).
[110] Regulation (EU) 2021/1153 of 7 July 2021 establishing the Connecting Europe Facility and repealing Regulations (EU) No 1316/2013 and (EU) No 283/2014 [2021] OJ L 249/38 (CEF Regulation).
[111] ibid, art 7.

with the Union's climate and energy policy goals, and a willingness by the non-EU state to comply with 'a similar timeline for accelerated implementation and other policy and regulatory support mechanisms' applying to PCIs in the Union.[112] Non-EU Member States involved with PCIs may also be able to access CEF funds in certain circumstances.[113]

Improving Coordination between Development Consent Processes – In addition to addressing aspects of the regulatory challenge considered in section III H, the 2022 TEEI Regulation follows its 2013 predecessor in requiring that specified approaches should be employed for authorisation in law of PCI development. Its requirements aim to address the all-too-common substantial delays with decision-making on transboundary infrastructure development in the EU. Often-lengthy permitting processes are attributed to the need to obtain multiple permits for development from national authorities acting independently of each other and to the public opposition that new network development can give rise to.[114] These problems and legal responses to them will be considered (in the context of obtaining consents for new generating plant) in Chapter 7. The Regulation contributes to addressing these problems as they affect transboundary grid developments in the following respects:

- *Article 7* – PCIs are to be prioritised in permitting processes. Their 'necessity' should not be questioned. They should be accorded the most rapid treatment legally possible under Union and national law.[115]
- *Article 8(1)* – Member States should designate a single authority to facilitate and coordinate permit granting processes for PCIs. More than one permit may be required, but one authority should manage the permitting process ('one-stop-shop' approach).

The various competent authorities for transboundary projects should take 'all necessary steps' to coordinate permitting for transboundary projects and should 'endeavour' to provide for joint procedures for environmental impact assessment.[116] Public consultations in different states should be coordinated and completed within two months of each other.[117]

Permit-granting processes must be completed within a maximum of three years and six months (with a possible maximum extension to four years and three months). The process is split into a pre-application phase of a maximum period of two years during which public consultations and environmental assessments should be conducted and a decision phase of one year and six months.[118]

---

[112] 2022 TEEI Regulations (n 98) art 4(2).
[113] CEF Regulation (n 110) art 5.
[114] SEC (2011) 1233 (n 35) 9–12.
[115] 2022 TEEI Regulation (n 98) arts 7(1) and 7(2).
[116] ibid, art 8(5).
[117] ibid, art 9(5).
[118] ibid, art 10.

Classroom Questions

(1) How is electricity conveyed from where it is produced to consumers? Identify the main actors and related activities involved with (a) conveying electricity from producers to consumers; and (b) related sales of electricity in markets.
(2) Why is network regulation required in liberalised electricity systems? What role do national regulators play in such systems?
(3) Identify each of the several different challenges with integrating renewable electricity into existing networks. For each challenge you identify, explain why the relevant difficulty arises. Is this due to physical limitations of existing networks to accommodate the new supply sources, to differences between renewable electricity and the fossil fuel electricity which networks were designed to carry, with laws and institutions that were adopted before significant renewable electricity production was a serious prospect, or a combination of these reasons?
(4) Identify ways in which law can be used to address each of the challenges you identify in your answer to Question 3. For each of the challenges, explain how the legal response assists with addressing it, and give examples of relevant uses of law.

Scenarios

Freedonia is a sovereign state with a liberalised electricity system in which generators and suppliers compete for market share. Freedonia has a state-wide transmission network under the ownership and operation of Voltacorp, the sole licensed transmission system operator in Freedonia. It also has several licensed distribution system operators who own and operate systems that take electricity from Freedonia's transmission system and distribute it to consumers in the different regions of Freedonia. As with other system operators in liberalised systems, Voltacorp and the DSOs are not in competition with other providers and are therefore subject to regulation and scrutiny from the Freedonia Office of Ampere Transportation (FOAT). Tariffs for use of the transmission and distribution systems are set by FOAT following negotiations with system operators over the extent to which system development and other costs can be recovered from system users.

The Freedonian executive has policies, backed by supportive legislation, to increase renewable energy generation significantly in the decade ahead. Fully involving its citizenry in renewable electrification is a central plank of its policies with a view to promoting public acceptability of the alterations in energy supplies. However, the policy push will be constrained without radical change to the governance, operation, and physical fabric of the existing transmission and distribution networks. The networks were established during the second half of the twentieth century to convey the electricity production from fossil fuel sources (coal, gas and oil) which still dominate the country's energy system in the present. The country's laws for governing transmission and distribution system operation also date from a period before major renewable energy integration was contemplated by legislation. Current generation is connected to the transmission system with the distribution networks being used purely to channel electricity from the transmission system to consumers.

Freedonia's neighbouring state, Sylvania, is mountainous. Much of its power is hydroelectric. Freedonia is in discussion with Sylvania about developing an electricity interconnector between them to allow the interstate exchange of electricity. Freedonia currently lacks options for storing electricity (eg, electrolysis and battery facilities).

The Committee of Freedonia's parliament on energy policy and law has convened a session to examine options in policy and law for supporting the integration of renewable electricity into Freedonia's energy system. You are a legal scholar undertaking research in energy law at the national university of Freedonia and have been invited to give evidence on possible legal responses to certain of the challenges arising with integrating renewable electricity into Freedonia's networks. The particular aspects you are asked to consider before the Committee hearing are as follows:

1. *Operational*: Freedonia's distribution system operators are receiving frequent requests from renewable generators to connect generating units to their networks for purposes including conveying electricity produced via the transmission system to reach other consumers. DSOs are finding this challenging because their experience is solely with distributing electricity taken from the national transmission system to end consumers linked to their systems. Transmission and distribution system operators are also expecting difficulties with keeping electricity systems in balance because of the intermittency of wind and solar electricity. It is recognised that physical change to networks will be needed, but modifications to system operation are needed in the short term to accommodate growing volumes of renewable electricity whilst physical alterations are being planned and conducted.

Advise the Committee on how law could be used to reduce possible constraints due to the above challenges on integrating renewable electricity into Freedonia's energy system before it is modified physically by requiring that system operators alter their operational practices.

2. *Legal Market Structures*: Freedonia's policymakers and legislators are keen to take advantage of the scope created by renewable electricity for introducing new classes of actors such as prosumers, aggregators and storage providers into the electricity system and its markets for trading power. However, it will not be possible to do this under its current legal framework. It was adopted before the renewable technology revolution and does not allow participation in the system by the new actors and new services that technological change has made possible. Even if this were possible, a significant proportion of the contribution that they could make would be lost because of Freedonia's market arrangements. Its electricity markets currently close the day ahead of

generation because supplies have largely been derived from controllable fossil fuel sources. Its balancing markets are at a rudimentary state of development for the same reason.

Advise the Committee on how law could be used to address such obstacles to renewable energy generation.

3. *Planning/regulation*: Freedonia's policymakers and system operators recognise that operational fixes alone will not be sufficient to accommodate increasing energy supplies from renewable sources. Significant physical modification of networks will be needed to provide capacities required for transmitting and distributing renewable electricity in view of its production in different places, by a more diverse group of generators and at different scales to centralised fossil fuel power. Development is also required to introduce new technologies and facilities (storage, hydrogen production, digitalisation for smart electricity systems, interconnections with other electricity systems) that will assist with managing the variability of intermittent renewable electricity production. The envisaged development includes the electricity interconnector with the neighbouring state Sylvania which is mentioned above.

Questions arise over the adequacy of Freedonia's current legal provision on system operator duties for preparing and implementing plans for network development to ensure that its electricity networks are always capable of providing secure and efficient transmission even during periods of change in electricity generation and transmission technologies. The legal framework was developed at a time of stability in the means of producing and transporting electricity when significant network modification was not required. In addition, the law establishing the regulator and setting out its responsibilities when regulating system operators places strong emphases on regulatory duties to restrain use of network charges placed on national consumers including by close scrutiny of cost recovery proposals for planned development, and on promoting reductions in those costs where possible. Policymakers fear that the national regulator may feel reluctant to allow cost recovery through use of system charges for some of the major infrastructure works that must be undertaken to accommodate renewables. The law establishing the regulator does contain a provision empowering the government to give direction to the regulator on preferred regulatory policy.

As with the other matters to be examined by the Committee, you are asked to speak on ways in which law could be used to overcome these possible constraints from inadequate provision in law on network planning and from a regulatory regime dating from an era when improving network efficiency was prioritised over changing networks to enable renewable-energy-led decarbonisation.

Suggested Reading

Book Chapters

Aileen McHarg, 'Evolution and Revolution in British Energy Network Regulation: From RPI-X to RIIO' in Martha Roggenkamp, Lila Barrera-Hernández, Donald Zillman and Iñigo del Guayo (eds) *Energy Networks and the Law: Innovative Solutions in Changing Markets* (Oxford University Press, 2012) 332.

LeRoy Paddock and Karyan San Martano, 'Energy Supply Planning in a Distributed Energy Resources World' in Donald Zillman, Martha Roggenkamp, LeRoy Paddock and Lee Godden (eds) *Innovation in Energy Law and Technology* (Oxford University Press, 2018) 371.

Ignacio Perez-Arriaga, Tomás Gómez, Luis Olmos and Michel Rivier, 'Transmission and Distribution Networks for a Sustainable Electricity Supply' in Ibon Galarraga, Mikel Gonzalez-Eguino and Anil Markandya (eds) *Handbook of Sustainable Energy* (Edward Elgar, 2011) 116.

Letha Tawney, 'Revolutionizing the Electricity Sector: Renewable Energy and Low Carbon Grid Infrastructure' in Frauke Urban and Johan Nordersvard (eds) *Low Carbon Development: Key Issues* (Routledge, 2013) 154.

Articles

Christian Hoerter, Nils Feyel and Alexandria Awad, 'The Smart Grid: Energy Network of Tomorrow – Legal Barriers and Solutions to Implementing the Smart Grid in the EU and US' (2015) 8 *International Energy Law Review* 291.

Bruce Stram, *Key Challenges to Expanding Renewable Energy* (2016) 96 *Energy Policy* 728.

Policy

International Energy Agency Energy Technology Systems Analysis Programme & International Renewable Energy Agency, *Renewable Energy Integration in Power Grids: Technology Brief* (IEA-ETSAP & IRENA Technology Brief E15, April 2015) Renewable Energy Integration in Power Grids (irena.org) (accessed 9 October 2022).

Report

Athir Nouicer and Leonardo Meeus (lead authors), *The EU Clean Energy Package* (European University Institute, Technical Report, 2019 edn, October 2019) EU-CEP-2019.pdf (eui.eu) (accessed 9 October 2022).

7

Planning, Licensing and Public Opposition

I. Introduction

It will almost invariably be necessary for developers to obtain authorisations for the construction and sometimes the operation of renewable energy generating plant under national legal regimes. Permitting processes allow public authorities to control and, where necessary, reject or apply conditions to development proposals. It may also be necessary for an environmental impact assessment of a proposed renewable energy development to be conducted under which the developer has to produce a report on likely environmental impacts of the proposed project for consideration by those with responsibility for reviewing permit applications. Earlier environmental assessment may be required at strategic levels of decision making of policies, plans and programmes, typically of central and local governments, that set the framework within which development that is likely to be environmentally consequential will proceed. Relevant laws ensure that environmental information is available to decision makers before they adopt or approve a proposed policy, plan, programme or project, and, it is hoped, contribute to the avoidance or reduction of development's negative environmental effects. They can also serve a cultural purpose of entrenching environmental considerations in the planning and processes of authorities and businesses.[1]

Principle 10 of the Rio Declaration on Environment and Development captures a normative position which was emerging in 1992 and which has been very influential since on legal frameworks for developmental planning and decision making: that '[e]nvironmental issues are best handled with the participation of all concerned citizens, at the relevant level' based on 'appropriate access to information concerning the environment that is held by public authorities ... and the opportunity to participate in decision-making processes'.[2] Laws on planning, permitting and environmental

---

[1] Jane Holder and Maria Lee, *Environmental Protection, Law and Policy* 2nd edn (Cambridge University Press, 2007), 550–56.
[2] *Rio Declaration on Environment and Development*, Report of the *United Nations Conference on Environment and Development*, UN Doc. A/CONF. 151/6/Rev. 1, (1992), 31 ILM 874 (1992), Principle 10.

assessment are often used as a vehicle for involving members of the public in decision making over whether plans and projects should be authorised. A common approach is for legally prescribed information about a proposal and information about its anticipated environmental effect which the actor making the proposal is obliged to provide under environmental assessment laws to be made publicly available. Members of the public are then invited to 'participate' in the decision making process whether by submitting comments through a remote consultation process or public-facing processes such as inquiries and hearings or deliberative engagement.

Planning and permitting processes and public engagement conducted through them serve essential purposes. They safeguard public interests, avoid inappropriate land use, prevent environmentally harmful development and enable public engagement as a core component of good environmental decision making. However, they can also be criticised by pro-renewable businesses and central and local public authorities. Their criticisms are based on a sometimes-justified perception that legal requirements for planning, permitting and public engagement are *unnecessarily* complex or time consuming, often therefore causing *delay* and adding to development costs. Section III of this chapter examines frequently cited grounds for concern over planning, permitting and public engagement for renewable energy development. Section V then considers types of legal response which are often used to address them.

A major source of governmental and business concern over the feasibility and rate of renewable energy development stems from the public opposition sometimes raised by relevant plans and projects including for new power lines required to carry electricity produced by them. Strong opposition may lead publicly elected decision makers to find grounds for rejecting a proposal even where the information in front of them supports its authorisation. A second major use of policy and law on planning and permitting for renewable development has therefore been to enhance its public acceptability. Section IV of the chapter examines common reasons for public opposition to renewable energy development. They fall into two categories: concern over the development itself and about the quality of the decision-making process. Section VI of the chapter explores legal approaches which have been used to address sources of opposition. They also fall into two categories: earlier public involvement to address potential issues before a development proposal is set in stone; and the use of shares in projects and other financial incentives to engender more positive attitudes towards a project and its proposer.

'Unnecessarily' and 'delay' are not objective terms. Rather, they are informed by the commentator's perspective. For example, what may be viewed as a source of 'delay' by a developer may be viewed as an essential component of good environmental decision making by someone whose community the development will affect. Reforms aimed at streamlining planning and permitting processes or making them more likely to yield pro-development decisions could be counterproductive if they add to grounds for concern over the quality of environmental decision-making processes, thereby strengthening public opposition. Measures seeking to promote more positive attitudes can also have the opposite effect if they are not conducted with care. A theme considered throughout the chapter is the need for careful design and implementation of relevant laws if they are to achieve their purposes.

The chapter focuses on planning and permitting for onshore wind farms. The reason for this is that onshore wind offers a good example of the strong views that renewable energy development can give rise to, and particularly where it is perceived to be incongruous with the place where development is proposed. Some details considered in the chapter such as concerns with flicker effects are specific to the technology. However, the example illustrates well how characteristics of any renewable technology can raise concerns and therefore of the need for a careful response, including in law, if initial fears which could be assuaged are not to become grounds for strident opposition.

Reference is made in the chapter to EU Regulation 2022/869 on Trans-European Energy Infrastructure.[3] This is concerned with energy transportation networks rather than power generation developments but is considered as the legal solutions which it requires Member States to use afford good examples of responses in law to the perceived concerns of developers and governments with permitting processes.

II. Planning and Permitting for Onshore Wind Energy

Governments use legal frameworks to control the quality and location of development. Legal control over development assists governments with promoting policy objectives whilst constraining activities which could have negative impacts on matters of public importance including the quality of built and natural environments. The most common means of legal control is by requiring that persons wishing to undertake development must obtain an authorisation, permit or licence from a specified public authority. Laws introducing such requirements typically specify information to be provided in support of an application, the actor(s) who will make the decision, the decision-making process, opportunities for public engagement in decision making, and the availability of appeal processes for persons with concerns over a decision's validity.

Permitting laws may have a relationship in law with planning regimes under which a specified, usually public, actor has a duty to prepare a plan for an area (eg, a city, a county) indicating attitudes towards different development types and promoting or discouraging them depending on their perceived compatibility with the area.[4] Plans embody strategic thinking and decision making on the future development of areas. Permitting laws may be aligned with planning law in order to effect publicly reviewed and endorsed plans by advising decision makers that their decisions should be guided by the plan. The influence of the plan on the decision will depend on the extent to which the law advises that it should be considered and followed in decision making.

---

[3] Regulation 2022/869 of 30 May 2022 on guidelines for trans-European energy infrastructure, amending Regulations (EC) No 715/2009, (EU) 2019/942 and (EU) 2019/943, Directives 2009/73/EC and (EU) 2019/944 and repealing Regulation (EU) 347/2013 [2022] OJ L 152/45 (2022 TEEIR Regulation).

[4] See Holder and Lee (n 1) 505.

As noted in Section I, permitting processes are used as a legal vehicle for integrating environmental considerations into decision making. Principle 17 of 1992's Rio Declaration on Environment and Development requires states to introduce environmental impact assessment in national law 'for proposed activities that are likely to have a significant negative impact on the environment' and that 'are subject to a decision of a competent national authority'.[5] Environmental impact assessment has since become recognised internationally as an essential aspect of good decision making from an environmental perspective. The International Court of Justice and the International Tribunal on the Law of the Sea have both found that the conduct of environmental impact assessment is obligatory under customary international law for activities which present risks of significant transboundary harm.[6]

Environmental impact assessment is relevant to both aspects of this topic. Obligations which relevant laws typically place on developers to prepare and submit information on environmental conditions and anticipated impacts with development consent applications and on decision makers to make provision for public participation in decision-making processes are prone to criticism from persons whose interests lie in expediting projects. Conversely affording opportunities for affected publics to engage with decision making under environmental impact assessment is essential for ensuring that decision makers are fully informed on a development's likely environmental impacts including on values held by people in the places which development affects. It can also be essential for diffusing potential public opposition to proposals.

Developers will usually be required in law to obtain a permit before undertaking a renewable energy development. Multiple permits will sometimes be needed. For example, governments may require that licences be obtained both to construct and to operate a renewable energy generating plant. The complexity of decision-making processes and the burdens they place on developers may vary by reference to the size of the development concerned. Permitting regimes may be less exacting for smaller developments conducted by householders and communities than for ones classed as being on a commercial/industrial scale. Licences may not be required in law at all for development whose intrusiveness falls below specified levels (eg, a solar panel on a roof). Such development may be allowed without authorisation in the UK by virtue of a Permitted Development Order.[7]

Similarly, environmental impact assessment may not be required for smaller scale development. Environmental impact assessment laws such as the EU's Environmental Impact Assessment Directive give direction on determining whether or not assessment is needed.[8] Assessment is mandatory under the EU's Environmental

---

[5] Rio Declaration (n 2) Principle 17.
[6] Philippe Sands and Jacqueline Peel with Adriana Fabra and Ruth Mackenzie, *Principles of International Environmental Law* 4th edn (Cambridge University Press, 2018) 658, 676–80.
[7] The Town and Country Planning (General Permitted Development) (England) Order 2015 (SI 2015/596), Sch 2, Pt 14.
[8] Directive 2011/92/EU of 13 December 2011 on the assessment of the effects of certain public and private projects on the environment [2012] OJ L26, art 4.

Impact Assessment Directive for certain classes of development, but is not required under the Directive where it is judged that a project's likely impacts would not reach the 'significant' level which triggers the duty it places on Member States to ensure that environmental information is before decision makers and assessed by them before deciding on a permit application.[9] For renewable energy developments (apart from large hydro-electric schemes for which assessment is compulsory) the Directive allows Member States to determine whether the 'significant' level is reached by setting a threshold or on a case-by-case basis applying criteria set out in Annex III to the Directive. Where environmental impact assessment is required, information generated through environmental assessment must be made publicly available. Early and effective opportunities must be afforded to the public to participate in environmental decision making.[10] This will typically be done through public consultation under which members of the public have an opportunity to submit a statement of their views on a proposed project under consideration. Decision makers must take representations made by consultees into account when reaching their decision, and must give reasons for reaching the decision made by them.[11]

III. Concerns with Authorisation Processes for Renewable Energy Development

Decisions by developers to conduct renewable energy projects and by investors to provide support for them, and, if so, at what rate of return, are based on assessment of risks associated with their conduct and related prospects for making an above-inflation profit on monies expended and loaned. Such risk analyses will focus in part on the number of permits required for the project and the processes that must be gone through to obtain them. A project for which only one licence is required from one licensing authority may be viewed as low risk. Conversely, processes involving multiple stages and authorities may ring alarm bells, and sometimes with good reason. Practical experience garnered during the first two decades of the renewables sector's growth links greater complexity in authorisation with longer timescales before a development is able to start recovering monies and higher project costs, whether due to higher interest rates or the need to pay financing charges, before the project has a revenue stream.

In view of the above, it is unsurprising that energy sector businesses and governments pursuing pro-renewables policies are sometimes critical of licensing regimes, accusing them of adding unnecessarily to development costs and of retarding the

---

[9] ibid.
[10] ibid, art 6(4).
[11] ibid, arts 8, 8(a), and 9.

low carbon energy transition's progress. Common reasons given for criticising legal requirements for licensing are as follows.

A. Complexity

A link is often made between perceived delay in permitting and the number of steps to be taken before a licence is issued, the number of separate permits to be obtained for each development, and the number of authorities involved in assessing applications whether as consultees on a proposal or because official approval is required from them.[12] Separate processes running consecutively or at the same time but without coordination add to the length and inefficiency of project authorisation. Higher numbers in procedural steps, requirements for permits and involved authorities cannot be correlated exactly with longer timescales but it would clearly be desirable to strip out procedural stages where they are genuinely unnecessary and to avoid duplication by coordinating separate licensing processes and/or combining them where possible.

Other complicating aspects identified by businesses and political authorities include: a lack of upfront clarity about information and documents concerning a development which licensing and/or environmental impact assessment laws require with resulting requests for clarification and further tests by reviewing authorities after applications are submitted; and inconsistency between licensing procedures due not only to requirements for multiple permits by authorities of a state but also to a lack of coordination between processes of separate states or regional authorities for projects crossing administrative borders.[13]

B. Lack of Time Limits

A lack of time limits for the review of applications is seen by businesses and authorities as an open invitation to delay in licensing processes. For example, the European Commission's definition of problems justifying its introduction of an expedited regime for trans-European energy networks laments the lack of 'binding time limits' in Member State permitting laws for electricity infrastructure 'to ensure that decisions are taken in a timely fashion'.[14] It also finds that laws setting time limits are not always backed by review and enforcement mechanisms to ensure that decision makers adhere to them.[15]

---

[12] International Energy Agency – Renewable Energy Technology Deployment ('IEA-RETD'), *Document the Cost of Regulatory Delays (RE-Delays)* (Report, Utrecht, 2016) 22–23; European Commission, 'Guidance to Member States on good practices to speed up permit-granting procedures for renewable energy projects and on facilitating power purchase agreements', SWD (2022) 149 final, 18 May 2022, 10.

[13] IEA-RETD (n 12) 4, 21–23. European Commission, 'Impact assessment Accompanying the document Proposal for a Regulation on guidelines for trans-European energy infrastructure and repealing Decision No 1364/2006/EC', SEC (2011) 1233 final, 11; European Commission, SWD (2022) 149 final (n 12) 22.

[14] European Commission, SEC (2011) 1233 final (n 13) 11. See also IEA-RETD (n 12) 4, 21–22.

[15] ibid.

When setting time limits, one consideration is whether they should include not only the initial decision-making process but also the conduct of any following appeal process. Swift and rationalised appeal processes are advocated by commentators calling for reductions in delay from permitting.[16] Care is needed when making relevant reforms to ensure that access to justice is not obstructed by the desire for haste.

C. Public Participation Processes

Tensions arise for renewable energy developers and governments with pro-renewables policies, both desiring as swift a decision as possible on project proposals, with requirements in law for public participation in decision making. Public involvement may be broadly accepted as an essential component of a good environmental decision, but there are different levels of participation with differing degrees of engagement ranging from the mere provision of information to affected publics having a veto on the final decision.[17] Requirements for public participation are vulnerable in general to being labelled as causes of delay in permitting processes by those who question their value, but this is particularly the case for more ambitious means of engagement than giving an opportunity to register a view on a development proposal in a remote consultation process. For example, inquiries in which members of the public have an opportunity to present their views in public meetings have been cited in the UK as delay factors necessitating reform of planning law with examples of notoriously lengthy hearings such as those for Heathrow Terminal 5 and Sizewell B Power Station being used to support the point.[18] Inquiries for electricity infrastructure being developed in part to enable network access for renewables such as the Beauly-Denny Transmission Link in Scotland and multiple transboundary projects connecting national electricity systems in the EU are mentioned as contributors to unduly lengthy licensing processes.[19]

Perception of public participation as a source of delay in decision making is a driver for the adoption of laws considered in Section 5 which seek to prevent authorisation processes from retarding the renewable sector's growth. This focus in reforming planning and licensing law would be reasonable and justified where provision for participation is genuinely unnecessarily complex and lengthy, but should otherwise be used with caution. It is all too easy to lay blame at participation's door for the duration of decision-making processes where their length is actually due to the number and complexity of issues which development proposals often raise.[20] In addition, curtailing participation in the interests of renewable energy growth could be counterproductive if it leads to opposition due to a lack of public confidence in decision-making processes.

---

[16] IEA-RETD (n 12) 7, 41.
[17] Holder and Lee (n 1) 85–87.
[18] Tim Marshall and Richard Cowell, 'Infrastructure, Planning and the Command of Time' (2016) 34 *Environment and Planning C: Government and Policy* 1843, 1853–55.
[19] Georgina Crowhurst and Simone Davidson, 'Planning: A Roadblock to Renewable Energy in the UK' (2008) 10 *Environmental Law Review* 181, 188.
[20] Marshall and Cowell (n 18) 1847–49.

D. Rejection by Decision Makers

The fact that decision making on renewable energy permits sometimes leads to their rejection should not be viewed as a weakness. The role of decision-making processes is to ensure that the diverse interests affected by a development proposal are taken into account in decision making so that an informed evaluation can be made, potentially leading to refusal if the balance of evidence points to that conclusion.[21] However, risks inevitably arise where decisions are made by representatives of elected local authorities that choices will be influenced by electoral considerations. In particular, local authorities may be minded to reject development proposals generating much public opposition even where governmental policy statements and targets militate for their approval and where the weight of evidence does not justify that outcome fully. The appeal of a decision to a higher authority may be available, but that may not be an attractive proposition in view of the additional time and expense. The view that local decision makers are rejecting too many applications based on political considerations rather than their merit is one reason for the trend in reform of planning and permitting laws which steer decision making toward governments' preferred outcomes.

Significant levels of public opposition in general (or amongst an electorally significant group) to a type of development can also influence governmental policy. For example, the UK Conservative Governments of 2015–2022 have effectively stifled the growth of onshore wind energy generation by giving communities in which such development was proposed a right of veto.[22]

IV. Reasons for Public Opposition to Renewable Energy Development

Surveys of public attitudes on renewable energy record strong and increasing support for meeting energy demand from renewable sources. For example, statistics on public attitudes collected by the UK Government in 2022 recorded 85 per cent support for renewable energy;[23] 78 per cent were in favour of onshore wind generation with only 4 per cent opposed to its use.[24] Similarly, the European Commission's 2019 review of public attitudes towards its energy policies found 90 per cent support amongst

---

[21] Brian Preston and Tristan Orgill, 'Adapting to a Sustainable Energy Future: The Role of Planning and Environmental Law', 13 October 2016. Available at: SSRN: https://ssrn.com/abstract=2856730 (accessed 8 October 2022), 32–33.

[22] UK Government, Department for Communities and Local Government, House of Commons: Written Statement (HCWS42), 18 June 2015.

[23] UK Government, *BEIS Public Attitudes Tracker: Energy Infrastructure and Energy Sources, Spring 2022, UK* (Department of Business Energy and Industrial Strategy, 16 June 2022) BEIS PAT Spring 2022 Energy Infrastucture and Energy Sources (publishing.service.gov.uk) (accessed 8 October 2022).

[24] ibid.

Europeans for the proposition that the European Union should encourage more investment in renewable energy.[25] However, people who back renewables in general are often less supportive when confronted with a proposal for renewable energy development which will impact on them directly. The label NIMBY (standing for 'not in my backyard') is sometimes used to describe those who favour renewable energy development as long as they are not affected by it.

Negative attitudes towards development proposals can contribute to the complexity and timescale of decision-making processes. They can also lead to a proposal's rejection and have been known in some cases to lead to the watering down or withdrawal of pro-development policies because opposition has reached an electorally significant level.[26] It is desirable, therefore, for those promoting relevant development to understand why projects are opposed. Having this understanding will assist them in tackling reasons for opposition at their source in the design of processes for public engagement and of laws which establish them as obligatory components of the decision-making processes.

'NIMBY' attitudes may well have contributed to opposition that renewable projects have met to some extent, but use of the term to suggest that opponents are motivated primarily by self-interest has met with strong criticism from academic commentators on grounds for public concern over renewable energy development.[27] They argue that reasons for opposition are much more complex than the NIMBY stereotype would suggest and will differ for each project. That said, analyses of opposed renewables projects reveal some recurring categories of concern. This is particularly the case for onshore wind turbines, a technology type which has become associated in the public mind with negative traits such as noisiness and visual intrusion.

A. Place-based, Visual and Amenity Concerns

As with any other type of development, renewable energy projects interact with values held by people in places. People form attachments to the places they are familiar with and enjoy, often to the extent that they contribute to their own sense of identity.[28] They hold values in the unaltered continuity of places to which they are attached. Development which alters a place may therefore be regarded with concern by those whose values are threatened. Every development is likely to affront some peoples' sense of place, but may be viewed as less problematic by others whose attachment to place is less challenged. Indeed, projects which some regard with dismay may be

---

[25] European Union, *Europeans' Attitudes on EU Energy Policy*, Special Eurobarometer 492, Report, May 2019.

[26] Richard Cowell and Susan Owens, 'Governing Space: Planning Reform and the Politics of Sustainability' (2006) 24 *Environmental Planning C: Government Policy* 406; see also the reaction of the UK's Conservative party to opposition to onshore wind development from a proportion of its electorate at n 22 above.

[27] Maria Petrova, 'NIMBYism Revisited: Public Acceptance of Wind Energy in the United States' (2013) 4 *WIREs Climate Change* 575, 577.

[28] Olivia Woolley, 'Trouble on the Horizon? Addressing Place-Based Values in Planning for Offshore Wind Energy' (2010) 22 *Journal of Environmental Law* 223, 230–32.

welcomed by others. However, developments may raise majority concerns amongst affected communities where many people share values in a place's characteristics. This is often the case with places valued by people for their peacefulness and lack of experience with development on an 'industrial' scale whether as 'green' spots in an urbanised environment or as rural areas.[29] As we have already noted, renewable energy production is often most viable in distributed locations without recent experience of responsibility for meeting energy demands and of hosting related facilities. It is unsurprising therefore that renewable energy development can raise concerns amongst affected populations. This knowledge highlights the desirability of exploring values held by potentially affected communities through public engagement before development is formally approved.

Conflict with often strongly-held values in places' aesthetic qualities are a particular source of concern over renewable energy development. Wind turbines may seem incongruous in previously unoccupied skylines. Their height enables them to tap into the strongest wind currents, but means that they can be seen over long distances in otherwise undeveloped landscapes. Less intrusive but also potentially jarring solar arrays have also encountered opposition on grounds of visual impact. Some governments have preferred to concentrate on offshore wind energy because of the strength of feeling which wind farms engender, but offshore wind has also encountered opposition because of its effect on seascapes.[30] The UK Government responded to such concerns by preferring wind farm development beyond the 12 nautical miles limit of the UK's territorial sea at which distance there is little or no visual impact.[31] Values held in views and seascapes should be a particular consideration when exploring how proposed development may interact with peoples' values.

Renewable energy development may be viewed as most threatening by those who fear that it will affect their homes and health directly. Onshore wind raises concerns of this nature in three respects. First, worries arise over noise from turbines.[32] The Centre for Sustainable Energy report advises that noise from modern onshore wind turbines is typically 'comparable to outdoor background noise' and that atypical situations where more intrusive noise may be produced can be identified and addressed during project design and implementation.[33] Even so, noise still crops up as a reason for concern over onshore wind energy projects. Second, views held by some commentators, but contested by others, that ultrasound from wind turbines could have health effects have added to public concerns.[34] Third, flicker effects from turbine blade shadows may cause irritation for neighbours at certain times of day and affect persons suffering from photosensitivity (this also being contested by others in medical academic literature).[35]

---

[29] Patrick Devine-Wright, 'Place Attachment and Public Acceptance of Renewable Energy: A Tidal Energy Case Study' (2011) 31 *Journal of Environmental Psychology* 336, 337–38.
[30] Woolley (n 28).
[31] ibid, 228.
[32] Centre for Sustainable Energy, *Common Concerns about Wind Power* (Centre for Sustainable Energy report, 2nd edn, June 2017) common_concerns_about_wind_power (cse.org.uk) (accessed 8 October 2022), 105–15.
[33] ibid, 105.
[34] ibid, 117–25.
[35] ibid, 101–03.

Production of biogas from anaerobic digestion has also been opposed over fears that gathering large amounts of organic waste in one place will impair public amenity both through lorry traffic and unpleasant odours.[36] Debate may arise over whether some of these concerns are well-founded, but effects from mechanical sound, flicker, increased road transport and waste have some grounding in reality and should be taken into account in thinking on the design of processes and laws for public engagement as well as in project planning.

B. Socio-economic Factors

Renewable energy development may be opposed by affected persons on economic grounds. Home owners may fear that their properties will lose value because of a project's proximity. Studies suggest that wind farm development does not lead to feared falls in property prices,[37] but the concern is understandable. Policies and laws have been adopted in some jurisdictions which seek to allay this concern by requiring that householders should be compensated for loss of value in their properties.[38]

It is important to bear socio-economic considerations in mind when seeking public views on proposed development. People may be concerned over how a renewable energy project could affect a community's economic interests and therefore its inhabitants' quality of life. Worries of this nature are likely to arise for communities whose economies depend on tourism, especially where this derives from a place's wilderness nature or from uninterrupted views onshore and offshore.[39] For example, the Gwynt Y Mor development off Llandudno raised questions about its compatibility with a traditional Victorian resort as well as the cluttering of its seascape.[40] Socio-economic considerations can also lend support for proposed development. Petrova notes that potential economic benefits for individuals and communities from a new industry, including the prospect of new employment, may make renewable energy development attractive for communities, particularly in rural areas where agriculture has become uncompetitive.[41]

The greater appeal which renewable energy development may have when it benefits communities financially can also be seen in legal requirements for communities to be given shares in renewable energy developments and in other forms of financial benefit for communities such as lower electricity prices as an enticement for acceptance of relevant development.[42]

---

[36] Christian Krekel and others, 'Quantifying the Externalities of Renewable Energy Plant using Wellbeing Data: The Case of Biogas' (Centre for Economic Performance, LSE, December 2020) Quantifying the Externalities of Renewable Energy Plants Using Wellbeing Data: The Case of Biogas (lse.ac.uk) (accessed 8 October 2022).
[37] Centre for Sustainable Energy (n 32) 69–74; Petrova (n 27) 582–84.
[38] See section VIB (ii) below.
[39] Petrova (n 27) 582–84.
[40] Woolley (n 28) 229, 231.
[41] Petrova (n 27) 583.
[42] ibid; see sections VI B (i) and (ii).

Care is needed over financial benefits from projects, including those required in policy and law, to avoid increased opposition amongst those who sense that they are being treated inequitably within their communities and in relation to other places. People are certain to question why a development is being conducted in their community rather than elsewhere and a resulting perception that they have been treated unfairly may be heightened where some members of communities enjoy greater financial reward from a project than others. Perceived disproportionate benefits for owners of land on which development is conducted and wealthy members of communities who are better able to benefit from share offerings for renewable energy and other financial incentives than others are likely to prompt more discontent than they avoid.[43]

C. Environmental Effects

The environmental benefits hoped for from mitigating climate change provide a principal reason for policies promoting renewable energy but relevant developments can also have negative environmental impacts. For example, unavoidable risks of bird and bat collision arise with wind turbines although they have been reduced by learning from early unfortunate experiences.[44] Dam and tidal barrage projects typically involve major alteration of ecosystems with significant attendant risks of environmental harm. The introduction of noise to the marine environment by offshore renewables adds to fears for the well-being of marine mammals such as whales that depend on their hearing for navigation and prey location.[45] Concerns over environmental impacts from renewable energy development have led to opposition to some projects from individuals and organisations such as the UK's Royal Society for the Protection of Birds. Projects have also been opposed where places are valued by people because of their environmental qualities such as hosting rich biodiversity. This was a factor in opposition to the proposal for the US first offshore wind farm in Cape Cod.[46]

That development may be opposed by members of the public on environmental grounds should not be viewed as a problem. The very purpose of legal requirements for strategic environmental assessment and environmental impact assessment is to ensure that decision makers are informed about the likely effects of a plan or project when making a decision on whether it should be approved, authorised with conditions aimed at addressing feared environmental impacts or rejected. It is hoped that the practice of considering, reporting on and reviewing environmental effects of

---

[43] ibid, 584; Marie Jørgensen, Helle Anker and Jesper Lassen, 'Distributive Fairness and Local Acceptance of Wind Turbines: The Role of Compensation Schemes' (2020) 138 *Energy Policy* 111294, 6; Katinka Johansen and Jens Emborg, 'Wind Farm Acceptance for Sale? Evidence from the Danish Wind Farm Co-ownership Scheme' (2018) 117 *Energy Policy* 413, 420.

[44] Centre for Sustainable Energy (n 32) 79–93.

[45] George Boehlert and Andrew Gill, 'Environmental and Ecological Effects of Ocean Renewable Energy Development' (2010) 23 *Oceanography* 68, 73.

[46] Jeremy Firestone and Willett Kempton, 'Public Opinion about Large Offshore Wind Power: Underlying Factors' (2007) 35 *Energy Policy* 1584, 1588–89.

development plans will promote a culture of environmental harm prevention amongst developers and central and local planning authorities. However, the need to take both environmental benefits from mitigating climate change and environmental effects when evaluating plans and projects for renewable energy does present a particular challenge for decision makers.[47] Laws adopted by some States with pro-renewable energy policies seek to assist decision makers with addressing the challenge by directing that projects implementing them should be authorised unless strong reasons are present for their rejection. Such laws run the risk of creating a critical mass of public opposition to pro-renewable energy policies held by governments by driving through authorisations in the face of popular concerns including over environmental impacts.[48]

D. The Quality of Developmental and Decision-making Processes

Persons who do not hold strong views on environmental effects or whose views are not set in stone may still become opponents to proposed projects because of the way in which development and decision-making processes are conducted.[49] Such concerns can entrench instinctive mistrust of developers external to affected communities (particularly large energy companies), and especially if communication with local communities is poor. External developers (and supportive governments/local authorities) may be seen as imposing projects on communities for profit. A failure to provide adequate opportunities for public participation may turn potential supporters into opponents because they question the legitimacy of the decision-making process. Opposition also arises even where people are able to make known their views where they feel that there is little or no likelihood that they will influence the outcome of decision making on the development proposal.[50] Particular attention should be given to the potential for poor public engagement to create hostility when designing decision-making processes as risks of public opposition due to concerns over developers' motivations and mistrust of authorities can be much reduced by interaction with communities and providing meaningful opportunities for them both to participate with developers on shaping a project and in decision making on its authorisation.

V. Legal Responses to Concerns with Authorisation Regimes

Governments and legislatures address concerns that authorisation processes may be retarding renewable energy development by reforming them. This may be done, where

---

[47] Olivia Woolley, 'Climate Law and Environmental Law: Is Conflict between them Inevitable?' in Benoit Mayer and Alexander Zahar (eds) *Debating Climate Law* 398, 404–06.
[48] Cowell and Owens (n 26); Woolley (n 28) 239–40.
[49] Petrova (n 27) 586–87; Woolley (n 28) 232–33.
[50] Woolley (n 28) 234–35.

the processes are set down in law, by removing aspects of decision making that are viewed as unnecessary. Complexity and related scope for delay are stripped out by streamlining decision-making processes including by coordinating the authorisation of renewable energy development and limiting the timeframe available to responsible authorities to reach their decisions. Governments take advantage of legal duties for responsible authorities to take specified matters into account in decision making to influence the outcome. This may be done by adopting policy statements concerning the treatment of certain development types in planning decisions. In addition, separate legal frameworks may be introduced for classes of largescale development viewed as nationally significant by governments, typically because they are central to delivery of their policy objectives, which positively require that relevant projects be authorised unless grounds exist for their rejection.

These legal interventions are effective for removing perceived sources of delay. However, their use could be counterproductive if they erode the public acceptability of renewable energy development by introducing new grounds to criticise the quality of decision-making processes and to question their legitimacy. The following sections look in greater detail at the legal approaches mentioned above, and at the need for care in legal design to prevent them from adding to rather than avoiding problems with pursuing renewable energy development.

A. Streamlining Development Consent Regimes

The term 'streamlining' entails the reform of permitting regimes where they are judged to be inappropriate or excessive for a type and scale of development. It is used in laws of the European Union which require Member States to review and where necessary revise their authorisation procedures for renewable energy projects. Article 15(1) of the 2018 Renewable Energy Directive repeats language used in its 2009 predecessor by obliging Member States to ensure that authorisation, certification and licensing arrangements for plant used to produce renewable energy and organic and non-organic transport fuels 'are proportionate and necessary'.[51] To achieve this overarching goal they must ensure that administrative procedures are streamlined and expedited at the appropriate administrative level, that rules are transparent and proportionate, that administrative charges are cost-related, and that simplified and less burdensome processes are introduced for smaller-scale developments included by requiring only that notice be given of decentralised power production and of infrastructure for storing renewable energy.[52]

The term is also used widely in academic literature on legal reforms of decision-making processes to enhance their efficiency. Jenkins describes the purpose of the Trans European Energy Infrastructure Regulation as being to 'facilitate the timely implementation of' infrastructure projects 'by streamlining, coordinating more closely

---

[51] Directive 2018/2001 of 11/12/2018 on the promotion of the use of energy from renewable sources, OJ L 382/82 21.12.2018 ('2018 RES Directive') art 15(1).
[52] ibid.

and accelerating permit-granting and enhancing public participation'.[53] Schumacher describes laws adopted to streamline decision-making processes for larger renewable energy developments including by coordinating separate strands of review and setting timescales for decision making in New Zealand and in Washington state in the US.[54]

As is the case with EU law on streamlining described above, relevant legal requirements will commonly make a distinction between aspects of decision making which a development type or project merits and others which are not merited. That is the basis on which laws in need of reform are identified. For example, the 2018 Renewable Energy Directive implicitly singles out laws that are 'disproportionate' or 'unnecessary' for revision.[55] However, views on the necessity of a stage in decision making may vary depending on the view-holder's interests. Care is needed in observing such strictures to avoid cutting aspects of processes out that are essential for good decision making with resulting potential to delegitimise outcomes in the eyes of those affected by them.

B. 'One-stop-shops'

Significant potential for complex and lengthy decision making may be created where several separate permits must be obtained for a project from separate authorities whose powers derive from separate legal regimes. This potential can be addressed by requiring that decision making under the separate regimes is coordinated, and, where feasible, by reducing the number of licences that a project must attain. The EU favours coordination through the establishment of 'one-stop-shop' authorities. It encouraged Member States to do this in its 2009 RES Directive and goes further under the 2018 Directive, having been frustrated by slow Member State progress with modifying permitting regimes for renewable energy.[56] Article 16 of the 2018 Directive obliges Member States to establish designated contact points that will, at an applicant's request, guide the applicant through and facilitate the entire permitting process.[57] This does not mean that there will be only one decision or permit. Rather, the applicant's transaction costs are reduced by having to deal with one contact point only which will then work with the different authorities and communicate with the applicant on papers and information needed and on progress with the application.

The Trans-European Energy Infrastructure Regulation employs this approach by requiring Member States to designate one national competent authority to be responsible for facilitating and coordinating the permit-granting process for projects of

---

[53] Victoria Jenkins, 'Regulation No 347/2013 on Guidelines for Trans-European Energy Infrastructure: The Provisions on Permit Granting and Public Participation and Their Implementation in the UK' (2015) 17 *Environmental Law Review* 44, 46.

[54] Kim Schumacher, 'Approval Procedures for Large-scale Renewable Energy Installations: Comparison of National Legal Frameworks in Japan, New Zealand, the EU and the US' (2019) 129 *Energy Policy* 139.

[55] 2018 RES Directive (n 51) art 15(1).

[56] Directive 2009/28/EC of 23 April 2009 on the promotion of the use of energy from renewable sources and amending and subsequently repealing Directives 2001/77/EC and 2003/30/EC [2009] OJ L140/16 (2009 RES Directive) arts 22(3)(a) and 23(6).

[57] 2018 RES Directive (n 51) art 16(1).

community interest, but goes beyond it in obliging them to coordinate the process using one of three options.[58] Under the 'integrated' option, one authority is responsible for issuing a single overall permit. Under the 'coordinated' option, authorities continue to reach their own decisions but they are coordinated in doing so by the single competent authority with a view to publishing the separate decisions together alongside one overall decision. The competent authority is to be given powers to support coordination by setting reasonable time limits for individual decisions, taking a decision where a body has not made it by the deadline, and disregarding decisions which it considers are not sufficiently substantiated by the underlying evidence. Third, the 'collaborative' option is less intrusive with the competent authority having the power only to establish reasonable time limits for the separate decision-making processes.

The 'one-stop-shop' approach offers a sensible means of reducing risks of delay for renewable energy development where multiple authorisations are needed. Care is needed however with its legal design. The involvement of many different actors and authorities with decision making on renewable energy projects will often be necessary because of the wide range of impacts they can give rise to. Coordination carries risks, if it is not sensitive to the often-complex effects of renewable energy development, of leading to decisions that are not well-founded because essential expertise has been excluded from the process, and whose legitimacy are questioned by those with associated concerns.

C. Limiting Timescales for Decisions

A common legal response to concerns over the time taken by authorisation processes is to limit the time allowed for decision makers to reach a conclusion after receiving the permit application. Relevant laws typically set a default limit but make allowance for the process to go beyond this if necessary on a case-by-case basis. Appeals of decisions are also usually excluded from the timeframe. Examples of this practice abound in the European Union and the UK. The EU's 2018 Renewable Energy Directive obliges Member States to limit permit granting processes to a maximum of two years for power plants and one year for small-scale electricity generating installations (capacities of less than 150Kw) and for refitting already authorised power plants with equipment capable of producing more power from the same resource (a practice known as repowering).[59] Time limits may only be extended where 'extraordinary circumstances' justify a longer timescale.[60] Decision making by planning authorities on onshore wind farms in England and Wales is less generous with a maximum of 13 weeks being allowed for 'major' decisions and eight weeks for others.[61]

---

[58] 2022 TEEIR Regulation (n 3) art 8.
[59] 2018 RES Directive (n 51) arts 16(4) to 16(6).
[60] ibid.
[61] Town and Country Planning (Development Management Procedure) (England) Order 2015 (SI 2015/595), reg 34.

It is from experience with lengthy decision-making stages for major infrastructure developments that general concerns with them as a source of delay stem.[62] It is unsurprising, therefore, that separate planning regimes for major infrastructure projects limit the time allowed for decision making. The UK's Planning Act 2008 and the EU's Trans-European Energy Infrastructure Regulation respectively set default periods of nine months and 18 months from the application's submission.[63]

Limiting the length of the decision-making process impacts on time allowed for public participation. As discussed earlier in this chapter, opportunities for public comment on proposed projects are provided once the full details of a proposed development and a report on its projected environmental impacts are available for review. Indeed, public participation stages of decision making can be particularly targeted for curtailment because of their reputation, not necessarily founded in fact, for being major culprits in 'delaying' the conclusion of relevant processes.[64] One way of limiting duration is by excluding consideration of public views on the need for a means of producing energy compared to other means of energy production (offshore wind instead of onshore wind, nuclear power instead of renewables) which may obviate the need for the project under consideration on grounds that relevant decisions are made by national governments when formulating policy. For example, the Planning Act 2008 gives the examining authority the power to 'disregard representations' that 'relate to the merits of policy set out in a national policy statement'.[65] The designation of particular projects as possessing priority status under the EU's Trans-European Energy Infrastructure Regulation places discussion of their necessity from an energy policy perspective off-limits in decision making, without prejudice to 'the exact location, routing or technology of the project'.[66]

Relevant laws often attempt in their design to compensate for possible constraints on public engagement after submission of a formal application by requiring that greater provision be made for earlier participation. Both of the UK laws and the EU's Trans-European Energy Infrastructure Regulation which this section mentions require developers to undertake pre-application consultation with communities likely to be affected by proposed projects and to include reports on the consultation and its outcome with their application papers.[67] As considered below, pre-application consultation can enhance the acceptability of renewable energy development amongst affected persons if developers are genuinely interested in exploring views on a proposed development with affected communities and prepared to modify their plans in light of feedback received on them. In addition, the UK's Planning Act 2008 makes up for constraints on public participation after submission of the development consent application by making provision for public comment on the policy statements concerning infrastructure types that decision makers are expected to follow when making decisions

---

[62] See section III C above.
[63] Planning Act 2008, s 98; TEEIR Regulation (n 3) art 10(1).
[64] Marshall and Cowell (n 18) 1847, 1861–62.
[65] Planning Act 2008, s 87(3)(b).
[66] 2022 TEEIR (n 3) art 7(1).
[67] Planning Act 2008, ss 47 to 50; 2022 TEEIR (n 3) art 9 and Annex VI.

on relevant projects.[68] Public engagement at strategic levels of decision making can be beneficial for public acceptability although with some significant provisos.[69] Even so, limited timescales for decision making could have negative consequences for renewable energy's expansion including by reinforcing public opposition where this derives from concerns with the quality of decision-making processes. Limited opportunity is left for public engagement after receipt of the formal application with potentially negative effects on public acceptance.[70] With regard to decision making over the largest infrastructure projects, these require an appropriate allocation of time to address complex and sensitive issues. Arbitrary curtailment could exacerbate public discontent or lead to bad decisions or both.[71]

D. Planning Policy Statements

Land use planning systems allow governments of states and regional and local governments operating under them to influence decision making on renewable energy. Legal requirements for decision makers on the adoption of strategic plans and approval of applications for development consent to 'have regard to' or to 'take into account' considerations specified in the law establishing the planning regime when making decisions creates an opportunity for governments to favour development types by adopting policy statements on how they should be viewed by responsible authorities when observing their decision-making duties.[72] The position will vary from state to state, depending on the provisions of relevant laws and their interpretation, but states may therefore be able to support renewables by adopting policy statements on relevant developments which encourage decision makers to use their powers to promote and favour them. This can be done at two levels. First, governmental policy statements may require responsible authorities to promote renewable energy when formulating long-term strategic plans which influence the subsequent development of areas covered by them. For example, the UK's national planning policy framework advises that plans should support 'the use and supply of renewable and low carbon energy and heat' including by providing 'a positive strategy for energy from these sources, that maximises the potential for sustainable development, while ensuring that adverse impacts are addressed satisfactorily'; and by 'identifying suitable areas for renewable and low carbon energy sources, and supporting infrastructure'.[73]

---

[68] Planning Act 2008, s 7, although note that the Infrastructure Planning (National Policy Statement Consultation) Regulations 2009 prescribing who should be consulted were revoked by the Town and Country Planning (Revocations) Regulations 2014 (SI 2014/692) and have not been replaced.
[69] Olivia Woolley, *Ecological Governance: Reappraising Law's Role in Protecting Ecosystem Functionality* (Cambridge University Press 2014) 90.
[70] Theresa Schneider and Antonella Battaglini, 'Efficiency and Public Acceptance of European Grid Expansion Projects: Lessons Learned across Europe' (2013) 4 *Renewable Energy Law and Policy* 42, 44 and 47.
[71] Woolley (n 28) 247–48; Schneider and Battaglini (n 70) 44 and 47.
[72] Holder and Lee (n 1) 511–13 and 703–09.
[73] Ministry of Housing, Communities and Local Government, *National Planning Policy Framework* (UK Government, 2021 revision) National Planning Policy Framework – GOV.UK (www.gov.uk) (accessed 8 October 2022), para 155.

Second, governments use planning policy statements to ensure that their preferences are taken into account when it comes to decision making on individual renewable energy developments. Policy statements may encourage authorities to favour renewable projects where possible. For example, the UK's national planning policy statement directs local planning authorities to approve applications if their impacts are or can be made acceptable and to 'recognise that even small-scale projects provide a valuable contribution to cutting greenhouse gas emissions'.[74] In addition, planning policy can be used to promote renewables indirectly by advising that developers seeking authorisation should be equipped for a renewable future. UK planning policy advises both that plans should identify opportunities for development to draw its energy supply from 'decentralised, renewable or low carbon energy' and that new development should be expected to comply with development plan policies on local requirements for decentralised energy supply unless the application demonstrates that this is not feasible or viable.[75]

Planning policy statements can serve a role in increasing the public acceptability of renewable energy development. The selection of areas for wind energy development can reduce scope for public concern, and particularly where there has been strong public involvement with plan formation and publicity for resulting plans. However, they may also exacerbate hostility amongst affected populations where strong governmental guidance in favour of renewable energy over which the public have had no influence, coupled with legal requirements for decision makers to take it into account, create the impression that local views are unlikely to have much influence on decisions on development consent. Local decision makers may prefer to reject proposals in the face of strong opposition rather than follow unpopular guidance.

E. Limiting Scope for the Rejection of Renewable Energy Development

Planning policy statements in the UK example given above are only one 'material consideration' amongst others to be evaluated by decision makers when adopting a plan or deciding on an application for development consent. Planning laws may give governmental planning policy statements more weight than other considerations when decisions concern categories of development identified as nationally significant because of their significance for implementing policy in areas such as energy, transport and trade. For example, decisions on development consent applications under the UK's Planning Act 2008 must be made in accordance with National Policy Statements (NPS) except where exceptions specified in the Act apply.[76] The NPS on renewable energy gives a strong steer to decision makers on supporting relevant development.[77] The decision maker (the Secretary of State) can follow a different course to that recommended

---

[74] ibid, para 158.
[75] ibid, paras 155(c) and 157(a).
[76] Planning Act 2008, s 104(3).
[77] Maria Lee and others, 'Public Participation and Climate Change Infrastructure' (2012) 25 *Journal of Environmental Law* 33, 60.

in the NPS but only 'if satisfied that the adverse impacts of the proposed development would outweigh its benefits'.[78] The legal direction significantly reduces scope for challenging projects that NPSs support. One reason for this is that impacts which may only become fully apparent once a project is under construction and operational such as environmental effects in combination with other human activities and alteration of a valued view may seem intangible for decision makers compared to benefits for economies, for energy security and for reducing greenhouse gas emissions that a renewable energy development is expected to deliver.

Closing down room for opposition to individual projects in this way may enable them to proceed quickly but could also have a negative effect on public willingness to accept them because of a lack of any meaningful opportunity to influence development proposals that policies already rubber stamp. A long-term consequence of this practice could be to see a veto effect emerging due to public antipathy to development types as numbers of decisions made under this process increase.[79]

VI. Legal Responses to Reasons for Public Opposition

The essential starting point for reducing risks of public opposition is to engage with communities that a planned project may affect. Knowledge garnered through engagement enables developers to respond in ways that address and alleviate grounds for concern. Public consultation on proposed development is often required in law following submission of application documents as part of their review by decision makers,[80] but this comes at a stage when room to modify a project is often limited. Developers may be unwilling to alter project details significantly, hence the 'decide announce defend' practice of backing a proposal in the face of concerns.[81] Indeed, their room for manoeuvre may be limited at this stage due to being boxed in by terms agreed with investors and by project details as presented in applications for subsidies and tenders. Participation in such circumstances can provoke rather than avoid public opposition because affected communities are not able to have a meaningful influence on the outcome. In view of this, developers have chosen voluntarily or have been required in law by governments with pro-renewables policies to engage with affected communities in ways other than consultation after a development consent application is submitted. The following sections consider two prominent means of alternative engagement: pre-application consultation and using financial incentives to promote positive attitudes towards development plans.

---

[78] Planning Act 2008, s 104(7).
[79] See n 48 above.
[80] Stuart Bell, Donald McGillivray, Ole Pedersen, Emma Lees and Elen Stokes, *Environmental Law* 9th edn (Oxford University Press, 2017) 324–26.
[81] Derek Bell, Tim Gray and Claire Haggett, 'The Social Gap' in Wind Farm Siting Decisions: Explanations and Policy Responses' (2005) 14 *Environmental Politics* 460, 462.

A. Early Public Engagement

Public antipathy to renewable energy development may stem initially from instinctive distrust of projects being pursued by developers external to communities to implement central government policy. Unwillingness by developers to alter their plans, as exemplified by the 'decide announce defend approach' compounds initial attitudes, transforming nascent negativity into outright opposition. Conversely, engagement by developers with communities *before* the development consent application is submitted can reduce scope for opposition where this enables affected members of the public to influence the development proposal as this takes shape. Participation at a stage when the location and design of a project and the relationship between the developer and community are still susceptible to change can assist with creating trust as a basis for more positive interaction.[82] In this regard, Hall, Ashworth and Devine-Wright review literature which explores how trust can be created between community members and wind developers and also in the technology by giving communities 'a more participatory and empowering role'.[83] The greater the influence affected persons and communities have on a development proposal, the more likely it is that they will be willing to accept it. Hall and colleagues draw an important distinction for acceptability between 'local determination to decide to accept a wind farm' and their being subject to 'what was perceived to be a fait accompli'.[84] Pre-application consultation was conducted for the AAT project in Wales.[85] Leitch argues that experience with this project evidences the importance of influence over the conduct of a development for swaying community attitudes.[86] In this case, unusually, the developer gave the community a veto over its final development proposals if it was not content with them.

The UK Government and the EU have recognised the potential value of early engagement for project acceptability by requiring that developers consult with affected stakeholders before the development consent application is submitted. The Planning Act 2008 requires developers to draw up a pre-application consultation scheme, and to engage with the public in accordance with it before the application is formally submitted.[87] The intended application must also be publicised.[88] Applicants must have regard to consultation responses when drawing up their application, and this should be accompanied by a consultation report.[89]

Pre-application consultation was extended in December 2013 to onshore wind developments involving more than two turbines or with any turbine exceeding a

---

[82] Vikki Leitch, 'Securing Planning Permission for Onshore Wind Farms: The Imperativeness of Public Participation' (2010) 12 *Environmental Law Review* 182; Petrova (n 27) 589–91.
[83] Nina Hall, Peta Ashworth and Patrick Devine-Wright, 'Societal Acceptance of Wind Farms: Analysis of Four Common Themes across Australian Case Studies' (2013) 58 *Energy Policy* 200, 204.
[84] ibid, 205.
[85] Leitch (n 82).
[86] ibid.
[87] Planning Act 2008, s 47.
[88] ibid, s 48.
[89] ibid, ss 37 and 49.

height of 15 metres.[90] As with the Planning Act, the application must be publicised and certain persons must be consulted by law. The final application must be submitted with a consultation report advising how this was approached and how responses were taken into account.[91]

Article 9 of the EU's Trans-Europe Energy Infrastructure Regulation requires project proposers to prepare and implement a pre-application participation concept with a report on consultations to be provided on formal submission of the application (this does not require the proposer to explain how it has taken public views into account).[92] At least one pre-application consultation must be carried out by the proposer or competent authority.[93] Part of the stated purpose of this consultation is 'to identify the most suitable location, [or] trajectory' for a proposal.[94]

The realisation of the potential for pre-application consultations to alter public attitudes to proposed projects will depend on how this is conducted. PACs may contribute to reducing scope for opposition if they provide a meaningful opportunity for affected communities to influence the proposed development including its location, and wind turbine numbers or configurations. However, PACs may not reduce opposition and may even create it where they are used as a 'tick-box' exercise to satisfy legal requirements rather than as a serious attempt at co-development with affected communities.[95] The strong support for projects that comply with NPSs under the Planning Act 2008 creates the risk that developers will pay lip service to pre-application consultation, but not take this seriously because approval of the project is very likely. Conversely, pre-application consultation may be more meaningful for developments for which decision making proceeds under the standard planning regime in view of the less strident support for renewable energy developments in current planning policy statements of the UK Government.

B. Financial Incentives

Perception that there is an imbalance between the benefits of renewable energy projects accruing to their developers, the burdens borne by communities in places where they are constructed, and the advantages for communities that benefit from clean electricity but without the impacts associated with construction and operation of the generating plant that produces it all contribute to public opposition. Developers seek to redress perceived imbalances by providing affected communities with monetary payments

---

[90] Town and Country Planning (Development Management Procedure and Section 62A Applications (England) (Amendment)) Order 2013 (SI 2013/2392, since replaced by SI 2015/595) (n 61).
[91] Louise Smith, House of Commons Library, *Planning for Onshore Wind* (Briefing Paper Number 04370, 13 July 2016) Planning for onshore wind (parliament.uk) (accessed 8 October 2022), 5–7.
[92] 2022 TEEIR (n 3), arts 9(3) and 9(4).
[93] ibid, art 9(4).
[94] ibid.
[95] Mhairi Aitken, Claire Haggett and David Rudolph, 'Practices and Rationales of Community Engagement with Wind Farms: Awareness Raising, Consultation, Empowerment' (2016) 17 *Planning Theory and Practice* 557.

and in-kind support such as enhancing facilities. This may be done by them voluntarily, but may also be encouraged or required in policy or law by governments with pro-renewables policies. The following sections examine means by which financial incentives for communities to view renewable energy development in a more positive light are made available. A common theme of this review is that they may contribute to enhancing the acceptability of renewable energy development in the eyes of recipients, but that care is needed in the design of schemes and rules to prevent incentives from creating more opposition than the benefits prevent. As Jørgensen notes, incentives must address the 'project-related concerns and the needs of local citizens' if they are to have a positive effect on how proposed projects are viewed.[96] Incentives which are advanced by developers without exploring with communities the reasons for concerns may be viewed simply as bribes and serve to deepen mistrust. In addition, it is important to avoid creating more losers than winners, the likely consequence of which is that net discontent will increase.

(i) Share Ownership

Opposition to renewable energy projects may derive from the lack of connection between their developers and affected communities. This adds to the impression that external actors take all of the benefits from projects by profiting from them whilst all of the burdens are borne by places where they are constructed. A way of responding to this perceived imbalance is to confer or make available the opportunity to acquire a stake in renewable energy developments to individuals and communities impacted by them. Experience with share ownership shows that it can have a positive effect on the acceptability of projects.[97] Community ownership assists with breaking down the image of non-community developers as outsiders interested in a location only because of the resource it offers, and with adjusting the view that benefits from a project flow only to external actors.[98] More advanced share ownership practices in which local stakeholders not only have a share in development but also a meaningful role with conduct and management of the relevant development can also create trust between communities and developers and the senses of control and of allowing renewable energy instead of having it visited upon them that aid acceptance.[99]

Denmark has a long history of encouraging community development and ownership of wind farms through subsidies and tax exemptions. Corporate investment in wind farms and their size is growing in Denmark to meet targets for decarbonisation (50% of electricity from wind by 2020). The Danish Renewable Energy Act (No 1392 of 2008) requires that a minimum of 20 per cent of shares in new wind energy projects should be offered preferentially to local people living within 4.5km from the installation

---

[96] Jørgensen, Anker and Lassen (n 43).
[97] Petrova (n 27) 583–54.
[98] ibid, 584.
[99] Fleur Goedkop and Patrick Devine-Wright, 'Partnership or Placation? The Role of Trust and Justice in the Shared Ownership of Renewable Energy Projects' (2016) 17 *Energy Research and Social Science* 135, 138.

site and, if they are not sold out, to citizens with a permanent residence in the affected municipality.[100]

The UK Government published its first Community Energy strategy in January 2014. The strategy requested the renewables industry and the community energy sector to work on creating a voluntary framework for shared ownership.[101] To back this up, the Infrastructure Act 2015 confers a power for the Secretary of State to make regulations giving individuals/groups a right to acquire a stake in renewable developments in or adjacent to the community. Developers would be required to make a minimum offering of a 5 per cent share in the development if regulations are made.[102]

Care is needed with the design of policies and laws requiring that renewable energy developments should make shares available, as they can exacerbate negative attitudes if used incautiously including by creating more losers than winners. For example, schemes that enable already wealthy and influential citizens to benefit from share offerings but which are inaccessible in practice to those without funds would not contribute significantly to creating a positive community attitude toward a proposed development.[103] On the contrary, hostile attitudes may be strengthened by the reinforcement of existing divides between rich and poor in communities. Legal definition of the group that benefits from share ownership can also have the effect of alienating those who are not included within it including on grounds of their homes being marginally too distant from the relevant development.[104]

(ii) Compensating Individuals

'Compensation' is often used broadly in relevant literature to refer to the several different ways in which financial benefits are provided by developers.[105] This section employs a narrower definition to distinguish between measures directly targeting those who have suffered financial loss because of the renewable energy development and those which serve in general to counter the impression that the flow of benefits is in one direction only. The Danish Renewable Energy Act provides an example of targeted compensation.[106] Wind farm developers are obliged to compensate those who can provide the evidence required in law that their properties' values have fallen due to the project's impact. Such measures can complement benefits for communities by acting with environmental justice toward persons whose interests have been affected negatively by development benefitting populations at large. However, care is needed in legal design to avoid typical risks with such schemes of strengthening opposition.

---

[100] Jørgensen, Anker and Lassen (n 43); Birgitte Olsen, 'Regulatory financial obligations for promoting local acceptance of renewable energy projects' in Marjan Peeters and Thomas Schomerus, *Renewable Energy Law in the EU: Legal Perspectives on Bottom-up Approaches* 189–209.

[101] Department of Energy and Climate Change, *Community Energy Strategy: Full Report* (UK Government, 27 January 2014) 20140126 Community_Energy_Strategy.pdf (publishing.service.gov.uk) (accessed 8 October 2022).

[102] Infrastructure Act 2015, s 38.

[103] Jørgensen, Anker and Lassen (n 43) 9–10; Goedkop and Devine-Wright (n 99) 143.

[104] Olsen (n 100) 202.

[105] Jørgensen, Anker and Lassen (n 43) 2–3; Petrova (n 27) 583.

[106] Consolidated Act No 1074 of 8 November 2011 on Renewable Energy.

This can be created or reinforced by excluding persons from entitlement to compensation on arbitrary terms (eg limiting it by using a distance cut off), by a lack of transparency on how compensation is calculated, or by setting requirements with high transaction costs for attaining compensation with the result that only those with social and financial advantages are able to access them (eg varying according to state of house/ use of property).[107] The impact on wind farm developers should also be considered. Adding an obligation to pay compensation to other costs could deter development by making financial support harder to obtain at reasonable rates or eroding profit margins. In addition, why should wind farm developers compensate householders when developers of other development types are not obliged to provide affected persons with compensation? Engagement over the need to mitigate climate change would be preferable to sending out a message that there is something inherently wrong with renewable energy development.

(iii) Community Benefits

Developers provide financial and non-material benefits for communities over and above those deriving directly from projects (eg local employment) to reduce risks of public discontent and opposition. This may be done by supporting facilities which benefit communities, by providing funds for allocation by the community to projects, or by giving particular benefits to communities where possible such as lower cost electricity.[108] Community benefits may be provided by projects' promoters voluntarily, but this practice may also be encouraged in policy statements or even required in law by governments with pro-renewables policies because of its positive effects. For example, the UK Government encourages wind farm developers to make voluntary contributions to community projects under the Community Benefit Protocol of Renewable Energy UK (the sector's trade body) of £5000 per MW per year.[109]

Developers may also agree to provide certain benefits where they are needed to make a project acceptable to decision makers which they would not otherwise be willing to authorise. Section 106 of the UK's Town and Country Planning Act 1990 allows developers and planning authorities to enter into planning obligation agreements in order to secure planning permissions in circumstances where it would otherwise be unacceptable.[110] Planning obligation agreements could be used in connection with

---

[107] Jørgensen, Anker and Lassen (n 43) 7–10; Olsen (n 100) 202–07.

[108] Department for Business, Energy and Industrial Strategy, *Community Engagement and Benefits from Onshore Wind Energy* (UK Government, December 2021) Community Engagement and Benefits from Onshore Wind Developments: Good Practice Guidance for England (publishing.service.gov.uk) (accessed 8 October 2022), 31–39; Chiara Armeni, 'Participation in Environmental Decision-making: Reflecting on Planning and Community Benefits for Major Wind Farms' (2016) 28 *Journal of Environmental Law* 415, 429; Benjamin Walker, Bouke Wiersma, and Etienne Bailey, 'Community Benefits, Framing and the Social Acceptance of Offshore Wind Farms: An Experimental Study in England' (2014) 3 *Energy Research and Social Science* 46, 47–48.

[109] Renewable UK, *Onshore Wind: Our Community Commitment* (Renewable UK Website, October 2013) community_benefits_report.pdf (ymaws.com) (accessed 8 October 2022); Smith (n 91) 19.

[110] Smith (n 91), 17.

wind farms to develop environmental compensation schemes for disturbed habitats and visual effects or to improve roads in view of likely traffic increases. Decisions reached on this basis may be vulnerable to legal challenge unless the agreed benefits are genuinely required for the award of planning permissions.[111] For example, the landscaping of the area occupied by an onshore wind farm may be legitimate to make up for the visual impact, whereas construction of a swimming pool which has no connection with a wind farm may not.

As with other financial incentives, community benefits assist with improving public perception of the developer and therefore with strengthening support for its projects. As part of this, engagement by the developers with communities to learn more about them and to agree support with inhabitants that would enjoy wide support can create confidence in the procedural fairness of decision making and trust in the developer.[112] However, community benefits may not sway attitudes amongst those whom feel strongly about the likely effects of a development proposal.[113] For others whose opposition is more deeply rooted, an element of control over the development (including with negotiating packages of benefits as a condition for support) is likely to be necessary to alter attitudes. Indeed, financial incentives as well as opportunities for early engagement with decision making on individual projects may have little impact on the views of persons whose opposition to renewable energy development in certain locations is strongly rooted. With this in mind, public participation at strategic levels including the formulation of policy, plans and programmes may assist with identifying types of projects and areas in which development may prove particularly problematic as well as creating an early partnering relationship with communities that are more likely to be receptive to prospects of onshore renewable energy development in their vicinity.[114]

Classroom Questions

(1) Explain how legal regimes for guiding decision making on land use through plan formation, for decision making on whether development should be authorised and for assessing the environmental impacts of proposed development can be used to (i) promote renewable energy development; (ii) regulate renewable energy development; and (iii) ensure that views of members of the public likely to be affected by renewable energy development are explored and taken into account in decision-making processes.

---

[111] Richard Cowell, Gill Bristow and Max Munday, 'Acceptance, Acceptability and Environmental Justice: The Role of Community Benefits in Wind Energy Development' (2011) 54 *Journal of Environmental Planning and Management* 539, 544.
[112] Walker, Wiersma and Bailey (n 108) 47–48, 52.
[113] Armeni (n 108) 428; Cowell, Bristow and Munday (n 111) 541–43, 552–53.
[114] Woolley (n 28) 240–47: Woolley (n 69), 89–96, 131–39.

182 PLANNING, LICENSING AND PUBLIC OPPOSITION

(2) Identify the ways in which some actors (particularly businesses/central government) see requirements for authorisation of development and associated procedures (such as environmental assessment) as constraints on the expansion of renewable energy.
(3) On what grounds are onshore wind farm developments typically opposed by members of the public?
(4) What legal approaches are used to address the concerns with authorisation regimes mentioned in Question 2? Support your answer with examples of relevant laws.
   (a) Could these approaches give rise to problems with securing consent for renewable energy development (eg, a heightened risk of public opposition)?
(5) What legal approaches are used to address the reasons for public opposition that you identified in your answer to Question 3? Support your answer with examples of relevant laws.

Consider the benefits and disadvantages of these approaches for improving public acceptance.

Scenarios

(1) The government of Costaguana has ambitious policies for increasing renewable energy production. It provides generous subsidies to attract investment in new developments and has reformed its laws on network operation to promote the integration of renewables into its energy systems as far as possible. However, to date, it has failed to secure the support it had hoped for. Analysis commissioned by the Costaguanan government about reasons for this failure attributes it, amongst other causes, to the state's laws on authorisation of renewable energy development. Seven permits are required for each development from seven separate authorities whose licensing regimes are not coordinated. The duration of permitting procedures is very variable with some taking three or more years to complete. Part of the timeframe for their conduct is taken up by responsible authorities' compliance with legal duties for enabling public participation in decision making. Several permit applications for onshore wind farms have been rejected in recent years by the local government of the Piano Grande province. The Costaguanan government suspects that they were rejected by the local government not because of anticipated negative impacts, but for electoral reasons.

The Costaguanan government has instructed you, a partner in an energy specialist law firm, to advise on how its legal permitting laws could be reformed to remove features which deter renewable energy investment.

Note that public opposition to renewable energy development is not a problem in this scenario. However, the Costaguanan government is concerned that legal reforms to permitting laws to make them more attractive to investors could lead to heightened public opposition. Advise it on risks that legal reform could lead to opposition and on how those risks can be mitigated through careful legal design.

2. The Costaguanan government is exploring possibilities for implementing a pro-onshore wind policy in the country's Aeolian region. It is concerned that projects pursued within this region may encounter public opposition. The region contains some areas which are prized by its residents for their beauty and environmental value, while other areas which are not valued so highly. The inhabitants of the region are inclined (as is the case for all inhabitants of Costaguana) to distrust the government and also the major power corporations that are likely to be developing individual projects. The region is a rural area and most inhabitants of its villages and small towns are not well off. However, there has been a recent trend of wealthier city dwellers moving into the area from Costaguana's capital city. Some of the latter were vocal in opposing a previous proposal by the Costaguanan government for biogas production on grounds that it would affect property prices. Other residents, whilst seeing the possibility of new economic activity as a potential positive for employment and for the faltering regional economy, are concerned that energy development in the region could have negative impacts on communities' qualities of life.

Advise the Costaguanan government on how it could use the law to reduce risks this combination of circumstances gives rise to that its onshore wind programme in the region will encounter significant public opposition.

Suggested Reading

Books

Patrick Devine-Wright (ed), *Renewable Energy and the Public: From NIMBY to Participation* (Earthscan, 2011).

Book Chapters

Birgitte Olsen, 'Regulatory Financial Obligations for Promoting Local Acceptance of Renewable Energy Projects' in Marjan Peeters and Thomas Schomerus, *Renewable Energy Law in the EU: Legal Perspectives on Bottom-up Approaches* (Edward Elgar, 2014), 189–209.

Articles

Chiara Armeni, 'Participation in Environmental Decision-making: Reflecting on Planning and Community Benefits for Major Wind Farms' (2016) 28 *Journal of Environmental Law* 415.

Richard Cowell, Gill Bristow and Max Munday, 'Acceptance, Acceptability and Environmental Justice: The Role of Community Benefits in Wind Energy Development' (2011) 54 *Journal of Environmental Planning and Management* 539.

Victoria Jenkins, 'Regulation No. 347/2013 on Guidelines for Trans-European Energy Infrastructure: The Provisions on Permit Granting and Public Participation and Their Implementation in the UK' (2015) 17 *Environmental Law Review* 44.

Marie Jørgensen, Helle Anker and Jesper Lassen, 'Distributive Fairness and Local Acceptance of Wind Turbines: The Role of Compensation Schemes' (2020) 138 *Energy Policy* 111294.

Maria Lee, Chiara Armeni, Javier de Cendra, Sarah Chaytor, Simon Lock, Mark Maslin, Catherine Redgwell and Yvonne Rydin, 'Public Participation and Climate Change Infrastructure' (2012) 25 *Journal of Environmental Law* 33.

Tim Marshall and Richard Cowell, 'Infrastructure, Planning and the Command of Time' (2016) 34 *Environment and Planning C: Government and Policy* 1843.

Maria Petrova, 'NIMBYism Revisited: Public Acceptance of Wind Energy in the United States' (2013) 4 *WIREs Climate Change* 575.

Olivia Woolley, 'Trouble on the Horizon? Addressing Place-Based Values in Planning for Offshore Wind Energy' (2010) 22 *Journal of Environmental Law* 223.

8
Offshore Renewables*

I. Introduction: Offshore Power Potential

The world's seas and oceans offer enormous potential for renewable electricity production.[1] Offshore renewable electricity sources include winds which are typically stronger and more constant than onshore winds. Underwater tidal currents can be used to drive turbines for power generation. Differences in water level between low and high tides can, when the differential is large enough, be used to generate power by retaining waters behind tidal barrages (a similar concept to damming rivers for hydroelectric power) whose release then drives power producing equipment. Electricity can be produced from waves by taking advantage of the undulation of surface waters to harness their kinetic energy. Differences in temperatures between ocean surface waters and deep ocean waters can be exploited for power production using ocean thermal energy conversion technology. The greater space that is sometimes available offshore compared to built-up areas onshore for power production can be used to deploy largescale solar photovoltaic arrays. Artificial energy islands are also seen as a means of employing offshore power exceeding demand or available capacity to transport it to consumers by using the excess to activate equipment for power retention such as electrolysis to produce 'green' hydrogen and battery storage.

A. Fixed Offshore Wind Technology

Technologies for producing power from offshore wind energy have evolved rapidly during the twenty-first century. First emerging in the early 2000s, total offshore wind electricity capacity grew worldwide from 3000MW in 2010 to 34000MW in June 2021.[2] The UK is currently the leading offshore wind power producer with up to around two-fifths of its electricity deriving from this source. China is the second largest producer of offshore wind power and is likely to become world leader in offshore capacity during

---

*This chapter includes content which was first published in Olivia Woolley, 'Renewable Energy and the Law of the Sea' in J Kraska and Y-K Park (eds), *Emerging Technology and the Law of the Sea* (Cambridge University Press, 2022), 35–62.
[1] IRENA, *Offshore Renewables: An action agenda for deployment*, (IRENA, July 2021), 27.
[2] ibid, 11.

the 2020s. Other leading producers are found in the EU including Germany, Denmark, the Netherlands and Belgium. The EU has massive plans for growing offshore wind energy capacity to 60GW by 2030 and to 300GW by 2050.[3] Other jurisdictions such as the US, India, and Japan are behind the UK, the EU and China, but themselves have major plans for establishing offshore power production capacities of around 30GW by 2030.[4] In effect, the world's search for low carbon energy is driving a revolutionary shift in electricity production offshore.

The growth in offshore wind power to date has largely been from the installation of turbines that are fixed permanently in place to the seabed by foundations. Fixed offshore wind is now a well-established technology. Improvements in the efficiency and capacities of offshore wind turbines through learning by doing have enabled significant reductions in the costs of offshore wind power. The massive size of offshore wind farms compared to most onshore wind farms also enables economies of scale both in power production and in the creation of facilities for manufacturing the technology and supporting its deployment. As a result, offshore wind power costs have dropped dramatically over a short space of time. For example, the bid prices for offshore wind in the UK's contracts for difference funding rounds fell from £114.39 for wind farms commencing operation in 2018–2019 under Round 1 to £37.35 for five wind farms with a combined notional capacity of 7GW commencing operation in 2026–2027 under Round 4.[5] The technology's increasing competitiveness on price enhances its appeal as an alternative to fossil fuel energy.

B. Floating Turbine Technology

Fixed turbines can only be deployed in shallow water depths of up to around 70 metres. States with deeper coastal waters such as Norway, Japan and the west coast states of the US have therefore been unable to participate in the fixed offshore wind boom. Instead, they have become pioneers in developing floating wind turbine technology which can be used in waters deeper than 70 metres. Floating wind turbines are held in place temporarily to the seabed using anchors, cables and other means of keeping them in situ. At the time of writing (September 2022), the six turbine 50MW capacity Kincardine project off Scotland's Aberdeenshire coast is the world's largest floating wind farm. Much larger developments are likely to follow during the 2020s due to the technology's appeal both for states with deeper coastal waters and for other states due to the potential opening up of deeper waters further from coastlines than were previously accessible for power production.[6] Academic commentators are already contemplating possibilities for power production from floating turbines in far distant High Seas areas lying beyond states' exclusive economic zones, a global commons area

---

[3] ibid.
[4] ibid.
[5] Department for Business, Energy and Industrial Strategy, 'Policy Paper: Contracts for Difference' (UK Government website, 13 May 2022) Contracts for Difference – GOV.UK (www.gov.uk) (accessed 7 October 2022).
[6] IRENA, *Floating Foundations: A Game Changer for Offshore Wind Power* (IRENA, 2016).

which cannot be made subject to the jurisdiction of any state under international law.[7] The challenge here may be less with electricity production than the difficulties and expense of developing the infrastructure for transmitting it from places far removed from human populations to consumers.

C. Ocean Energy Technologies Lag Behind

Energy production from seawater retention using tidal barrages is well-established but is limited to areas where water depths at low and high tides differ sufficiently for commercially viable electricity generation.[8] Other ocean energy technologies are still passing through pre-commercialisation phases of research and development and prototype testing. Operational tidal stream and wave energy projects remain at modest scales with the largest capacity projects as at the publication of IRENA's 2021 offshore renewables report being 2MW (UK, Orkney Islands) and 1MW (US, Hawaii) respectively.[9] However, lengthy gestation periods for both technologies are now expected to bear fruit with commercialisation, significant growth, and cost reductions for currently expensive means of producing power being expected during the 2020s.[10] OTEC has the largest potential power production capacity amongst ocean energy sources, but high capital costs, a lack of practical experience and environmental concerns continue to prevent progress beyond small-scale prototypes.[11] Finally significant growth is expected for offshore solar power in the decade ahead.[12] Tidal stream, wave and offshore solar technologies offer particular promise for meeting the energy needs of developing island states from renewable sources.

D. Offshore Network Development is Key for the Expansion of Offshore Wind and Ocean Energy

As with all other electricity generating station projects, corresponding development is needed of cable networks for conveying electricity from where it is produced to consumers. No transmission capacity exists offshore due to the newness of the relevant renewable energy technologies. Offshore generation therefore necessitates the laying of new cables to transmit electricity to onshore networks. It also prompts longer term thought about how the potential advantages of 'greenfield' development for new transmission infrastructure including economic efficiency, environmental efficiency, and flexibility (eg, to route electricity to more than one market depending on where it is

---

[7] Paul Elsner and Suzette Suarez, 'Renewable Energy from the High Seas: Geo-spatial Modelling of Resource Potential and Legal Implications for Developing Offshore Wind Projects Beyond the National Jurisdiction of Coastal States' (2019) 128 *Energy Policy* 919.
[8] IRENA (n 1) 52.
[9] ibid 12.
[10] ibid 51–56.
[11] IRENA, *Ocean Thermal Energy Conversion: Technology Brief* (IRENA, 2014).
[12] IRENA (n 1) 12.

most needed at the time) can best be taken advantage of. For proximate states such as those surrounding the North Sea, this has led to collaborative exploration of possibilities for developing a common offshore electricity grid.[13]

Fixed offshore wind farms are already being constructed in waters very far removed from coastlines where water depths allow this. For example, the 1.2GW Hornsea One wind farm which began operation in the UK's North Sea EEZ area in 2020 is located 120km from the coastline.[14] It is advantageous, therefore, that the emergence of technologies for producing power in remote offshore areas has coincided with major advances in direct current cable technologies for transmitting electricity from where it is produced to consumers. High voltage direct current (HVDC) cables now offer a preferable alternative to alternative current (AC) cables for the transmission of electricity from wind farms situated far out to sea because they lose less power than AC comparators.[15] Emerging HVDC Voltage Source Converter (VSC) technologies also offer more scope than was previously available for linking separate offshore transmission cables to create a meshed grid which is capable of conveying power from offshore wind farms to several potential destinations.[16] These technological developments afford states practical tools to realise the potential cost reducing, environmental efficiency, and flexibility benefits of collaborating on their offshore generation and transmission energy development programmes.

E. Structure of the Chapter

The chapter examines the key legal questions and challenges raised by offshore power production and transmission. Section II reviews the different legal bases offshore, deriving from the international law of the sea, which replace the familiar world of onshore development under the territorial sovereignty and jurisdiction of the states concerned. It identifies relevant legal rights to undertake the development and operation of related infrastructure as well as some respects in which further legal development may be required to clarify grey areas.

Section III examines potential for offshore renewable energy development to conflict with other sea uses in practice and also in law due to protections for states' rights to undertake certain activities offshore even in waters under the sovereignty or functional jurisdiction of other states under public international law. In this regard, a tendency to view the seas as limitless places for power production compared to developed landmasses is misplaced. Long-established marine activities play essential roles in trade and travel by shipping, food supplies from fisheries, and support for construction and industries including from the extraction of gravel and minerals. Balances between

---

[13] European Commission, 'The North Seas Energy Cooperation' (European Commission, Website) (The North Seas Energy Cooperation (https://europa.eu) (accessed 7 October 2022).

[14] Orsted, 'About the project', (Hornsea One, Website) About the project (hornseaprojectone.co.uk) (accessed 7 October 2022).

[15] Asimenia Korompili, Qiuwei Wu and Haoran Zhao, 'Review of VSC HVDC Connection for Offshore Wind Power Integration' (2016) 59 *Renewable and Sustainable Energy Reviews* 1405.

[16] ibid.

offshore power and these activities must be struck to respect both legal protections for them and the roles they play in meeting societal needs.

Section IV considers offshore renewable energy development within the broader contexts of marine ecosystems and of laws which place duties on states and their nationals to protect them. Predicted and actual environmental effects may lead to constraints on human activities offshore or other consequences where legal duties for marine environmental protection are triggered. The section outlines negative effects which offshore wind energy can have on marine environments and reviews duties of states under public international law and of EU Member States under European Law that may oblige the regulation and, where necessary, the restriction of offshore renewables.

Section V explores ways in which states use law to try and make their offshore renewable development programmes compatible with other sea uses and with obligations for preventing harm to marine environments. Section VA concentrates on marine spatial planning, whose use has become widespread during the last two decades as a legal tool for enabling multiple growing demands on the seas to coexist whilst respecting environmental protection laws. The focus for sections VB to VD is on legal tools which require that proposed development should be assessed to ensure that information on its likely environmental effects and its compatibility with environmental conditions is before decision-makers when they come to make a decision on whether a plan, programme, or project should be authorised. Laws requiring environmental assessment at strategic and project licensing levels of decision-making in general and when negative impacts on an area which has been designated as protected because of its particular environmental value are considered.

II. Legal Foundations in Public International Law for Offshore Power Production

The section examines rules under the international law of the sea that determine which states have rights to exploit and transmit electricity from offshore wind and to exercise jurisdiction over these activities in different parts of the world's seas. Section IIA outlines the zoning approach laid down by treaties and by rules of customary international law by which all rights of states for resource exploitation and to exercise jurisdiction over marine activities are conferred. Section IIB then sets out rights allocated by the law of the sea of relevance for offshore wind generation specifically.

A. The Zoning Approach to Rights Allocation

Rights to exploit resources and to authorise related development onshore lie with the state which exercises sovereignty over the land concerned under public international law. For development offshore, such rights are allocated to states under public international law by rules of the law of the sea. The main source of these rules is the

United Nations Convention on the Law of the Sea.[17] The treaty was agreed in 1982 and has 168 ratifying parties, around 85 per cent of the world's sovereign states. Major coastal states who have not ratified UNCLOS include the US and Turkey.

UNCLOS uses a 'zoning' approach to allocate rights to exploit resources and exercise jurisdiction over activities conducted for this purpose. The territorial sea extends from states' coastal baselines to 12 nautical miles out to sea.[18] Coastal states exercise full sovereignty over this zone with one notable exception for navigation. States are permitted to declare an Exclusive Economic Zone extending from the Territorial Sea to up to 200 nautical miles in which they enjoy exclusive rights to exploit resources to the extent provided for under UNCLOS and have functional jurisdiction (eg, to the extent necessary to enjoy exclusive rights and comply with duties such as those for environmental protection in the zone).[19] The zone comprises the waters included within it and the overlying airspace.

Coastal states have exclusive rights to exploit resources of the seabed lying beyond the territorial sea under the continental shelf regime established by Part VI UNCLOS. As defined under UNCLOS, the continental shelf can extend up to 350 nautical miles from states' coastal baselines and sometimes beyond this.[20] The exclusive economic zone regime under Part V UNCLOS integrates the Part VI regime to the extent that the seabed lies under EEZ waters.[21] Part VI applies alone to continental shelves extending beyond EEZs. The Area is a seabed zone lying beyond continental shelves in which stated resources are to be exploited on behalf of all states as the common heritage of mankind.[22] Finally, all waters lying beyond states' exclusive economic zones fall under the High Seas regime.[23] Individual states cannot claim exclusive rights in this zone with all states being free to exploit resources of the High Seas.

Some states that have not ratified UNCLOS did ratify treaties amongst the suite of instruments of 1958 that preceded UNCLOS.[24] Some states have not ratified any of the law of the sea treaties. Complicated situations arise as a result when determining which set of rules apply to disputes between states including over rights to exploit resources. Rules under UNCLOS apply where both states have ratified it. Where both states have ratified a 1958 Convention but only one of them has ratified UNCLOS, the rules of the 1958 Convention will apply unless rules under UNCLOS have become recognised as rules of customary international law. Some of UNCLOS' provisions have arguably become rules of customary international law due to its ratification by a significant proportion of the world's states.[25] None of the conventions will be applicable for disputes involving the few states which have not ratified either UNCLOS or

---

[17] United Nations Convention on the Law of the Sea (adopted 10 December 1982, entered into force 16 November 1994) 1833 UNTS 397 (UNCLOS).
[18] UNCLOS, art 3.
[19] UNCLOS, Part V Exclusive Economic Zone, arts 55–75.
[20] UNCLOS, art 76.
[21] ibid, art 56(3).
[22] UNCLOS, Part XI The Area, arts 136 and 137.
[23] ibid, art 86.
[24] Robin Churchill, 'The UN Convention on the Law of the Sea' in Donald Rothwell and others (eds) *The Oxford Handbook of the Law of the Sea* (Oxford University Press, 2015) 24, 35–38.
[25] ibid, 37–38 and 45.

the 1958 Conventions, but provisions of these treaties will be relevant where they are recognised as rules of customary international law.

B. Rights to Generate and Transmit Electricity

Coastal states have exclusive rights to conduct activities in their territorial seas including the generation and transmission of electricity and the construction and regulation of installations and infrastructure required for this.[26] The position with regard to electricity generation in the exclusive economic zone (EEZ) is also clear. Article 56 UNCLOS includes 'the production of energy from the water, currents and winds' amongst 'other activities for the economic exploitation and exploration of the zone' which the relevant coastal state has exclusive sovereign rights to conduct.[27] Coastal states also have the exclusive right in their EEZs to construct and to authorize and regulate the construction, operation and use of installations and structures for the purposes provided for in Article 56.[28] The position is less clear where the continental shelf subject to the jurisdiction of a coastal state extends beyond its EEZ as Part VI UNCLOS does not expressly confer permission for energy production from the waters, currents and winds. This is not surprising as the continental shelf regime laid down in Part VI of UNCLOS is concerned with exploitation of the seabed and subsoil and as waters lying above it where it extends beyond a coastal state's EEZ belong to the High Seas. Questions also arise over the legal basis for offshore power production in the High Seas. Concerns of this nature were of academic interest only until recently due to the limitations of offshore renewable energy technologies (eg, offshore wind energy could only be exploited in areas with a maximum sea-bed depth because of their fixed foundations) but have been made more tangible by the development of floating wind turbine technology.[29]

UNCLOS is silent on the laying of cables for transmitting electricity from generating stations which it gives coastal states the exclusive right to establish in their EEZs. It has been argued that this was not seen as necessary as the exclusive right to produce energy in the EEZ must carry with it a right to lay cables from generating stations to the coastal state's onshore transmission system if it is to be given effect.[30] The later confirmation that UNCLOS rules at Article 79 on laying cables on the seabed where this is subject to the jurisdiction of a coastal state do not interfere with the coastal state's 'jurisdiction over cables ... constructed or used in connection with the ... operation of artificial islands, installations and structures under its jurisdiction' appears to confirm this assumption.[31] In any event, Article 79 advises that '[a]ll States are entitled to lay submarine cables ... on the continental shelf' subject to coastal state regulation

---

[26] UNCLOS, art 2.
[27] ibid, art 56(1)(a).
[28] ibid, art 60(1)(b).
[29] IRENA (n 6).
[30] Hannah Muller, *A Legal Framework for a Transnational Offshore Grid in the North Sea* (Intersentia 2015) 34–38.
[31] UNCLOS (n 17), art 79(4); Muller (n 30) 36.

and other considerations which the article mentions.[32] This means that power from generating stations situated in one state's EEZ could be transmitted through another's if that were more convenient than exclusive direct connection to the onshore grid of the state in whose EEZ the generating station is situated. All states enjoy freedom to lay submarine cables in the high seas. This freedom is subject to Part VI UNCLOS where cables are laid on parts of the continental shelf under the jurisdiction of a coastal state.[33] It has again been argued, although it is not stated in UNCLOS, that the freedom must include the right to use cables laid to transmit electricity if it is to be given effect.[34] It is important to note, however, that this freedom and also the entitlement under Article 79 could not be exercised in practice where the purpose of transmission is to transmit electricity produced in waters subject to the jurisdiction of one state directly to the onshore electricity grid of another state without ultimate agreement from terminus states for cables to be laid in their territorial seas and connected to their onshore electricity systems for onwards transmission to consumers.

III. Offshore Wind Energy and Conflict with Other Sea Uses

The introduction of offshore power production on an industrial scale to marine environments significantly increases potential for conflict between uses of the sea. The very large offshore wind farms now being constructed further out in UK waters will occupy over 500 km^2 of the seabed.[35] Coastal states are permitted by UNCLOS to establish safety zones of up to a 500-metre radius around each turbine lying in their EEZs, which vessels are not permitted to enter in the interests of safe navigation.[36] This can render the affected areas off limits to other sea uses including navigation and fishing in practice. It also creates potential for offshore renewable energy development to breach states' rights to undertake activities offshore in international law. Clarity is therefore desirable on where conflict in practice and in law may arise as well as thought on how this could be managed.

All states and their nationals are free in marine areas under the High Seas regime (including waters lying above continental shelves extending beyond a coastal state's EEZ) to undertake activities including navigation, overflight, laying submarine cables and pipelines, the construction of artificial islands and installations, fishing and scientific research.[37] Exercise of the freedoms is constrained by the duty to show due regard both 'for the interests of other states in their exercise of the freedom of the high seas'

---

[32] ibid, art 79(1).
[33] ibid, art 87(1)(c).
[34] Muller (n 30) 42.
[35] For example, see Dogger Bank Wind Farm, 'About the Project' (Dogger Bank Wind Farm, Website) About The Dogger Bank Wind Farm Projects | Dogger Bank Wind Farm (accessed 7 October 2022).
[36] UNCLOS (n 17), art 60(4) and (5).
[37] ibid, arts 78(2) and 87(1).

and for other states' rights with respect to activities in the Area.[38] Article 58 preserves these entitlements to an extent in EEZs by allowing continued enjoyment in them for all states of freedoms to navigate, of overflight, and of laying cables and pipelines as well as 'other internationally lawful uses of the seas related to these freedoms'.[39] The coastal state and other states must have due regard to each other's rights and duties as well as respectively acting 'in a manner compatible with' the Convention's provisions and in compliance with laws and regulations adopted by the coastal state in accordance with the Convention's provisions and other rules of international law insofar as they are not 'incompatible with Part V of UNCLOS'. Article 78(2) states that the exercise of rights held by coastal states in their continental shelves 'must not infringe or result in any unjustifiable interference with navigation and other rights and freedoms of other states as provided for in this Convention'.

In addition to these general duties, other provisions of UNCLOS require coastal states and other states to avoid obstruction of particular sea uses to a specified extent. Coastal states must respect the rights of ships under other states' flags to enjoy 'innocent passage' through their territorial seas.[40] Article 60(7) UNCLOS advises that coastal states may not erect artificial islands, structures, and installations or adopt safety zones around them 'where interference may be caused to the use of recognized sea lanes essential to international navigation'.[41] Article 79(5) obliges all states when laying cables to have due regard to cables and pipelines already in place including by not prejudicing possibilities for their repair.[42]

A number of questions are left unanswered by UNCLOS as to how conflicts between sea uses should be addressed. These concern the extent to which states' exercise of rights in their EEZs and continental shelves should be constrained because they would unlawfully impede navigation or to comply with requirements to show due regard for and avoid undue interference with other states' rights and freedoms. How may offshore energy production and transmission be affected by such constraints? To what extent must other sea uses be preserved where threatened by offshore energy development?

On navigation, vessels of all states have a right to make innocent passage through the territorial seas of coastal states.[43] Given that the territorial sea is a maximum of 12 nautical miles in breadth and that offshore wind farms can occupy large areas, commentators have questioned how far renewable energy development could impede innocent passage without this becoming unlawful.[44] UNCLOS does not offer complete clarity on the position, but it is made clear that ships of states conducting innocent passage must adhere to coastal state regulations.[45] These may include requirements such as the use of sea lanes and traffic separation schemes for reasons including the

---

[38] ibid, art 87(2).
[39] ibid, art 58(1).
[40] ibid, art 17.
[41] ibid, art 60(7).
[42] ibid, art 79(5).
[43] ibid, art 17.
[44] Hossein Esmaeili, *The Legal Regime of Offshore Oil Rigs in International Law* (Ashgate 2001) 73; David Leary and Miguel Esteban, 'Climate Change and Renewable Energy from the Oceans and Tides: Calming the Sea of Regulatory Uncertainty' (2009) 24 *The International Journal of Marine and Coastal Law* 617, 632–33.
[45] UNCLOS (n 17) art 21.

safety of shipping in the vicinity of offshore installations.[46] Commentators conclude from this that states conducting innocent passage should accept a certain amount of interference by coastal states in order to exploit energy production possibilities in sovereign waters although not to the extent that this would preclude innocent passage completely or otherwise interfere with it unreasonably.[47]

In the EEZs and waters overlying the continental shelves of coastal states, UNCLOS advises that installations and structures may not interfere with recognised sea lanes essential for international navigation, but does not give guidance on compliance with the constraint.[48] There is no definition of the sea lanes concerned, and no international body is recognised as the authority for designating them.[49] Some educated guesses can be made as to the extent of the constraint this may impose. Sea lanes for which the IMO has adopted routeing schemes and traffic separation schemes are likely to fall amongst those which should not be interfered with.[50] IMO guidelines advise states that structures must not be erected within them or near their terminations or seriously obstruct sea approaches to and from them.[51] It is a reasonable assumption therefore that non-interference with IMO approved schemes is likely to represent a minimum requirement for respecting Article 60(7). Even so, further clarity on the provision's ramifications would be desirable in view of the likely significant expansion of potential for conflict between offshore renewables and well-established sea routes.

The general due regard requirements aimed at achieving a balance of interests between states in pursuing their interests are necessarily non-prescriptive. What may amount to showing due regard depends on the particulars of cases under consideration.[52] There is an implicit expectation underlying this desire for balance that states will collaborate to prevent sea uses from precluding the exercise of rights and freedoms by other states.[53] Arbitral interpretation of the 'due regard' duty under Part V UNCLOS found that its discharge may involve 'elements of notice and meaningful consultation between the States involved'.[54] Growing potential for conflict between sea uses adds to the desirability of transboundary environmental impact assessment and

---

[46] Sarah McDonald and David VanderZwaag, 'Renewable Ocean Energy and the International Law and Policy Seascape: Global Currents, Regional Surges' (2015) 29 *Ocean Yearbook Online* 299, 304–06; Yen-Chiang Chang, 'Marine Renewable Energy – The Essential Legal Considerations' (2015) 8 *Journal of World Energy Law and Business* 26, 28–29.

[47] ibid; Leary and Esteban (n 44) 632–33; Karen Scott, 'Tilting at Offshore Windmills: Regulating Wind Farm Development Within the Renewable Energy Zone' (2006) 18 *Journal of Environmental Law* 89, 102–03.

[48] UNCLOS (n 17), art 60(7).

[49] Scott (n 47), 100–01.

[50] ibid.

[51] International Maritime Organisation, 'General Provisions on Ships' Routing', Resolution A.572(14) (adopted 20/11/1985); and International Maritime Organisation, 'Safety Zones and Safety of Navigation around Offshore Installations and Structures', Resolution A.671(16) (adopted 19/10/1989). See discussion of the relevant resolutions at Chang (n 46) 34–35; and Scott (n 47) 100–02.

[52] Douglas Burnett and Lionel Carter, *International Submarine Cables and Biodiversity of Areas Beyond National Jurisdiction: The Cloud Beneath the Sea* (Brill 2017) 19.

[53] Richard Barnes, 'Energy Sovereignty in Marine Spaces' (2019) 29 *International Journal of Marine and Coastal Law* 573, 590–92.

[54] Burnett and Carter (n 52) 19.

transboundary involvement with and cooperation on marine spatial planning exercises as ways by states of observing their due regard requirements to their mutual satisfaction.[55] The roles of marine spatial planning and environmental impact assessment as tools for managing conflict between sea uses, reducing risks of environmental harm and supporting compliance with duties under international law are examined in section V below.

Growing potential for conflict also promotes exploration by relevant international organisations of how sea uses within their remit and offshore renewable energy development could be accommodated. The International Maritime Organisation's role in achieving such an accommodation with regard to navigation is noted above. The International Civil Aviation Organisation has used powers under the Chicago Convention to lay down rules on marking and lighting for wind turbines if they are determined to be obstacles.[56] It has also advised with regard to the potential for wind turbines to affect communications between air traffic control centres and flights that initial screening should be used to determine whether reference to an engineering authority for fuller analysis is required.[57] A conclusion that a wind farm development would affect aviation communications could lead to relocation of the proposed project. Alternatively, the ICAO has a reserved right under the Chicago Convention to restrict or prohibit flights over delineated areas for reasons of public safety.[58] There is no equivalent international authority to the IMO and ICAO for cable laying and operation. The International Cable Protection Committee, a body representing the great majority of companies operating in the offshore telecommunications and power cables sector, has sought to fill this gap.[59] It recommends that those laying new power cables should observe a default 500 metre exclusion zone for existing cables.[60] It has also explored ways of observing reasonable regard for existing cables and new cable laying in relation to seabed minerals exploitation in the Area and vice versa with the International Seabed Authority.[61]

To conclude, initial growth in offshore renewable energy is already driving thought and action on how vague international law requirements on relations between different sea uses can be given effect. Need for further steps will only increase as demand for offshore power production grows. The ramifications for this are likely to be two-fold. First, further refinement and detailing of initial statements by sectoral authorities on

---

[55] Olivia Woolley, Peter Schaumberg, and Graham St Michel, 'Establishing an Offshore Electricity Grid: A Legal Analysis of Grid Developments in the North Sea and in U. S. Waters' in Martha Roggenkamp et al. (eds) *Energy Networks and the Law: Innovative Solutions in Changing Markets* (Oxford University Press, 2012) 180, 192–93.
[56] McDonald and VanderZwaag (n 46) 312–14.
[57] ibid.
[58] ibid.
[59] The International Cable Protection Committee's (ICPC) website is at www.iscpc.org (accessed 7 October 2022).
[60] ICPC, 'The Proximity of Offshore Renewable Energy Installations and Submarine Cable Infrastructure in National Waters' (ICPC Resolution 13 (version 2B), 2013).
[61] International Seabed Authority, *Submarine Cables and Deep Seabed Mining: Advancing Common Interests and Addressing UNCLOS "Due Regard" Obligations* (ISA Technical Study No 14, 2015).

how due regard towards activities for which they are responsible should be shown and of circumstances that would not be viewed as showing due regard and/or which would be prohibited by specific provisions of UNCLOS such as Article 60(7). Second, growth in state practice indicating that marine spatial planning for all sea uses in areas covered and strategic and environmental impact assessment are essential components for showing 'due regard' or avoiding 'undue interference' under UNCLOS.

IV. Offshore Renewable Energy and Negative Environmental Impacts

The exploitation of offshore renewable energy provides a good illustration of the adage that there is no such thing as a free lunch when it comes to energy production.[62] Offshore power production from renewable energy sources appeals as a major alternative to fossil fuel electricity, but concerns also arise over the potential for related development to have negative impacts on the marine environment including on species, their habitats, and the functioning of ecosystems of which they form part.[63] For example, offshore wind farms may have negative impacts if located incautiously. Particular care is needed where their construction could affect areas commonly used by species for breeding, feeding, moulting and other key life stages. There are several unresolved questions over how offshore wind farms may affect marine species including cetaceans, waterbirds and certain species of fish. In this regard, scientific certainty is lacking on how mechanical noise introduced to seas and oceans by the operation of wind turbines may affect species such as whales, dolphins and porpoises who rely on their hearing for navigation.[64] In addition, there is considerable uncertainty around the cumulative effects that major programmes of wind-farm development may have on marine biodiversity and, consequently, on ecosystem functionality. Possibilities for combined impacts are a very real concern in view of the current shared enthusiasm of coastal states for offshore wind electricity generation.[65]

Decision makers in states that value the healthy functioning of marine ecosystems, the wellbeing of their species, and habitat types (eg, coral reefs) may choose to limit offshore energy development where this could have negative environmental effects. They may also be legally obligated to limit such development whatever their values because permitting it would breach legal duties held by them to protect the marine

---

[62] George Pring, Alexandra Haas and Benton Drinkwine, 'The Impact of Energy and Health, Environment and Sustainable Development: The TANSTAAFL Problem' in Donald Zillman and others (eds) *Beyond the Carbon Economy: Energy Law in Transition* (Oxford University Press, 2008) 13.
[63] Andrew Gill, 'Offshore Renewable Energy: Ecological Implications of Generating Electricity in the Coastal Zone' (2005) 42(4) *Journal of Applied Ecology* 605; George Boehlert and Andrew Gill, 'Environmental and Ecological Effects of Ocean Renewable Energy Development: A Current Synthesis' (2010) 23 *Oceanography* 68.
[64] Gill (n 63) 609; Boehlert and Gill (n 63) 73.
[65] Gill (n 63), 612; Boehlert and Gill (n 63), 68, 70–71, 73, 77–78.

environment. Legal duties for environmental protection, as with duties to respect other sea uses examined in section III, are a key constraint for offshore renewables. For example, wind farm construction may not be permitted where this would affect a marine area which is protected in law because of its high environmental value. Potential sources of legal constraint on offshore renewable energy development at international, regional and national levels of law are considered in the following section.

A. Duties for Environmental Protection under UNCLOS

How may international law on protecting the marine environment affect renewable energy development?[66] To answer this question, we must first look at UNCLOS. Part XII of the Treaty on Protection and Preservation of the Marine Environment creates a global driver for adoption of and framework for relevant national laws in view of UNCLOS' wide ratification. Article 192 of UNCLOS confers a very broad duty on all states to 'protect and preserve the marine environment'.[67] It also places more specific requirements on them for preventing, reducing and controlling pollution of the marine environment.[68] This is defined as 'the introduction by man, directly or indirectly, of substances or energy into the marine environment, including estuaries, which results or is likely to result in such deleterious effects as harm to living resources and marine life, hazards to human health, hindrance to marine activities, including fishing and other legitimate uses of the sea, impairment of quality for use of sea water and reduction of amenities' (Art 1(4)). Noise is not mentioned in the definition, but Scott makes a convincing argument that 'energy' should be understood as covering not only heat but also sound waves 'as a flow of acoustic energy'.[69] The same argument could be applied to electromagnetic fields (EMF) from cables,[70] although scientific studies have not established conclusively whether cable-derived-EMF are likely to harm marine species.[71]

The impact of offshore energy may fall within UNCLOS' regime for environmental protection, but this offers little detailed guidance on what should be done. It leaves the development of regimes for addressing particular effects of sea uses to states to determine individually and in collaboration including through regimes established to regulate

---

[66] See Carlos Soria-Rodriguez, 'The International Regulation for the Protection of the Environment in the Development of Marine Renewable Energy in the EU' (2021) 30 *Review of European, Comparative and International Environmental Law* 46 for an overview of international law on protecting the marine environment from the effects of offshore wind energy development. This focuses on the position in EU waters but examines treaties such as UNCLOS and the Convention on Biological Diversity with worldwide applicability.
[67] UNCLOS (n 17) art 192.
[68] ibid, arts 194 and 207–212.
[69] Karen Scott, 'International Regulation of Undersea Noise' (2004) 53 *International and Comparative Law Quarterly* 287, 292–94. See also James Harrison, *Saving the Oceans Through Law* (Oxford University Press 2017), 26–27.
[70] World Health Organisation, 'Electromagnetic Fields' (WHO, Website) www.who.int/peh-emf/about/WhatisEMF/en/ (accessed 7 October 2022).
[71] Burnett and Carter (n 52) 41–42.

uses of regional seas and to address specific sources of environmental concern.[72] To the extent that there is detailed guidance, this concerns polluting activities. However, some of the most significant effects of offshore renewable energy development such as bird strikes and presenting barriers to wide-ranging marine mammals are not due to pollution, but to the conduct of the authorised activity itself.[73] It is unsurprising, therefore, that treaty regimes concerned with the protection of birds, bats and migratory species for which offshore renewables specifically can pose environmental threats if incautiously sited have been proactive in developing guidance for state parties on how relevant development should be conducted and operated thereafter.[74] Relevant treaty regimes include the Convention on Biological Diversity, the Convention on Migratory Species and treaties made under it for the conservation of European Bats, African-Eurasian Migratory Waterbirds, the Convention on Biological Diversity and cetaceans of the north, Baltic and Mediterranean Seas.[75]

B. Regional Seas Conventions and Plans

The implementation by states of their duties under UNCLOS will need to be tailored by them to reflect differences in the Earth's marine regions. A one-size-fits all approach to implementing Chapter XII of UNCLOS would not be effective for securing marine environmental protection. Relevant differences include the composition and condition of marine environments and of their biodiversity, human uses of them, and the level of development of coastal states. The Regional Seas Programme of the United Nations Environment Programme, established in 1974, responds to this need by bringing together 'stakeholders including governments, scientific communities and civil societies' to collaborate on planning and implementing region-specific activities aimed at the conservation of marine and coastal environments.[76] It has led to the formulation of regional action plans for marine environmental protection and in some cases to the negotiation and ratification by relevant coastal states of regional seas conventions. UNEP identifies 18 regional initiatives being pursued under its auspices: seven that were established under and are directly administered by UNEP (Caribbean, East Asian Seas, Eastern Africa, Mediterranean, North-West Pacific, Western Africa, Caspian Sea); seven that were established under UNEP but which now have independent administration (Black Sea, North-East Pacific, Red Sea and Gulf of Aden, ROPME (Persian Gulf and Arabian Sea), South Asian seas, South-East Pacific, Pacific); and four that were established and are administered independently from UNEP but which cooperate with the Regional Seas Programme (Arctic, Antarctic, Baltic, North-East Atlantic).[77]

---

[72] McDonald and VanderZwaag (n 46) 303–04.
[73] Scott (n 47) 104.
[74] Soria-Rodriguez (n 66) 102–06.
[75] Olivia Woolley, 'Renewable Energy and the Law of the Sea' in James Kraska and Young-Kil Park (eds) *Emerging Technology and the Law of the Sea* (Cambridge University Press, 2022) 35, 55–58.
[76] United Nations Environment Programme (UNEP), 'Regional Seas Programme', (UNEP Website, What we do – Oceans and Seas) Regional Seas Programme | UNEP – UN Environment Programme (accessed 7 October 2022).
[77] ibid.

The Regional Seas Conventions and Plans establish frameworks for cooperation on addressing marine environmental concerns between the coastal states with jurisdiction over the marine areas concerned. Their formulation with 'the political, legal and ecological needs' of particular marine areas in mind can make cooperation easier to achieve and more effective for addressing environmental problems than at the global level with its tendency to lowest common denominator compromises.[78] The focus at the regional seas level is typically on responding to two sources of marine environmental deterioration: pollution from onshore, offshore and atmospheric sources; and human activities posing threat to marine biodiversity for reasons other than pollution (eg, offshore development). Each individual regime must be examined separately to identify how activities which pollute or otherwise harm the marine environment may be affected by it. Parties who ratify conventions take on legal obligations whilst agreements made in regions which are not subject to conventions, although they may have normative effects, are typically not legally binding. Some conventions tackle pollution alone whilst others are wider ranging in their responses to drivers of damage to marine environments.

Duties placed by Regional Seas Conventions on states and rules and guidance developed under relevant regimes can add to obstacles to and influences on offshore renewable energy development deriving from higher-level international obligations. Indeed, knowledge of local conditions and problems that informs the development of relevant regimes and the often greater opportunities for meaningful cooperation that shared difficulties and interests create may lead them to 'bite harder' when it comes to regulating marine activities.[79] For example, the OSPAR Convention must be borne in mind for offshore wind projects in the North Sea and the North-East Atlantic, the world's busiest area for such marine development at the time of writing.[80] The Convention's 16 parties commit to 'take all possible steps to prevent and eliminate pollution' and also to 'take the necessary measures to protect the maritime area against the adverse effects of human activities so as to ... conserve marine ecosystems and, when practicable, restore marine areas which have been adversely affected ...'.[81] They are obliged to advance this end by adopting 'individually and jointly ... programmes and measures' and by harmonising 'their policies and strategies'.[82] Interstate collaboration led to the broadening of OSPAR's initial pollution focus by the adoption of an Annex introducing more focused legal provision on the protection and conservation of the ecosystems and biodiversity of the maritime area than the Convention provided for initially. Parties are required to take the necessary measures to protect and conserve the ecosystems and the biological diversity of the maritime area and to cooperate in adopting programmes and measures for those purposes for the control of human activities that could have actual or potential adverse effects.[83] The fuller detailing of

---

[78] Harrison (n 69) 36–37 and 53–62; Carlos Soria-Rodriguez, 'Marine Renewable Energies and the European Regional Seas Conventions' (2016) 6 *Climate Law* 314.
[79] ibid.
[80] Convention for the Protection of the Marine Environment of the North-East Atlantic (adopted 22 September 1992, entry into force 25 March 1998), 2354 UNTS 67 (OSPAR).
[81] OSPAR, art 2(1)(a).
[82] ibid, art 2(1)(b).
[83] ibid, Annex V, art 2.

OSPAR's regime for environmental protection creates more palpable possibilities of legal constraint, whether through the adoption of national laws to implement international obligations or of common positions at the Convention level, on offshore renewable development. For example, OSPAR's parties agreed on recommendations for offshore wind development in 2008[84] and are exploring whether further action is needed in view of their combined plans for massive growth in offshore renewable energy development.[85] The 2008 recommendations are not themselves legally binding but are of clear relevance when assessing the compliance of parties with obligations such as those found under Annex V of the treaty. Other regional seas regimes are currently or are in the future likely to be similarly proactive on regulating offshore renewables as this means of energy production expands.

C. Legal Measures to Meet International Duties and Offshore Wind

Questions arise about the compatibility of offshore renewables with general duties for marine environmental protection, but tangible constraints are most likely to result from measures in national laws for implementing them. Laws which oblige authorities to protect marine habitats and areas of importance for the lives of marine species (eg, for breeding, feeding, moulting) and for the functioning of marine ecosystems (eg, coral reefs) may require the application of controls including outright bans where it is feared that offshore development may impact negatively on the protected site. For example, plans or projects that are thought likely to have a significant effect on a protected site under the European Union's Habitats Directive must be made subject to an 'appropriate assessment' by the relevant Member State.[86] They should not be authorised unless the Member State's responsible authorities have ascertained that they 'will not adversely affect the integrity of the site concerned'.[87] Protected area laws vary significantly in legal consequences flowing from evidence that an activity may have negative environmental effects.[88] Even so, the potential for this legal approach to limit offshore renewables is certain to grow in the decades ahead both because of the expected massive growth in this sector and the parallel growth in areas of the seas subject to protection in law. The Convention on Biological Diversity's draft goals for 2030 call on its parties to ensure that marine areas 'conserved through ecologically representative and well-connected systems of protected areas' increase from the 10 per cent goal for 2020 to 30 per cent by 2030.[89]

---

[84] OSPAR Commission, *OSPAR Guidelines on Environmental Considerations for Offshore Wind Farm Development* (2008).

[85] ibid, 'Offshore Renewables' (OSPAR Website) Offshore Renewables | OSPAR Commission (accessed 7 October 2022).

[86] Council Directive 92/43/EEC of 21 May 1992 on the conservation of natural habitats and wild flora and fauna [1992] OJ L 206/7, art 6(3).

[87] ibid.

[88] Barbara Lausche, *Guidelines for Protected Areas Legislation* (International Union of Nature Conservation, 2011) 174–86.

[89] Open-ended Working Group on the Post-2020 Global Biodiversity Framework, *First Draft of the Post-2020 Global Biodiversity Framework*, (CBD/WG2020/3/3, 5 July 2021) First draft of the post-2020 global biodiversity framework (cbd.int) (accessed 7 October 2022) Annex, para 12.1 – Target 3.

Laws which require that permits be obtained for construction and operation allow decision-makers to control the development of offshore generating plant regardless of whether it threatens a protected site. Applications may be refused or licences made conditional on compliance with specified conditions where necessary to secure compliance with legal duties for environmental protection. The capacity of permitting regimes for preventing environmental harm is enhanced significantly by laws obligating authorities to ensure during the decision-making process laid down in law that environmental information concerning the proposed development and the area in which it is to be conducted should be gathered, that the environmental knowledge and opinions of experts and affected populations concerning the development proposal should be sought, and that the information and opinions be taken into account in decision making. The role of environmental impact assessment law in authorisation regimes for offshore renewables is considered further at section VC below.

Regulation of offshore renewable developments can be made difficult by a lack of scientific certainty over their likely environmental impacts individually and cumulatively. Uncertainty may be due to the novelty of technologies, poor understanding of marine species and of the functioning of ecosystems of which they form part, the complex pathways by which impacts from wind farms combine with other sources of impact to affect ecosystems and their species, the intrinsic unknowability of how dynamic natural systems may evolve, or a combination of these causes. How should holders of duties for environmental protection act in cases where they lack the information to determine whether their development programmes are compatible with them? Law may assist decision makers in such situations to an extent by providing guidance on how to proceed where scientific uncertainty exists over the consequences of a proposed activity. Principle 15 of the legally non-binding but highly influential Rio Declaration of 1992 calls on states to adopt a precautionary approach by not using 'lack of full scientific certainty ... as a reason for postponing cost-effective measures to prevent environmental degradation' where threats of 'serious or irreversible damage' are present.[90] Variants of this provision, referred to collectively as the precautionary principle or approach, have since been included in multiple international treaties and national laws.[91] Each individual use must be interpreted separately by reference to the law and legal system in which it features. Careful reading of individual uses is also necessary because of significant differences between them on the point at which the principle should be applied (eg, the significance of harm needed to trigger the principle) and the guidance provided on what actors should do when a situation demanding precautionary action occurs.[92] For example, the OSPAR Convention obliges its parties to act precautionarily in relation both to pollution and to the ecosystem and biodiversity of its parties' maritime areas.[93] It goes beyond Principle 15 by positively requiring

---

[90] 1992 Rio Declaration on Environment and Development, UN Doc. A/CONF.151/26 (vol. I), 31 ILM 874 (1992).
[91] Nicholas de Sadeleer, *Environmental Principles: From Political Slogans to Legal Rules* 2nd edn (Oxford University Press, 2021) 137–53.
[92] Alan Boyle and Catherine Redgwell, *Birnie, Boyle and Redgwell's International Law and the Environment*, 4th edn (Oxford University Press, 2021) 170–83.
[93] OSPAR (n 80) art 2(2)(a).

that measures for preventing harm and for environmental protection should be taken in the circumstances identified in the relevant provisions. Recourse to the precautionary principle when interpreting Article 6(3) of the Habitats Directive led the European Court of Justice to find that Member State authorities should only authorise activities made subject to an appropriate assessment where no reasonable scientific doubt as to the absence of adverse effects on the integrity of a protected site remained.[94] Guidance given on how to act precautionarily in this instance, therefore, has significant potential to limit scope for pursuing offshore renewable development where scientific uncertainty as to its effects exists. However, other variants of the principle, including Principle 15 referred to above, lead to less tangible constraints due to a lack of guidance on what acting precautionarily involves.

V. Planning for Offshore Renewables in Congested Seas

Perceptions of seas as open spaces offering opportunities for exploitation without the difficulties encountered in developed terrestrial areas are misplaced. Sea uses, including designating areas for environmental protection, increasingly compete with each other for marine space. Renewable energy development adds significantly to these pressures in view of coastal states' plans for massive growth in offshore electricity generation and of the large areas that offshore wind farms occupy. Spatial conflicts and breaches of legal duties to respect sea uses sponsored by other states of the type examined in section III will become more common as the offshore renewables roll-out progresses. Risks of negative environmental effects and of related breaches of legal duties for marine environmental protection due to disturbance of areas protected for their environmental value and to impacts both individually and cumulatively from offshore development are also very likely to grow.

States must have different sea uses, the potential for environmental consequences (both negative and positive), and their legal duties in mind when developing programmes for offshore renewables to ensure that best use is made of whatever spatial resource for power generation is left once practical and legal constraints have been taken into account. This section examines legal tools that are used by them to explore how and to what extent offshore power production can be accommodated in marine areas alongside other sea uses whilst respecting legal commitments for protecting the marine environment. Section VA reviews marine spatial planning, a legal tool used to try and manage different human demands on marine areas in ways that advance economic, social and environmental policy objectives simultaneously. Sections VB, VC and VD respectively consider strategic environmental assessment, environmental impact assessment and habitats protection assessment, three layers of legally required review which are used to identify and therefore create the opportunity for developers

---

[94] *Landelijke Vereniging tot Behoud van de Waddenzee, Nederlandse Vereniging tot Bescherming van Vogels v Staatssecretaris van Landbouw, Natuurbeheer en Visserij* (C-127/02) [2005] Env LR 14; Stuart Bell, Donald McGillivray, Ole Pedersen, Emma Lees, and Ellen Stokes, *Environmental Law* 9th edn (Oxford University Press, 2017) 730–31.

and decision-makers to respond to anticipated environmental consequences of development before it is authorised in law. The sections highlight the significant influence that the design of laws which establish these approaches can have on maximising or impairing their ability to reduce risks of environmental harm due to offshore renewable energy development.

A. Marine Spatial Planning

Marine spatial planning (MSP) has been described as a process of 'analyzing and allocating parts of three-dimensional marine spaces to specific uses, to achieve ecological, economic and social objectives that are usually specified through a political process'.[95] With regard to environmental protection, MSP is often associated with employing an 'ecosystem-based approach'. Such an approach aspires to keep the cumulative effects of human activities within levels (natural carrying capacities) that do not impair the functionality of marine ecosystems. The preparation of marine plans typically involves detailed exploration of the areas to which plans are to apply including their geology, fauna and flora, environmental conditions, current uses, expected future uses, and potential value for meeting policy objectives.[96] Widespread stakeholder consultation of relevant populations, sectors, and experts is vital for developing a solid knowledge base and for producing plans which are accepted because of their perceived legitimacy. A common aim for MSP is to produce plans presenting a vision of how economic and social objectives involving sea uses and development can be met whilst preserving and where necessary restoring good environmental conditions in the plan area. Plans often take the form of policy statements whose role is to guide decision making on development and environmental protection. Zoning plans giving more detail on preferred uses of spaces within the plan area may form part of the overall plan or be prepared under it to guide particular sectors.[97]

Marine spatial planning began to emerge as a response to increasing pressures on seas from human sea uses and related environmental deterioration in the 2000s. O'Hagan reports that around 70 countries now employ some form of this practice with many of them having adopted laws to create frameworks for the preparation of plans covering their coastal waters.[98] The UK and Scotland respectively introduced laws requiring designated authorities to prepare plans for their coastal waters and laying down the procedures to be followed in 2009 (Marine and Coastal Access Act)

---

[95] Charles Ehler and Fanny Douvere, *Visions for a Sea Change: Report of the First International Workshop on Marine Spatial Planning* (UNESCO, Report, November 2006) Visions for a sea change; report – UNESCO Digital Library (accessed 7 October 2022), 24.

[96] Michaela Young, 'Building the Blue Economy: The Role of Marine Spatial Planning in Facilitating Offshore Renewable Energy Development' (2015) 30 *International Journal of Marine and Coastal Law* 148, 155–56; Ehler and Douvere (n 95) 47–48 and 51.

[97] Anne Marie O'Hagan, 'Marine Spatial Planning and Marine Renewable Energy' in Andrea Copping and Lenaig Hemery (eds) *OES-Environmental 2020 State of the Science Report: Environmental Effects of Marine Renewable Energy Development Around the World*, Report for Ocean Energy Systems, 214–41 at 237–41.

[98] ibid, 216.

and 2010 (Marine (Scotland) Act). The EU's Marine Spatial Planning Directive required Member States to bring into force the laws, regulations and administrative procedures required to establish and implement marine spatial planning by September 2016.[99] Experience with introducing jurisdiction-wide marine spatial planning laws elsewhere is patchy, but O'Hagan identifies relevant initiatives at the sub-national state level in Australia, India and the US.[100]

Interest in marine spatial planning is being spurred by coastal state plans for offshore renewable energy. It is seen as a key tool for managing potential for very large turbine arrays to conflict with other sea uses, for reducing risks that they will further impair marine environmental conditions, and for promoting compliance with duties under international law to respect the marine activities of other states and their nationals and to prevent environmental harm. Commentators identify five principal respects in which the preparation of marine spatial plans, including zoning plans, may assist with avoiding physical and legal conflict and reducing the risks of environmental harm due to offshore wind energy.[101] They are by: (i) allocating areas for offshore renewables development where this would be unlikely to conflict with other sea uses or harm the environment; (ii) identifying areas that should be avoided because of their importance for other valued sea uses (eg, internationally important shipping routes) or their environmental sensitivity; (iii) supporting the regulation of the cumulative environmental effects of offshore renewables development with other sea uses by helping policy advocates and developers with forming an overview of combined pressures on marine areas from human activities; (iv) identifying areas for co-locating offshore renewables and other sea uses both to avoid conflict between sea uses and to reduce pressures on the marine environment; and (v) identifying possibilities for using areas rendered off limits by offshore renewables to advance environmental policy goals. Some evidence from offshore renewables development to date suggests that the de facto exclusion of fisheries and the reef-effect that can result when stone gravity foundations are used for turbines can support the revival of marine biodiversity in marine places occupied by turbine arrays.[102]

Whether or not marine spatial planning will have these beneficial effects in practice very much depends on how it is conducted. The design of marine spatial planning laws, particularly the legal rigour they introduce on necessary steps for conflict avoidance and reducing the risk of harm, are therefore crucial for securing the positive outcomes that the practice can bring. Marine spatial planning can contribute to avoiding conflict and reducing ecological pressures on the seas where it is holistic (eg, it encompasses all policies, programmes and activities affecting the seas).[103] A holistic integrative approach enables planners to: form an overview of the uses of the seas and influences acting on them, and to: (a) allocate space to and restrict the conduct of

---

[99] Directive 2014/89/EU of the European Parliament and of the Council of 23 July 2014 establishing a framework for marine spatial planning [2014] OJ L 257/135.
[100] O'Hagan (n 97) 237–41.
[101] Young (n 96) 55–58; O'Hagan (n 97) 228–30, 233–41.
[102] Boehlert and Gill (n 63) 71.
[103] Olivia Woolley, 'Ecological Governance for Offshore Wind Energy in United Kingdom Waters: Has an Effective Legal Framework Been Established for Preventing Ecologically Harmful Development?' (2015) 30 *The International Journal of Marine and Coastal Law* 765, 780, 782 and 784.

activities with a view to avoiding incompatible interaction with other sea uses and environmentally harmful cumulative levels of marine activities; and (b) reject projects that would be inconsistent with marine policies and plans. If a plan is not comprehensive at the outset, then a fundamental flaw is present in its ability to guide future development in ways that avoid or mitigate threats of conflict and of harm due to the combined impacts of sea uses. Even if a plan is comprehensive, its value for preventing harm will be weakened where legal controls on authorising sea uses are either not in place or do not insist that decision makers follow the previously adopted plan when deciding on whether a development proposal should be authorised.[104] Plans are likely to be rendered obsolete where planning and development for future sea uses is not required to be conducted in accordance with guidance provided by the plan.

The UK's experience with adoption of the Marine and Coastal Access Act 2009 for UK waters illustrates how weaknesses in legal design can impair a law's ability to secure hoped for benefits from marine spatial planning when used to guide offshore renewables development.[105] The Marine and Coastal Access Act 2009 requires planning authorities to produce marine plans that will thereafter provide a reference point for decision-making on and planning for specific uses of the seas. Decisions that fall under the Act's definition of authorisation or enforcement decisions by public authorities must be taken 'in accordance with the appropriate marine policy documents unless relevant considerations indicate otherwise'.[106] Decisions by public authorities which do not fall under this definition are only required to 'have regard to' the appropriate documentation.[107]

The Act provides little guidance itself on plan making. Instead, detailed direction is to be given by a marine policy statement with which marine plans must be 'in conformity ... unless relevant considerations indicate otherwise'.[108] The contents of the policy statement are therefore of central importance to the planning regime's effectiveness for improving marine environmental protection. The UK Government and the devolved administrations jointly adopted their first marine policy statement in March 2011. The marine policy statement adopts an 'ecosystem-based approach' to the management of human activities. The purpose of such an approach is to ensure that the capacity of marine ecosystems to respond to human-induced change is not compromised by the collective pressures that sea uses place on them. It also advises that the overarching purpose of marine planning is to deliver the high-level marine objectives of the UK Government and devolved administrations that were adopted in 2009 including:

(a) living within environmental limits;
(b) halting the loss of marine biodiversity; and
(c) preserving habitats to support biodiversity and the healthy functioning of marine ecosystems.[109]

---

[104] ibid, 784–85.
[105] ibid.
[106] Marine and Coastal Access Act 2009, s 58(1).
[107] ibid, s 58(3).
[108] ibid, s 51(6).
[109] HM Government, *Our Seas – A Shared Resource: High Level Marine Objectives* (Department for Environment, Food and Rural Affairs, 2009) Our seas: a shared resource, high level marine objectives – GOV.UK (www.gov.uk) (accessed 7 October 2022), 7.

The marine policy statement encourages planners to reflect on how negative ecological effects can be avoided (ie, by identifying areas where sea uses should be constrained; by considering how the cumulative effects of activities should be managed; and by seeking to avoid environmental harm as a principle of plan-making including through careful selection of locations, mitigation and the consideration of reasonable alternatives).[110] Even so, the Act falls short of establishing a regime that would provide effective ecological governance for the development of offshore wind energy in two key respects:

(i) It does not establish a holistic planning regime under which one planning authority allocates space for the whole marine environment. The allocation of marine space for offshore wind energy takes place independently from the spatial planning process. Planners may be reluctant to alter zones agreed under this independent process with developers even where they clash with other sea uses/environmental policies for the seas. Developers awarded zones also prepare their plans for exploiting them independently. The resulting developments will fall to be reviewed against marine plans by decision-makers for development consent applications, but this requirement to take marine plans into account may exercise a weak influence on developers' actions for reasons explored below.[111]

(ii) In England and Wales, decision-making on large offshore wind farms (100MW+) will be conducted by a different body to the marine planning authority (the Secretary of State for Energy and Climate Change) and under the regime established by the Planning Act 2008. Under this Act, the Secretary of State should make decisions in accordance with national policy statements for energy infrastructure and renewable energy, both of which encourage the authorisation of proposed large offshore wind farms.[112] The Marine and Coastal Access Act directs that the Secretary of State need only 'have regard' to marine policies/plans in making decisions.[113] The relevant national policy statements also state that they take precedence where there is a conflict between them and documents produced under the marine planning regime.[114] Appleby and Jones argue that this will allow sectoral authorities to continue to operate 'under the status quo of focusing largely on their sectoral priorities', undermining the potential for a strategic, integrated, ecosystem-based approach to marine spatial planning.[115]

Two additional limits on marine spatial planning's ability to reduce risks of environmental harm should be mentioned. First, marine ecosystems transcend borders. The medium of marine ecosystems is fluid, meaning that impacts of marine development in an area under one state's jurisdiction may be felt in waters of another state. Impacts of plans of multiple states for offshore development in semi-enclosed seas such as the North, Baltic, Mediterranean and Black Seas will combine to have a cumulative

---

[110] HM Government, *UK Marine Policy Statement* (The Stationery Office, 2011) 13.
[111] Woolley (n 103) 769–85.
[112] Planning Act 2008, s 104(3).
[113] Marine and Coastal Access Act 2009, s 58(3).
[114] Woolley (n 103) 785.
[115] Tom Appleby and Peter Jones, 'The Marine and Coastal Access Act: A Hornet's Nest?' (2012) 36 *Marine Policy* 73, 76.

transnational effect. Marine species, especially those which migrate, frequently move between areas subject to different states' jurisdictions. Interstate collaboration on planning is therefore needed to enable the holistic overview required for reducing risks of environmental harm from offshore renewables.[116] UNCLOS and regional seas conventions promote collaboration between states on environmental protection. However, it will be challenging for marine spatial planning, which has only emerged at national levels in recent decades, to provide a reliable regional overview in the near term. Second, inherent ignorance of how human activities combine to affect ecosystems makes it difficult, even with the most comprehensive planning process, to identify and reduce risks of harm in advance of development.[117] As considered in section VE below, legal provision for *ex post* monitoring and adaptive management of development can assist with addressing this fundamental problem but cannot provide a complete answer to it. The author argues in other publications that creative thinking is needed about how to go about environmental protection using law where significant uncertainties verging on ignorance are present.[118] This should include thought on elevating environmental regulation to policy level decision-making on appropriate options for advancing objectives in view of the limitations of project regulation by reference to prediction of likely impacts for preventing environmentally harmful outcomes.

B. Strategic Environmental Assessment

Article 4 of the 1992 Rio Declaration advises that '[I]n order to achieve sustainable development, environmental protection shall constitute an integral part of the development process and cannot be considered in isolation from it'.[119] So widespread has been the acceptance of this proposition internationally that the principle of integration is thought to have become a component of customary international environmental law.[120] Its guidance has led worldwide to the introduction of national laws under which consideration of environmental effects must be integrated into decision making on development processes if they are to be viewed as conducive for securing sustainable outcomes. Environmental impact assessment of proposed projects offers the main means of integration, but it has its limitations as a practice for preventing environmental harm. One such limitation is that room for manoeuvre for altering a project proposal may be limited by choices made at earlier stages of decision-making leading to time taken in following a particular course of action and expense. This weakness led to interest in introducing environmental considerations into earlier 'strategic' stages of decision-making allowing greater flexibility to choose alternative development options if it became apparent that a course of action could lead to environmental harm.

---

[116] Woolley (n 103), 792.
[117] ibid, 787–78, 792–93.
[118] Olivia Woolley, *Ecological Governance: Reappraising Law's Role in Protecting Ecosystem Functionality* (Cambridge University Press, 2014) 53–67.
[119] Rio Declaration (n 90) art 4.
[120] Philippe Sands and Jacqueline Peel with Adriana Fabra and Ruth Mackenzie, *Principles of International Environmental Law*, 4th edn (Cambridge University Press, 2018) 227–29.

Strategic environmental assessment in practice and in law has been adopted in many jurisdictions since the 2000s.[121] Relevant laws typically require that the likely environmental effects of plans, programmes and sometimes policies produced under public decision making that could have a significant impact and which create a framework within which lower project-level decision making takes place should be assessed, and that information considered should be taken into account in public decision making on how to proceed. A first major impetus for use of this approach in law was provided by the EU's Strategic Environmental Assessment Directive of 2001 which required Member States to enact laws obliging public decision makers to undertake the environmental assessment of certain plans and programmes.[122] The Directive was implemented in England in 2004 and in Scotland in 2005.[123]

Fischer and Gonzalez reported in 2021 that strategic environmental assessment has been taken up worldwide. Over 60 countries (including Australia, Brazil, China, Ghana and Vietnam) have introduced some formal strategic environmental assessment requirements.[124] Procedural stages often required by strategic environmental assessment laws include screening to identify whether assessment is needed, scoping to establish the necessary scope of assessment, the gathering and evaluation of relevant environmental information, the preparation of an environmental report by the actor responsible for the policy, plan or programme under review, consultation informed by the report on the plan, programme or policy with relevant experts and affected members of the public, decision-making informed by the report and consultation responses, and the giving of reasons for the decision reached in light of information revealed by the assessment. EU law requires that the process should examine not only the preferred plan but also reasonable alternatives to it, thereby enhancing the ability of the process to avoid environmental harm by revealing to decision-makers options that could achieve similar ends with fewer negative impacts.[125]

Offshore renewable energy development is being driven by state policies for, inter alia, decarbonisation. Detailed plans and programmes for implementing policies through offshore development in waters subject to a state's jurisdiction will tend to be drawn up publicly because of the importance of the infrastructure for maintaining secure energy supplies during decarbonisation and the greater likelihood compared to the position onshore that property rights over offshore areas lie with the state. Offshore development programmes are also likely to have significant environmental effects. It is likely therefore where strategic environmental assessment laws have been adopted, although the position will vary depending on the terms of each law, that plans, programmes and sometimes policies detailing state intentions for offshore renewable energy rollouts will be subject to strategic environmental assessment.

---

[121] Thomas Fischer and Ainhoa Gonzalez, 'Introduction to Handbook on Strategic Environmental Assessment' in Thomas Fischer and Ainhoa Gonzalez (eds) *Handbook on Strategic Environmental Assessment* (Edward Elgar, 2021) 2–3.
[122] Directive 2001/42/EC of the European Parliament and of the Council of 27 June 2001 on the assessment of the effects of certain plans and programmes on the environment [2001] OJ L 197/30 (SEA Directive).
[123] The Environmental Assessment of Plans and Programmes Regulations 2004 (SI 2004/1633); the Environmental Assessment (Scotland) Act 2005.
[124] Fischer and Gonzalez (n 121), 2–3.
[125] Directive 2001/42/EC (n 122), arts 5(1) and 9(1)(b).

As will be clear from the foregoing, strategic environmental assessment can be used by states and their public authorities to support compliance with legal duties for marine environmental protection, including for the preservation of protected areas, by identifying and avoiding or reducing risks of harm at a stage in decision making when flexibility remains to prefer alternatives which are less likely to pose environmental threats. However, whether or not potential benefits are realised depends on the seriousness with which responsible authorities use the process to attain environmentally positive outcomes. That seriousness may be influenced by the precision with which the process is laid down in law and by whether provision is made for an independent authority to review the quality of the process. The temptation will be there, where legal provisions are imprecise and independent review is lacking, for responsible authorities to undertake assessment as a tick-box exercise, one which meets the letter of the law but does not make a serious effort to secure environmentally beneficial outcomes. The UK's experience with conducting strategic environmental assessment of its early plans for offshore renewables offers an example of a failure to use it in a way calculated to realise the utility of the process for environmental protection fully.[126]

It should also be borne in mind that strategic environmental assessment laws are typically procedural. This means that they lay down a decision-making process that should be followed, but do not place any substantive obligations on decision makers to reach particular decisions (eg, to reject a plan where an assessment reveals that it could have negative environmental effects or that an environmentally preferable alternative is available). This does not mean that no legal consequences will flow from decisions which fail to follow guidance given in an assessment or which seem perverse in light of information revealed by it. Such decisions may be open to challenge under the administrative laws of the relevant jurisdiction. Information produced by an assessment will also be relevant for determining compliance with substantive obligations that states and their authorities may have taken on under environmental protection laws of the type considered at section IV above.

C. Environmental Impact Assessment

Laws requiring that environmental impact assessment is conducted as part of decision-making procedures for permitting individual projects provide the main means of effecting guidance from the integration principle referred to in section VB. The widespread recognition of environmental impact assessment through the adoption of national laws providing for this supports claims that its conduct has become obligatory under customary international law where grounds exist for believing that a proposed project is likely to have a significant impact on the environment.[127] Environmental impact assessment laws typically identify the circumstances in which an assessment should be conducted including by identifying categories of assessable activities (eg, the EU's Environmental Impact Assessment Directive requires that projects under Annex I

---

[126] Woolley (n 103) 771–75.
[127] Sands (n 120) 657–58.

categories must be reviewed).[128] The categories cover 24 types of development typically conducted on an industrial scale or which are likely to present (or be perceived as presenting) environmental, health or safety risks. For Annex II categories, Member States are required to make provision under national environmental impact assessment laws to determine whether projects falling under them should be assessed on a case-by-case basis or by using thresholds or criteria. Criteria set out in Annex III of the Directive must be taken into account when a case-by-case decision is made or when a threshold or criteria is set. The information attained and conclusions drawn through the assessment should be presented in an environmental report. This should be submitted with the application for development consent so that decision makers can take into account information concerning possible environmental effects of a proposed project in reaching their decision. Renewable energy developments fall under Annex II of the EU's Environmental Impact Assessment Directive (apart from large hydro-electric schemes for which environmental impact assessment is compulsory). This means that Member States can decide whether an assessment is required by setting a threshold or criteria or on a case-by-case basis. The directive was implemented in England and Wales by the Electricity Works (Environmental Impact Assessment) (England and Wales) Regulations 2017 (which have replaced the 2000 Regulations).[129] Generating plant over 300MW must be assessed under the regulations. Other projects can be considered on a case-by-case basis. The directive was implemented in Scotland by the Electricity Works (Environmental Impact Assessment) (Scotland) Regulations 2017 (which have replaced the 2000 Regulations). The need for assessment is considered on a case-by-case basis.[130]

Environmental impact assessment can assist with identifying risks that wind farm developments would give rise to environmental harm. The availability of environmental information can enable decision makers to prevent harmful development or to attach conditions to consents that require developers to take steps that avoid or mitigate the anticipated harm. It is therefore a highly important process for compliance by states and their authorities with environmental duties as it offers what may be a final opportunity to influence the development concerned in the interests of environmental protection based on a more detailed review of local environments that may be affected than strategic level reviews under spatial planning and strategic environmental assessment are likely to provide. Questions arise, however, over how capable environmental impact assessment is of preventing projects from being authorised even where they could lead to significant environmental harm. This process is ill-equipped to examine the broad ecological impacts of development programmes because of its focus on individual projects. Even where they are required to identify and assess likely cumulative impacts in their environmental reports, developers are not likely to possess the information needed to assess fully the cumulative impacts that may derive from

---

[128] Directive 2011/92/EU of the European Parliament and of the Council of 13 December 2011 on the assessment of the effects of certain public and private projects on the environment [2012] OJ L 26/1 (EIA Directive) art 4(1).

[129] Electricity Works (Environmental Impact Assessment) (England and Wales) Regulations 2017 (SI 2017/580).

[130] Electricity Works (Environmental Impact Assessment) (Scotland) Regulations 2000 (SI 2017/101).

the interaction of the project they propose with all other relevant developments and sea uses.[131] It is also difficult at this level of decision making to revisit decisions made at a strategic level, particularly where substantial investment in developing particular sites may already have been made.[132] As with the Strategic Environmental Assessment Directive, the Environmental Impact Assessment Directive places only procedural obligations on decision makers. Information contained in environmental reports and obtained through mandatory consultation with statutory consultees, typically authorities with relevant expertise, and affected members of the public, must be taken into account in the decision. Reasons must also be given for the decision reached, leaving decision makers vulnerable if information clearly calling the validity of the decision into question has been ignored. However, environmental impact assessment laws tend not to place any substantive obligations on decision makers for environmental protection. As noted at the conclusion of section VB, such information will be relevant for determining compliance with substantive obligations that states and their authorities may have taken on under other laws.

D. Protected Areas Assessment

As examined in section IVC, decision makers may have additional duties to those imposed by environmental impact assessment laws to assess the likely effects of a proposed plan or project where it could have a negative impact on sites protected for their environmental value. A common feature of habitat protection laws is the duty to assess proposed activities if threats of harm are perceived and to take specified steps if it appears that those concerns are well-founded.[133] For example, the EU's Habitats Directive obliges Member States to provide in national laws that a plan or project that is likely to 'have a significant effect' on protected sites either individually or in combination with other plans/projects should be made subject to an appropriate assessment 'of its implications for the site in view of the site's conservation objectives'.[134] Assessment of offshore plans/projects in the UK's Exclusive Economic Zone that affect protected areas under the Habitats Directive is required by the Offshore Marine Conservation (Natural Habitats etc.) Regulations 2017 and in the territorial sea by the Conservation (Natural Habitats etc.) Regulations 1994.[135]

Habitat assessment can be used to identify and prevent offshore wind energy development that would harm sites protected in law environmentally. A key difference between habitat assessment and environmental impact assessment, of course depending on the provisions of relevant laws, is that laws for the protection of identified

---

[131] Woolley (n 103), 776; Catherine Caine, 'The Race to the Water for Offshore Renewable Energy: Assessing Cumulative and In-Combination Impacts for Offshore Renewable Energy Development' (2020) *Journal of Environmental Law* 83, 96–98.

[132] ibid; Kate Johnson, Sandy Kerr and Jonathan Side, 'Accommodating Wave and Tidal Energy – Control and Decision in Scotland' (2012) 65 *Ocean and Coastal Management* 26, 27.

[133] Lausche (n 88), 174–86.

[134] Directive 92/43/EEC (n 86), art 6(3).

[135] Offshore Marine Conservation (Natural Habitats etc) Regulations 2017 (SI 2017/1013); Conservation (Natural Habitats etc) Regulations 1994 (SI 1994/2710).

sites because of their environmental value are more likely to prescribe a substantive outcome when assessment reveals that a proposed activity could have negative environmental effects on a protected site. For example, the EU's Habitats Directive provides that a plan or project which is made subject to an assessment should only be agreed to by the responsible authority where it has 'ascertained that it will not adversely affect the integrity of the site concerned ...'.[136] This can be contrasted with strategic environmental assessment and environmental impact assessment laws, both of which typically require that procedures be followed, but without specifying the outcome that should follow a negative assessment.

E. Adaptive Management

Finally, one approach to dealing with uncertainty over the environmental effects of offshore renewables could be to attach conditions to development consents for the approval of projects which require that their impacts be monitored. An adaptive management approach aims to generate information so that policies and plans can be revised as knowledge about the effects of development improves.[137] Such approaches may be allied with a precautionary approach to the roll-out of offshore renewables involving the monitoring of a small-scale initial development programme to explore its effects before proceeding to implement development plans and programmes in full. Adaptive management could certainly be beneficial for adjusting offshore renewables development to reduce environmental risks, but it has its limitations for promoting this purpose. The adaptive approach presupposes that it will be possible to alter policies, plans and programmes once implementation has commenced. Decision makers may be under pressure by that time not to insist that developments which have already been constructed and significant investment sunk in them should modify or cease their operation and substantial time and monies may already have been invested in preparing for following development stages.[138] Developers may also be reluctant to undertake monitoring seriously where the outcome could be that the project concerned has to be shut down or curtailed or that other projects cannot be pursued.[139]

Classroom Questions

1. What are the different maritime zones established by UNCLOS? What rights do states have within those zones including with regard to offshore renewable energy development?
2. Identify sea uses with which offshore renewable energy development may come into conflict.

---

[136] Directive 92/43/EEC (n 86), art 6(3).
[137] Celia Le Lievre, 'Sustainably Reconciling Offshore Renewable Energy with Natura 2000 Sites: An Interim Adaptive Management Framework' (2019) *Energy Policy* 491.
[138] Woolley (n 118) 216–17.
[139] Johnson, Kerr and Side (n 132) 27.

3. What provision does UNCLOS make for managing conflict between offshore wind energy and other sea uses in (a) the Exclusive Economic Zone; (b) on the Continental Shelf; and (c) in the High Seas?
4. What types of environmental effects may offshore wind farms have? What questions does knowledge of such effects raise for states with duties under international law to protect the marine environment including by preventing pollution?
5. How do states use legal tools to reduce risks of (a) conflict between offshore renewables and other sea uses; and (b) of offshore renewable energy development giving rise to breaches of their environmental duties? What is marine spatial planning and how can this assist with conflict avoidance?
6. How can strategic environmental assessment, environmental impact assessment, protected areas assessment, and adaptive management be used to reduce risks of conflict between offshore renewable energy development and legal duties for protecting the marine environment?

Scenario

The Thalassan Sea is a semi-enclosed marine ecosystem with seven coastal states, one of which is Boreas. Eurus, an island state, lies 25 nautical miles to the east of Boreas. Boreas and Eurus are separated by the Lynch Strait through which a major shipping route used for regional trade and transportation passes. Several important telecommunications cables between Boreas and Eurus lie on the seabed of the Lynch Strait. Boreas has a full Territorial Sea of 12 nautical miles. It has also declared an Exclusive Economic Zone. This does not extend to 200 nautical miles from Boreas' coastline as the coastlines of Thalassan Sea states are too close to each other for coastal states to claim Exclusive Economic Zones to the furthest extent permissible under UNCLOS. Instead, the Thalassan coastal states have agreed the maritime boundaries of their Exclusive Economic Zones and Continental Shelves with each other. Both Boreas and Eurus have several marine protected areas in waters subject to their jurisdiction protecting coral reefs and breeding areas for the Lesser Speckled Snipe, the endangered national bird of Boreas. Assume for the purposes of both scenarios that the legal regime for habitat protection for all of the marine protected areas is the same as that established by the EU's Habitat Directive examined at sections IVC and VD.

Boreas and the other Thalassan coastal states have ratified the United Nations Convention on the Law of the Sea and have obligations under it, alongside all other ratifying parties, for marine environmental protection. They have also negotiated and ratified a convention for their shared regional sea under which they take on more detailed and exacting legal obligations for preserving and where necessary restoring the functioning of the Thalassan marine ecosystem. Assume for the purposes of the scenarios that Boreas' legal obligations under the regional seas convention are the same as those of ratifying parties under the OSPAR Convention (see section IVB).

1. The government of Boreas wishes to exploit the state's excellent potential for electricity generation from offshore sources including wind, wave, tidal stream, and offshore solar. It approaches you, a noted expert on law relating to offshore renewables, for guidance in several respects on the legal position with its policy proposals for offshore renewables. Advise the government of Boreas on the following:
    - Its rights to install offshore renewable electricity generating plant and cables in waters under its jurisdiction, and to use them to produce and transmit electricity.
    - Boreas also wishes to explore the option of connecting some of its offshore generating stations directly to a new interconnector cable that will be built as part of the offshore development programme and that will link the electricity systems of Boreas and Eurus. Constructing the interconnector will enable electricity produced by Boreas' offshore generating plants to be transmitted directly either to Boreas or Eurus for sale in their electricity markets depending on where the best price for electricity can be obtained. What rights does Boreas have to lay and use cables for transmitting electricity in waters subject to Eurus' jurisdiction?
    - Eurus has raised concerns about how Boreas' planned development may affect shipping traffic passing between them and the operation of the telecommunication cables, both of which are important for Eurus' economy. It has requested Boreas to respect its rights under international law concerning these existing activities. Advise Boreas on its duties under public international law to take these activities into account when planning and implementing its development programme. To what extent could its observance of its duties constrain Boreas' offshore renewable development policies?
2. Save the Sealife, a non-governmental organisation, has reminded the government of Boreas of its obligations under UNCLOS and the regional seas convention to which it belongs to preserve and restore the Thalassan marine ecosystem and of the several protected areas lying in the vicinity of Boreas' and Eurus' coastlines. A report commissioned by Save the Sealife identifies significant risks that the planned programme of offshore development could have negative impacts on the functioning of the Thalassan marine ecosystem and on the environmental features which the protected areas were created to protect. The report is based on the high-level policy statement in which the government of Boreas expresses a general desire to construct offshore renewable generating plant in waters subject to its jurisdiction. Boreas has yet to develop a detailed plan or programmes identifying areas for development for implementing its policy on marine renewables.

The government of Boreas appoints you to advise on legal issues concerning the potential environmental effects of its offshore renewable energy development programme. Advise the Borean government on how it may use legal tools to assist with reducing risks that its offshore renewables programme will conflict with its duties for marine environmental protection under international law and in relation to the marine protected areas. Assume for the purposes of this exercise that Boreas already has in place laws on strategic environmental assessment and environmental impact assessment with the same provisions as those found under the corresponding EU legal instruments, and that the laws apply to offshore development in all waters subject to the jurisdiction of Boreas. Assume also that Boreas has enacted a law on marine spatial planning which is the same as the Marine and Coastal Access Act 2009 of England and Wales save that planning and permitting for offshore renewables is conducted exclusively under this Act rather than under a separate regime.

Suggested Reading

Book Chapters

Olivia Woolley, 'Renewable Energy and the Law of the Sea' in James Kraska and Yong-Kil Park (eds) *Emerging Technology and the Law of the Sea* (Cambridge University Press, 2022) 35.

Articles

Sarah McDonald and David VanderZwaag, 'Renewable Ocean Energy and the International Law and Policy Seascape: Global Currents, Regional Surges' (2015) 29 *Ocean Yearbook Online* 299.

Carlos Soria-Rodriguez, 'The International Regulation for the Protection of the Environment in the Development of Marine Renewable Energy in the EU' (2021) 30 *Review of European, Comparative and International Environmental Law* 46.

Olivia Woolley, 'Ecological Governance for Offshore Wind Energy in United Kingdom Waters: Has an Effective Legal Framework Been Established for Preventing Ecologically Harmful Development?' (2015) 30 *The International Journal of Marine and Coastal Law* 765.

Michaela Young, 'Building the Blue Economy: The Role of Marine Spatial Planning in Facilitating Offshore Renewable Energy Development' (2015) 30 *International Journal of Marine and Coastal Law* 148.

Policy Papers

IRENA, *Offshore Renewables: An Action Agenda for Deployment* (IRENA July 2021).
European Commission, 'An EU Strategy to Harness the Potential of Offshore Renewable Energy for a Climate Neutral Future' COM (2020) 741 final, 19 November 2020.

9

Decarbonising Road Transport

I. Introduction

Energy consumption for transport is a major source of greenhouse gas emissions globally. Transportation was estimated by the IPCC working group on climate change mitigation to be responsible for 15 per cent of global greenhouse gas emissions and 23 per cent of carbon dioxide emissions in 2019.[1] Seventy per cent of those emissions were attributed to road transport compared to 1, 11 and 12 per cent for rail, shipping and aviation respectively.[2] This chapter focuses on uses of law to reduce greenhouse gas emissions from energy consumption for road transport.

Emissions from transport have seen massive growth in the last 30 years, and are projected to see further growth of up to 50 per cent by 2050 without radical change in human transportation systems including technologies and fuels used by them.[3] It is essential, therefore, that non-greenhouse-gas-emitting means of transportation from renewable and other sources should be found and promoted as replacements for petrol and diesel alongside efforts to increase the efficiency of transport fuels consumption and to reduce demand for mobility. Finding alternatives to petrol and diesel can also be desirable for the energy security of regions and states which lack indigenous fossil fuel supplies. For example, the EU imported 96.8 per cent of its oil and petroleum products in 2019.[4] This leaves the EU economy, based as it is on the mobility of goods, highly vulnerable to geopolitical events and to the behaviour of countries who possess oil reserves. Oil price rises in the early 2020s for reasons including Russia's invasion of Ukraine have highlighted this vulnerability, prompting the EU to accelerate action on reducing its oil dependency.

Despite these clear motivations for switching to renewable energy as a vehicle fuel, the proportion of energy consumed for transport from renewables remains very low

---

[1] Intergovernmental Panel on Climate Change – Working Group III, *Climate Change 2022 – Mitigation of Climate Change* (Cambridge University Press, 2022) TS22 and TS67.
[2] ibid, TS67.
[3] ibid, TS68.
[4] European Commission, *EU Energy in Figures: Statistical Pocketbook 2021* (Publications Office of the European Union, 2021) 75.

at 3.7 per cent.[5] Ninety per cent of renewable energy consumed for transport derives from fuels produced from organic materials such as plants and wood, collectively referred to as biofuels. Recent years have seen rapid growth in the uptake of electric vehicles with sales tripling since 2019, but electric mobility's contribution remains minor with only 1 per cent of the global passenger car fleet and 4 per cent of the bus fleet running on electricity.[6] It must also be remembered when talking about electricity as a transport fuel that it is only renewable to the extent that it was produced from renewable sources. Much of the fuel for electricity production (more than 60 per cent) still comes from fossil fuels and the proportion of fossil fuels in electricity supplies could even increase if the growth in electric vehicle use is not coordinated with the replacement of coal, gas and oil in power production with renewable sources. Finally, high hopes have been placed in hydrogen and biomethane as major vehicle fuels of the future, but they have only marginal roles in meeting energy demand for transport at present.[7] The term biomethane is used to describe gas produced from organic sources (biogas) which has been 'upgraded' to natural gas specifications so that it can be injected into existing pipelines and used in natural gas-consuming equipment including vehicle engines. Natural gas mobility is already well established in many jurisdictions without access to indigenous oil supplies. Hydrogen's role is as an energy carrier which can be used to produce electricity for mobility indirectly (by burning it) or directly (through conversion in vehicles by a fuel cell or adapted internal combustion engine). Hydrogen itself may be produced using electricity to power electrolysis or by well-established industrial processes for 'reforming' fossil fuels. As with renewable electricity, hydrogen can only be viewed as renewable to the extent that it was produced from renewable sources.

Progress with increasing the proportion of renewable energy in transport fuel supplies is hampered by several significant obstacles.[8] First, energy for transport from fossil fuels is very closely bound into the operation of the socio-economic systems of most, if not all, of the world's states. Petroleum products met 96 per cent of energy transport needs in 2015 with the transport energy sector consuming 64.7 per cent of world oil consumption.[9] The growth of consumption of petroleum and diesel globally during the last three decades in connection with a doubling of trade volume in that time and much increased demand for personal mobility compounded an existing problem. Petrol and diesel are very well established as transport fuels, using longstanding technologies which have benefitted from cost reductions and efficiencies from their use for over a century. The infrastructure is in place to support petrol and diesel transportation, the business model of manufacturers is largely oriented to such vehicles, and consumers have little awareness of other possibilities. Replacing fossil fuel dependence for transport would represent a significant departure from the socio-economic status quo to the extent that renewable alternatives cannot be supplied and consumed using current infrastructure and equipment (eg, the internal combustion engine).

---

[5] REN 21, *Renewables 2022: Global Status Report* (REN21 Secretariat 2022) 21.
[6] ibid 65–66.
[7] ibid, 66.
[8] See discussion of obstacles to the growth of renewables in transport at REN 21 (n 5) 72–73; and IRENA, *Renewable Energy Policies in a Time of Transition* (IRENA 2018) 13, 21, 54–55.
[9] IRENA, 'Renewable Energy Policies' (n 8) 13.

Second, fossil fuel energy for transport is not easily replaceable by renewable energy as there are currently few alternative renewable fuel sources. As noted above, biofuels are the main renewable alternative currently.[10] This contribution is mostly from the now well-established production of first-generation biofuels from food crops such as corn, sugar beet and soybeans. In addition to their more advanced technological development than for other renewable transport fuels, early growth of biofuels consumption has been driven by the 'blending' of petrol and diesel with biofuels. Petrol and diesel-fuelled engines for road transport vehicles can run on fuels containing a small proportion (often lying between 10 and 20 per cent with the maximum size depending on the types of fuel and engine) of biofuels.[11] New engines are required for vehicles running on biofuels alone or on blends with a higher proportion of biofuels. Biofuels will undoubtedly play a substantial role in replacing fossil fuels for transport with renewable alternatives. However, early hopes that first generation biofuels could provide a ready and rapid replacement for petrol and diesel have been dashed by concerns over the sustainability of biofuels produced from certain feedstocks, particularly from those which can also be used to meet human or farm animal demand for food.[12] In view of this, the focus is shifting in developed economies to promoting more sustainable second- and third-generation biofuels from organic waste and algae and to other alternative fuels such as electricity, hydrogen and biomethane. However, sectors for producing some of these fuels are in the first stages of growth. Major public support is needed to enable their further technological development and progress, including by leveraging private investment, which would not otherwise be made because of perceived risks with investing in newer technologies that are not yet able to compete fully with established incumbents.

Third, introducing renewables to energy for transportation is not simply a matter of promoting alternative fuel sources. As importantly, significant capacities for producing affordable vehicles that consume those fuels must be established. New vehicle types which can run solely on electricity, hydrogen and biofuels are needed to replace the currently dominant production of vehicles which run on petrol and diesel. However, vehicle manufacturers are either not making available vehicles that consume renewable fuel sources or are only doing so at prices which may be unattractive for consumers. This is unsurprising in view of the currently low proportions of alternative fuel sources in energy consumed for transport. The market does not provide an incentive for manufacturers to develop the capacities required to produce alternative fuel vehicles in bulk that would enable vehicle price reduction through growing experience with the manufacture and use of relevant technologies and economies of scale in their manufacture. Stimuli from sources outside of markets such as public funds may be needed to address this 'chicken and egg' situation. The position outlined in this paragraph is changing rapidly for electric vehicles with surging sales during the last three years leading to a 9 per cent market share in 2021.[13] However, further progress is needed to reduce the

---

[10] See the fuller discussion of biofuels at section III below.
[11] REN21 (n 5) 95.
[12] IRENA (n 8) 46–47.
[13] See the account at REN 21 (n 5) 68–69.

costs of electric cars whose median price differentials remain substantially higher than those for equivalent fossil fuel models in the US and EU.[14]

Fourth, two factors related to confidence in renewable fuels mobility may retard the growth of markets in renewable fuels and vehicles even where they could be made available. Awareness of opportunities for mobility through renewable fuels vehicles and of the reasons why change is desirable may be limited amongst consumers. Again, that is unsurprising in a world which has been so long dominated and shaped by fossil fuel transportation. Concerted efforts are needed to support renewable fuels use by communicating why their availability is promoted and explaining their advantages over established options. In addition, existing refuelling infrastructure was developed to support a fossil fuel transport system. The infrastructure required to service vehicles using alternative fuels such as biomethane, hydrogen and electricity is lacking, and efforts to remedy that situation are in their infancy. In the absence of substantial demand for renewable fuels consumption, it may not emerge without legal intervention and support from public funds to create a minimum initial level of infrastructure support required for reliable mobility using alternative fuel vehicles.

Significant legal intervention is required both to support the growth of renewable energy for transportation from its currently early stages if renewable fuels are to enable continued mobility approaching levels to which humanity has become accustomed in the fossil fuels era. Principal focuses for law will be on supporting sectoral expansion from technological development to commercialisation including by overcoming the challenges described above. This chapter examines different ways in which law can be used for these purposes. Section II examines types of legal interventions which can be made to support the emergence of renewable alternatives to petrol and diesel. A key aim of this section is to highlight the need for coordinated legal interventions to be made simultaneously at several levels to secure emergence of renewable fuels as viable alternatives to petrol and diesel. Action must be taken at the same time to promote renewable energy transportation in the manufacture of fuels and of vehicles that consume them, in the provision of the refuelling infrastructure to support renewable mobility, and in consumer awareness.[15] Securing the growth of renewables in one part of the transportation energy system will not be valuable if other elements remain firmly stuck in a fossil fuels paradigm. For example, ready availability of renewable fuels would be of little use without the corresponding availability of affordable renewable vehicles and of the infrastructure needed to maintain mobility.

Section III draws from the EU's promotion in the 2000s and 2010s of first-generation biofuels production and consumption to explore problems which biofuels exploitation can create, ways in which law has been and can be used to address them and limits to law's utility for tackling the problems. Particular attention is given to concerns over the sustainability of biofuels production and attempts made by the EU to address them by regulating the biofuels sector. The more recent concentration of the EU on using law to promote second and third generation biofuels and other alternative renewable energy fuels derives, in part, from legal limitations discovered by the EU for preventing unsustainable outcomes from the production of certain first-generation biofuels.

---

[14] ibid.
[15] IRENA (n 8) 13, 44.

II. Promoting Renewable Fuel Consumption in Road Transport through Law

This section considers how law can be used to address the challenges identified in Section I with a view to promoting the consumption of renewable fuels. As noted above, a key message from the section is that legal interventions need to operate at several levels simultaneously to address the challenges of decarbonising road transport. First, at the national legislative level by the introduction of supportive framework legal structures for replacing fossil fuel mobility with renewable fuels transport. Legal frameworks for renewable transport must form part of holistic frameworks for replacing fossil fuels with renewables in energy consumption in totality in view of competing demands from electricity, transport and heating for renewable power, renewable hydrogen and sustainable biofuels. Second, at the level of vehicle manufacturers by prompting them to introduce capacities for producing renewable fuel vehicles alongside and in preference to their petrol/diesel models. Third, at the fuel producer level to promote the availability of renewable fuels. Fourth, at the fuel provider level to ensure that the infrastructure is available to support renewable energy mobility. Fifth, at the consumer level by encouraging vehicle users to move from petrol/diesel vehicles to renewable fuel vehicles. Examples from law in the EU, California, the UK and Norway are used to illustrate ways in which law can be used to reach these different audiences at the same time.

A. Setting Legal Targets for Renewable Energy in Transport

Replacing fossil fuels with renewable sources in energy consumption for transportation is more difficult than it is for electricity generation due to the challenges outlined above. States may therefore choose to adopt policy targets for energy from renewable sources in energy consumed for transport alongside policy targets for renewables as a proportion of overall energy consumption. Chapter 4 of the book examines how the achievement of policy targets can be supported and enhanced by backing up political commitments with legal support. Potential benefits examined in that chapter include creating investor confidence that a sector will undergo change over a set timescale, thereby creating demand for new products, and forcing governments with legally binding duties to adopt policies and enact laws that will enable them to be met. However, if targets set in law are to have these positive effects, it is essential (a) that they are supported by requirements for transparency by the target holder on progress towards the required outcome; (b) that steps can be taken to hold the target holder to account if progress towards the target is deficient; (c) that targets can be enforced when they fall due; and (d) that penalties for non-achievement are sufficient to have a deterrent effect.

Renewable transport targets must also be linked with targets and duties in legal frameworks for increasing renewable electricity production and for its integration into transmission and distribution networks.[16] Growth in electric mobility may lead to increased greenhouse gas emissions from fossil fuel generation if renewable electricity production does not keep pace with greater electricity demand. In addition, the rollout of electric transport must be coordinated with transmission and distribution network planning, with market design and with governmental policies on new building, on adapting existing buildings and on land use planning.[17] Coordination between them is needed to ensure that peoples' homes are equipped with battery-recharging facilities, that distribution networks are able to carry the additional demand for electricity and that they are also able to carry flows of electricity from properties where consumers assist with maintaining the balance between network inputs and outputs by selling capacities to release electricity stored in car batteries in balancing markets.[18]

The focus in this section is on setting targets in law requiring that the proportion of energy consumed in the transport sector as a whole is increased to a set level by a set date. Targets are also set in laws targeting separate components of the energy transport system. For example, a common legal approach is to place targets on fuel suppliers requiring that the proportion of renewable fuels placed by them on the market reaches a specified level by a specified time or over a prescribed period. Targets may also be set in law for the proportion of vehicles made available by manufacturers that consume only renewable energy or for increasing the number of facilities available for refuelling renewable energy vehicles. Uses of targets to drive change in components of the transport system are considered in sections concerning the relevant sub-sectors below. The approach developed in Chapter 4 for assessing the likely effectiveness of renewable energy targets set in law can also be applied to these sub-sectoral targets without modification.

EU law furnishes examples of targets for renewable energy in transport backed up by law. Member States were obliged by the EU's Biofuels Directive to ensure that a minimum proportion of biofuels and other renewable fuels was placed on their national fuels market by 2010.[19] National targets indicating the level to be reached were to be set by them using reference values of 2 per cent by 2005 and 5.75 per cent by 2010 of the energy content of petrol and diesel for transport purposes placed on their markets.[20] However, there was no obligation for Member States under EU law to reach the reference values. The Directive also lacked support from a detailed legal framework requiring that coordinated measures targeted at different sectoral components be adopted to secure growth in biofuels consumption. It is unsurprising, therefore, that 22 out of the 27 EU Member States had failed to achieve the EU's 5.75 per cent target by 2010.[21]

As with the failure of its 2001 Renewable Electricity Directive to drive across the board growth in its Member States, the poor level of achievement led to calls for a strengthening of legal obligation to achieve the EU's desired level of renewables in

---

[16] IRENA (n 8) 48.
[17] IRENA, *Global Energy Transformation: A Roadmap to 2050* (IRENA, 2019) 46–48.
[18] See Chapter 6, section IVC.
[19] Council Directive 2003/30/EC of 8 May 2003 on the promotion of the use of biofuels or other renewable fuels for transport [2003] OJ L123/42.
[20] ibid, art 3(1).
[21] Commission, 'Renewable Energy Progress Report' COM (2013) 175 final, 4.

energy consumed for transport in the successor Directive. All EU Member States were given a legally binding target under the 2009 Renewable Energy Directive for increasing the proportion of energy from renewable sources consumed for transport to 10 per cent by 2020.[22] The target was set at the same level for all states because of: (a) the need for a common contribution in a spirit of solidarity to this challenging area for decarbonisation; and (b) the ability of states to meet the target by importing biofuels, meaning, in contrast to renewable electricity, that it could be met by Member States without access to indigenous supplies of the fuel source. The more exacting legal obligation may have contributed to an improved performance with the share in energy for transport consumed in the EU from renewable sources increasing from less than 2 per cent in 2010 to 10.2 per cent in 2020.[23] However, this was due to overperformance by Sweden (at 31.9 per cent) and by 11 Member States exceeding their 10 per cent target overall. Sixteen Member States failed to meet their legally binding targets.[24] This failure can be contrasted with the success of all but one state in reaching their overall national targets. Their performance raises questions about the ability of targets alone, even where they are clear, legally binding and enforceable, to secure action required to meet obligations in a sector for which the overwhelming domination of fossil fuel energy poses much greater challenges, including greater prospects of disrupting peoples' lives, than the easier to decarbonise power generation. In the case of the 2009 Directive, the threat of penalisation under EU law was not able to overcome the lack of political will amongst Member States to adopt measures capable of securing sufficient change to the status quo for reaching the 10 per cent minimum level.

This experience may have informed the EU's choice not to adopt a Union-wide target for renewable energy in transport under the 2018 Directive. Instead, the Directive targets a key component of the energy transport system by obliging Member States to adopt laws ensuring that their fuel suppliers reach at least a minimum proportion of renewable fuels in supplies by 2030.[25] A proposal for reforming the Directive keeps the focus on fuel suppliers, but replaces the minimum proportion with a minimum level of reduction in the greenhouse gas intensity of fuels (eg, the amount of greenhouse gases released by fuel consumption) of at least 13 per cent.[26] Measures requiring direct change in components of the energy transport system may well have a greater immediate impact on renewable energy growth than legally binding targets lacking support from key measures such as renewable supply obligations; however, the point made earlier must be borne in mind: simultaneous targeting of systemic actors is required to prevent progress on one front being thwarted by a lack of progress on others. The ideal

---

[22] Council Directive 2009/28/EC of 23 April 2009 on the promotion of the use of energy from renewable sources and amending and subsequently repealing Directive 2001/77/EC and 2003/30/EC [2009] OJ L140/16 (the 2009 RES Directive), art 3(4).
[23] Eurostat, *Renewable energy statistics*, January 2022. Available at: Renewable energy statistics – Statistics Explained (europa.eu) ((accessed 7 October 2022)).
[24] ibid.
[25] Directive (EU) 2018/2001 of the European Parliament and of the Council of 11 December 2018 on the promotion of the use of energy from renewable sources [2018] OJ L 328/82 (the 2018 RES Directive) art 25.
[26] European Commission, 'Proposal for a Directive amending Directive (EU) 2018/2001, Regulation (EU) 2018/1999 and Directive 98/70/EC and repealing Council Directive (EU) 2015/652', COM (2021) 557 final, 41–42.

would be an overarching legal framework for introducing renewables to road transport centred around a legally binding target with the credibility to secure adoption of effective measures for its attainment.

Setting targets in law for increasing renewable energy enables the use of multipliers to encourage those responsible in law for achieving targets to favour certain fuels over others. A multiplier enables a target to be met despite overall consumption falling below the level set in law by multiplying the contribution from favoured sources. Multipliers introduced to the 2009 Renewable Energy Directive by amendment in 2015 because of problems experienced with unsustainable first generation biofuels were used to encourage Member States to promote the production of biofuels from more sustainable sources.[27] Annex IX of the 2009 Directive advised that biofuels produced from the listed fuel sources 'shall be considered to be twice their energy content' when calculating whether the 10 per cent target has been met (eg, the target would be achieved even if only 5 per cent of energy consumed for transport was from renewable sources if all of that 5 per cent was derived from biofuels listed in Annex IX).[28] Similarly, Article 3(4)(c) of the Directive provided strong encouragement for Member States to adopt policies and laws promoting electric vehicles by advising that a multiplier of five would be applied to electricity consumed for transport that can be attributed to renewable sources when calculating compliance with the 10 per cent target.[29] Multipliers were also set for these renewable fuels for the obligation placed on fuel suppliers by the 2019 Directive,[30] but the proposal for a reformed Directive replaces them with a minimum obligation for reducing the intensity of greenhouse gas releases from fuel consumption which is designed to accelerate support for electric mobility from renewables specifically. The new approach reflects EU views that renewable electricity will be the dominant road transport fuel of the future, with advanced biofuels having a more valuable role to play due to want of viable alternatives in decarbonising fuels for heavy duty road transport, shipping and aviation.[31]

B. Promoting the Availability of Alternative Fuel Vehicles

Vehicle manufacturers must introduce new models which run on renewable fuels to enable the growth of renewables in energy consumed for transport. However, they may choose not to do this either because consumer demand is insufficient, or they wish to concentrate on supplying established markets for fossil fuel vehicles in which they already have significant sunk investment. Even if they do choose to do this to supply a niche market of well-off, green-minded consumers and are able to reduce

---

[27] Directive 2015/1513 of 9 September 2015 amending Directive 98/70/EC relating to the quality of petrol and diesel fuels and amending Directive 2009/28/EC on the promotion of the use of energy from renewable sources [2015] OJ L239/1.
[28] 2009 RES Directive (n 22), Annex IX.
[29] ibid, art 3(4)(c).
[30] 2018 RES Directive (n 25), art 27(2).
[31] Sean Caroll, 'EU drops "accounting trick" to boost green fuel in road transport' (EurActiv website, 29 July 2021) EU drops 'accounting trick' to boost green fuel in road transport – EURACTIV.com (accessed 7 October 2022).

manufacturing costs through learning by doing, prices for renewable fuel vehicles may remain high compared to those for fossil fuel vehicles due to demand remaining too low to invest in the manufacturing capacities that would enable significant economies of scale and corresponding reductions in price for renewable models.

Electric passenger cars and vans are seen as the major alternative to fossil fuel equivalents. Substantial production capacity already exists for electric vehicles and is increasing in response to sharp rises in sales including in China and the US.[32] However, electric vehicles still remain a small proportion both of cars and vans in circulation and in new car and van sales.[33] Massive growth in electricity as a vehicle fuel is needed for road transport decarbonisation: IRENA posits an increase from the current 1 per cent level to over 40 per cent by 2050.[34] The continued higher median price of electric vehicles compared to established fossil fuel models restricts their appeal for consumers.[35] Costs have declined significantly because of recent growth, with China reaching a median price for electric vehicles of only 9 per cent higher than fossil fuel cars and vans, but the difference in the US and the EU remains at around 50 per cent. The position with cars and vans consuming other alternative vehicle fuels including hydrogen, biomethane, and biofuels at levels that cannot be accommodated in internal combustion engines, is much further behind. Costs are high and the demand from consumers needed to spur cost reductions through experience-based technological improvement and economies of scale in production are not yet present.

Renewable energy sources have also made limited headway with displacing fossil fuels in heavy duty vehicles such as lorries, buses and coaches. Some positive progress has been made with the electrification of bus fleets for urban travel, but concerns over the range that electric vehicles can cover, although being challenged by improvements in battery technology, constrain electrification of longer-distance road transport.[36] Advanced biofuels are seen as a better prospect for heavy duty vehicles, but a stronger focus is needed on producing the engine technologies for vehicles that can run on high biofuel blends.[37]

Law can be used to address vehicle manufacturers' current inability or reluctance to produce alternative fuel vehicles at declining prices in four main ways. First, investment support subsidies are needed from public funds to aid actors with developing and improving technologies that would be capable of meeting public mobility needs.[38] As with renewable electricity production, investment support enables the development of promising new technologies at lower cost. The second is by mandating vehicle manufacturers to include a proportion of alternative fuel-consuming models in fleets of vehicles they make available for sale. Laws of this kind seek to secure the availability of alternative fuel vehicles at more attractive costs for consumers by obliging vehicle manufacturers to establish production capacity although initial demand may be absent and to take steps, including through investment in research and development, to make models affordable and appealing for consumers. California's Zero Emission Vehicle

---

[32] REN 21 (n 5) 68.
[33] ibid, 65–67.
[34] IRENA (n 17), 28.
[35] REN 21 (n 5), 68–69.
[36] ibid, 71–72.
[37] IRENA (n 8), 47.
[38] See Chapter 5, section II.

Regulation places an obligation to include a specified proportion of zero and low emission vehicles such as full battery-electric, hydrogen fuel cell and plug-in hybrid-electric vehicles for sale in manufacturers' fleets.[39] The obligation lies at 22 per cent by 2025. Manufacturers demonstrate compliance with the obligation by acquiring credits and are penalised if the mandated level is not met. More credits are acquired for vehicles aimed at the harder-to-decarbonise long-range vehicle market. The ambition of California's ZEV programme has recently increased drastically, with Governor Gavin Newsom having issued an executive order requiring that all new passenger vehicles sold should be zero emission by 2035.[40] The UK Government has announced that it also intends to introduce a zero-emissions vehicle mandate from 2024 under which annual targets will be set for the percentage of new car and van sales from zero emission vehicles.[41]

Third, laws which require manufacturers to meet legal standards for carbon dioxide emissions from the fleets of vehicles which they make available for purchase are used to encourage manufacturers, or to oblige them if the standard is set low enough, to produce very low carbon vehicles such as those consuming renewable energy. The EU has made prominent use of this legal approach as part of its decarbonisation legislative packages. Its legal standards require manufacturers selling vehicles in the EU to ensure that average emissions from vehicles in their fleet (all vehicles placed on the market by a manufacturer in a calendar year) are below a specified level. Regulation 2019/631/EC sets average emission performance standards for new passenger cars and for light commercial vehicles: 95g CO_2/km and 147g CO_2/km respectively from 2020 to the end of 2024.[42] Tailored limits are set for each manufacturer using the standards set in law as a reference but modifying them to take into account factors such as how heavy vehicles are, it being easier for manufacturers selling lower weight vehicles to meet the emission standards. From January 2025, manufacturers must further reduce fleet emissions by 15 per cent of an average of individually tailored standards set for 2021, increasing to 37.5 per cent and 31 per cent reductions for cars and vans respectively from 2030.[43] Manufacturers failing to achieve the average will be penalised financially with the fine depending on the size of the excess. The legislative package made necessary by the EU's subsequent increase of its greenhouse gas emissions reduction goal for 2030 from 40 per cent to 55 per cent includes a proposal to increase the 2030 standard to 55 per cent for cars and 50 per cent for vans.[44] This hike is the precursor to a

---

[39] 13 California Code of Regulations, ss 1962.1 and 1962.2. See also California Air Resources Board, *Zero-Emission Vehicle Program* (CARB website) Zero-Emission Vehicle Program | California Air Resources Board (accessed 7 October 2022); Barry Barton and Peter Schütte, 'Electric Vehicle Law and Policy: A Comparative Analysis' (2017) 35 *Journal of Energy and Natural Resources Law* 147, 153–55; Lewis Pickett et al., *Electric Vehicles and Infrastructure* (House of Commons Library (CBP-7480), 20 December 2021) Electric vehicles and infrastructure – House of Commons Library (parliament.uk) (accessed 7 October 2022), 60–61.
[40] Executive Department State of California, Executive Order N-79-20, 23 September 2020.
[41] HM Government, *Net Zero Strategy: Build Back Greener*, October 2021, 24; Pickett and others, (n 39) 28–29.
[42] Regulation (EU) 2019/631 of 17 April 2019 setting CO_2 emission performance standards for new passenger cars and for new light commercial vehicles, and repealing Regulations (EC) No 443/2009 and (EU) No 510/2011 [2019] OJ L111/13, art 1(2).
[43] ibid, arts 1(4) and (5).
[44] European Commission, Proposal for a Directive amending Directive (EU) 2018/2001 on the promotion of the use of energy from renewable sources, Directive 2010/31/EU on the energy performance of buildings and Directive 2012/27/EU on energy efficiency, COM (2022) 222 final.

much more ambitious goal of 100 per cent cuts by 2035. The proposal was still under review in September 2022.

Regulation 2019/1242 sets average emission performance standards for new heavy-duty vehicles placed by manufacturers on the market.[45] This is the first such regulation adopted in the EU. The Regulation requires that average emissions from manufacturers' fleets should be reduced by 15 per cent by 2025 and 30 per cent by 2030 against reference values to be established on bases set out in the Regulation.[46] Again, manufacturers failing to achieve the reduction will be fined, with the fine depending on the size of excess. This is a rare recent example of standards being set in law for reducing emissions from heavy-duty vehicles.[47]

Targets under the EU laws may encourage manufacturers to increase the proportion of vehicles consuming renewable fuels in their fleets in two ways. Firstly, the average emissions from all covered vehicles in a manufacturer's fleet are taken into account when considering whether the maximum permissible emissions level has been complied with. One way of reducing the average emissions for a fleet is to include more low carbon emission vehicles in the fleet to bring the average down. Secondly, all the laws mentioned above have previously or currently allow 'super credits' to be used for vehicles with zero or very low emissions (as defined in the relevant laws).[48] This means that a multiplier can be applied to such vehicles under which each qualifying unit is multiplied when the average is calculated, thus reducing the average. This incentivises manufacturers to introduce more zero/very low emissions vehicles including those consuming renewable sources to stay under the maximum level set by the standard. Super credits are to be replaced from 2025 by an alternative incentive to manufacture zero and low emission vehicles. Under the alternative, the laws set benchmarks to be achieved by manufacturers for low and zero emission vehicles.[49] They are set at 15 per cent and 35 per cent for cars and vans for 2025 and 2030 respectively. Achievement of the benchmark allows a slight relaxation of the overall standard to be achieved.

Fourth, some countries and cities have placed bans on the future sale of vehicles consuming fossil fuels and restrictions on their ability to access specified areas.[50] Simply forbidding the purchase and use of fossil fuel vehicles by consumers may force manufacturers to produce vehicles consuming renewables and other low carbon fuels instead, but it is a blunt legal tool which should be used with care. There is no guarantee that manufacturers will turn to alternative vehicle production instead. Bans may also be socially regressive by preventing the poorest members of communities, who may not be able to afford alternative options, from using vehicles they already own or replacing them with second-hand fossil fuel models. Consequences of this kind must be borne in mind when designing relevant laws. Bans are also best used as part of larger packages of policies and laws aimed at promoting widespread access to low-cost

---

[45] Regulation (EU) 2019/1242 of 20 June 2019 setting CO_2 emission performance standards for new heavy-duty vehicles and amending Regulations (EC) No 595/2009 and (EU) 2018/956 of the European Parliament and of the Council and Council Directive 96/53/EC [2019] OJ L 198/202.
[46] ibid, art 1.
[47] REN 21 (n 5) 72.
[48] Regulation 2019/631 (n 42) art 5; Regulation 2019/1242 (n 45) art 5.
[49] Regulation 2019/631 (n 42) arts 1(6) and 1(7); Regulation 2019/1242 (n 45) arts 5(3) and 5(4).
[50] IRENA (n 8), 13; REN21 (n 5), 33, 65, 80.

vehicles which consume low-cost renewable fuels such as laws examined in this section that incentivise manufacturers to introduce low emission vehicles into their fleets.

C. Promoting Alternative Fuels

Dramatic change is needed in the fuel production and supply sectors if renewable and other alternative fuels are to make significant incursions in and to displace petrol and diesel. Fossil fuels currently meet 96 per cent of global energy consumption for transport.[51] Strong legal interventions are therefore required to enable the growth in alternative fuels despite this dominance. They must be accompanied by corresponding interventions to secure change in vehicle manufacture and supply and infrastructure sectors, and in consumer preferences.[52]

A commonly employed legal approach for promoting growth in renewable fuels is to place a legal obligation on national fuel suppliers which requires them to include a specified proportion of fuels from renewable sources in their total fuel supplies over a specified period. Compliance will typically be demonstrated by submitting certificates attesting to the supply of renewable fuels. The UK's Renewable Transport Fuel Obligation, in place since 2008, is set at 13.507 per cent in 2022, increasing to 21.066 per cent from 2032 onwards.[53] The EU's 2018 RES Directive requires Member States to impose an obligation on fuel suppliers to reach at least 14 per cent renewable fuels in their supplies by 2030.[54] It is also common for states to adopt biofuels blending mandates under which suppliers must include a proportion of biofuels amongst their fuel supplies.[55] IRENA refers to 68 states having adopted such mandates by 2016, all but seven of which were below 10 per cent.

Commentators call for greater use to be made of fuel obligations to support advanced biofuels including by offering more certificates for newer fuel supplies than for established supply sources.[56] Advanced biofuels are seen as promising for future use in hard to decarbonise transport sub-sectors such as long haul heavy-duty vehicles, shipping and aviation, but the fuels and supply chains for producing them are described as 'immature'.[57] The use of obligations at this early stage of their development would assist with scaling up production capacities and acquiring experience with their use, hopefully leading in both cases to falling fuel costs. IRENA noted in 2017 that only limited use of advanced biofuels obligations had been made to that point, naming Denmark, Italy and the US as being amongst the few jurisdictions to take this step.[58] Others have followed since. The UK's Renewable Transport Fuel Obligation includes a development fuel target, set at 0.908 per cent in 2022 and increasing to 3.390 per cent

---

[51] ibid, 13.
[52] ibid.
[53] The Renewable Transport Fuel Obligations Order 2007 (SI 2007/3072).
[54] 2018 RES Directive (n 25), art 25(1).
[55] IRENA (n 8), 45–47; REN21 (n 5), 95.
[56] IRENA (n 8) 13, 47–48; REN 21 (n 5) 95.
[57] IRENA (n 8), 46–48.
[58] ibid, 23.

in 2032.[59] Development fuels include fuels made from sustainable wastes or residues and biofuels which can be used in blends with petrol of at least 25 per cent. They also cover hydrogen, biomethane and certain aviation fuels. They are double counted when assessing compliance with the obligation. The EU's 2018 RES Directive requires Member States to set obligatory shares of advanced biofuels in overall fuel supplies of 0.2 per cent in 2022, rising to 3.5 per cent in 2030.[60] Multipliers are applied to biofuels produced from certain feedstocks and to renewable electricity when consumed for transport.

Fuel obligations have been important for driving the early growth of renewable transport but may not be useful for securing further growth without change in vehicle supplies. Their role to date has largely been to promote the practice of 'blending'.[61] Internal combustion engines can run without modification on petrol and diesel blended with a small proportion of biofuels. Blends with higher proportions of biofuels can have a negative impact on engines including impairing their fuel efficiency. Jurisdictions with strong experience of using biofuels may have enough vehicles with engines adapted to run on blends with higher proportions of biofuels to set more exacting obligations. For example, Brazil's biofuel mandate has allowed for 27 per cent from ethanol in standard gasoline and 10 per cent from biodiesel in diesel.[62] However, blends of below 10 per cent are the norm in most jurisdictions.

For renewable electricity, the main expected contributor to renewable energy in passenger cars and vans, the fuel derives from electricity generation. In view of this, coordination is needed between measures promoting electricity consumption for transport, the growth of renewable electricity production, and the adaptation of networks to carry higher proportions of renewable electricity.[63] Risks arise if coordination is lacking that fossil fuel generation will rise to meet increased demand or that networks will lack the capacity to carry electricity for transport as well as for established uses. In this regard, both IRENA and REN21 note with concern the lack of legal provision directly linking policies supporting electric vehicle use with others supporting growth in renewable electricity production.[64]

Laws setting fuel quality standards (eg, the level of emissions associated with each unit of fuel consumed) impose duties on fuel suppliers to keep the greenhouse gas intensity of supplied fuels (the amount of greenhouse gases associated with each unit of consumed fuel) below specified levels. The obligation to achieve the standard and the prospect of a fine if it is not met drive efforts by suppliers to reduce the greenhouse gas intensity of fuels. They may include bringing lower greenhouse gas emission fuels into their portfolio including biofuels, biomethane, renewable hydrogen and renewable electricity. Greenhouse gas intensity may be measured on a life cycle basis, taking into

---

[59] Department for Transport, *Renewable Transport Fuel Obligation: Compliance Guidance 2022: 01/01/2022 to 31/12/2022*, (UK Government, January 2022) renewable-transport-fuel-obligation-compliance-guidance.pdf (publishing.service.gov.uk) (accessed 7 October 2022).
[60] 2018 RES Directive (n 25), art 25(1).
[61] IRENA (n 8), 47; REN 21 (n 5), 94.
[62] IRENA, (n 8), 47.
[63] IRENA (n 8) 48; REN 21 (n 5) 71.
[64] ibid.

account not only emissions at the point of consumption, but also all emissions that the production and supply of the fuel gave rise to.

The EU's Fuel Quality Directive required Member States to achieve a 6 per cent reduction in the life cycle greenhouse gas intensity of fuels made available for purchase in their territories by 2020.[65] The target has not been increased since the deadline for meeting it passed at the end of 2020. However, the draft amendment to the 2018 RES Directive proposes to replace the provision on the promotion of renewable fuels with a duty for Member States to place an obligation on national fuel suppliers leading to a greenhouse gas intensity reduction of at least 13 per cent by 2030.[66] The main means of doing this, as the provision notes, would be by increasing supplies of renewable fuels and renewable electricity. It is believed that this would lead to more substantial growth in renewable and alternative fuels production than the renewable fuels obligation. A low carbon fuel standard is also used under the law of California.[67] This, too, seeks to drive reduction in the carbon intensity of fuels by encouraging the inclusion of options with a lower carbon intensity than the specified level in fuel supplies. Credits are issued for fuels with carbon intensity below the standard and debits for fuels whose intensity exceeds the level. The approach under Californian law is also being followed by other North American west coast states (Oregon, Washington, British Columbia). The California Air Resources Board reports that it is working with these states under the Pacific Coast Collaborative 'to strategically align policies to reduce GHG and promote clean energy' including by building an integrated West Coast market for low carbon fuels.[68]

D. Infrastructure for Alternative Fuel Vehicles

Another major challenge for securing increases in alternative fuel vehicle production by manufacturers and purchase by consumers is that the infrastructure is not in place to support their usage. Nearly all the existing refuelling capacity is for petrol and diesel. Currently limited infrastructure for fuelling and refuelling deters investment in alternative fuel vehicles. For electric vehicles, it exacerbates concerns that batteries lack the capacity to support long-distance travel (range anxiety). As governments with policies in favour of mobility powered by electricity and other alternative fuels recognise, a rapid roll-out of refuelling infrastructure is needed over the next decade. Careful thought about the technologies to be introduced is also important for creating consumer confidence and for taking full advantage of the benefits of electric mobility. Car batteries recharge at different rates depending on the capacity of charging facilities. High-capacity fast recharging is preferable for publicly accessible recharging infrastructure. Smart charging or vehicle to grid technologies must also be used to take advantage of opportunities for lowering peak demand and keeping electricity systems in balance as electric vehicle charging adds to electricity consumption.[69]

---

[65] Directive 98/70/EC of 13 October 1998 relating to the quality of petrol and diesel fuels and amending Council Directive 93/12/EEC [1998] OJ L 350/58.
[66] European Commission, Proposal for a Directive amending Directive (EU) 2018/2001 (n 44) 41.
[67] California Air Resources Board, 'Low Carbon Fuel Standard' (CARB Website) Low Carbon Fuel Standard | California Air Resources Board (accessed 7 October 2022).
[68] ibid.
[69] Pickett and others (n 39) 66–68.

The first focus for electric vehicles must be on installing charging facilities in peoples' homes. Much electric vehicle charging is expected to take place domestically with public facilities being used to top up batteries as necessary. Laws which regulate building can be used alongside those controlling the issue of development permits to ensure that all new buildings including existing buildings undergoing refurbishment are fitted with electric charging points. For example, the building regulations for England lay down requirements applying from 2022 on fitting charging points in new buildings and in existing buildings undergoing renovation and changes in use.[70] Governments may be reluctant to oblige owners of existing buildings not being renovated to fit charging equipment. Instead, subsidies may be used to encourage property owners to install a charging point. For example, the UK's Electric Vehicle Chargepoint Grant provides funding of up to 75 per cent for installing a charging points in domestic properties.[71]

Law can be used in several ways to establish the refuelling facilities needed to maintain traffic circulation without fear of running out of fuel or charge not only for electric vehicles but also for those fuelled by hydrogen and biomethane. Options include infrastructure obligations for fuel suppliers (eg, at motorway service stations), financial incentives for installing facilities and national law placing obligations on local authorities to introduce minimum levels of infrastructure in areas under their jurisdiction. The latter legal approach is needed to ensure that facilities are consistently available and comprehensive, thereby ensuring the availability of alternative fuels to all and quelling fears about travelling in more rural areas. The EU's Alternative Fuels Infrastructure Directive places a duty on Member States obliging them to develop and implement strategies employing the legal tools mentioned above and others with a view to reaching the minimum levels of availability specified in the law.[72] A proposal to replace the Directive with a regulation, which was still under consideration in September 2022, would set higher targets and introduce more rigorous governance arrangements for reviewing proposals for infrastructure development and monitoring progress on implementing them.[73] The UK Government proposes to follow suit in 2023 by placing a legal obligation on local authorities to develop and implement strategies for electric vehicle charging.[74]

Consistency in the technical specifications for charging and refuelling infrastructure and in the information provided on using them are essential for cross-border travel using alternative fuel vehicles. The EU Directive on Alternative Fuels Infrastructure makes corresponding provision. Member States must use common technical specifications for refuelling and recharging points throughout the EU, thereby preventing cross-border travel from being disrupted by differences in refuelling technology.[75]

---

[70] Building Regulations 2010 (SI 2010/2214), regs 44D–44K and Part S of Sch 1.

[71] Office for Zero Emission Buildings, 'Grant schemes for electric vehicle charging infrastructure' (UK Government website, 18 August 2022) Grant schemes for electric vehicle charging infrastructure – GOV.UK (www.gov.uk) (accessed 7 October 2022).

[72] Directive 2014/94/EU of 22 October 2014 on the deployment of alternative fuels infrastructure [2014] OJ L307/1.

[73] European Commission, Proposal for a Regulation on the deployment of alternative fuels infrastructure, and repealing Directive 2014/94/EU of the European Parliament and of the Council, COM (2021) 559 final.

[74] HM Government, 'Taking charge: the electric vehicle infrastructure strategy' (UK Government Website 2022) Taking charge: the electric vehicle infrastructure strategy (https://assets.publishing.service.gov.uk) (accessed 27 September 2022), 8, 70.

[75] Directive 2014/94/EU (n 72), arts 4(4), 5(2), and 6(9).

Common consumer information must also be provided for refuelling facilities, again with a view to enabling ease of use for those crossing borders.[76] In addition, early experience with alternative fuels infrastructure has revealed potential for disruption from inconsistent and uncoordinated arrangements on payment for using refuelling and recharging points. The proposed Alternative Fuels Infrastructure Regulation includes provisions requiring that methods for charging for the use of relevant facilities are harmonised.[77] This is not only a transboundary issue. The UK electric vehicle infrastructure strategy similarly recognises the need for legal intervention to harmonise arrangements on charging for infrastructure use and payment between different areas.[78]

E. Encouraging the Purchase of Alternative Fuel Source Vehicles

Measures to promote the availability of alternative fuels and of alternative fuel vehicles as well as the establishment of related infrastructure networks will enhance their appeal for consumers by removing range anxiety and enabling a reduced-price differential with fossil fuels and petrol and diesel vehicles. Complementary legal measures which address reasons for consumer loyalty to fossil fuel vehicles will further assist with creating a market for alternative mobility options. First consumers may simply not be aware that possibilities other than petrol and diesel vehicles exist. They may also lack knowledge that the environmental consequences of vehicle use differ radically depending on factors such as the fuel consumed, the greenhouse gas emissions associated with each unit of fuel consumption and engine efficiency. The EU's Passenger Car Labelling Directive contributes to addressing this lack of awareness by requiring Member States to adopt laws ensuring that retailers of passenger cars make consumers aware of their environmental consequences.[79] Under the Directive, all new cars for sale must bear labels providing information about their fuel economy and their emissions of CO_2. The information allows consumers to make a comparison between vehicles which would reveal the comparative advantage, on both fronts, of alternative fuel vehicles. The provision of information may, therefore, have an indirect benefit for alternative fuel vehicles by making consumers aware of their better environmental performance.

Second, improved awareness may not overcome the major difficulty with persuading consumers to choose alternative fuel vehicles: that, despite declining electric vehicle production costs, they still tend to be more expensive than petrol and diesel vehicles due to the long experience with fossil fuel motor technology and the enormous market for this which allows major economies of scale in production. Subsidies and benefits (often with financial advantages) are used to prevent automatic rejection of alternative fuel vehicles as expensive options by making them more competitive with conventional

---

[76] ibid, art 7.
[77] European Commission, COM (2021) 559 final (n 73) 33–36.
[78] HM Government, 'Taking charge' (n 74) 3, 57, 68.
[79] Directive 1999/94/EC of 13 December 1999 relating to the availability of consumer information on fuel economy and CO_2 emissions in respect of the marketing of new passenger cars [2000] OJ L 12/16.

vehicles. Subsidies are often provided by lowering taxes charged for alternative fuel vehicles compared to fossil fuel vehicles when they are registered and at annual licensing. Commentators give examples of vehicle and fuel tax concessions for alternative vehicles being used in Brazil, California, the EU including France and Germany, Iceland, Norway, South Africa, Thailand and the UK.[80] Loans and grants at much lower interest rates than could be obtained commercially are also made available for the purchase of electric and other alternative fuel vehicles. This has been a longstanding practice of the UK and Scottish governments although the accessibility of grants and their size are often varied.[81] In addition, the Scottish Government grants interest free loans for the purchase of second-hand electric vehicles.[82]

Relaxations of national and subnational rules on road use and on access to and costs for using civil amenities are also employed to attract interest in alternative vehicles. Benefits offered to alternative fuel vehicle drivers compared to fossil fuel drivers have included access to road lanes usually preserved for buses and multi-occupancy vehicles, reserved parking spaces, free parking and exemptions from congestion charging.[83] Norway, currently the world's jurisdiction with the highest proportion of electric vehicles on the road, also offers reduced road tolls and free ferry tickets for electric vehicle drivers.[84]

Subsidies and benefits for alternative fuel vehicle drivers have raised social justice concerns. At present, drivers of these vehicles tend to be wealthier members of communities whilst less well-off drivers are denied benefits and may also be penalised for driving older less-efficient fossil fuel vehicles (eg, by congestion zone charges). Careful consideration must be given in legal design to address unfair outcomes that support for alternative fuel mobility through such measures may give rise to.

III. Biofuels

Biofuels are defined in the EU's 2018 RES Directive as 'liquid fuel for transport produced from biomass'. Biomass is defined as 'the biodegradable fraction of products, wastes and residues from biological origin from agriculture, including vegetal and animal substances, from forestry and related industries, including fisheries and aquaculture, as well as the biodegradable fraction of waste, including industrial and municipal waste of biological origin'.[85] It is important to keep in mind that the label 'biofuels' includes a great variety of fuels deriving from hundreds if not thousands of different feedstocks, each one possessing its own characteristics, advantages and problems. Biofuels are often separated into three categories: first generation, largely

---

[80] IRENA (n 8) 47–48, 50; REN21 (n 5) 95; Barton and Schütte (n 39) 152–64; Pickett and others (n 39) 55–61.
[81] Pickett and others (n 39) 44–49.
[82] ibid.
[83] See the references at n 79.
[84] Barton and Schütte (n 39) 152–53; Pickett et al (n 39) 56–58.
[85] 2018 RES Directive (n 25), arts 2(24) and (33).

derived from crops that may otherwise be used in food production for humans and animals; and second generation, derived more often from non-food crops and waste including from agriculture, food industries, and forestry. A third generation of biofuels may emerge through production using algae during the coming decades, but this possibility is still being examined through research and development and is some way off commercialisation.[86]

The primary benefit offered by biofuels is that their consumption can result in significant reductions of greenhouse gas emissions when compared to emissions from petrol and diesel. The combustion of biofuels releases carbon dioxide into the atmosphere, but they are not additional emissions as the carbon released is absorbed from the atmosphere by the organic matter whilst it is growing. Contrast this with fossil fuels where all emissions are additional. However, there are also a range of 'sustainability' concerns associated with the consumption of biofuels from some feedstocks.[87] Several of these concerns relate to feedstocks for biofuels production imported into the EU and other jurisdictions with insufficient indigenous capability for biofuels production to meet demand including from South America and Southeast Asia. The import of biofuels is a key consideration when thinking about how problems associated with the sustainability of exported biofuels can be addressed. States can adopt laws that regulate how biofuels are produced within their own territory but they cannot legislate to control directly how feedstocks for biofuels are produced externally. They can only use laws for imports that seek to exercise some control over the quality of biofuels being imported.

A. Sustainability Concerns[88]

The principal sustainability concerns that arise with biofuels are as follows:

Greenhouse gas emissions: The main virtue of biofuels, as noted above, is that their consumption may result in significant greenhouse gas emission savings when biofuel consumption displaces fossil fuel consumption for transport. Greenhouse gas emission savings should be calculated not only at the point at which biofuels are combusted but also by taking into account the full life-cycle emissions associated with the process leading up to consumption (eg, land clearance to grow biofuels releasing carbon stored in soils and forests; the use of fertilisers; harvesting crops; transporting crops to refineries (when importing biofuels this may involve shipping over thousands of miles using vessels consuming diesel fuel); and transporting biofuels to points of sale. When all these considerations are taken into account, greenhouse gas emission savings from some feedstocks for biofuels (particularly those associated with land clearance) may not be much of an improvement over fossil fuel consumption. Some means is therefore required of differentiating between biofuels by reference to the greenhouse

---

[86] IRENA, *Advanced Biofuels? What holds them back?* (IRENA 2019) 33–34, 70.
[87] Piergiuseppe Morone, Andrzej Strzalkowski, and Almona Tani, 'Biofuel Transitions: An Overview of Regulations and Standards for a More Sustainable Framework' in Jingzheng Ren and others (eds), *Biofuels for a More Sustainable Future* (Elsevier 2020) 21.
[88] For literature on biofuels and sustainability concerns, see Morone et al (n 87); and Seita Romppanen, 'The EU's Biofuels: Certified as Sustainable?' (2012) 3 *Renewable Energy Law and Policy Review* 173, 173–76.

gas emissions associated with their production. Calculating life cycle emissions also enables accurate comparison of biofuels with fossil fuels when assessing the relative merits of options for mitigating climate change.

Effects on biodiversity: Demand for biofuels consumption may result in the clearance of land (eg, rain forest, grassland), particularly in developing world countries, that is valued for the support it provides for a diversity of species. Measures are required to try and avoid a perverse outcome of gains in reducing greenhouse gas emissions being counterbalanced by significant and irreparable environmental harm, often associated with the release of greenhouse gas emissions from carbon sinks including forests, peat bogs, wetlands and soil in previously uncultivated areas.

Competition with food crops and price effects: First generation biofuels are often produced from feedstocks that are already used to produce food for humans and animals. Diverting food crops from use for food production to energy production will lead to rising food prices with negative impacts being most likely to be felt in low income developing countries.

Indirect land use:[89] Demand for crops to produce energy is likely to result in land that was previously used for food production being used for energy production instead. However, demand for food remains the same. Indeed, it is growing globally. The consequence of this is that new land will be brought into cultivation to meet food demand with resulting releases of carbon from soil and deforestation and impacts on biodiversity. This phenomenon presents a major problem when attempting to establish life cycle emissions associated with biofuels and their sustainability. It is at least feasible to assess the sustainability of biofuels through information about how they were produced. However, it is extremely difficult to have accurate knowledge of the knock-on consequences of land being used for energy crop production. This will be the case anywhere, but it will be a particular problem in jurisdictions that lack effective legal systems for controlling land use and the exploitation of property rights. Accordingly, the credibility of estimates for life cycle emissions of greenhouse gases may be called into question.

Social impacts: This concern relates to biofuels production in developing world countries. Corporations interested in benefiting from the drive for biofuels consumption from developed economies may dispossess indigenous peoples of their land and mistreat labour hired to cultivate feedstock.

B. The EU's Legal Response to Concerns with Biofuels: The Sustainability Criteria Regime[90]

The sustainability concerns outlined above do not affect all biofuels. They relate to some feedstocks used for producing certain first-generation biofuels, but other biofuels

---

[89] European Commission, 'Report from the Commission on indirect land-use change related to biofuels and bioliquids' COM (2010) 811 final, 22 December 2020.

[90] See accounts of EU law on biofuels sustainability at Romppanen (n 88); Renske Giljam, 'Towards a Holistic Approach in EU Biomass Regulation' (2016) 28 *Journal of Environmental Law* 95; and Emily Webster, 'Transnational Legal Processes, the EU and RED II: Strengthening the Global Governance of Bioenergy' (2020) 29 *Review of European, Comparative and International Environmental Law* 86.

produced from different feedstocks are viewed as positively advantageous from a sustainability perspective. It is clear from the above, however, that some means of regulating the supply of biofuels is needed to have confidence that they can be consumed without compromising decarbonisation efforts and the pursuit of sustainability, the very goals their use is meant to serve. Relevant laws will need to set up bases for assessing the sustainability of biofuels including the greenhouse gas emissions associated with their production and consumption. They will also need to identify when a biofuel would be regarded as unacceptable because of sustainability concerns and to spell out the legal consequences of a biofuel and/or biofuels from a certain feedstock being labelled as unsustainable. This section uses relevant provisions of the EU's Renewable Energy Directives of 2009 and 2018 as examples of legal provision on these matters. EU law on biofuels is not presented as an exemplar for others to follow. Rather, the study is useful for exploring challenges for legal design with avoiding negative environmental and social outcomes from biofuels consumption by regulating its supply.

(i) Consequences of Unsustainability in EU Law

The EU moved early and was proactive in its support for biofuels consumption as a means of decarbonising energy consumed for transportation. The 2003 Biofuels Directive sought to advance this policy position by directing Member States to take measures aimed at reaching 5.75 per cent renewables in energy supplies for transport by 2010.[91] Biofuels were also expected to make up the bulk of the 10 per cent of energy from renewables in energy consumed for transport that Member States were obliged to achieve by 2020 under the 2009 Renewable Energy Directive.[92] However, it had already become apparent by the time of this Directive's adoption that promoting biofuels consumption could have negative environmental and social impacts. The Directive responded to fears that the 10 per cent target could cause unsustainable outcomes by including sustainability criteria provisions. The criteria do not regulate biofuels production directly. The EU cannot legislate for how biofuels are produced outside of its territory. Instead, the Directive seeks to discourage the production of 'unsustainable' biofuels by advising that biofuels which do not fulfil 'sustainability criteria' will not:[93]

- be taken into account when measuring compliance with legally binding national targets under the Directive;
- be taken into account under national support schemes which require energy sector actors to include a proportion of renewable energy in their supplies (obligation/certificate schemes); and
- be eligible for the receipt of financial support made available to promote the consumption of biofuels and bioliquids.

The 2018 RES Directive adopts this approach, with unsustainable biofuels not counting towards Member States' contributions to achieving the EU's renewable energy goal

---

[91] Directive 2003/30/EC (n 19).
[92] Directive 2009/28/EC (n 22), art 3(4).
[93] ibid, art 17(1).

or to meeting obligations for renewable energy consumption in energy sectors, and not being eligible for subsidies.[94]

It may be asked why the EU did not simply ban the consumption of unsustainable biofuels at this juncture. This may have been due to concerns over the legality of a complete ban under the rules of world trade law.[95] It may also have been due to a reluctance by the EU to pull the rug out from under producers of biofuels using unsustainable feedstocks in the EU that had come into existence to meet expectations of demand created by initial EU enthusiasm for biofuels from all feedstocks. However, as discussed at section IIID. below, it was forced to introduce a de facto ban on the growth of biofuels consumption from certain feedstocks in 2015 because its regulatory regime was not able to prevent biofuels production from having negative environmental effects.

(ii) The Sustainability Criteria

The criteria that biofuels were required to meet to be regarded as sustainable under the 2009 RES Directive are set out below. Modifications to the criteria made by the 2018 RES Directive are also stated.

Greenhouse gas emission savings: The 2009 Directive required that biofuels, to be considered as sustainable, must make a minimum level of greenhouse gas emissions savings over fossil fuels.[96] The savings were calculated on a life-cycle basis using formulae set out in Article 19. Default emissions values were set out for biofuels from certain feedstocks in Annex V of the Directive, meaning that biofuels from certain feedstocks would generally be regarded as unsustainable under EU law. The minimum saving under the original Directive was 35 per cent, rising to 50 per cent from January 2017 and 60 per cent from January 2018 for installations commencing biofuels production from January 2017. Following reforms to the Directive in 2015 (see IIID below), the minimum savings were 35 per cent rising to 50 per cent from 2018 for installations in operation before 5 October 2015 and 60 per cent for installations starting operation after 5 October 2015.[97]

The 2018 RES Directive retains the 50 per cent and 60 per cent savings criteria for biofuels from installations in operation before 6 October 2015 and 31 December 2020 respectively. Savings of at least 65 per cent must be realised for biofuels from installations starting operation after 1 January 2021.[98]

Land of high biodiversity value: Biofuels will not be regarded as sustainable if they are made from raw materials obtained from land with high biodiversity value which possessed specified statuses in and after January 2008.[99] The 2018 RES Directive

---

[94] 2018 RES Directive (n 25), art 29(1).
[95] Emily Lydgate, 'Biofuels, Sustainability, and Trade-Related Regulatory Chill' (2012) 15 *Journal of International Economic Law* 157.
[96] 2009 RES Directive (n 22), art 17(2).
[97] Directive (EU) 2015/1513 (n 27), art 2(5).
[98] 2018 RES Directive (n 25), art 29(10).
[99] 2009 RES Directive (n 22), art 17(3).

repeats this criterion, but applies it to biomass produced from agriculture, the main threat to the identified land types being from clearance for crop growth. Listed statuses under the 2018 Directive, all providing detail on when they are satisfied as well as exceptions to the default position are: primary forest and other wooded areas whose ecological processes have not been significantly disturbed by human activity; highly biodiverse forest and other wooded areas which are species rich and not degraded; areas designated by law for nature protection purposes or for the protection of rare or threatened ecosystems and species; and highly biodiverse grassland.[100]

High carbon stock land including peatland: Biofuels will not be regarded as sustainable if they are made from raw material obtained from land types typically possessing high carbon stocks and which had one of the following statuses in or after January 2008, but have since lost it.[101] The land types identified under the 2018 RES Directive, all providing detail on when they are satisfied as well as exceptions to the default position, are wetlands and continuously forested areas as well as other areas with trees which include minimum heights and levels of canopy cover. As with land of high biodiversity value, the 2018 Directive limits the criterion's application to agricultural biomass. Agricultural biofuels made from raw material obtained from land classified as peatland in or after January 2008 is also unsustainable unless evidence is provided that the cultivation and harvesting of that raw material does not involve drainage of previously undrained soil.[102]

Biofuels produced from forested biomass: The 2018 Directive adds additional sustainability criteria for biofuels produced from forest biomass to minimise the risk of using biofuels derived from unsustainably produced feedstocks.[103] States in which the forested land from which the biomass used for producing the biofuel was harvested must have in place national or sub-national laws for regulating harvesting activities, and arrangements for monitoring their observance and enforcing them. They must also be parties to the Paris Agreement and have submitted a nationally determined contribution which ensures that changes in carbon stock associated with biomass harvesting are accounted for or have national laws in place to secure the compatibility of harvesting with relevant provisions of the Paris Agreement on conserving and enhancing carbon sinks. Alternatively, management systems must be in place that ensure compliance with these criteria.

Economic operators (eg, biofuels producers in the EU and importers) are required to provide evidence that consignments of biofuels satisfy the sustainability criteria by following verification processes.[104] Provision is made to make verification easier by the Commission's approval of voluntary schemes for biofuels verification.[105] Several voluntary schemes have been approved by the Commission to date.[106]

---

[100] 2018 RES Directive (n 25), art 29(3).
[101] 2009 RES Directive (n 22), art 17(4); 2018 RES Directive (n 25), art 29(4).
[102] 2009 RES Directive (n 22), art 17(5); 2018 RES Directive (n 25), art 29(5).
[103] 2018 RES Directive (n 25), arts 29(6) and 29(7).
[104] 2009 RES Directive (n 22), art 18; 2018 RES Directive (n 25), art 30.
[105] 2009 RES Directive (n 22), art 18(4); 2018 RES Directive (n 25), art 30(4).
[106] European Commission, 'Voluntary Schemes', (European Commission website, Energy) Voluntary schemes (europa.eu) (accessed 7 October 2022).

C. Reporting Obligations

The sustainability criteria address only some of the concerns mentioned in section IIIA. Others were too uncertain or controversial when the 2009 RES Directive was adopted to address through legally binding criteria. In view of this, the 2009 Directive placed multiple reporting obligations on the European Commission.[107] It was required to report every two years on matters including observance of the sustainability criteria and social sustainability impacts (food prices, ratification and implementation of international conventions on treatment of labour and land use rights). Member States were required to report on the consequences of biofuels consumption in their own territories.[108]

The Commission was further obligated to report on matters relating to the calculation of life-cycle emissions under Article 19. As part of this raft of obligations, the Commission had a duty to submit a report on the impact of indirect land use change on greenhouse gas emissions and ways of minimising this in December 2010.[109] The report concluded that it was extremely difficult to make reliable provision in life-cycle carbon emission calculations for the effects of indirect land use change and advised that a precautionary approach should be adopted.[110] This entails that action should be taken to prevent environmental harm (where a more than hypothetical threat of this is present) notwithstanding that the information required either to establish the negative consequences of biofuels production or the likelihood that those consequences will result and over what timescale are not available.[111]

Reporting obligations for some of the matters to be covered under the 2009 Directive are not repeated under its 2018 successor. One reason for this is that Member State and Commission reporting and investigations under duties imposed by the 2009 Directive revealed significant difficulties with preventing unsustainable biofuels production by trying to establish the sustainability or otherwise of biofuels, and that legal reforms were made to the 2009 Directive and then adopted and strengthened under the 2018 Directive to tackle major drivers of the indirect land use concern. In particular, tougher provisions on biofuels from feedstocks that are also used for feeding animals and humans have been introduced as discussed in the following section. Even so, the sustainability of biofuels production remains under close review. Much of the additional information to be reported by Member States in the National Climate and Energy Plans on renewable energy concerns the consumption and impacts of biofuels including on commodity prices and land use.[112] The Commission is required to report biennially from 2023 to the European Parliament and to the Council on the sustainability of bioenergy in the Union.[113]

---

[107] 2009 RES Directive (n 22), art 17(7).
[108] ibid, arts 22(g) to 22(j).
[109] ibid, art 19(6).
[110] European Commission (n 89).
[111] See section IIIA above for further discussion of difficulties with measuring sustainability impacts due to indirect land use change.
[112] Regulation (EU) 2018/1999 of 11 December 2018 on the Governance of the Energy Union and Climate Action, amending Regulations (EC) No 663/2009 and (EC) No 715/2009 of the European Parliament and of the Council, Directives 94/22/EC, 98/70/EC, 2009/31/EC, 2009/73/EC, 2010/31/EU, 2012/27/EU and 2013/30/EU of the European Parliament and of the Council, Council Directives 2009/119/EC and (EU) 2015/652 and repealing Regulation (EU) No 525/2013 of the European Parliament and of the Council [2018] OJ L 328/1, Art 20 and Annex IX.
[113] ibid, art 35(2)(d) and Annex X; 2018 RES Directive (n 25), art 33.

D. Amendments to the Sustainability Criteria Regime

The conclusions of the 2010 report concerning indirect land use change prompted a proposal for reforms to Directive 2009/28/EC to make further provision on promoting sustainable biofuels and discouraging the production of unsustainable biofuels.[114] The proposed reforms were controversial, the main concern being the effect that they would have on the by-now-established biofuels production sector in the EU. They were debated over a period of three years, eventually resulting in Directive 2015/1513 of 9 September 2015.[115] The key reforms introduced by this Directive were as follows:

(i) The total permissible contribution to the 10 per cent renewable energy target for transport of first-generation biofuels from certain types of sources was limited to 7 per cent.[116] The sources identified include cereals, starch-rich crops, sugars, oil crops, and crops grown as main crops primarily on agricultural land (unless specified circumstances apply).

(ii) Minimum greenhouse gas emissions savings for biofuels produced from installations established after 5/10/2015 were raised to 60 per cent.[117]

(iii) A requirement was included for the Commission to include provisional estimates for ILUC emissions (based on values set out in new Annex VIII) in its reports on GHG emission savings from biofuels. This allowed trialling of approaches for assessing ILUC emissions so that a legal requirement could be introduced subsequently for calculating life-cycle emissions if there was sufficient confidence in the method of calculation.[118] The 2018 RES Directive also includes an Annex on provisional estimation of emissions from indirect land use whilst recognising that 'it is ... not possible to fully characterise the uncertainty range associated with such estimates'.[119] The Commission's biennial bioenergy sustainability report is to include 'an assessment of whether the range of uncertainty identified in the analysis underlying the estimations of indirect land-use change emissions may be narrowed ...'.[120]

(iv) Measures were included to promote movement away from first-generation biofuels by promoting second and third-generation biofuels. Biofuels from sources listed in Annex IX were to be counted twice when calculating compliance with the 10 per cent target. These sources (predominantly second and third generation) included algae, municipal/domestic/industrial/forestry waste, manure, straw, and woody crops. This was a little disappointing as biofuels 'produced from wastes, residues, non-food ligno-cellulosic material, and lingo-cellulosic materials' were already counted twice when calculating compliance with the target under the 2009 Directive.[121] All that the new provision did was to expand

---

[114] European Commission, 'Proposal for a Directive amending Directive 98/70/EC relating to the quality of petrol and diesel fuels and amending Directive 2009/28/EC on the promotion of the use of energy from renewables sources', COM (2012) 595 final.
[115] Directive 2015/1513 (n 27).
[116] 2009 RES Directive (n 22) art 3(4)(d).
[117] ibid, art 17(2).
[118] ibid, art 23(4).
[119] 2018 RES Directive (n 25) Annex VIII.
[120] Regulation (EU) 2018/1999 (n 111) Annex X, para. (e).
[121] 2009 RES Directive (n 22), art 21(2).

the range of biofuels that would be doubled up when calculating compliance with the target.

(v) Member States had an obligation to set national targets for energy from second and third generation biofuels. The national target was to be set using a reference value of 0.5 per cent of energy consumed for transport unless Member States could rely on a ground stated in the law for setting a lower target.[122] The obligation of Member States was to 'endeavour to achieve the target'. This provision represented a disappointing watering down of proposals made in the draft directive and put forwards by the European Parliament during the legislative process.

The 2018 RES Directive maintains and strengthens legal provision on ending reliance on biofuels that raise sustainability concerns because they are made from crops also used for human and animal food or otherwise pose higher than acceptable risks of indirect land use change. The share of biofuels consumed in energy for transport in each Member State from food and feed crops must not exceed 1 per cent higher than their share in the final consumption of energy in the road and rail transport sectors in 2020, and in any event must not exceed 7 per cent, the maximum level set by the 2015 reforms to the 2009 Directive.[123] The share may be increased to 2 per cent where it lay below 1 per cent in 2020. In addition, the share of 'high indirect land use change risk' biofuels produced from food and feed crops for which a significant expansion of the production area into land with high carbon stocks is observed must not exceed the level of consumption of such fuels in 2020.[124] Consumption of fuels of this type is to be gradually reduced from December 2023 and ultimately eradicated by 2030.

E. WTO Law and the Sustainability Criteria

The exclusion of some biofuels from access to subsidies and from counting towards the EU's renewable energy targets has had a negative impact on the jurisdictions in which production of the biofuels concerned is concentrated. Argentina, Indonesia and Malaysia, three jurisdictions heavily affected by the EU's measures, have brought claims before the World Trade Organisation's Dispute Resolution Body that aspects of the sustainability criteria regime contravene international trade law rules. Argentina initiated a dispute concerning the 2009 RES Directive in 2013, but it did not proceed beyond the first stage of consultations.[125] The 2018 RES Directive's strong discouragement of biofuels sourced from palm oil (unless producers can prove that this was done sustainably) have led to claims initiated by Indonesia and Malaysia.[126] The disputes have progressed

---

[122] ibid, art 3(4)(e).
[123] 2018 RES Directive (n 25), art 26(1).
[124] ibid, art 26(2).
[125] DS459, European Union and Certain Member States – Certain Measures on the Import and Marketing of Biodiesel and Measures Supporting the Biodiesel Industry.
[126] DS593 European Union – Certain measures concerning palm oil and oil palm crop-based biofuels; DS600 European Union and Certain Member States – Certain measures concerning palm oil and oil palm crop-based biofuels.

further than the earlier claim with Panels of the Dispute Resolution Body having been established in both cases. The outcomes of these disputes will have significant ramifications for states' ability to dissuade biofuels production perceived as being unsustainable through regulations modelled on the sustainability criteria. Both cases have attracted significant interest amongst other states because they have their own biofuels sectors or use regulations on the sustainability of biofuels or both in some cases with many of them having joined the proceedings as third parties.

All of the disputes have based claims on breaches of the two key provisions of the General Agreement on Trade and Tariffs.[127] First, complainants allege that the EU has breached its duty under GATT to extend the advantages accorded to certain biofuels which do qualify for subsidy receipt and are allowed to contribute to EU targets to 'like' products originating in other Contracting Parties (the Most Favoured Nation clause).[128] A main consideration here is whether biofuels which differ in levels of associated greenhouse gases and in the sustainability of production methods can be said to be like. Second, claimants contend that the sustainability criteria favour domestic production of biofuels in the EU because it is more likely to meet the criteria than biofuels available for export from the claimant jurisdictions (the national treatment clause).[129] Claims are also brought under the WTO's Technical Barriers to Trade Agreement.[130]

The EU responds to the claims made under GATT by relying on Article XX of the treaty.[131] The Article allows states to adopt laws in breach of the above duties, where they fall under one of its listed categories and satisfy criteria that all laws relying on these exemptions must meet. Laws may be permitted under GATT's Article XX where they are: '(b) necessary to protect human, animal, or plant life or health' or they relate '(g) to the consumption of exhaustible natural resources if such measures are made effective in conjunction with restrictions on domestic production or consumption'. The criteria require that the measures concerned are not applied in a manner that would constitute either an arbitrary or unjustifiable discrimination between countries where the same conditions prevail or a disguised restriction on international trade.

Readers are referred to the extensive academic literature which explores issues raised by these claims under WTO law for further comment on whether the complainants' claims and the EU's reliance on Article XX have merit.[132] The Panels have yet to report on either of the current claims and it is eminently possible given their ramifications that initial rulings may subsequently be brought before the WTO's Appellate Body. In the meantime, these disputes represent a further question mark over the ability of states to use law to prevent biofuels production from having negative environmental outcomes by regulating relevant products on grounds of their sustainability.

---

[127] General Agreement on Tariffs and Trade (adopted 15 April 1994, entered into force 1 January 1995) 1867 UNTS 187 (GATT).
[128] GATT (n 127), art I:1.
[129] ibid, art III:4.
[130] Agreement on Technical Barriers to Trade (adopted 15 April 1994, entered into force 1 January 1995) 1868 UNTS 120.
[131] GATT (n 127), art XX.
[132] For example, see Lydgate (n 95); and Stefan Mayr, Birgit Hollaus and Verena Madner, 'Palm Oil, the RED II and WTO Law: EU Sustainable Biofuel Policy Tangled Up in Green?' (2021) 30 *Review of European, Comparative and International Environmental Law* 233.

Classroom Questions

1. What lower carbon alternative fuel sources can be used to replace petrol, diesel and other oil-based fuels for decarbonising road transport? To what extent can those alternatives be described as 'renewable"?
2. Identify the key actors and activities that should be targeted (including through legal intervention) by strategies to promote alternative fuel source consumption in connection with decarbonisation.
3. List the actors and activities that you have identified in your answer to Question 2. For each of them, consider how law can be used to involve them with promoting alternative fuel source consumption. Identify examples of laws from the EU and other jurisdictions which require or encourage the actors you have identified to promote alternative fuel consumption and explain how the laws seek to have this effect.
4. What problems have arisen with some first-generation biofuels? How (and to what extent) can law be used to address them?

Scenario

(1) The government of Granita has been in negotiations with Noel Bouquet, an electric car entrepreneur, about establishing production facilities in its jurisdiction. Bouquet is reluctant to make a commitment because Granita does not have a supportive legal framework for electric mobility. In particular, he is concerned about the following: (a) that Granita has not established targets in law for securing the growth of electricity consumption in transportation by a specified amount over a specified period; (b) that domestic and public infrastructure for charging electric vehicles is limited; (c) that laws are not used to promote electric vehicles to consumers as an alternative to fossil fuel vehicles.

The Granitan Minister of Transport seeks advice from you, a noted expert in renewable transport law, on the type of legal approaches it could employ to create a supportive legal framework for increasing the proportion of electric vehicles making up new national vehicle sales. Advise the Granitan government on legislative options it could use to address Noel Bouquet's concerns.

(2) Forestfuels, a renewable fuel producer in Granita, produces three types of biofuel. The first, Superfast, is made from a crop usually used for human food production. It has been assessed as achieving a 55 per cent greenhouse gas emission saving over fossil fuels. The installation used to produce the fuel commenced operation in January 2022. The fuel itself is made from a crop grown on land which was formerly part of the Grande Swamp, a large wetland in Granita which enjoys legal protection as a nature reserve under Granitan law. The area was drained after January 2008 so that it could be used for agricultural purposes.

The second, Speedwell, is not made from a food/feed crop. The installation used to produce the fuel commenced operation before October 2015. The land on which the feedstock for the fuel is grown was cleared for development (for the former Granitan President's new palace which was not subsequently built due to his deposition) in the 1990s and was not previously in use for agriculture.

The third, Rocketship, is produced from nut shells, a feedstock included in Annex IX of the EU's 2018 Renewable Energy Directive. Rocketship achieves a 75 per cent greenhouse gas emission saving over fossil fuels. It is produced from waste pistachio nut shells collected from the bars of Granita Town, the country's capital, and so its production does not involve land conversion.

Forestfuels wishes to start exporting its fuels to the European Union. Advise the company on whether EU law on biofuels would allow this. If so, how would its biofuels be treated under EU law? Is their import into the EU encouraged? What would Forestfuels need to do to secure access to the EU market?

Suggested Reading

Book chapters

Ian Skinner, 'The Mitigation of Transport's CO_2 Emissions in the EU: Policy Successes and Challenges' in Geert van Calster, Wim Vandenberghe and Leonie Reins (eds) *Research Handbook on Climate Mitigation Law* (Edward Elgar, 2015) 103–25.

Articles

Jaime Amezaga, S. L. Boyes and J. A. Harrison, *Biofuels Policy in the European Union* (Conference Paper 2010) www.researchgate.net/publication/265037791_Biofuels_Policy_in_the_European_Union (accessed 7 October 2022).

Barry Barton and Peter Schütte, 'Electric Vehicle Law and Policy: A Comparative Analysis' (2017) 35 *Journal of Energy and Natural Resources Law* 147.

Emily Lydgate, 'Biofuels, Sustainability, and Trade-Related Regulatory Chill' (2012) 15 *Journal of International Economic Law* 157.

Emily Webster, 'Transnational Legal Processes, the EU and RED II: Strengthening the Global Governance of Bioenergy' (2020) 29 *Review of European, Comparative and International Environmental Law* 86.

Policy Documents

IRENA, *Renewable Energy Policies in a Time of Transition* (IRENA, 2018) 38–55.
REN 21, *Renewables 2022: Global Status Report* (REN21 Secretariat 2022) 65–73, 94–97, 220–22.

Index

Introductory Note

References such as '178–79' indicate (not necessarily continuous) discussion of a topic across a range of pages. Wherever possible in the case of topics with many references, these have either been divided into sub-topics or only the most significant discussions of the topic are listed. Because the entire work is about 'renewable energy', the use of this term (and certain others which occur constantly throughout the book) as an entry point has been restricted. Information will be found under the corresponding detailed topics.

acceptability   172, 176, 178
   public   114, 157, 169, 173–74
active management   131, 139–40
adaptive management   207, 212
advanced biofuels   17, 223–24, 227–28
affected communities   165, 168, 172, 175, 177–78
affordability   18–19, 89
Africa   29, 37, 56, 69, 198, 232
Agenda 21   56, 59–62
aggregators   132, 142, 146
agriculture   166, 232–33, 237
air pollution   10–11, 14
algae   218, 233, 239
allocation   119, 137, 150, 173, 180, 206
   competitive   103, 108–9, 111–12, 117
   risk   104, 109, 119–20, 122
allowances   36–37, 39–40, 171
alternative fuel vehicles   17, 218–19, 223–27;
   see also **road transport**
   encouraging purchase   231–32
   infrastructure for   229–31
alternative fuels   3, 50, 100, 217–19, 229–31
   promotion   227–29
ambitions   29, 33, 63, 90–91, 93–94, 225
auctions   103, 108–9, 113–14, 117–22, 129
Australia   143–44, 204, 208
authorisation   151, 156–60, 205–6
   processes   160–63, 168, 171
      complexity   161
      lack of time limits   161–62
      legal responses to concerns   168–75
      public participation   162
      rejection by decision makers   163
authoritative knowledge   69

balancing markets   131–32, 139–40, 221
Baltic   198, 206
banding   107–8, 115–16
barriers   2–3, 6, 15–16, 21, 37–38, 47–48, 60, 125

batteries   132, 145, 221, 230
benefits   40–41, 107–8, 119–20, 132, 149–50, 175, 177–81, 231–32
   community   180–81
   environmental   167–68
   financial   166–67, 179
bids   103, 108, 113, 120, 137–38, 142
binding targets   30, 35, 39, 87–91, 93–94, 96, 222–23
biodiversity   11, 167, 198–99, 201, 234
   marine   196, 199, 204–5
biofuels   1, 102, 217–18, 221, 223–24, 227–28, 232–41
   advanced   17, 223–24, 227–28
   consumption   218, 221, 233–36, 238
   feedstocks   233
   first-generation   218–19, 234, 239
   production   219, 223, 233–36, 238, 241
   sustainability   219
      criteria   234–41
      EU legal response to concerns   234–37
   third-generation   218, 239
   unsustainable   235–36, 239
biomass   1, 6–7, 19, 22, 72, 117, 232, 237
   boilers   15, 100–2
   burning   7, 11
Brundtland Report   55, 58–59
budgets   117–20
businesses   64, 69, 79, 89, 105, 110, 156–57, 161

cables   18, 186, 188, 191–93, 195, 197
   laying   191, 193
   networks   18, 125–26, 129, 187
California   76, 141, 220, 229, 232
capacities   7, 20, 41–42, 44–45, 128–31, 145, 218, 228–29
capacity building   46, 48–50, 60, 62
   support   28, 50
   and technology transfer   28, 60, 62

INDEX

capital investment 126–27
carbon 7, 9–10, 20, 33, 35, 39, 79, 233–34
  intensity 73, 76, 229
  lock-in 17–18
  prices 39, 106
carriage of renewable electricity 130, 137; *see also* electricity, transmission
CDM (Clean Development Mechanism) 36–40
CEF (Connecting Europe Facility) 136, 150
certificate/obligation schemes 104, 106–8, 114–16, 121
certificates 103, 107–8, 111, 113, 115–16, 227
CFDs (Contracts for Difference) 107, 115, 117–22
China 14, 31, 37, 44, 70, 185–86, 208, 224
civil societies 57, 63–64, 95, 198
clarity 43, 192, 194
Clean Development Mechanism, *see* **CDM**
clean energy 53, 62, 70, 90, 138, 229
climate change 1, 3, 10, 12–14, 20–22, 66–67, 70–71, 73
  as driver for renewable energy development 9–10
  international law 26–50
  mitigation 30, 39, 44, 48, 72, 167–68, 234
  regime 26, 28, 35, 48–49
  treaties 26–51, 53
climate finance 28, 41–44, 47–48, 50, 62
  from developing states 44
  low transparency 43
  unclear commitments 42
coal 1, 16, 79, 125, 217; *see also* **fossil fuels**
coastal states 22, 190–94, 196, 198–99, 202
  EEZs 191–92
  regulations 191, 193
collaboration 26, 38, 64, 69–70, 86, 140, 197, 207
  interstate 26, 64, 199
commitments 26, 28–29, 31–32, 41–42, 66, 71–72, 76–77, 94–95
  hard 26, 66
  legal 77–78, 202
  political 85, 220
  unclear 42
communities 16, 19, 157, 159, 166–68, 172, 175–81, 226
  affected 165, 168, 172, 175, 177–78
community benefits 180–81
compatibility 93, 166, 189, 200, 237
compensation 20
  claims 71
  individual 179–80
competent authorities 151, 159, 170–71, 177
competition 117, 120, 127–28, 135, 141, 234
competitive allocation 103, 108–9, 111–12, 117
competitive processes 108–9

compliance 33–34, 43, 193–94, 200–1, 209–11, 225, 227–28, 237
  calculating 223, 239–40
confidence 77–78, 80, 82, 91, 94–95, 99, 102, 109–11
  creation 38, 82, 87, 95, 111
  investor 79, 82, 88, 105, 110, 112, 114, 119
conflict 55, 147, 165, 188, 192–95, 204–6
congested seas, planning for 202–12
congestion 138, 145, 149, 232
Connecting Europe Facility, *see* **CEF**
connection, costs 134, 144
consultations, public 151, 160, 175
consumer participation 141
  electricity systems 131–32
consumers 18–19, 100–1, 103–5, 107–8, 125–26, 129–32, 141–43, 224
consumption 1–2, 6–8, 20–22, 26–28, 59–60, 76–78, 233, 240–41
  biofuels 218, 221, 233–36, 238
continental shelves 190–94
contracting parties 28–30, 32–33, 50, 71–72, 241
Contracts for Difference, *see* **CFDs**
contributions
  nationally determined 29, 31–33, 46, 50
  planned 91, 94–95
control 28–29, 156, 158, 178, 181, 199, 201, 233
cooperation 38, 41, 60, 131, 140, 195, 199
coordination 47, 49, 131, 140, 161, 170–71, 221, 228
costs 16–17, 99–100, 102–5, 112–14, 118–19, 132–35, 144–45, 149
  connection 134, 144
  development 101, 104, 106, 114, 116, 118, 146, 149
  fixed up-front 100
  production 100, 103, 105
  renewable energy 5, 14, 103
  renewable energy production 90, 108
credibility 38, 94, 223, 234
credits 36–38, 40, 225, 229
critical mass of public opposition to pro-renewable energy policies 168
crops 165, 233–34, 239–40
cumulative effects 196, 203, 206
customary international law 22, 58, 159, 189–91, 209
  rules 22, 58, 189–91

decarbonisation 14, 17, 27–28, 34–35, 79, 90, 93, 208
  of road transport 216–41
decision-makers 156, 159–61, 163, 167–68, 171–75, 201, 205, 209–12

INDEX

decision-making 59, 64, 69, 145, 147, 150–51, 172–73, 205–7
  processes 156–59, 162–64, 168–70, 173, 201, 209
delays 149, 157, 161–62, 169, 171
demand 7–8, 12–13, 36–38, 129–31, 143, 145–46, 224, 233–34
  management 132, 145
  response 140–42
demonstration projects 109, 138
Denmark 178, 186, 227
deterrent effect 80, 82, 86, 220
developed state parties 20, 27, 30, 44, 46–47
developed states 20, 27, 29–33, 42–45, 47, 55, 109, 111
developers 101–3, 107–8, 118–22, 156–60, 168, 172, 174–81, 206
  wind farms 179–80
developing country parties 32, 44, 47–49
developing states 20, 28–29, 31–33, 40–50, 55–56, 59–60, 62, 67
  climate finance from 44
developing world challenges 20–21
development, *see also* **Introductory Note**
  consent
    applications 159, 172–76, 206, 210
    streamlining regimes 169–70
  costs 101, 104, 106, 114, 116, 118, 146, 149
    initial 16, 108
    recovery 99, 101, 120
  infrastructure 145, 148, 230
  large-scale 116, 122, 150, 169
  low carbon 28, 41, 46, 48
  networks 125, 127–28, 130, 136, 145–46
  offshore 187–88, 193, 199–202, 206, 208
  plans 168, 175, 212
  processes 56, 207
  programmes 59, 68, 201, 210
  proposals 157, 162–63, 168, 176, 181, 201, 205
  renewable 60, 133, 157, 179, 200–2
  social 20, 31, 53, 55–56
  sustainable, *see* sustainable development
  types 158, 169–70, 175, 180
  wind farms 165–66, 195, 210
diesel 17, 216–19, 221, 227–29, 233
  vehicles 231
discontent, public 110, 173, 180
disputes 12, 190, 240–41
distribution
  networks 139–40, 146, 221
  systems 126–27, 129–32, 145
    operators 110, 127, 131, 135, 139–40, 142, 145–46
drivers for renewable energy development 8–15
DSOs, *see* distribution, systems, operators

duties 80–82, 127–28, 135–36, 189–90, 192–93, 197–99, 228–30, 238
  legal 30, 133, 141, 146, 189, 196, 201–2, 209
  offshore wind 200–2

early public engagement 176–77
ECJ (European Court of Justice) 87, 202
economic benefits 13–14
economic growth 13–14, 20, 34, 53, 56
ecosystems 167, 196, 199, 201, 207
  marine 11, 189, 196, 200, 203, 205–6
EEZs (exclusive economic zone) 22, 186, 190–94, 211
effectiveness 16, 21, 29–30, 41, 48, 110, 116, 118
effects
  cumulative 196, 203, 206
  deterrent 80, 82, 86, 220
  environmental, *see* environmental effects
  negative 8, 173, 175, 189
  positive 43, 178, 180, 220
efficiency 59, 84, 107, 128, 138, 141, 169, 216–17
electric vehicles 11, 15, 140–41, 145, 217–18, 224, 229–30, 232; *see also* **road transport**
electricity 7–8, 15–19, 84–85, 104–7, 112–15, 118–22, 187–88, 217–21
  capacity constraints 130
  connection costs 134, 144
  consumption 84, 229
  fossil fuel 2, 196
  generation 85, 145, 187, 191, 220, 228
  markets 99, 118, 128, 131
  network access challenges 5, 130–36
    legal responses 136–51
  network and market operation 129, 133–34, 136–41
  networks and regulation 126–29
  from passive to active management 131
  production 7, 10–11, 16, 99, 133, 138, 141, 187
  pro-renewables grid development 146–47
  storage options 132–33
  suppliers 106, 114–15, 118
  supplies 17, 112, 129, 217
  systems 114, 125, 127, 129, 137, 141–43, 145, 229
    consumer participation 131–32
    liberalised 127–28, 138
    opening to new actors 141–44
    operation 127, 140–41, 146
    regulators 128
  trading 129
  transmission 125–51
    distribution systems and interconnectors 126–27
    intermittency 132–33
    investment challenge 134

248 INDEX

planning 144–46
pro-renewables grid development 146–47
regulatory challenge 135–36
supporting transboundary development 147–51
system operators 129, 131–32, 135, 138, 140, 142, 146, 148–49
systems 106, 126, 129–30, 140
electrolysis 8, 133, 143, 185, 217
emissions 9–10, 17–18, 28–33, 76–77, 93, 216, 228–29, 233–35
life cycle 233–34, 238
reduction
market mechanisms for 31, 35–41
targets 77–78
trading 36, 39
Energy Charter Treaty 71–72
energy consumption 1, 61, 79, 84–85, 88–90, 94, 216, 220
global 17, 227
energy markets 18, 102, 105
energy security 26, 30, 82, 175, 216
as driver for renewable energy development 11–13
energy supplies 8, 15, 26–27, 61, 63, 66–67, 82–84, 92–93
engagement 43, 162, 175–76, 180–81
public, *see* public engagement
environmental assessment 119, 151, 156, 160, 208
strategic 167, 202, 207–10, 212
environmental conditions 159, 189, 203–4
environmental effects 22, 168, 175, 189, 207–8, 212
and public opposition 167–68
environmental harm 55, 167, 195, 203–4, 206–8, 210, 238
environmental impact assessment 104, 109, 151, 156, 159–60, 194–96, 207, 209–11
laws 159, 161, 201, 209, 211–12
environmental information 156, 160, 201, 210
environmental limits 55–56, 205
environmental protection 56, 189–90, 197–98, 200–3, 205, 207, 209–11
environmental value 189, 202, 211–12
environmentally sound energy systems 59–60
established technologies 14, 117, 139
European Commission 83, 86, 102–3, 105–6, 144, 149, 161, 163
European Council 83–85
European Court of Justice (ECJ) 87, 202
European Parliament 83, 91, 238, 240
European Union 11–13, 23, 76–77, 82–83, 126, 147–48, 169–72, 234–37
Renewable Energy Directives 82–95, 137, 144, 169–71, 222, 235

exclusive economic zone, *see* **EEZs**
exclusive rights 22, 190–91
experience 2–3, 6, 95–96, 99–100, 115–16, 165, 176, 204–5
expertise 54, 69–70, 81, 142, 171, 211

feed-in premiums 102, 106–7
feed-in tariffs 101–7, 110–13, 116, 137
feedstocks 218, 228, 232–36, 238
finance 41–43, 45–47, 60, 104, 134, 149
climate 28, 41–44, 47–48, 50, 62
financial barriers 16–17
financial benefits 166–67, 179
financial incentives 101, 141, 147, 157, 167, 175, 177–81, 230
financial penalties 87, 104
financial support 2, 16, 42, 47, 115, 134–36, 235
financial viability 99, 110, 133, 145
first-generation biofuels 218–19, 234, 239
FIT schemes 104–5, 107, 113
fixed offshore wind, potential 185–86
fixed prices 104, 112, 115
fixed up-front costs 100
floating turbine technology, potential 186–87
floating turbines 186
food production 233–34
forests 10, 233–34
fossil fuel vehicles 223–24, 226, 231–32
fossil fuels 1–2, 6–7, 10–15, 17–20, 29, 217, 226–27, 233–34
consumption 1, 30, 58, 233
deterring investment 29–35, 72
replacement 10, 26, 67, 70, 218, 220
subsidies 18, 29
France 77, 88, 127, 232
fuel obligations 227–28
fuel suppliers 93–94, 107, 221–23, 227–28, 230
funding 21, 42–44, 49, 68, 70, 101–2, 104, 117–21
Future We Want, The 57, 61–62

gas 7, 9, 11, 16, 18–19, 38, 125, 217
natural 1, 9, 79, 100
networks 19
generating plant 16, 104–6, 109, 125, 130, 145, 156, 159
generating stations 137, 145, 191–92
generators 104, 106–7, 110–11, 118–20, 125, 128–29, 137–39, 146
renewable 103–4, 112, 119–20, 129, 131, 133, 139, 144
geothermal energy 6–7
Germany 68, 77, 103, 105, 126, 186, 232
feed-in tariff, premium schemes and competitive allocation 112–14

INDEX 249

goals 26, 32–34, 57, 63, 67–68, 83–84, 90–93, 95–96
greenhouse gases 2, 31, 35–36, 38, 77–78, 222–23, 228, 234
   emissions, *see* emissions
   growth 9–10, 16
   intensity 94, 222, 228–29
grids 16, 119, 125, 128, 130, 138, 140–41, 147
growth 2–7, 13–15, 21–22, 70–71, 76–80, 84–89, 144–46, 216–19
   economic 13–14, 20, 34, 53, 56
   greenhouse gas 9–10, 16
   renewable electricity 129, 138–39
   renewable energy 3, 5, 10, 26, 54, 66, 80
guidance 42, 106, 109, 199, 201–2, 205, 207, 209

hard commitments 26, 66
harm 10–12, 197, 199, 201, 204–5, 207, 209, 211
   environmental 55, 167, 195, 203–4, 206–8, 210, 238
health, human 10–11, 197
heat 7, 173, 197
heating 3, 7, 10, 17, 79, 85, 93–94, 100
high biodiversity value 236–37
high carbon stock land 237, 240
human health 10–11, 197
hydrogen 7–8, 132, 143, 148, 217–19, 224, 228, 230
   renewable 220, 228

imports 12, 86, 233
incentives 40, 99, 135, 140, 147, 178, 218
   financial 101, 141, 147, 157, 167, 175, 177–81, 230
India 14, 31, 37, 40, 44, 70, 186, 204
indicative targets 84, 87–89, 94
   national 84
indicative trajectories 85–86, 88, 92
indirect land use 234, 239
information 34, 43, 156–61, 201, 208–12, 230–31, 234, 238
   environmental 156, 160, 201, 210
infrastructure 17, 145, 147–48, 150, 187–88, 217, 219–20, 229–30
   for alternative fuel vehicles 229–31
   development 145, 148, 230
   projects 150, 169, 172–73
   refuelling 219, 229–30
initial development costs 16, 108
innocent passage 193–94
innovation 46, 48, 50, 69, 147
institutions 2, 5, 38, 41, 68, 70, 126, 131
integration 64, 67, 69, 140–42, 144, 146, 148, 207
   renewable electricity 5, 144–45
interconnectors 126–27, 136, 147

intermittency 5, 18, 135, 143, 148
   electricity transmission 132–33
internal combustion engines 217, 224, 228
international climate change law 26–50
international declarations on renewable energy 63–65
international institutions 27, 54, 67–70; *see also individual instiutions*
International Renewable Energy Agency, *see* IRENA
internationally determined mitigation outcomes, *see* ITMOs
interstate collaboration 26, 64, 199
interventions, legal 2–3, 15, 18, 21, 105, 113, 126–27, 219–20
investment 16, 38–39, 71–72, 101–4, 107–9, 111, 114–16, 118–19
   capital 126–27
   environments 4, 46, 109, 111
   in fossil fuel energy 29–35, 72
   private 37, 39, 218
   risk 108–9, 114, 118
   support 72, 101–3, 224
   treaties 111
investors 35, 37, 70–71, 78, 80, 82, 99–101, 108–11
   confidence 79, 82, 88, 105, 110, 112, 114, 119
   private 48, 70, 150
IRENA (International Renewable Energy Agency) 13, 15, 27, 33, 54, 68–70, 224, 227–28
ITMOs (internationally determined mitigation outcomes) 38–40

Japan 31, 77, 186
JI (joint implementation) 36, 40
Johannesburg 14, 56, 59–60
   Declaration 60
   Plan 56, 61–62
joint implementation (JI) 36, 40
jurisdictions 5–6, 36, 186–88, 191–92, 207–8, 227–28, 233–34, 240

knowledge 3, 6, 16, 18, 20, 69, 128, 133

land 167, 173, 189, 234, 236–37, 240
land clearance 233–34
land of high biodiversity value 236–37
land use, indirect 234, 239
largescale developments 150, 169
least developed countries 20, 37–38, 40–41
legal commitments 77–78, 202
legal design 83, 88, 114, 116, 169, 171, 232, 235
legal duties 30, 133, 141, 146, 189, 196, 201–2, 209

250 INDEX

legal frameworks 21–22, 48, 77, 79, 87, 89, 156, 158
legal interventions 2–3, 15, 18, 21, 105, 113, 126–27, 219–20
legal obligations 54, 58, 104, 118, 199, 221, 227, 230
legal reforms 116, 132, 144, 169, 238
legal requirements 136, 157, 161, 166–67, 174, 177, 239
legal responses 3, 5–6, 21, 107, 126, 157
  to biofuels sustainability concerns 234–37
  to concerns with authorisation regimes 168–75
  to electricity network access challenges 136–51
  opening the electricity system to new actors 141–44
  to reasons for public opposition 175–81
legal status 77, 81, 133
legal targets 78, 90
  in road transport 220–23
legitimacy 168–69, 171, 203
liberalised systems 128–29, 134, 141, 146
licences 33, 109, 156, 158–59, 161, 170, 201
limitation targets 32
limits, environmental 55–56, 205
location of renewable energy sources 19
low carbon development 28, 41, 46, 48
low carbon energy 3, 72–73, 173–74, 186
  development 20, 37, 41, 50
  sources 15, 31, 173
  transition 13–14, 20, 26, 64, 145
low emission vehicles 225–27

management 139, 144, 178, 205
  active 131, 139–40
  adaptive 207, 212
  demand 132, 145
  passive 131, 140
manufacturers 15, 100, 217–18, 221, 225–26, 229
marine activities 189, 197, 204–5
marine areas 147, 192, 197, 199–200, 202, 204
marine biodiversity 196, 199, 204–5
marine ecosystems 11, 189, 196, 200, 203, 205–6
marine environment 167, 189, 192, 196–99, 202, 204, 206
marine plans 203, 205–6
marine spatial planning (MSP) 189, 195–96, 202–7
market entrants, new 108, 116, 121
market exposure 103, 107–9, 113, 139
market mechanisms for emissions reduction 31, 35–41
market operation 15, 107, 130, 133
market risk 104, 107, 118–19, 122, 142

markets 18–19, 102–8, 112–13, 118–19, 128–29, 131–33, 137–39, 141–42
  balancing 131–32, 139–40, 221
  electricity 99, 118, 128, 131
  energy 18, 102, 105
meters, smart 143–44
mitigation 30, 32–33, 40, 206
mobility 216–17, 219, 229
monitoring 81, 207, 212, 237
MSP, *see* marine spatial planning
multipliers 223, 226, 228

national circumstances 28, 32–33
national indicative targets 84
national laws 137, 141, 146–47, 151, 200–1, 207, 209, 211
national policies 10, 59, 76, 83, 91, 113
national policy statements 172, 174, 206
National Policy Statements, *see* NPSs
national regulators 135–36, 146–47, 149–50
national renewable energy action plans, *see* NREAPs
national targets 78, 82–95, 110, 221–22, 235, 240
nationally determined contributions 29, 31–33, 46, 50
natural gas 1, 9, 79, 100
navigation 167, 190, 192–93, 195–96
NDCs 32–35, 38–39, 50
negative effects 8, 173, 175, 189
negative environmental impacts 11, 22, 156, 167, 209, 212, 236
  and offshore power 196–202
negative impacts 158–59, 189, 196, 208, 211, 228, 234, 240
negotiations 30–31, 44, 48, 50, 57, 73, 93, 198
  soft law 66
network development 125, 127–28, 130, 136, 145–46
  offshore 187–88
  plans 140, 145, 149
network modification 132, 135, 137, 142, 144
network operators 119, 127–28, 130, 133, 137
network upgrades 134–35, 144–45
networks 16, 18–19, 21, 45, 125–37, 139–40, 142–47, 228
  distribution 139–40, 146, 221
  operation 5, 127, 130, 140, 142
noise 165, 167, 197
North Sea 147, 188, 199
Norway 127, 186, 220, 232
NPSs (National Policy Statements) 174–75, 177, 206
NREAPs (national renewable energy action plans) 86, 94
nuclear energy 8

INDEX 251

objectives 32, 34–35, 57, 61, 66, 207
obligation/certificate schemes 103, 107–8
obligations
  fuel 227–28
  legal 54, 58, 104, 118, 199, 221, 227, 230
  substantive 95, 209, 211
obstacles for renewable energy development 15–18
ocean energy technologies 187
offshore development 187–88, 193, 199–202, 206, 208
offshore power 167, 185–212
  legal foundations in public international law 189–92
  and negative environmental impacts 196–202
  planning for congested seas 202–12
  potential 185–89
  production 188–89, 191–92, 195–96
offshore wind 115, 117, 120–21, 165, 185–89, 191–93, 195–96, 206
  and conflict with other sea uses 192–96
  and legal measures to meet international duties 200–2
  projects 121–22, 199
one-stop-shops 151, 170–71
onshore wind 99, 107, 109, 115–17, 120–21, 171–72, 176, 185–86
  planning and permitting for 158–60
operating support 101–11
  case studies 111–22
operators
  distribution system 110, 127, 131, 139, 145–46
  network 119, 127–28, 130, 133, 137
  system 104–5, 112, 128–29, 131, 133–38, 141–44, 146–47, 149–50
opposition, public 2, 19, 103, 105, 151, 156–81
options 27, 29–30, 61–62, 72–73, 79, 132–33, 137, 229–30
organic waste 7, 166, 218

participation, public 159, 162, 168, 172, 181
passive management 131, 140
PCIs (projects of common interest) 148–49
peatland 234, 237
peer pressure 33–34, 57
penalties 65, 80–82, 86–87, 110, 142, 220
  financial 87, 104
performance 65–66, 68, 70, 81, 83, 86, 88–90, 92
permitting
  laws 158, 161, 163
  for onshore wind energy 158–60
  processes 151, 156–59, 162, 170
  regimes 159, 169–70, 201
petrol 102, 217, 228, 231
pipelines 10, 192–93
planned contributions 91, 94–95

planning 96, 119, 131, 156–81, 198, 221
  authorities 171, 180, 205–6
  for congested seas 202–12
  electricity transmission 144–46
  law 158, 162, 174
  marine spatial planning (MSP) 189, 195–96, 202–7
  for onshore wind energy 158–60
  policy statements 173–74
policies 21, 48, 64, 76–77, 156–57, 166–67, 178–79, 208
  pro-renewables 6, 19, 21, 160, 162, 175, 178, 180
policy goals 80, 82, 89, 112, 128, 138
policy statements 65, 76, 90, 172, 174, 180, 203, 205
  national 172, 174, 206
  planning 173
  supportive 66
policy targets 220
policymakers 3, 103, 112, 136
political commitments 85, 220
pollution 10, 71, 197–99, 201
  air 10–11, 14
poverty 8, 53, 55–58, 61
  eradication 31, 38, 56–57
pre-application consultation 172, 175–77
precautionary approach 201, 212, 238
premiums 104, 113, 118, 121–22
  feed-in 102, 106–7
  schemes 101, 106–7, 112, 118, 120–21
price risk 104, 107–8, 113, 118
prices 105, 108, 115–16, 118, 120, 143, 218, 224
  fixed 104, 112, 115
priority access 112, 137–38
private actors 50, 62, 127
private investment 37, 39, 218
private investors 48, 70, 150
processes
  authorisation, *see* authorisation, processes
  competitive 108–9
  decision-making, *see* decision-making, processes
  remote consultation 157, 162
production 1–2, 17, 125, 129–30, 132–33, 137–39, 233–35, 239–40
  biofuels 219, 223, 233–36, 238, 241
  costs 100, 103, 105
profits 99, 105, 108, 113, 115, 135, 168
projects
  of common interest, *see* PCIs
  demonstration 109, 138
  infrastructure 150, 169, 172–73
  offshore wind 121–22, 199
  transboundary 135, 147, 149–51

252   INDEX

pro-renewable energy policies   21, 168
pro-renewables grid development   146–47
pro-renewables policies   6, 19, 21, 160, 162, 175, 178, 180
prosumers   131–32, 142, 146
protected areas   200, 209
  assessment   211–12
public acceptability   114, 157, 169, 173–74
public acceptance as obstacle to renewable energy development   19–20, 173
public attitudes   163, 177
public authorities   156, 205, 209
public consultations   151, 160, 175
public discontent   110, 173, 180
public engagement   157–58, 164–66, 168, 172–73
  early   176–77
public international law   4, 61, 65, 188–89, 191
public opposition   2, 19, 103, 105
  and environmental effects   167–68
  place-based, visual and amenity concerns   164–66
  and quality of developmental and decision-making processes   168
  reasons for   157, 163–68, 175, 177, 179, 181
  socio-economic factors   166–67
public participation   159, 168, 172, 181

raw materials   236–37
reference points   92–93, 95, 205
reference values   221, 226, 240
reforms   21, 26, 142, 147, 157, 162, 169–70, 239–40
  legal   116, 132, 144, 169, 238
refuelling infrastructure   219, 229–30
regional seas conventions and plans   198–200, 207
regulators   134–36, 140–42, 146–47, 149–50
  electricity system   128
  national   135–36, 146–47, 149–50
regulatory risk   109–11
rejection of renewable energy development   19
  limiting scope for   174–75
remote consultation processes   157, 162
renewable alternatives   3, 50, 100, 217–19
renewable developments   60, 133, 157, 179, 200–2
renewable electricity   17–19, 112–14, 125–26, 132–33, 136–39, 148, 222–23, 228–29; *see also Intoductory Note*
  carriage   130, 137
  growth   129, 138–39
  integration   5, 144–45
  production   11, 19, 100, 105, 135–37, 221, 224, 228
  sources   19, 185

renewable energy, *see also Introductory Note*
  consumption   29, 76–77, 84–86, 116, 236
  costs   5, 14, 103
  definition   6–8
  developers   19, 117, 144, 162
  development   16–22, 39–40, 48–50, 101, 156–60, 163–72, 174–81, 197–200
    drivers   8–15
    obstacles   15–18
  generators   103–4, 112, 119–20, 129, 131, 133, 139, 144
  growth   3, 5, 10, 26, 54, 79–81, 110, 112
  integration   127, 136, 139, 146
  investment   31, 33, 99
  law
    definition   21–22
    levels   22–23
    parameters   5–6
  law, *see also Introductory Note*
  offshore   167, 185–212
  policy goals   83, 87–88
  producers   105, 107–8
  production   26, 28, 58, 60, 73, 76, 107–8, 130
  projects   103–4, 108, 110, 118, 164, 166, 169, 177–78
  sources   1–2, 4–8, 10–11, 26–28, 84–85, 105–7, 217, 222–24
    characteristics as obstacle to renewable energy development   18–19
  targets   5, 10, 21, 78–96, 239–40
  technologies   11, 14, 45, 53, 67, 71, 99, 101–2
renewable hydrogen   220, 228
Renewables Obligations, *see* ROs
reporting   43, 48, 78, 94, 96, 167, 238
  obligations   92, 95, 238
resources   18, 20, 55, 61, 140, 145, 171, 189–90
responsible authorities   169, 173, 200, 209, 212
revenues   16, 100, 102, 104, 110, 113, 116, 118
rights   18, 21–22, 72, 110, 115, 188–94, 238
  exclusive   22, 190–91
Rio Declaration on Environment and Development   54, 56, 68, 156, 159, 201, 207
Rio+20   59, 61–62
risks   103–9, 112–14, 116, 118, 120–21, 168, 179–80, 202–4
  regulatory   109–11
  route to market   104, 107, 114, 118–19, 122
  volume   104
road transport   17, 102
  alternative fuel promotion   227–29
  biofuels, *see* biofuels
  decarbonisation   216–41
  encouraging purchase of alternative fuel vehicles   231–32

INDEX 253

infrastructure for alternative fuel vehicles 229–31
legal targets for renewable energy 220–23
promoting availability of alternative fuel vehicles 223–27
promoting renewable fuel consumption through law 220–32
ROCs (Renewable Obligation Certificates) 115
ROs (Renewables Obligations) 115–18, 120
route to market risk 104, 107, 114, 118–19, 122
Russia 11–12, 31

scale 1–2, 15, 17, 19, 99–100, 122, 186–87, 224
  industrial 19, 165, 192, 210
scheme types 101, 103, 106–8, 115
  certificate/obligation 106–7, 121
Scotland 121, 162, 203–4, 208, 210, 232
SDG7, *see* Sustainable Development Goals, Goal 7
sea lanes 193–94
security 8, 13, 15, 19, 53, 66, 127, 132
  system 136, 138–39
share ownership 178–79
smart grid technologies 132, 143, 145, 148
smart meters 143–44
social development 20, 31, 53, 55–56
social impacts 234–35
socio-economic systems 12, 18, 73, 217
soft law 54, 65–67
  instruments 22–23, 73
  negotiations 66
  statements 67, 73
solar energy 7, 13–16, 18, 100, 117, 120, 129, 132
solar panels 19, 110, 138, 159
solar radiation 1, 9, 12, 99
sovereignty 53, 66, 188, 190
standards 12, 35, 55–56, 226
state support 16–17
  for renewable energy, obliging 28–29
storage 79, 133, 140–45
storage operators 141–43, 146
strategic environmental assessment 167, 202, 207–10, 212
streamlining 169–70
strike prices 118–22
subsidies 39, 99–122, 133, 175, 178, 230–32, 236, 240
  feed-in premiums 102, 106–7
  feed-in tariffs 101–6, 111–13, 116
  fossil fuel 18, 29
  investment support 72, 101–3, 224
  obligation/certificate schemes 103, 107–8
  operating support 101–11
    case studies 111–22
  regulatory risk 109–11
  support schemes 99–101, 110–11, 116–17, 122
  support through tenders/auctions 108–9

suppliers 18, 104, 107, 114–15, 118–19, 129, 131, 227–28
  electricity 106, 114–15, 118
  fuel 93–94, 107, 221–23, 227–28, 230
supplies 12, 107, 127, 129, 222–23, 227, 229, 235
  electricity 17, 112, 129, 217
support 37–45, 47–50, 61–64, 68–69, 101–5, 107–15, 117–22, 219–23
  financial 2, 16, 42, 47, 115, 134–36, 235
  investment 72, 101–3, 224
  operating 101–11
  schemes 99–101, 110–11, 116–17, 122
  state 16–17, 28–29
  technological 20, 33, 44, 49
sustainability 53, 218
  biofuels 219, 233–34
  criteria 234–39
  and WTO law 240–41
sustainable development 15, 36, 38–40, 53–73, 173, 207
  discourse 27, 53
  as driver for renewable energy development 14–15
  international declarations on renewable energy 63–65
  introduction 54–58
  Johannesburg Declaration and Plan of Implementation 60–61
  and renewable energy 58–65
  Rio Declaration on Environment and Development and Agenda 21 59–60
  Rio+20 and The Future We Want 61–62
  Sustainable Energy for All and Sustainable Development Goal 7 62–63
Sustainable Development Goals 21, 57, 70
  Goal 7 (SDG7) 15, 54, 62–64, 70
Sustainable Energy for All 54, 62–63, 73
system operation 127, 140–41, 146
system operators 104–5, 112, 128–29, 131, 133–38, 141–44, 146–47, 149–50
system security 136, 138–39

target holders 81–82, 220
targets 27–28, 31, 36–37, 61–63, 65–66, 76–96, 220–23, 239–41
  binding 30, 35, 39, 87–91, 93–94, 96, 222–23
  characteristics 80–81
  emissions reduction 77–78
  greenhouse gas emissions 77
  higher 31, 90, 93–95, 230
  holding responsible actors to account 81–82
  legal 78, 90
  in road transport 220–23
  limitation 32
  national 78, 82–95, 110, 221–22, 235, 240

254 INDEX

policy 220
renewable energy 5, 10, 21, 78–96, 239–40
role in promoting renewable energy 78–79
value for supporting renewable energy 80–82
tariffs, feed-in 101–7, 110–13, 116, 137
technological support 20, 33, 44, 49
technologies 2, 7–8, 13–14, 16–17, 45–49, 99–103, 106–7, 185–88
development 45–46, 48–49, 132, 188, 218–19
established 14, 117, 139
renewable 11, 14, 45, 53, 67, 71, 99, 101–2
Technology Mechanism 45–47
technology transfer 37, 40, 43, 45–50
and capacity building 28, 60, 62
tenders 103, 108–9, 175
territorial seas 165, 190–93, 211
third-generation biofuels 218, 239
time limits 161–62, 171
timescales 35, 120, 164, 238
for decisions 170–73
trade law 3–4
trading, emissions 36, 39
trajectories, indicative 85–86, 88, 92
transboundary development, support for 147–51
transboundary projects 135, 147, 149–51
Trans-European Energy Infrastructure Regulation 136, 147–48, 170, 172
transmission, *see* electricity, transmission
transmission systems 106, 126, 129–30, 140
transparency 33, 43, 70, 86, 96, 140, 180, 220
transport 3, 17, 22, 78–79, 85, 88, 93, 100
renewable 88, 220, 228
road, *see* road transport
treaties 22–23, 26–28, 71–72, 82–83, 148, 189–91, 197–98, 200
TSOs, *see* electricity, transmission, system operators
turbines 7, 165, 167, 176, 186, 192, 195–96, 204
floating 186

Ukraine 12–13, 94, 148, 216
UNCLOS 22, 190–94, 196, 198
environmental protection duties 197–98

UNEP (United Nations Environment Programme) 198
Unied States 143–44, 167, 170, 186–87, 190, 219, 224, 227
United Kingdom 5–6, 110–11, 126–28, 162–63, 165, 173–74, 185–87, 230–32
Contracts for Difference (CFD) Scheme 117–22
Renewables Obligation Order (ROO) (certificate/obligation scheme) 114–16
United Nations Environment Programme, *see* UNEP
unsustainability, consequences in EU law 235–36
unsustainable biofuels 235–36, 239
upgrades, network 134–35, 144–45
utility 71, 101, 114, 209

values 63, 66, 70–71, 141, 143, 162, 164–66, 196
environmental 189, 202, 211–12
vehicles 8, 17–18, 38–39, 47, 50, 217–19, 224–29, 231–32
alternative fuel, *see* alternative fuel vehicles
low emission 225–27
manufacturers 218, 220, 223–24
zero emission 225–26
viability, financial 99, 110, 133, 145
volume risk 104

waste 11, 166, 232–33, 239
organic 7, 166, 218
weaknesses 46–47, 77, 88, 96, 101, 103, 121–22, 205
wholesalers 107, 118, 122, 142
wind 5–7, 11–14, 18, 178, 181, 185–86, 188, 191
developers 179–80
development 165–66, 195, 210
offshore 115, 117, 120–21, 165, 185–89, 191–93, 195–96, 206
onshore 99, 107, 109, 115–17, 120–21, 158, 171–72, 185–86
turbines, *see* turbines

zero emission vehicles 225–26
zoning approach 189–90